SEXUAL
HARASSMENT

Contemporary Issues

Series Editors: Robert M. Baird
                 Stuart E. Rosenbaum

Other titles in this series:

CONFRONTATIONS AND DECISIONS

SEXUAL HARASSMENT

REVISED EDITION

EDITED BY

EDMUND WALL

Prometheus Books

59 John Glenn Drive
Amherst, New York 14228-2197

10/01

43245821

Published 2000 by Prometheus Books

Inquiries should be addressed to
Prometheus Books
59 John Glenn Drive
Amherst, New York 14228–2197
VOICE: 716–691–0133, ext. 207
FAX: 716–564–2711
WWW.PROMETHEUSBOOKS.COM

04 03 02 01 00   5 4 3 2 1

Library of Congress Cataloging-in-Publication Data

Sexual harassment : confrontations and decisions / edited by Edmund Wall.—Rev. ed.
      p. cm. — (Contemporary issues)
   Includes bibliographical references (p.).
   ISBN 1–57392–830–5 (pbk. : alk. paper)
   1. Sexual harassment of women—United States. 2. Sexual harassment of women—Law and legislation—United States. I. Wall, Edmund. II. Contemporary issues (Buffalo, N.Y.)

HQ1237.5.U6 S48 2000
305.42—dc21   99–045206
                                                                                                          CIP

Printed in the United States of America on acid-free paper

CONTENTS

5

PART TWO: EXPLANATIONS AND CAUSES

PART THREE: LEGAL RESPONSES

The Civil Rights Act

Hostile-Environment Sexual Harassment and the First Amendment

ACKNOWLEDGMENTS

I would like to thank my mentor, Burleigh Wilkins, who first made me aware of the need for a sexual harassment anthology. Among his many valuable lessons to his students is one that he conveyed by example: integrity demands a genuine effort to consider all sides of a debate. Steven L. Mitchell, editor-in-chief at Prometheus Books, has honored that principle throughout the years. It has been a pleasure to work with him and the editorial staff at Prometheus Books.

INTRODUCTION

After an onslaught of legal, corporate, and other attempts to address the issue of sexual harassment, it seems that the problem is just as pervasive today as it was twenty years ago. The problem's nature and remedies continue to elude social researchers and public policymakers. But even though the problem appears to be intractable, we should not assume that, as a society, we have made no progress toward an understanding and resolution of this social ailment. Much more so today than in the past, researchers, public policymakers, and other citizens have demonstrated their genuine concern about sexual harassment and the mistreatment of human beings. Even though we have not arrived at a panacea, increased social awareness of the problem is cause for optimism (albeit guarded optimism). For the first step toward the elimination of a social problem is recognition that there is a problem.

In an effort to overcome ignorance and the denial of the problem, society has made a massive effort to "get the word out" that sexual harassment is a valid issue and that the demeaning treatment of others is not socially acceptable. Through books, workshops, posters, media events, and other social mechanisms, society has drawn attention to the evils of sexual harassment. This massive (if uncoordinated) attempt to educate people about sexual harassment may do much to set the groundwork for its eventual decline. For instance, few, if any, employers in our society can legitimately claim ignorance about the need for a sexual harassment policy, including a policy statement and grievance procedures (whether formal or informal). Any such claim by an employer is likely to amount to prevarication, negligence, or a calculated indifference to human rights.

Given that education plays a fundamental role in addressing sexual harassment, social researchers have a responsibility to delineate the dimensions of the problem so that eventually some relief can be afforded to the large number of people who have been mistreated by others. Since we now have some awareness of the dimensions of sexual harassment, we have incentive to work toward its prevention. Yet, one major hurdle can be found in the diversity of approaches to the problem. There is wide disagreement about the definition, causes, and effects of sexual harassment. It is, therefore, no surprise that the proposed remedies are just as diverse. Certainly, researchers want to overcome these differences and work toward some basic consensus, but that does not mean that the wide range of scholarly approaches should be considered unwelcome. We must go through this process of dialogue if we are to eventually see some improvements. And even if we never reach the point in which, generally speaking, people are safe from harassment and other forms of mistreatment, our debates on the issue have left us with something valuable, even beyond the fact that social awareness has been raised by these very debates. For in sharing our opposing views with others, we show respect for *their* views which, in turn, encourages an attitude in our society that makes occurrences of sexual harassment less likely. Mature debate is a staple in a healthy society.

Elisabeth A. Keller begins the debate by arguing that the right to privacy, implicit in various constitutional amendments, applies to consensual amorous relationships between faculty and students at public, postsecondary institutions. We are told that even though the prohibition of amorous faculty-student relationships in a secondary school setting is both prudent and constitutionally permissible, it is a different matter for public colleges and universities. Keller finds that public colleges and universities are only justified in proscribing intimate faculty-student relationships which arise within the instructional context (i.e., when the faculty member is [or will be] in some way supervising the student). And she finds that this prohibition is justified by the moral and constitutional right of students to decline the association. In that context, she advises us to presume that the student is coerced into such a relationship. With regard to nonsupervisory relationships, however, we are told that faculty and students are free to form intimate associations. In making her case, Keller reviews, among other things, Title VII of the congressional Civil Rights Act of 1964 and Title IX of the Educational Amendments of 1972.

Louise F. Fitzgerald argues against the significance of Keller's distinction between supervisory and nonsupervisory academic relationships. Fitzgerald finds that even when a professor is not supervising a student, he still holds considerable power over her. After laying out the implications of a professor's authority over students, she concludes that no faculty-student relationship should be tolerated at public colleges and universities.

As she makes clear in her first paragraph, Fitzgerald focuses her attention on vulnerable women students. This is not surprising. It is a dominant trend in the social and legal research on sexual harassment. However, Billie Wright Dziech and Michael W. Hawkins find that male students' perceptions and responses to sexual harassment have been more or less ignored in the sexual harassment literature. They point out that in sexual harassment studies, men's perceptions of sexual harassment are only considered as a baseline for comparison with women's perceptions of sexual harassment. Note that Dziech and Hawkins are not suggesting that the sexual harassment of women has been given adequate attention in sociological studies, only that men should be included in those studies as well. After reviewing the limited studies on the frequency, perceptions, and effects of sexual harassment on men, the authors point to the need for further research in this area. Unlike the typical approaches, they question the untested assumption that men are less likely than women to feel vulnerable in the face of unsolicited sexual overtures. And even if that assumption were true, they argue that the focus of sexual harassment studies should be on the *actual* damage done to men by the harassment rather than on a comparison with the damage done to women.

Moving from the academic environment to the workplace, Vaughana Macy Feary argues that sexual harassment in the corporate world is not only a communication problem, but a continuing moral problem. Feary appeals to our objective moral duties and reminds us that sexual harassment is more than just a phenomenon to be described and categorized, but an immoral use of power. In calling for a change of attitudes and beliefs in the corporate world, she underscores the importance of moral education in the battle against sexual harassment. After examining what she takes to be the problems with Edmund Wall's definition of sexual harassment in the previous selection, she defends the Equal Employment Opportunity Commission's (EEOC) definition. In her defense of that definition, she responds to Wall's contention that the sexual harassment of women by men does not necessarily constitute sex discrimination. There is a lot riding on the position that sexual harassment against women is a form of sex discrimination. That position provides the justification for lawsuits brought under Title VII of the Civil Rights Act which is viewed as a welcomed relief by many feminists. But if discrimination is not involved in cases of sexual harassment, or if discrimination is a mere secondary consideration in such cases, then many, if not all, of the lawsuits brought under Title VII are without foundation. In response to Feary's defense of the view that sexual harassment by men against women constitutes sex discrimination, Wall focuses, in his second selection, on Feary's account of "gender." Wall also develops the account of sexual harassment offered in his first selection, an account modeled on disrespectful communication. Among other things, he argues that the EEOC's definition of sexual harassment can lead to injustice.[1]

After these six selections on definitions and policy descriptions, we turn in Part Two to three basic models designed to explain why sexual harassment occurs. Sandra S. Tangri, Martha R. Burt, and Leanor B. Johnson outline three basic explanations of sexual harassment which they have garnered from legal cases and sociological studies. They identify a Natural/Biological Model which depicts sexual harassment as a natural sexual attraction between people. Although her analysis goes well beyond the mere attraction of men to women, the selection by Camille Paglia can be viewed as an approach that more or less falls under the Natural/Biological Model. Paglia argues that women are harassed and physically abused by men due to natural forces that incline men to do such things. In her estimation, there are no comprehensive solutions to a problem that has plagued society from time immemorial, but she believes that perhaps society can at least constrain violent and aggressive behavior.

One of the other two models is the Organizational Model which views sexual harassment as the result of social structures created by organizational relations. According to this account, organizations have a hierarchical structure that provides the opportunity for sexual harassment to occur. The other model is the Sociocultural Model. According to this model, sexual harassment reflects power and status imbalances between the sexes. Sexual harassment is one of the mechanisms for maintaining social and economic dominance over women. The selection by Catharine MacKinnon is more or less based on the Organizational and Sociocultural Models described in the selection by Tangri, Burt, and Johnson.

As an attorney and legal scholar who has influenced the development of sexual harassment law, there is no need to belabor MacKinnon's credentials. Nor are the penetrating insights of Paglia's books unfamiliar to many of us. Indeed, both scholars have done much to advance social awareness about the human condition. Nevertheless, let us not downplay a fundamental difference between the approaches of Paglia and MacKinnon. MacKinnon believes that sexual harassment is a *social* problem, something that can, in principle, be worked out through a restructuring of society. In her estimation, social attitudes, beliefs, and practices can be altered, and resources reallocated. But if Paglia is correct, any social steps we may take to end sexual harassment are only attempts to control the symptoms and manifestations of the problem. For sexual aggression against women, in her estimation, is rooted in the very *nature* of men (and women). Her unsettling selection focuses on the less appealing aspects of human nature.

Part Three moves to the topic of legal responses, but actually the first selection in it, which was written by MacKinnon, should be read in the same sitting with the last selection of Part Two, also written by MacKinnon. According to MacKinnon, the causes of sexual harassment, intimately related, as she takes them to be, to social and economic inequalities, indicate why the remedy ought to be a legal one focusing on discriminatory practices against women. Prior to the use of Title VII for sexual harassment lawsuits, women were virtually unprotected against sexual harassment. They could, in some cases, make an attempt to seek remedies under tort law (i.e., the law of private harms), but tort law was not designed to offer relief specifically to sexual harassment victims. With the use of Title VII, women can now sue specifically for sexual harassment, on the assumption that the harassment constitutes sex discrimination. In the selection in Part Three MacKinnon compares the use of Title VII for sexual harassment with that of tort law, pointing out what she takes to be the slanted assumptions behind the use of tort law.

The selection by Ellen Frankel Paul is clearly at odds with MacKinnon's approach. Paul focuses on what she takes to be the infringement of *employer's* rights under Title VII. She finds that under a Title VII approach to sexual harassment, which, she believes, overprotects and patronizes women in the workplace, the federal government is being invited to regulate personal relationships. There is a distinction, she argues, between merely offensive behavior and genuine harm to persons. Instead of Title VII, she wants to see tort law revised to accommodate cases of sexual harassment involving genuine harm.[2] Comparing the two selections, we find just how much MacKinnon and Paul differ in their expectations of women.

After the selections by MacKinnon and Paul, Alba Conte offers a summary of sexual harassment law as it has developed over the years. She defines relevant legal concepts, traces out the impact of federal and state legislation on sexual harassment claims,[3] and places court decisions within the context of the law's evolution. Among other cases, Conte summarizes the findings in *Meritor Savings Bank* v. *Vinson* in which the U. S. Supreme Court upheld the EEOC's definition of sexual harassment as well as the view, maintained by MacKinnon, Feary, and other feminists, that the question should not be whether a plaintiff voluntarily *consented* to the inappropriate sexual advances, but whether those advances were *unwelcome*. The high court also held that even though a plaintiff's intimate associations and other workplace behavior are not to be used as evidence of voluntary consent to the sexual advances in question, they can constitute evidence of whether the advances were unwanted.

The *Meritor* finding evolved from a decision reached by a federal appellate court in Washington, D.C. The majority opinion in *Vinson* v. *Taylor* not only found the sexual harassment test to be whether the sexual advances were merely *unwanted*, but also that the plaintiff/appellant's own workplace conduct was irrelevant. As indicated above, the U.S. Supreme Court did not agree. They found that such conduct could constitute evidence of whether the advances were unwanted. The dissenting opinion in the *Vinson* case, written by Judge Robert Bork, is more at odds with the majority opinion than is the Supreme Court's opinion. Judge Bork, a staunch defender of "original understanding" as the guide for judicial decision making, found no legal basis for the use of Title VII antidiscrimination legislation for sexual harassment cases. In his estimation, there is good reason to believe that sexual harassment was not thought to be included by Congress in the Title VII legislation of 1964. In *The Tempting of America*, Bork later develops his position against what he takes to be judicial activism.[4] According to his book, when judges circumvent written law and make decisions according to their own principles or other standards, they thereby thwart the will of the people who have elected legislators to design the laws. Bork explains that unlike legislators, judges are not elected to make the law. There are no safeguards on a judge's arrogant law-making activities. Bork views judicial activism as a dangerous and antidemocratic trend in our society. For those who have read his book or have heard him interviewed, his dissenting opinion in *Vinson* provides his actual response as a judge to the type of judicial approach he has long opposed.

Susan Deller Ross's analysis of more recent legal trends would not provide any comfort to those who take a position similar to that of Judge Bork. Ross suspects that the Hill-Thomas hearings have influenced some current legal decisions in sexual harassment law. Although Anita Hill, in Ross's estimation, has inspired many women to persevere in their struggle to achieve equal rights, Ross also feels that Hill's actions may have had some influence on the outcome of the congressional Civil Rights Act of 1991. After the confirmation hearings before the Senate Judiciary Committee on Clarence Thomas's nomination for the U.S. Supreme Court, hearings in which Anita Hill testified that she had been sexually harassed repeatedly by Thomas (to whom she reported while they both worked at the Equal Employment Opportunity Commission), the new Civil Rights Act was passed enabling victims of sexual harassment to receive monetary damages under Title VII. Ross believes that the Hill-Thomas hearings may have played a significant role in those developments. She also suggests that, by solidifying public opinion in favor of further protection for women, Hill's courageous appearance before the Senate Judiciary Committee may have influenced the U.S. Supreme Court decision in *Franklin* v. *Gwinnett County Public Schools*.[5] In that case, the court found that, under Title IX, students in federally funded education programs who are victimized by sexual harassment can sue for damages.

Ross observes that *unanimous* Supreme Court opinions in *Franklin* as well as in *Harris* v. *Forklift Systems* were issued after the Hill-Thomas hearings. Although Ross's case is admittedly speculative, it is interesting that, even those justices on the high court whose dissent may have been expected, supported opinions in each of the two cases that would be viewed favorably by feminists such as Hill.[6]

In the *Harris* case, Justice Sandra Day O'Connor delivered the opinion of the Court. The Court found that Title VII protection against hostile environments is not limited to economic or tangible discrimination. Psychological harm is not required; neither is interference with a victim's work performance. The Court sees a middle ground between mere offensive conduct on the one hand and conduct causing psychological injury on the other. According to the Court, for Title VII hostile-environment lawsuits to be successful, it must be the case that a reasonable person would have found the environment to be hostile or abusive.

In a separate opinion, Justice Antonin Scalia concurred with the Court's conclusion, even though he found the reasonable person standard endorsed by the Court to be murky. Scalia focuses attention on the fuzzy meaning of the Title VII legislation. But, despite the vagueness in the language of Title VII, Scalia cannot find a suitable alternative to the reasonable person test endorsed by the Court.

In the last section of this anthology, we find that sexual harassment claims under Title VII raise questions about the nature and extent of the First Amendment right to freedom of speech. In the first selection of this section, MacKinnon maintains that "the First Amendment was conceived by white men from the point of view of their social position." According to MacKinnon, these men wrote the First Amendment so that *their* speech would not be threatened. She maintains that for those who have been denied access to the social channels of speech and expression, the First Amendment guarantees them a right to speech in theory only.

MacKinnon views what she calls "First Amendment absolutism" (i.e., the view that speech must be absolutely protected) with suspicion. She is not surprised that First Amendment absolutism has developed through obscenity legislation. She says that "pornography is exactly that speech of men that silences the speech of women." She believes that pornography is a male practice which constitutes sex discrimination against women. In fact, she defines pornography as the sexual subordination of women through words or pictures. She believes that its prevalence contributes to the rape and harassment of women.

Whether pornography leads to sexual harassment and crimes against women has been debated. But MacKinnon's approach to pornography raises conceptual questions about sexual harassment. If an employee brings sexually explicit materials into the workplace (e.g., he hangs a sexually explicit poster over his office desk), could he be sexually harassing his coworkers? Would we want his behavior to be legally actionable under Title VII as a hostile-environment case? In addition to questions about the definition of pornography (e.g., would sexually explicit creations by artists be considered pornography?), questions would arise about the respective weights that should be given to protection against harassment and freedom of speech. Nevertheless, MacKinnon's work on this topic reminds us that pornography and First Amendment concerns can be placed in the larger context of an ongoing social struggle by women to be treated equally—with equal respect and equal access to social resources such as speech.

The editors of the *New Republic* argue that sexual harassment claims should be tied to tangible harm to victims. The editors believe that hostile-environment claims not only violate freedom of speech, but also trivialize legitimate sexual harassment claims. The editors point to the legal distinction between speech and conduct. As they see it, the posting of pinup calendars is protected speech, not harmful conduct. Instead of hostile-environment claims, they support the more specific test of whether sexual advances unreasonably interfered with job performance.

Like the editors of the *New Republic*, the U.S. Supreme Court in *Harris* supports the use of a reasonable person standard, but unlike the editors, the Court believes that this standard can be used for hostile-environment claims without violating First Amendment rights. As indicated above, the Court also finds that psychological harm and interference with work performance are not requirements of valid hostile-environment claims. As for the editors' point about the distinction between speech and conduct, MacKinnon's selection offers the response that case law suggests a considerable overlap between the two constructs.

The editors of the *New Republic* disagree with a federal district court in Florida which decided that verbal remarks and the pervasive posting of inappropriate pictures can constitute a legitimate Title VII claim. In *Robinson* v. *Jacksonville Shipyards*, the court argued that the state has a compelling interest in eliminating workplace discrimination. In its estimation, even though pictures and pinups can be considered speech, the state can regulate such speech. The court argued that a male-dominated work environment in which men make blatant sexual remarks to women and extensively post pictures of nude women would be considered abusive by a reasonable woman and could unreasonably interfere with her work performance. Unlike the editors of the *New Republic*, and in step with the later U.S. Supreme Court decision in *Harris*, this federal district court found that relief from a hostile environment (limited to verbal comments and the posting of pinups) need not run afoul of the constitutional right to free speech. It is interesting that, unlike the editors of the *New Republic*, the federal district court found that inappropriate sexual remarks and pictures *can* cause actual psychological damage to women and *can* interfere with their work performance. Of course, the Supreme Court ruling in *Harris*, two years later, does not require such effects for valid hostile-environment claims, and it is interesting that the high court arrives at this broader hostile-environment protection without recourse to a reasonable woman standard. Thus the Supreme Court appears to offer broader protection for women than the Florida district court which endorsed a reasonable woman standard. In our last selection, the editors of the *Harvard Law Review* examine the *Robinson* case and argue that the elimination of pornographic materials from the workplace is necessary to realize the Title VII guarantee of a discrimination-free workplace,

Some of the commentators place more weight on the protection of human rights and the advancement of equality in our society. Others emphasize individual liberty and responsibility. Some are not averse to using the power of the federal government to protect human rights. Others find that the federal government is anything but an ally in the human struggle to maintain moral commitments. It is obvious that the differences run deep in these debates. But the authors in this anthology would all agree that human beings have rights that are worth defending.

NOTES

1. In addition to the debates among legal scholars and philosophers on the definition of sexual harassment, we have seen in the previous edition of this anthology that there is considerable disagreement about definitions among social researchers as well. For those who wish to see how the work of James E. Gruber, Louise F. Fitzgerald, and other social scientists has progressed on the task of finding a common empirical definition of sexual harassment, Fitzgerald et al. offer a useful overview of various definitions, including a defense of Fitzgerald's own definition against the one proposed by Gruber. For that discussion, see Louise F. Fitzgerald, Suzanne Swan, and Vicki J. Magley, "But Was It Really Sexual Harassment? Legal, Behavioral, and Psychological Definitions of the Workplace Victimization of Women," in *Sexual Harassment: Theory, Research, and Treatment*, ed. William O'Donohue (Boston: Allyn and Bacon, 1997), pp. 5–28.

2. Ellen Frankel Paul, "Sexual Harassment as Sex Discrimination: A Defective Par-

adigm," *Yale Law & Policy Review* 8, no. 2 (Fall 1990): 333–65. In that paper, Paul develops her proposed tort approach to sexual harassment.

3. For those who want to trace out the effects of the Civil Rights Act of 1991 on sexual harassment litigation, Conte's selection in this anthology explains how this federal legislation affects plaintiffs and defendants in the courtroom.

4. Robert H. Bork, *The Tempting of America* (New York: Simon & Schuster, 1990).

5. 112 S. Ct. 1028.

6. For the role of personal and ideological considerations in U.S. Supreme Court decisions, see Edward Lazarus, *Closed Chambers* (New York: Random House, 1998).

DEFINITIONS AND POLICY DESCRIPTIONS

The University

CONSENSUAL AMOROUS RELATIONSHIPS BETWEEN FACULTY AND STUDENTS

The Constitutional Right to Privacy

ELISABETH A. KELLER

INTRODUCTION

Surveys of college students in the United States revealed that a significant number of students thought they had been victims of some form of sexual harassment. Thirty percent of the female seniors at the University of California at Berkeley reported harassment by at least one male instructor.[1] A survey of graduate and undergraduate female students at Iowa State University found that 43.2 percent of the students thought they received undue attention from a professor; 17.4 percent experienced verbal sexual advances; 6.4 percent experienced physical advances of fondling, kissing, pinching, or hugging; and 2.1 percent were subject to sexual bribery that included promises of rewards for compliance.[2] The results of a survey reported in the *Journal of College and Student Personnel* showed that 75 percent of students believed that most female students would be reluctant to report a professor's sexually harassing conduct. None of those surveyed who considered themselves harassed

An abstract of this article, which won the NACUA National Legal Writing Competition, was printed in The NACUA Publication Series, *Sexual Harassment on Campus: A Legal Compendium* (1988).

From the *Journal of College and University Law* 15, no. 1: 21–42. Copyright NACUA (National Association of College and University Attorneys). Reprinted by permission.

reported such harassment to a university official.[3] Thus, a lack of sexual harassment reports does not necessarily indicate absence of such a problem.

Growing awareness of the magnitude, dimensions, and effects of sexual harassment at educational institutions and the potential for institutional liability have prompted educators to adopt policies to avert such problems, Many private and public colleges and universities include these policies in their faculty and student handbooks. The policies typically prohibit sexual harassment of employees and students and alert the university community to the serious effects of sexual harassment and the potential for student exploitation. Many institutions have used a definition of sexual harassment in academe similar to that of the National Advisory Council of Women's Educational Programs: "Academic sexual harassment is the use of authority to emphasize sexuality or sexual identity of a student in a manner which prevents or impairs that student's enjoyment of educational benefits, climates, and opportunities."[4]

Some universities have gone beyond establishing regulations directed at the widely litigated problems of sexual harassment and have promulgated policies addressing the problematic issues surrounding consensual amorous relationships between faculty and students. For example, the University of Iowa adopted a policy stating: "No faculty member shall have an amorous relationship (consensual or otherwise) with a student who is enrolled in a course being taught by the faculty member or whose academic work (including work as a teaching assistant) is being supervised by the faculty member."[5] The policy further declares that "[a]morous relationships between faculty members and students occurring outside the instructional context may lead to difficulties," but are not prohibited so long as the faculty member avoids participation in decisions that could penalize or reward the student.[6] The University of Minnesota does not forbid consensual relationships between faculty and students, but its policy statement on sexual harassment clearly states that such relationships are considered "very unwise."[7]

The Faculty Senate of the University of California defeated a proposed amendment to the Faculty Code of Conduct which declared it unethical for professors to engage in amorous relationships with students.[8] A similar proposal was rejected by the faculty of the University of Texas at Arlington.[9] Some faculty members at both universities considered the issue "none of the university's business."[10] A University of California professor suggested that restrictions on amorous relationships between faculty and students may violate civil rights.[11] Such a comment highlights the potential conflict between concerns for preventing victimization of students through sexual harassment and concerns for the individual's right to enter intimate relationships.

This article contends that the constitutional right to privacy applies to consensual amorous relationships between faculty and students in public colleges and universities. Accordingly, such institutions must recognize this right when regulating faculty-student amorous relationships. The analysis begins with a review of recent law regarding sexual harassment, followed by an examination of possible responses of private and public institutions to these developments. Finally, court decisions challenging institutional actions regarding consensual amorous relationships are analyzed in light of the constitutional guarantees of privacy and proper limits of institutional policies.

I. SEXUAL HARASSMENT UNDER TITLE VII AND TITLE IX

Institutions which have included statements regarding amorous relationships in their sexual harassment policies acknowledge the difficulty of drawing a line between sexual harassment and intimate consensual relationships. Therefore, consenting relationships and sexual harassment cannot be dealt with as entirely distinct concerns. The legal developments surrounding Title VII of the Civil Rights Act of 1964[12] and Title IX of the Educational Amendments of 1972[13] set the stage for the formulation of university policies regarding sexual harassment and amorous relationships between faculty and students.

Congress enacted Title VII to prevent sexual discrimination in the employer-employee relationship and Title IX to prevent sexual discrimination in the educational environment. Under both acts sexual harassment has been considered tantamount to sexual discrimination.[14] Due to the broader application of Title VII, a greater number of actions in this area have been filed under Title VII than under Title IX.[15] Consequently, the law under Title VII has developed more rapidly and more fully. In considering charges of harassment under Title IX, the courts have turned to case law under Title VII for assistance.[16]

A. Title VII

The Equal Employment Opportunity Commission (EEOC) guidelines, enacted pursuant to Title VII, define sexual harassment as:

> Unwelcome sexual advances, requests for sexual favors, and other verbal or physical conduct of a sexual nature . . . when (1) submission to such conduct is made either explicitly or implicitly a term or condition of an individual's employment, (2) submission to or rejection of such conduct by an individual is used as the basis for employment decisions affecting such individual, or (3) such conduct has the purpose or effect of unreasonably interfering with an individual's work performance or creating an intimidating, hostile, or offensive working environment.[17]

The courts have adopted the EEOC definition and have classified sexual harassment under Title VII into two categories: (1) "quid pro quo" situations, in which a supervisor conditions tangible employment benefits on the granting of sexual favors or in which a supervisor makes threats of retaliation for noncompliance;[18] and (2) "hostile environment" situations, in which harassment takes the form of suggestive language and/or intimidating conduct that creates an offensive atmosphere in the work setting which unreasonably interferes with the work performance of the employee.[19] In both categories of sexual harassment, the harassing behavior must be inflicted by persons in positions of authority against persons in subordinate roles over whom the former can exert authority. In hostile environment cases under Title VII, courts require evidence of repeated questionable conduct in the workplace. This standard operates to discourage blatant or persistent sexual misconduct but not to deter normal friendship and communication between coworkers. Thus, to establish a hostile environment claim under Title VII, the harassment must be so severe and persistent as to affect seriously the employee's psychological well-being.[20]

The only sexual harassment case to come before the United States Supreme Court was *Meritor Savings Bank, FSB* v. *Vinson*.[21] A former employee of Meritor Savings brought an action under Title VII against the bank and the bank's supervisor, claiming that during her employment she was subjected to repeated demands from her supervisor for sexual relations, to which she unwillingly acquiesced. The district court found no tangible economic injury to the employee and refused to recognize the existence of a valid claim of sexual harassment in violation of Title VII, despite the presence of a "hostile environment."[22] The Supreme Court reversed, holding that hostile environment claims are actionable under Title VII, even in the absence of alleged economic harm such as demotion, loss of wages, or loss of employment.[23]

Courts have not uniformly applied the standards for employer liability in sexual harassment cases under Title VII. Moreover, the Court, in *Meritor*, did not provide definitive standards for employer liability. Prior to *Meritor*, some courts applied a two-tiered standard of liability for employers. Those courts held the employer strictly liable for the conduct of supervisors in instances of quid pro quo harassment. In claims of hostile environment harassment, however, courts held liable only that employer who had knowledge of the supervisor's conduct.[24]

The Eleventh Circuit justified a different standard of liability in *Hensen* v. *City of Dundee*.[25] The court reasoned that in order to cause quid pro quo harassment, a supervisor must use the authority in which the employer has "clothed" the supervisor. The power given to the supervisor by the employer to hire, fire, and promote allows the supervisor to condition continued employment and advancement on submission to sexual demands.[26] Without this express use of the authority, vested by the employer, no quid pro quo sexual harassment exists. A coworker lacking such authority to retaliate could not effect this type of harassment.[27] Therefore, authority given to the supervisor by the employer justified the strict liability standard.

On the other hand, the capacity to create a hostile environment in the workplace "is not necessarily enhanced or diminished by any degree of authority which the employer confers upon th[e] individual . . ."[28] and, therefore, strict liability should not apply. Rather, the ability to create a hostile environment is a function of the proximity of the harasser to the harassed. This is outside the actual or apparent authority of the harasser. Employers, however, are required to maintain a safe work environment, which would include an environment free of sexual harassment. Thus, it may be argued that employers should be held to the strict liability standard. Other courts[29] have imposed strict liability on employers for both types of harassment for another reason. Since employers are held strictly liable for ethnic and religious harassment under Title VII, some judges and commentators believe that the same standard of strict liability should apply to all forms of sexual harassment.[30]

In *Meritor*, although presenting no definitive standard of employer liability, the Court does offer some guidance. The Court rejected the imposition of strict liability in all cases, but suggested that an employer's lack of notice of hostile environment harassment would not necessarily insulate the employer from liability.[31] Thus, a vague liability standard under Title VII emerged which took a middle ground, adopting neither the two-tiered approach nor the automatic liability standard.

B. Title IX

A student who is not an employee of the university and is sexually harassed by a faculty member has no recourse under Title VII, which applies only to employer-employee relations. For relief, the student must proceed under Title IX. Title IX states: "No person in the United States shall, on the basis of sex, be excluded from participation in, be denied the benefits of, or be subjected to discrimination under any educational program or activity receiving federal financial assistance."[32] Title IX further requires universities and other federally funded educational institutions to establish adequate grievance procedures for alleged violations.[33] Universities must guarantee prompt investigation of complaints and proper remedial measures. Failure to adopt and publish such procedures may result in the loss of federal funds and invite civil liability.[34]

Alexander v. *Yale University*[35] was the first case to recognize that sexual harassment violates Title IX and that students have the right to sue directly in federal court. Five former Yale University students sued the university for violating Title IX through failure to consider seriously and to investigate adequately complaints of sexual harassment brought by female students. The university's inaction, it was claimed, in effect condoned the sexual harassment.[36] The court found that only one of the claims of sexual harassment fell within Title IX protection:[37] the quid pro quo claim of a female student who received a poor grade because she rejected the sexual demands made by a course instructor. The court considered the hostile environment claims of other students insufficient to warrant judicial action.[38]

In *Brown* v. *California State Personnel Board*,[39] a California court found that a single sexual invitation to a student unaccompanied by a threat of retaliation or promise of gain, did not constitute sexual harassment.[40] The court commented that in the absence of a rule against faculty student dating, one such incident did not constitute sexual harassment and, therefore, was not sufficient grounds for dismissal of the faculty member.[41] Although *Brown* involved an appeal in an action for wrongful dismissal, not Title IX, it suggests that in order to make a case of hostile environment harassment in the education context, a pattern of abusive behavior must be demonstrated, similar to the pattern under Title VII.

Both types of sexual harassment in the workplace may provide reasonable analogies for the academic setting, where faculty members are vested with institutional authority over students. For example, a professor offering a student a good grade or a good recommendation in exchange for sexual favors would commit quid pro quo sexual harassment.[42] Hostile environment harassment would seldom involve a single incident. It would rather be characterized by repeated exposure to offensive conduct and language and/or sanction-free sexual advances.

The direction of Title IX litigation and university policies will likely be influenced by *Meritor*.[43] The relevance of *Meritor* to the liability of educational institutions in sexual harassment claims by students, however, remains unclear. It has been suggested that a university "must always be held liable for the sexually harassing behavior of its faculty in either quid pro quo or hostile environment cases because Title IX imposes upon the institution the nondelegable duty of nondiscrimination."[44] In view of the great power differential between faculty and students, and the relative autonomy of faculty as compared with supervisors in the usual employment context, a strict liability standard may ensure greater university efforts to comply with Title IX's mandate.[45]

Perhaps the most significant aspect of *Meritor* to the issue of consensual amorous relationships was the Court's determination that an employee's voluntary participation in sexual intercourse with a supervisor provides no defense to the employer.[46] The inquiry more importantly focuses on whether the sexual advances by a person in authority are unwelcome rather than on whether the participation in sexual conduct was voluntary. The Court recognized the dilemma of the employee who fears that lack of compliance with a supervisor's sexual demands may result in lack of advancement, demotion, or loss of job.

Courts may view the asymmetry of power between faculty and students as analogous to the power differential existing between a supervisor and an employee. Students are keenly aware of their vulnerability to the broad discretionary power of faculty.[47] Regardless of faculty intention, potential coercion can influence students to consent to sexual involvement with faculty. Students may consent to unwanted sexual liaisons because of uncertainty regarding the academic consequences of noncompliance. Therefore, what may appear to be an adult, consensual, private relationship may be the product of implicit or explicit duress and thus may constitute the basis for individual or institutional liability.[48] Additionally, truly consensual relationships may change and lead to rancor, disappointment, and retaliatory claims of sexual harassment.

Concern for protecting students and faculty and avoiding potential liability may encourage colleges and universities to consider a total ban on all amorous relationships between faculty and students. Such a ban, however, raises other legal issues unrelated to those concerning sexual harassment, and may, depending upon the public or private identity of the institution, raise constitutional issues as well.

II. CONSENSUAL RELATIONSHIPS

A. *Private and Public Institutions*

Actions by private colleges and universities to prohibit consensual intimate relationships between faculty and students would be treated similarly to private company rules prohibiting such relationships between managerial and nonmanagerial personnel. Court challenges to such rules have been unsuccessful, even though employees dismissed for violation of so-called nonfraternization rules have usually alleged wrongful discharge and tortious invasion of privacy.[49] For example, in *Rogers* v. *IBM*, the plaintiff was discharged after fourteen years of service for engaging in a relationship with a subordinate employee that "exceeded reasonable business associations."[50] The court reasoned that the dismissal was appropriate because an employer may be legitimately concerned with the appearance of favoritism, possible claims of sexual harassment, and employee dissension resulting from amorous relationships between management and nonmanagement employees.[51] Similarly, another court, to support the contention that employers have a legitimate interest in enforcing "no-dating" policies, cited a federal regulation that states: "[A]n employer should take all steps necessary to prevent sexual harassment from occurring."[52]

While employer-employee relationships in private institutions are governed by contract principles and state constitutional provisions, generally such institutions are not subject to the federal constitutional provisions, which require state action. However, public institutions with policies banning amorous relationships must consider the principles which protect an individual's constitutional rights, since a public institution's enforcement of administrative policies constitutes state action.

B. *Freedom of Association*

The constitutional guarantees of freedom of association would appear to apply to policies which improperly prohibit consensual amorous relationships between faculty and students in public institutions. The Eleventh Circuit Court of Appeals in *Wilson* v. *Taylor* concluded that "dating is a type of association which must be protected by the First Amendment's freedom of association."[53] In *Wilson* a police officer employed by the City of Winter Park, Florida, was dismissed for dating the daughter of a convicted felon, a reputed key figure in organized crime in Florida.[54] Relying on earlier First Amendment cases that recognized that freedom of association may apply to relationships which promote social and personal ties, rather than just those that advance political and religious beliefs,[55] the court held that the right of a public employee to date falls under the protection of the First Amendment. Thus, the court held that the police officer was fired for "a reason infringing upon his constitutionally protected freedom of association."[56]

Although the constitutional rights at issue in consensual amorous relationships may be thought to be First Amendment rights of association, they are more properly considered as protected under the penumbral right to privacy. One month after the *Wilson* decision, the United States Supreme Court, in *Roberts* v. *United States Jaycees*,[57] for the first time outlined the existence of two distinct associational freedoms under the United States Constitution: (1) expressive association and (2) intimate association. In *Roberts*, the United States Jaycees challenged a Minnesota law[58] which prohibited charitable organizations from denying membership on the basis of gender. The Court held the state did not abridge either the Jaycees' male members' freedom of intimate association or their freedom of expressive association. The freedom of expressive association, according to the Court, guarantees the "right to associate for the purpose of engaging in those activities protected by the First Amendment—speech, assembly, petition for the redress of grievances, and the exercise of religion."[59] Intimate association, an intrinsic element of personal liberty,[60] is not grounded solely in the First Amendment but is secured generally by the Bill of Rights and the Fourteenth Amendment. Referring to a line of decisions which speak to the constitutional right to privacy, the Court explained that "choices to enter into and maintain certain intimate relationships must be secured against undue intrusion by the State."[61]

Roberts thus makes clear that the analysis of the right to engage in intimate consensual relationships free from governmental interference does not properly focus on the First Amendment freedom of association. Rather, universities contemplating restrictions on the personal associations of faculty and students must consider the constitutional right to privacy. Accordingly, while the Eleventh Circuit's reliance on the First Amendment in *Wilson* may have been inappropriate, the "right to date" recognized in *Wilson* should still be entitled to constitutional protection under the fundamental right to privacy.

C. Right to Privacy

While the right to privacy is not explicitly mentioned in the Constitution, numerous Supreme Court decisions rest on this principle and explore its scope. One of the earliest statements of the fundamental right to privacy appears in the dissenting opinion of Justice Brandeis in *Olmstead* v. *United States*.[62] In *Olmstead*, the Court considered the government's gathering of criminal evidence through unauthorized wiretapping. The majority found that no violation of the defendant's Fourth or Fifth Amendment rights resulted from this conduct. Brandeis's dissent stated that "[t]he makers of our Constitution . . . conferred, as against the government, the right to be let alone—the most comprehensive of rights and the right most valued by civilized men."[63] This dissent was later relied upon to overrule the case.[64]

Two cases, *Meyer* v. *Nebraska*[65] and *Pierce* v. *The Society of Sisters*,[66] contemporaries of *Olmstead*, support the idea that the right to personal privacy inheres in the concept of liberty protected by the Fourteenth Amendment. In *Meyer*, the Court invalidated a statute making it illegal to teach a foreign language to any child who had not completed the eighth grade. In *Pierce*, the Court struck down an Oregon law requiring children to attend public school. While neither case specifically found a constitutional right to privacy, the recognition of a liberty interest in family-related matters, such as child-rearing and education, became the foundation for the more modern recognition of a constitutional right to privacy.

Not until 1965, in *Griswold* v. *Connecticut*,[67] was the privacy concept identified as an independent constitutional right. In *Griswold*, the Court declared unconstitutional a Connecticut statute forbidding the use of contraceptives by married persons. Justice Douglas, writing the majority opinion, considered the constitutional right to privacy to have roots in the penumbras of the First, Third, Fourth, Fifth, and Ninth Amendments.[68] Other justices believed that the right to privacy emanated from the Ninth Amendment or the concept of personal liberty in the Fourteenth Amendment.[69] Although the specific textual source of the constitutional right to privacy may still be debated, a line of Supreme Court decisions, beginning with *Griswold*, clearly established an independent constitutional right to privacy, the scope of which is still being explored and defined. In *Griswold*, Justice Douglas asserted that marriage is a relationship that lies within the zone of privacy created by the emanations of several fundamental constitutional guarantees. He wrote:

> We deal with a right of privacy older than the Bill of Rights—older than our political parties, older than our school system. Marriage is coming together for better or for worse, hopefully enduring, and intimate to the degree of being sacred. It is an association that promotes a way of life, not causes; a harmony in living, not political faiths; a bilateral loyalty, not commercial or social projects. Yet it is an association for as noble a purpose as any involved in our prior decisions.[70]

Two years later, in *Loving* v. *Virginia*,[71] which involved an equal protection challenge to a Virginia statute prohibiting interracial marriages, the Supreme Court strongly reiterated that a constitutional protection surrounds marriage. "The freedom to marry has long been recognized as one of the vital personal rights essential to orderly pursuit of happiness by free men."[72] Seven years after *Griswold*, in *Eisenstadt* v. *Baird*,[73] the Court extended the zone of privacy beyond marital relations. The Court invalidated a statute which made it illegal to distribute contraceptives to unmarried persons. "If the right of privacy means anything, it is the right of the *individual*, married or single, to be free from unwarranted governmental intrusion into matters so fundamentally affecting a person as the decision whether to bear or beget a child."[74]

Given the emphasis placed by the Court on the interrelationship among the right to privacy, marriage, and child-bearing, the formation of consensual intimate relationships, viewed as natural precursors to the more formal bond of marriage, should similarly be protected by the right to privacy. Otherwise, one might argue, the specific rights of privacy previously announced by the Court are hollow.

It has been suggested that the right to privacy may be the "least stable terrain of modern constitutional doctrine."[75] There is little doubt, however, that Americans believe that their civil rights include the right to engage in highly personal relationships free from governmental intrusion.[76] In our daily lives, "the values of intimate association loom larger than the value of freedom of expression or political association."[77] Many faculty have immediately deemed university policies prohibiting faculty-student dating, violative of their civil rights, thus reflecting the "natural law" quality of the right to privacy.

The Court has recently hesitated to expand the substantive reach of the right to privacy. This may be attributed in part to an effort to avoid the appearance of reviving the judicial activism associated with the 1930s and, thus, appearing to make law without express constitutional authority.[78] This concern is reflected in *Bowers* v. *Hardwick*[79] a 1986 Supreme Court opinion addressing a challenge to Georgia's criminal sodomy statute which gave the Court another opportunity to define the scope of the right to privacy. Justice White, writing for the majority, commented that "the Court is most vulnerable and comes nearest to illegitimacy when it deals with judge-made constitutional law having little or no cognizable roots in the language or design of the Constitution."[80] While deciding that the Constitution confers no right upon homosexuals to engage in sodomy, the Court did reaffirm the privacy rights previously recognized by it, rights that touch upon traditional family matters. Restrictions on dating, unlike the prohibition of sodomy, would arguably render meaningless the Court's reaffirmation of privacy rights relating to family matters. *Bowers* seems limited to the power of the State to proscribe specific sexual acts; it did not recognize state power to intrude upon the rights of adults to establish consensual relationships.

The analysis of the Court in *Roberts* v. *United States Jaycees* is instructive in examining the right to privacy and consensual dating policies. In distinguishing the freedom of intimate association from that of expressive association, the Court characterized the personal affiliations that come under the shelter of the constitutionally protected freedom of intimate association and the right to privacy. These relationships are "distinguished by such attributes as relative smallness, a high degree of selectivity in decisions to begin and maintain the affiliation, and seclusion from others in critical aspects of the relationship."[81]

The Court noted the spectrum of human relationships, from the smallest and most selective and seclusive, at one end of the spectrum, to large business enterprises, at the other."[82] The location of a specific relationship on this spectrum determines the limits of State authority to interfere with such associations.[83] Intimate consensual relationships may well be considered relationships that require a high degree of selectivity, smallness, and seclusiveness. Under the analysis in *Roberts*, therefore, an amorous relationship formed by two adults would lie at the end of the spectrum affording the greatest claim to constitutional protection from incursions by the State.

The right of privacy, however, is not absolute. As with any constitutionally guaranteed individual right, a compelling state interest permits certain infringements of that right.[84] Laws which limit the fundamental freedoms of an individual must serve a compelling state interest and also must be narrowly drawn to serve only that interest.[85] The context of an educational institution may reveal such a compelling interest. Case law, however, has not been very helpful in this regard since courts have not properly addressed these issues or have avoided them by focusing on the particular facts or egregious behaviors before them.

III. CONSENSUAL AMOROUS RELATIONSHIPS BETWEEN TEACHERS AND THEIR STUDENTS—CASE LAW

In a New York case, *Goldin* v. *Board of Education*,[86] a high school guidance counselor claimed that school officials violated his constitutional right to privacy by sanctioning him for his sexual relationship with a former student.[87] The teacher was suspended without pay, pending a hearing, when school officials discovered that he had spent the night at the home of a former student while her parents were away. The student was over eighteen years of age and had graduated two months prior to the incident.[88] The court upheld the suspension but expressed no opinion regarding the ultimate outcome of the hearing.[89] The majority opinion stressed that the hearing should focus on "whether the plaintiff used his position as a teacher to establish that relationship and whether that relationship has adversely affected the plaintiff's fitness as a teacher within the community. . . ."[90] The teacher's recent professional supervision of the student made his conduct "susceptible to the presumption that the intimate relationship did not develop overnight."[91] A teacher's guarantee of privacy may yield to the valid government purpose of inquiring into "the character and integrity of its teachers in the educational process. . . ."[92]

The dissenting judge reasserted that this incident involved voluntary intimate conduct at a private residence between a teacher and an adult former student. Absent proof that the teacher used his position of authority over the student to establish a "meretricious relationship," the plaintiff is entitled to protection from inquiry under the principle enunciated in *Griswold*.[93] The dissent also noted that "it is apparent that proof of such prior relationship is not available to the board or it most certainly would have been the subject of another and separate charge."[94]

Both the majority and the dissent would confine the proper scope of inquiry at the suspension hearing to the teacher's activities while the student was still under his educational guidance. Thus, the scope of appropriate state interference with a protected right was limited to the academic setting. The court recognized a legitimate school board concern that intimate relationships between teachers and students may undermine confidence in the integrity of the teachers and the school. To justify the inquiry into a seemingly consensual relationship between two adults outside the school, however, the majority indulged the inference that the relationship may have been initiated earlier as a teacher-student romance. Without this presumption, the board of education's actions may have violated the teacher's right to privacy.

Few would deny that in a high school, as opposed to a postsecondary institution, factors such as age and maturity of the students make a broader scope of inquiry permissible. The place of the high school in the community also requires greater awareness of and sensitivity to local public opinion. The board of education's interest in maintaining an atmosphere that preserves the integrity of the educational process overrides the right of the teacher to be let alone.[95] The parameters of permissible infringement on the constitutional right to privacy thus depend on the setting. In a secondary school setting, broad proscriptions regarding amorous relationships between faculty and students may be both wise and constitutionally permissible. However, in postsecondary public institutions such proscriptions may be subject to a different constitutional test.

Cases involving consensual sexual relationships between faculty and students in institutions of higher education may also involve allegations of sexual harassment or other such egregious behavior on the part of faculty compelling schools to take action. Because court decisions often focus on such behavior, it is difficult to discern the limits of permissible infringement on the rights of faculty and students to private relationships. For example, *Board of Trustees* v. *Stubblefield*[96] concerned patently outrageous behavior on the part of a junior college professor. The professor offered to drive a student home after an evening class. The professor subsequently parked the car on a public street and engaged in sexual relations with the student.[97] When the local sheriff approached the car, the professor shouted expletives and sped away, knocking down but not seriously injuring the sheriff. The student had to force the professor to bring the vehicle to a stop.[98] A California court upheld the school's decision to dismiss the professor on the basis of the professor's unacceptable behavior with the sheriff and the notoriety surrounding the incident that likely would impair the professor's ability to carry out his academic role.[99] Additionally, the court felt that this apparently consensual sexual relationship threatened "[t]he integrity of the educational system under which teachers wield considerable power in the grading of students and the granting or withholding of certificates and diplomas . . . ."[100] While the court articulated the state's legitimate concerns regarding amorous involvement of faculty and students generally, this was not its focus; the court was clearly more concerned with the professor's bizarre behavior.

In *Korf* v. *Ball State University*,[101] current and former students accused an associate professor of making unwelcomed homosexual advances and offering good grades for sexual favors. Professor Korf denied the allegations but admitted having sex with one of the students. Korf characterized his relationship with the student as consensual.[102] He claimed that the university, in dismissing him, violated his constitutional rights to substantive and procedural due process, equal protection, free speech, freedom of association, and privacy. In addition, Korf made state claims for breach of contract and infliction of emotional distress.

A hearing committee at the university found evidence supporting the charge that Korf was guilty of unethical conduct because he "used his position and influence as a teacher to exploit students for his private advantage."[103] The testimony and affidavits of the students alleged quid pro quo harassment. The court acknowledged the possibility that one of the relationships was consensual, finding no proof to the contrary."[104]

On appeal, the Seventh Circuit, dismissed all the professor's claims despite the fact that Ball State University had no specific policy regarding intimate relations between faculty and students. The university relied on a statement of the American Association of University Professors (AAUP), which it had adopted and printed in the Faculty Handbook: "(1) The professor, guided by a deep conviction of the worth and dignity of the advancement of knowledge recognizes the special responsibilities placed upon him . . . ; (2) He demonstrates respect for the student as an individual and adheres to his proper role as intellectual guide and counselor . . . ."[105] The court held that such relationships breached the professor's ethical obligations under the AAUP guidelines.[106]

In *Korf*, [as] in *Stubblefield*, the determination that the professor breached his ethical obligations was not necessary to support the court's decision. The testimony of seven other students clearly indicated Professor Korf's sexual harassment and exploitive conduct. This case too, then, does not adequately define the extent of constitutional protection in consensual relationships between faculty and students in institutions of higher education.[107]

In 1984, the Fifth Circuit Court of Appeals heard a case involving a consensual adult sexual relationship with no allegations of harassment or outrageous public misconduct, unlike the circumstances in *Goldin*, *Stubblefield*, and *Korf*. In *Naragon v. Wharton*,[108] the plaintiff, Naragon, a music instructor at Louisiana State University, had a lesbian relationship with a freshman student over eighteen years of age.[109] The instructor was not in a position to evaluate, recommend, or otherwise affect the academic progress of the student. The student was not enrolled in any of the instructor's classes and was unlikely to be in these classes in the course of her studies.[110] While the student never lodged a complaint against the instructor, the student's parents expressed their concern to university officials. Upon university investigation, the instructor maintained that her relationship with the student was a private matter and therefore none of the university's business.[111] The university took no immediate action and at the end of the term a faculty committee recommended continuation of the instructor's teaching assignment.[112] However, the university administrators ultimately responsible for appointments decided, in the "best interests of the university," to relieve the instructor of teaching assignments and reassign her to research activities.[113] Although the university had no written policy prohibiting amorous relationships between faculty and students, the administrators relied on general standards of professional conduct and ethics, considering avoidance of such relationships an obvious standard of the academic profession.[114] The instructor's appointment ended at the close of the term and, therefore, the university had no legal obligation to renew her employment.

Naragon sought an injunction to compel the university to restore her teaching duties. Naragon alleged violation of a variety of constitutional rights, including the right to association under the First Amendment and the right to equal protection under the Fourteenth Amendment. The plaintiff alleged that she was treated differently from heterosexuals in the same situation. The trial court tied Naragon's constitutional claims to the issue of whether the university based its decision on Naragon's sexual preference. The trial court and the court of appeals found no evidence that the reassignment was motivated by considerations of sexual preference.[115] Therefore, the court of appeals did not resolve whether the "Equal Protection Clause of the Fourteenth Amendment prohibits or circumscribes discrimination based upon an individual's sexual preference."[116]

While the court never explicitly addressed the instructor's constitutional right to privacy, much of the court's analysis of the university's actions spoke implicitly to this issue. The court examined the interests of the university which might override the instructor's right to engage in intimate relationships free from interference. The university asserted that it based its decision to reassign Naragon on the belief that intimate relationships between teachers and students are unprofessional and likely to be detrimental to the students and to the University. The court stated that the university was legitimately concerned:

> that a romantic relationship between a teacher and student may give the impression of an abuse of authority; it may appear to create a conflict of interest even if in fact no such conflict directly results; it tends to create in the mind of other students a perception of unfairness; it tends to and most probably does affect other students' opinions of the teacher. . . .[117]

The inherent asymmetry in faculty-student power is manifest primarily in the instructional context, which includes course work, advisorships, student evaluation, recommendations, and similar processes. When amorous involvement and academic responsibilities intersect, a student's meaningful consent to an intimate relationship is suspect. The voluntary nature of the association cannot be assured. Even when the faculty member intends no coercion, these concerns are still valid. However, when a faculty member does not academically supervise a student, these concerns cannot be entirely substantiated.

In *Naragon*, the university's concern over the appearance of abuse of authority and potential harm to the university's mission caused by faculty-student amorous relationships would be compelling only in the instructional context, where the risk of harm is greatest. However, Naragon's relationship with the student occurred outside the instructional context and, therefore, the potentially coercive factors arguably did not taint the relationship.

Serious inconsistencies emerge in *Naragon* if one accepts the university's contention that all amorous relationships between faculty and students are unethical.[118] The university's dean acknowledged that no action was taken and no sanctions imposed against a well-known heterosexual teacher-student relationship.[119] The university justified its inaction, noting that the student had been previously married, that her parents knew of the relationship, and that the school received no complaints. In *Naragon*, only the parents of the adult student lodged complaints.

Arguably, the university interfered improperly in a private relationship in *Naragon*, without sufficient compelling interest. The court's determination that no constitutional violation occurred may have turned on the fact that the university action imposed minimal deprivation. The university gave Naragon an equivalent position in research, rather than teaching, with no economic loss or significant damage to her career. The university's action, however, foreclosed Naragon's opportunity to teach, solely because of a consensual adult relationship, in violation of Naragon's right to privacy.

IV. DEFINING THE LIMITS OF THE PROHIBITION ON INTIMATE ASSOCIATIONS

Upon examination of the Supreme Court decisions which define the constitutional right to privacy, the foregoing consensual relationship cases pose privacy questions not adequately addressed by the courts that decided them. In *Roberts v. United States Jaycees*,[120] the Court described the characteristics of intimate association, i.e., smallness, selectivity, and seclusiveness, which confer the right to privacy. This right places constraints upon the power of the state to interfere in such intimate associations. Once a right to privacy is established as protecting consensual amorous relationships between faculty and students, public universities, as state actors, may only intrude upon these relationships to serve compelling interests.

In the landmark abortion case, *Roe v. Wade*,[121] the Court deemed it appropriate for states to interfere with the mother's right to abortion for only a limited time during the pregnancy. The Court utilized a time line to delineate the boundary of permissible state regulation in areas otherwise protected by the mother's right to privacy. The timeline in *Roe v. Wade* illustrates when it is appropriate for the state to regulate areas protected by the right to privacy.[122] This approach could be adapted to establish the permissible limits of university authority to regulate intimate consensual relationships between faculty and students. In the university setting, however, a situational paradigm would be more appropriate than a temporal one.

The overall university setting should be viewed as a large circle encompassing all its activities and interrelationships. Within the larger circle, a smaller circle sets off the activities and interrelationships that fall within the "instructional" context that could appropriately be regulated. Intimate associations between faculty and students arising within the "zone of instruction" carry the presumption of coercion and render the consensual nature of the relationships suspect. Here the university has a compelling interest in preserving academic integrity and safeguarding students from duress and exploitation. Within the instructional context, students fearing adverse consequences from noncompliance may feel compelled to enter or to continue undesired intimate relationships with faculty members, even when such duress is not intended by the faculty member. Other students may also assume that such relationships result in unfair academic advantage. Since such perceptions damage the academic climate and the exact nature of such relationships is difficult to determine, the university may legitimately proscribe all such associations.

Outside the instructional context, the presumption that an intimate faculty-student relationship results from coercion cannot be justified. Since the faculty member does not academically supervise the student, the university has no reason to question the consensual nature of the association. The faculty person cannot use the threat of reprisal or the promise of reward to manipulate the student. Also little reason would exist for others to suspect academic favoritism. Consequently, proscribing such relationships would serve no compelling interest.

A bright-line test can thus be formulated for public universities, defining the area of permissible state intrusion into constitutionally protected private relationships; the university may proscribe the formation of intimate faculty-student relationships within the instructional context, namely, when the faculty member academically supervises the student. Intimate consensual relationships falling outside the instructional context are constitutionally protected from university interference.

Under this bright-line test, the university in *Naragon* apparently impermissibly infringed upon the instructor's constitutional right to privacy. The relationship between the instructor and the student arose outside the instructional context, there were no allegations of harassment or exploitation, and it was highly unlikely that the instructor would ever academically supervise the student. Consequently, the university had no authority to intervene.

The bright-line test suggests the constitutional minimum which public institutions should incorporate into a policy. However, universities may need to address other concerns before adopting a policy on amorous relationships. Frances Hoffman, writing in the *Harvard Educational Review*, discussed some of the implications of such policies.[123] Hoffman believes that amorous relationships between faculty and students are generally inappropriate and risky. She labels all such relationships inappropriate when there is an abuse of power.[124] However, Hoffman suggests that policies should not "reinforce status hierarchies and ignore or deny the right of individuals to establish relationships when, with whom, and where they choose."[125] The paternalistic attitude of policies on amorous relationships runs counter to higher education's abandonment of the in loco parentis role.[126] Female students have a strong interest in protecting their right to forge alliances with faculty, in order to generate the personal ties of trust and friendship crucial for personal and political strength within an organization and beyond. "It is not in women's interest to concede to institutions the right to delimit the formation of personal ties among community members."[127]

The entire definition of amorous relationships is fraught with ambiguity, which may result in a further chilling effect on mentorship and the social interactions that are part of a nurturing academic environment. Therefore, policymakers should carefully delineate the realm of unacceptable behavior, which is a difficult task. Consequently, some institutions may choose to have no explicit policy and others may prefer to articulate a very general statement with no mention of sanctions.

CONCLUSION

The freedom to decline or resist intimate association is inextricably bound up with the freedom to form intimate association. Upholding both these freedoms in the university setting generates inherent conflict. Clearly, "coerced intimate association is the most repugnant of all forms of compulsory association."[128] However, the right to form adult consensual intimate relationships is a fundamental personal freedom. A strong and effective university policy against sexual harassment, together with the recognition of the right to privacy of faculty and students, will, within the parameters of constitutional guarantees, serve both the interests of the university and those of the individual.

NOTES

1. Smith, "Must Higher Education Be a Hands-On Experience? Sexual Harassment by Professors," *Education Law Reports* 28 (1986): 693, 696 (referring to Middleton, "Sexual Harassment by Professors: An Increasingly Visible Problem," *Chronicle of Higher Education* [September 15, 1980]: 1, 4).

2. J. W. Adams, J. L. Kottke, and J. S. Padgitt, "Sexual Harassment of University Students," *Journal of College Student Personnel* 24 (1983): 484, 488.

3. Ibid.

4. Amy Somers, "Sexual Harassment in Academe: Legal Issues and Definitions," *Journal of Social Issues* 38 (1982): 22, 24.

5. University of Iowa, Policy on Sexual Harassment and Consensual Relationships, Division 2, § 7 (1986) (Consensual Relationships in the Instructional Context).

6. Ibid. at § 8.

7. University of Minnesota, Policies and Procedures on Sexual Harassment, Policy Statement on Sexual Harassment (1984) (approved by University Senate, May 17, 1984).

8. *Chronicle of Higher Education* (September 3, 1986): 44.

9. McMillen, "Many Colleges Taking a New Look at Policies on Sexual Harassment," *Chronicle of Higher Education* (December 17, 1986): 1, 16.

10. Ibid., p. 16.

11. *Chronicle of Higher Education*, see note 8, p. 44.

12. 42 U.S.C. §§ 2000e–2000e-17 (1982).

13. 20 U.S.C. § 1681 (1982). See infra note 32 and accompanying text.

14. See, e.g., *Alexander* v. *Yale University*, 631 F.2d 178 (2d Cir. 1980); *Barnes* v. *Costle*, 561 F.2d 983 (D.C. Cir. 1977).

15. Employers with more than fifteen employees are subject to Title VII provisions. 42 U.S.C. § 2000e(b) (1982).

16. See, e.g., "Though the sexual harassment doctrine has generally developed in the context of Title VII, [the Equal Employment Opportunity Commission's] guidelines seem equally applicable to Title IX." *Moire* v. *Temple University School of Medicine*, 613 F. Supp. 1360, 1366–67, n.2 (E.D. Pa. 1985), *aff'd without opinion*, 800 F.2d 1136 (3d Cir. 1986) (referring to the 1980 Guidelines on Sexual Harassment, 29 C.F.R. § 1604.11 [1984]); see also *Alexander* v. *Yale University*, 631 F.2d 178 (2d Cir. 1980) (citing *Barnes* v. *Costle*, 561 F.2d 983 [D.C. Cir. 1977]).

17. 29 C.F.R. § 1604.11 (1984).

18. See, e.g., *Barnes* v. *Costle*, 561 F.2d 983 (D.C. Cir. 1977).

19. See, e.g., *Hensen* v. *City of Dundee*, 682 F.2d 897 (11th Cir. 1982); *Bundy* v. *Jackson*, 641 F.2d 934 (D.C. Cir. 1981).

20. *Hensen*, 682 F.2d at 904.

21. 477 U.S. 57, 106 S. Ct. 2399 (1986).

22. 23 Fair Emp. Prac. Cas. (BNA) 37 (D. D.C. 1980).

23. 477 U.S. at 67–68, 106 S. Ct. at 2406 (affirming the circuit court's ruling on hostile environment claims under Title VII).

24. See, e.g., *Katz* v. *Dole*, 709 F.2d 251 (4th Cir. 1983); *Hensen*, 682 F.2d 897 (11th Cir. 1982); *Bundy*, 641 F.2d 934 (D.C. Cir. 1981). See Note, "Employment Discrimination—Defining an Employer's Liability Under Title VII for On-the-Job Sexual Harassment: Adoption of a Bifurcated Standard," *North Carolina Law Review* 62 (1984): 795.

25. 682 F.2d 897 (11th Cir. 1982).

26. Ibid. at 910 (citing *Miller* v. *Bank of America*, 600 F.2d 211, 213 [9th Cir. 1979]).

27. Note, see note 24, p. 808.

28. *Hensen*, 682 F.2d at 910. But see *Meritor*, 477 U.S. at 74–78, 106 S. Ct. at 2409–10 (Marshall J. concurring).

29. See, e.g., *Miller* v. *Bank of America*, 600 F.2d 211 (9th Cir. 1979).

30. Note, see note 24, p. 801.

31. *Meritor*, 477 U.S. at 72, 106 S. Ct. at 2408.

32. 20 U.S.C. § 1681 (1982).

33. 34 C.F.R. § 106.8 (1987).

34. The matter of federal funding may also limit the protection of students under Title IX. *Grove City College* v. *Bell*, 465 U.S. 555, 104 S. Ct. 1211 (1980), established that only the programs, within an educational institution, that receive federal funds are subject to Title IX. Thus, the fact that a particular program receives federal funds does not trigger institution-wide Title IX coverage. A student claimant must demonstrate that a nexus exists between the sexual harassment and the federally assisted programs or activity within the institution. Ibid. at 573, 104 S. Ct. at 1221. The Civil Rights Restoration Act, Pub. L. No. 100-259 (1988), overrules *Grove City* by reinterpreting "program or activity" under Title IX. For purposes of the Educational Admendments of 1972, "program or activity" means "all of the operations of a college, university, or other postsecondary institution, or a public system of higher education." See also *Alexander* v. *Yale University*, 631 F.2d 178, 181 n.1 (2d Cir. 1980). But other grounds and avenues of recourse may be available to students, such as claims under applicable state constitutional provisions, torts of intentional infliction of emotional harm, or breach of contract. Therefore, universities should take note of the Court's view in *Meritor* that the mere existence of grievance procedures and a policy against sexual harassment will not insulate the employer from liability. *Meritor*, 477 U.S. at 71–73, 106 S. Ct. at 2408–09.

35. 631 F.2d 178 (2d Cir. 1980).

36. Ibid. at 181.

37. Ibid. at 185.

38. Ibid. at 184–85.

39. 213 Cal. Rptr. 53, 166 Cal. App. 3d 1151 (1985).

40. Ibid. at 61, 166 Cal. App. 3d at 1163.

41. Ibid.

42. *Alexander*, 631 F.2d at 184-85.

43. *McMillen*, see note 9, at 1, 16.

44. Schneider, "Sexual Harassment and Higher Education," *Texas Law Review* 65 (1987): 525, 567.

45. Ibid., p. 569.

46. 477 U.S. at 68, 106 S. Ct. at 2406 (1986).

47. Nancy Tuana, "Sexual Harassment in Academe: Issues of Power and Coercion," *College Teaching* 33 (1985): 58.

48. Wyatt, "Avoiding Sexual Abuse Claims After *Meritor*," *National Law Journal* (October 7, 1986): 19, col. 1.

49. See, e.g., *Rogers* v. *International Business Machines Corp.*, 500 F. Supp. 867

(W.D. Pa. 1980); *Crosier* v. *United Parcel Service, Inc.*, 150 Cal. App. 3d 1132, 198 Cal. Rptr. 361 (1983); *Ward* v. *Frito-Lay, Inc.*, 95 Wis. 2d 372, 290 N.W.2d 536 (1980)

50. 500 F. Supp. at 868

51. *Crosier*, 150 Cal. App. 3d at 1140. 198 Cal. Rptr. at 366

52. Ibid. at 1140 n.10, 198 Cal. Rptr. at 366 n.10 (1983) (quoting from 29 C.F.R. §1604.11[f] [1987]).

53. 733 F.2d 1539, 1544 (11th Cir. 1984).

54. Ibid. at 1540.

55. Ibid at 1543.

56. Ibid. at 1544.

57. 468 U.S. 609, 104 S. Ct. 3244 (1984).

58. Minn. Stat. § 363.03, subd. 3 (1982).

59. 468 U.S. at 618, 104 S. Ct. at 3249.

60. Ibid.

61. Ibid. at 617–18, 104 S. Ct. at 3249.

62. 277 U.S. 438, 48 S. Ct. 564 (1928) (overruled, 389 U.S. 347, 88 S. Ct. 507 [1967]).

63. Ibid. at 478, 48 S. Ct. at 572.

64. *Katz* v. *United States*, 389 U.S. 347, 353, 88 S. Ct. 507, 512 (1967).

65. 262 U.S. 390, 43 S. Ct. 625 (1923).

66. 268 U.S. 510, 45 S. Ct. 571 (1925).

67. 381 U.S. 479, 85 S. Ct. 1678 (1965).

68. Ibid. at 484, 85 S. Ct. at 1681.

69. Ibid. at 487, 85 S. Ct. at 1683 (Goldberg, J., concurring) (Ninth Amendment); see also *Roe* v. *Wade*, 410 U.S. 113, 153. 93 S. Ct. 705, 727 (1973), *reh'g denied*, 410 U.S. 959, 93 S. Ct. 1409 (1973) (Fourteenth Amendment).

70. *Griswold*, 381 U.S. at 486, 85 S. Ct. at 1682.

71. 388 U.S. 1, 87 S. Ct. 1817 (1966).

72. Ibid. at 12, 87 S. Ct. at 1824.

73. 405 U.S. 438, 92 S. Ct. 1029 (1972).

74. Ibid. at 453, 92 S. Ct. at 1038 (emphasis in original).

75. Kenneth L. Karst, "The Freedom of Intimate Association," *Yale Law Journal* 89 (1980): 624, 625.

76. Ibid.

77. Ibid., p. 655.

78. Ibid., p. 664.

79. 106 S. Ct. 2841 (1986), *reh'g denied*, 107 S. Ct. 29 (1986).

80. Ibid. at 2846.

81. 468 U.S. at 620, 104 S. Ct. at 3250.

82. Ibid., 104 S. Ct. at 3250–51.

83. Ibid., 104 S. Ct. at 3251.

84. See, e.g., *Roe* v. *Wade*, 410 U.S. 113, 155, 93 S. Ct. 705, 728 (1973); *Eisenstadt* v. *Baird*, 405 U.S. 438, 92 S. Ct. 1029 (1972); *Griswold* v. *Connecticut*, 381 U.S. 479, 485, 85 S. Ct. 1678, 1682 (1965).

85. For example, in *Roe* v. *Wade* the constitutionality of a state criminal abortion statute was challenged. The Supreme Court, in striking down this statute, decided that the statute violated the implicitly guaranteed constitutional right to privacy. The Court determined that the fundamental right to privacy is broad enough to encompass the right of a woman to decide whether to terminate a pregnancy. 410 U.S. 113, 153, 93 S. Ct. 705, 727 (1973). This right, however, is not unqualified. The Court acknowledges that some state

regulations in the areas protected by the right to privacy are appropriate. Ibid. at 153–54, 93 S. Ct. at 727. In its efforts to define the area of appropriate governmental regulation, the Court took into account the stage of the pregnancy at which the abortion is performed. The mother's right to privacy is paramount in the first trimester. After the first trimester, the state's interest in protecting the health of the pregnant woman and protecting the potentiality of human life becomes more compelling as the woman approaches term. Ibid. at 163, 93 S. Ct. at 731. The Texas antiabortion statute challenged in *Roe* v. *Wade* was found to sweep too broadly because it did not delineate the boundaries of permissible state regulation.

86. 45 A.D.2d 870, 357 N.Y.S.2d 867 (1974).

87. Ibid., 357 N.Y.S.2d at 869.

88. Ibid.

89. Ibid. at 873, 357 N.Y.S.2d at 873.

90. Ibid. at 872, 357 N.Y.S.2d at 872.

91. Ibid. at 871 357 N.Y.S.2d at 870.

92. Ibid. at 873, 357 N.Y.S.2d at 872 (concurring opinion).

93. Ibid., 357 N.Y.S.2d at 873 (dissenting opinion).

94. Ibid.

95. Ibid. at 873, 357 N.Y.S.2d at 872 (concurring opinion).

96. 16 Cal. App. 3d 820, 94 Cal. Rptr. 318 (1971).

97. Ibid. at 823, 94 Cal. Rptr. at 320.

98. Ibid.

99. Ibid. at 826, 94 Cal. Rptr. at 322.

100. Ibid. at 827, 94 Cal. Rptr. at 323.

101. 726 F.2d 1222 (7th Cir. 1984).

102. Ibid. at 1224.

103. Ibid.

104. Ibid. at 1227.

105. Ibid.

106. Ibid.

107. Korf also claimed that it was the homosexual nature of the relationship that led to his dismissal, in violation of his right to equal protection of the laws. However, the record failed to provide any suggestion that "the university would hesitate to discourage a professor who acted in a manner similar to Dr. Korf but directed his or her advances towards students of the opposite sex rather than the same sex." Ibid. at 1229. The court rejected Korf's equal protection claim as having no legal or factual basis. However, the court left unanswered the question of whether homosexuals would indeed have a valid equal protection claim.

108. 737 F.2d 1403 (5th Cir. 1984).

109. The student and the instructor were friendly before the student's eighteenth birthday. However, there was no sexual involvement between them until the student was eighteen. 572 F. Supp. 1117, 1119 (M.D. La. 1983), *aff'd*, 737 F.2d 1403 (5th Cir. 1984). Sexual relations with a minor may give rise to claims of statutory rape, which is not a problem in this case.

110. *Naragon* v. *Wharton*, 572 F. Supp. 1117, 1119 (M.D. La. 1983).

111. Ibid.

112. Ibid. at 1120.

113. Ibid.

114. 737 F.2d at 1403.

115. 572 F. Supp. at 1124; 737 F.2d at 1406.

116. 737 F.2d at 1408 (Goldberg, J., dissenting).

117. 572 F. Supp. at 1121.

118. 737 F.2d at 1406.

119. Ibid.

120. 468 U.S. 609, 104 S. Ct. 3244 (1984).

121. 410 U.S. 113, 93 S. Ct. 705 (1973).

122. The Supreme Court in *Roe* v. *Wade* delineated the boundaries of permissible state interference in another circumstance involving the right to privacy, namely, a pregnant woman's right to elect an abortion. The Court placed the interest of the individual versus the compelling interests of the state on a timeline. In the first trimester of pregnancy, the right of the individual to choose to terminate the pregnancy is paramount, as there is little or no risk to the mother and the fetus is not viable. In the second trimester, the important and legitimate state interest in protecting the health of the woman may abridge the individual right of the mother. Thus, the state is permitted to regulate abortion to the extent that it will protect and preserve maternal health. In the last trimester of pregnancy, the interest of the state in protecting fetal life, after viability, permits the state to go as far as to proscribe abortion. 410 U.S. at 160–62, 93 S. Ct. at 181–82.

123. F. L. Hoffman, "Sexual Harassment in Academia: Feminist Theory and Institutional Practice," *Harvard Educational Review* 50 (1986): 105.

124. Ibid.

125. Ibid.

126. Ibid., p. 112.

127. Ibid., p. 115.

128. Karst, see note 75, p. 638.

2 Consensual Amorous Relationships

Louise F. Fitzgerald

I resent horribly the exploitation of female students by male faculty. Too many male teachers use (this place) as a sexual supermarket, and I grieve for my female students who are (rightly) awed by these men, whom they see as so wonderfully appreciative of their minds, only to find out that this man simply gets off on the adoration of nineteen-year-old women. It's still offensive to see aging male faculty members with nubile pregnant wives who are former graduate students, many of whom will never finish. . . .

—Female professor, quoted in
Fitzgerald and Weitzman (1990)

As the issue of sexual harassment has become widely recognized as a serious social problem, some universities have gone beyond establishing prohibitions against the more commonly recognized problems and developed policies addressing what have come to be known as consensual relationships—situations where women students "willingly" enter into a sexual relationship with a professor; in this context, "willing" is taken to imply the absence of bribery, coercion, or any form of threat or inducement whether direct or subtle.

Keller (1988) provides an extensive analysis of such poli-

From Bernice Lott and Mary Ellen Reilly, eds., *Combatting Sexual Harassment in Higher Education* (Washington, D.C.: National Education Association, 1996). Copyright © 1996 National Education Association. Reprinted by permission.

cies from a legal perspective. She argues that the constitutional right to privacy, grounded in the penumbra of various constitutional amendments, offers some protection for consensual relationships between faculty and students at public institutions She notes, however, that "[this right] is not absolute. As with any constitutionally guaranteed individual right, compelling state interest permits certain infringements of that right. Laws which limit the fundamental freedoms of an individual must serve a compelling state interest and also must be narrowly drawn to serve only that interest. *The context of an educational institution may reveal such a compelling interest*" (pp. 33–34).

After reviewing relevant case law, Keller concludes that faculty-student relations within the "zone of instruction"—when the student is in the professor's class, when lie is her thesis director, or in some supervisory capacity—can legitimately be prohibited on the grounds that the element of coercion can never be completely eliminated when the faculty member has such power over the student. She notes that such associations "carry the presumption of coercion and render the consensual nature of the relationships suspect. . . . the university may legitimately proscribe all such associations" (p. 40).

If, however, the faculty member does not supervise the student in any way, the institution has no basis to question her consent, nor would any favoritism be implied. Thus, according to Keller, the state has no compelling interest that would justify such a prohibition. She proposes a "bright-line" test for determining when a university may legitimately prohibit faculty-student relationships: "namely, when the faculty member academically supervises the student. Intimate consensual relationships falling outside the instructional context are constitutionally protected from university interference" (p. 41).

At first reading, Keller's logic seems compelling. But readers familiar with life in academia will realize immediately that the bright line she proposes is neither as bright nor [as] definitive as she would have us believe. Even with respect to strictly formal power, any professor will realize that he does not have to directly teach, supervise, or advise a student to be able to influence or even determine her fate, for good or ill. This is particularly true within the somewhat intimate confines of graduate departments where a professor may not academically supervise a student in any way and have no authority over her, and yet still be in a position of considerable authority and influence. Although there may certainly be cases where the professor and student are so far professionally removed from one another that his power is minimal or trivial, Keller's bright-line distinction will not serve to identify them.

Zalk, Paludi, and Dederich (1990) offer a thoughtful analysis of the psychological power differentials inherent in any faculty-student relationship. Their analysis seems particularly suited for illuminating the situation of undergraduate women who become involved with professors. They write:

> The bases of the faculty member's almost absolute power are varied, and range from the entirely rational into broad areas of fantasy. Professors give grades, write recommendations for graduate schools, awards and the like, and can predispose colleague's attitudes toward students. But it goes beyond that.

Knowledge and wisdom are power—particularly in the academy, the setting within which the student must effectively operate. While superior knowledge, and thus presumably greater wisdom, are often ascribed to faculty members by society at large, the students' adolescent idealism exaggerates its extent. The knowledge and experience ascribed to age add to this source of power. The extension of the power of knowledge is often made into the realm of values and students often accept, uncritically, as true or right what the professor espouses (Stimpson 1988).

It is easy to see how this imbalance of power exacerbates the vulnerability of all students. One can also understand what a heady experience it is for the student who is singled out as "special" by a professor (pp. 109–10).

As a practical matter, universities that have consensual relationship statements have tended to incorporate Keller's distinction between supervisory and nonsupervisory academic relationships. For example, the strongest policy to date on consensual relationships is that of the University of Iowa, which states *"No faculty member shall have an amorous relationship (consensual or otherwise) with a student who is enrolled in a course being taught by the faculty member or whose academic work (including work as a teaching assistant) is being supervised by the faculty member."* The policy goes on to say that consensual relationships outside the instructional context can lead to great difficulties, particularly when the individuals are in the same or related departments. It cites problems with appearances of favoritism, possible conflicts of interest, and so forth.

Other statements, although not formally proscribing such relationships, indicate that they are generally inappropriate or problematic. The University of Wisconsin, Illinois, Pennsylvania, and Harvard, among others, have policies of this sort. Most of these policies also point out that if subsequent charges of harassment are brought, they will be extremely difficult to defend.

SUMMARY AND RECOMMENDATIONS

As our knowledge and understanding of the dynamics of sexual harassment have developed and expanded, so too have the policy statements designed to address it. Currently, colleges and universities are beginning to confront the difficult legal, moral, and ethical issues raised by apparently consensual sexual relationships between faculty and students.

Although history and custom have traditionally inhibited institutions from formally proscribing such relationships, such prohibitions are both advisable and legally defensible, at least within the instructional context broadly defined. The courts have ruled that faculty have no right to "exploit students for personal gain" whatever the student's consent may or may not have been (*Korf* v. *Ball State University*, 1984), and universities themselves should do no less.

POSTSCRIPT

Of all the issues raised by the problem of sexual harassment in higher education, none has proved thornier for colleges and universities than that of supposedly "consensual" relationships between faculty and students. In contrast to the progress that has been made on other aspects of the problem, attempts to address this particular issue continue to be met with resistance from a variety of sources. Even fairly conservative policies such as that recently implemented by the University of Virginia (which prohibits faculty members from dating students who are enrolled in their classes) are frequently opposed by those who argue that they infringe on professors' rights of privacy and association. The UVA Faculty Senate debate on the policy attracted national media attention, including attempts at live television coverage, front-page headlines, and lengthy (and frequently sarcastic) features in magazines such as *Newsweek*. Some elements within the media and academia have delighted in ridiculing the issue as "political correctness" run amok, and even some feminist academicians (e.g., Hoffman 1986) have argued that such policies patronize women by suggesting that they cannot make informed decisions about their personal lives.

Much of this resistance appears to represent a disproportionate (albeit well meaning) emphasis on the rights (as opposed to the responsibilities) of faculty combined with a certain innocence about professorial power and influence. However, as Rollo May (1972) pointed out some time ago "we need only ask any graduate student whether his [*sic*] professors have power over him, and he will laugh at our naiveté. The perpetual anxiety . . . as to whether they will be passed or not is proof enough. The professor's power is even more effective because it is clothed in scholarly garb. *It is the power of prestige, status, and the subtle coercions of others that follow from these*" (p. 102, emphasis added).

Consider the following scenario: Professor X meets and becomes attracted to Graduate Student Y when she takes his seminar in medieval ecclesiastical history. Scrupulously ethical, he waits until the end of the semester before he asks her out, but shortly after that, they become a couple. They go everywhere together, including departmental social events and faculty dinner parties. It becomes commonplace for her to interact on a personal and social level with the rest of the faculty, who are still her professors. She never takes another course from Professor A, and indeed, is specializing in a totally different historical period. In short, they are a fixture of departmental life. Everyone knows they plan to marry.

The following year, Student Y attempts her qualifying exam. To everyone's consternation, she does not do particularly well; a rewrite is required. This is somewhat embarrassing for all concerned, but not a major problem—after all, these things happen. Unfortunately, the rewrite is only marginally better. The committee is in a quandary. The unspoken theme that haunts their deliberations: how can they fail this woman who is, after all, their friend and engaged to their colleague? Finally, with much rationalization and some discomfort, she is passed and admitted to candidacy.

The following year, while beginning to work on her thesis, things begin to go quite wrong for Student Y. Her relationship is not going well; Professor X is restless, distracted, somewhat distant. After several weeks of quarrels, he breaks down and tells her that he doesn't want to get married—and, in fact, he has met someone else, a woman professor in his own area of expertise. He feels badly, but there it is. Student Y is devastated, crushed—she can't believe it's over. She calls him constantly, leaves notes in his mailbox. She is obsessed with the breakup of the relationship, and feels somehow betrayed in ways she only vaguely understands. Her advisor, who plays squash with Professor X, feels awkward, caught in the middle, and begins to dread working with her. Soon, the department is polarized; many feel sorry for Professor X, who is being "harassed" by a distraught, hysterical woman. Others feel badly for Student Y who is, after all, a friend of theirs and is now unable to get her work done and cries a great deal of the time. The undergraduates in the survey course she teaches complain that she is disorganized and missing class. At the end of the semester, to everyone's relief, she takes a leave of absence; the next year, her former advisor's wife runs into Student Y at a bookstore/coffeehouse where she is working—no, she doesn't plan to come back to school right now—it's still too painful. Maybe someday. End of story.

This story, and others like it, play themselves out every day in graduate departments all over this country and no doubt would pass Keller's (1988) "bright-line" test for a protected consensual relationship. *But what Keller's analysis ignores is that there are many forms of power, and the professor has them all—whether he acknowledges it or not, or even wishes to or not. It is a fact of life that all of us in academia recognize, if we are truthful, but often wish or choose to ignore.* It is disingenuous to pretend that because we do not chair someone's dissertation committee, act as advisor, or have the opportunity to give a grade in a particular class, a sexual relationship has no influence on a student's academic life, for good or ill. The truth is, of course, that such a relationship colors not only all of her professional interactions with her "partner," but also with every other professor in (at least) her academic department. Academic and professional opportunities and decisions that should depend solely on her talent and performance will be inappropriately enlarged or constricted for all the wrong reasons. Fellow students will sometimes fall silent when she enters the room. Is she a colleague or a "faculty fink?" Did she receive her fellowship because of her brilliant thesis proposal, or because she is sleeping with the most powerful professor in the department; did she *not* receive it because the thesis wasn't good enough or because the committee, with many deserving proposals to choose from, wished to avoid any suspicion of favoritism? The status lines are hopelessly confused. And, these are the consequences of so-called successful relationships, although "of course, nearly every observant academic admits that most teacher-student liaisons are temporary and that few end on an upbeat note?" (Wagner 1993, p. B2).

Wagner (1993) argues that such relationships can have tragic consequences not only for the individuals involved but, in the post-Franklin era, can be extremely costly for institutions as well. She notes: "Given the current case law on sexual harassment, the conclusion is inescapable: Colleges and universities whose federal funding brings them under Title IX cannot tolerate a faculty-student sexual relationship, regardless of the student's age . . . willingness to enter such a relationship, undergraduate or graduate status, . . . [or] whether the student comes under the direct supervision of the teacher or not." Although there are certain to be those who disagree, her logic is compelling.

REFERENCES

Fitzgerald, L. F., and L. M. Weitzman. "Men Who Harass: Speculation and Data." In *Ivory Power: Sexual Harassment on Campus*, edited by M. A. Paludi. Albany, N.Y.: State University of New York Press, 1990.

Hoffman, F. L. "Sexual Harassment in Academia: Feminist Theory and Institutional Practice." *Harvard Educational Review* 56 (1986): 105–21.

Keller, E. A. "Consensual Amorous Relationships between Faculty and Students: The Constitutional Right to Privacy." *Journal of College and University Law* 15 (1988): 21–42.

Korf v. *Ball State University*, 726 F.2d 1222 (7th Cir. 1989).

May, R. *Power and Innocence*. New York: Dell, 1972.

Wagner, E. N. "Fantasies of True Love in Academe." *Chronicle of Higher Education* (May 26, 1993): B2.

Zalk, S. R., M. A. Paludi, and J. Dederich. "Women Students' Assessment of Consensual Relationships with Their Professors: Ivory Power Reconsidered." In *Sexual Harassment on Campus: A Legal Compendium*, 2d ed., edited by E. K. Cole. Washington, D.C.: National Association of College and University Attorneys, 1990.

3 MALE STUDENTS

The Invisible Casualties

BILLIE WRIGHT DZIECH
AND MICHAEL W. HAWKINS

*Won't you come down here? . . . You haven't got to preach a
sermon. Come down beside me. . . . Have you a little time for
me?*

—Franz Kafka, *The Trial*

"**H**ave you a little time for me?" It is a question that resonates among male students on college campuses at the end of
the twentieth century, and it is particularly applicable when one
considers higher education's response to sexual harassment. If
institutions have been negligent about females' predicament,
they have also been guilty of neglecting males. The research
community has fared little better. After almost two decades of
studies, male perceptions of and responses to harassment are
discussed almost exclusively by comparing them to those of
females, and there has been either indifference to sexual harassment's impact on males or a curious willingness to accept
males' self-reports of having been unaffected by it.[1]

Though unwise, this approach was, to some extent, predictable. Designed for males, higher education historically
catered to their needs and ways of knowing and behaving. There
was and in many cases still is "little time" for females. Thus the

emergence of so-called female issues like harassment deterred educators and researchers from seeing it in anything but the most simplistic fashion. No one should apologize for the original emphasis on women. They are, after all, overwhelmingly the targets of the behavior, and concern about the "chilly" classroom climates they inhabit has led to greater sensitivity among professors and a better learning environment for all students.

Nevertheless, the time has come for a more inclusive examination of the problem. Few have acknowledged this need. A significant exception did occur in a 1995 article by Harsh K. Luthar, a Bryant College professor who argued that empirical studies of sexual harassment have produced "misleading" information because most have been tainted by "a female perspective and a feminist ideology."[2] Much of the current literature in sexual harassment "borrows heavily but selectively from the rape and sexual aggression literatures without acknowledging this lineage and the limitations associated with it,"[3] Luthar maintained. This has, he concluded, resulted in "intellectual paralysis of the worst kind"[4] and in a paucity of studies of men who have been falsely accused, who are the targets of powerful females in organizations, and who experience legal difficulties following job termination due to sexual harassment allegations. Rather than focusing on the very salient point that we know too little about males' experience with harassment and that we need to ensure gender neutrality in conducting research, Luthar himself used selective research and evidenced the very gender bias he decried.

Most important was that he neglected the small but generally reliable body of information which already exists on males and harassment. He did cite the U.S. Merit System Protection Board's finding that 15 percent of males reported having been targets of harassment in the preceding two years.[5] This statistic supports Barbara Gutek's earlier finding in a study of workplace harassment that "between 9 percent and 37 percent of men [were] sexually harassed by the opposite sex at least once during their working lives."[6] Studies of prevalence rates for males in educational or quasi-educational settings are limited because most of the studies of students have, in fact, concentrated on females, a condition pointed out in L. J. Rubin's and S. B. Borgers's "Sexual Harassment in the Universities During the 1980's."[7] As previously noted, a 1993 article of male medical residents found that 22 percent were subjected to harassment during training,[8] a statistic that is supported by 1991 and 1992 surveys of medical students.[9]

Gutek concluded that attempts to develop demographic profiles of both male and female targets were not "particularly fruitful,"[10] except in the case of marital status. Like women, married men in the workplace are, she observed, less likely to report incidents of harassment, possibly because those "who do not belong to someone else are apparently perceived as fair game and, perhaps, more approachable than other workers."[11] Whether or not a similar condition exists in the case of male students is uncertain, since there has been no research of the phenomenon. It is clear from studies of both the workplace and the campus that the majority of men have narrower definitions of sexual harassment and do not believe its effects to be as serious.[12] Nevertheless, as the Merit Board Survey indicated, they are as unlikely as females to employ formal or informal complaint responses. Very little is known about male responses or reactions, but most studies have found that males are less likely than females to confide in others about the problem.[13]

The area in which the literature on males is most deficient is that which treats consequences. N. J. Malovich and J. E. Stake summarized the prevailing wisdom about the effects of sexual harassment on males.

> It is well known that the number of men reporting harassment is much smaller than the number of women, and women have been viewed as the primary victims of harassment. In our sample of males, none could be properly labeled as a victim. Some did report harassment defined by our categories of inappropriate, sexually toned behavior from teachers, yet the responses of our male subjects suggested that rather than feeling harassed, they had enjoyed the experience. The men reported feeling flattered by the attention, and they seemed to view the incident as an interesting learning experience. These reactions are similar to those reported by men in the workplace. . . .
>
> That men respond more favorably than women to unsolicited sexual overtures is readily understood in light of the sex-role standards for sexual behavior in our society. A man's status is usually improved by having sexual relations with women, and if women show sexual interest in a man, he and others will usually interpret that interest as a sign of his success as a man. Furthermore, because of the status of men in our society, men are more likely to continue to feel safe and in control even when they are propositioned by a female teacher or supervisor.[14]

A limitation in Malovich's and Stake's comments is their leap from finding that male students feel flattered by instructors' "sexually toned" behavior to their assertion that men are less likely than women to feel vulnerable when propositioned. Evaluation of the consequences of sexual harassment should not rest on comparisons of gender abuse but on the individual costs the behavior exacts. Then, too, Malovich and Stake fail to observe that there is a huge difference between being the target of sexually toned behavior and actually being propositioned by a professor, just as there are marked differences between male responses. Whether male students in the aggregate feel safer and more in control than females when confronted with harassment is a moot point when research gives way to reality and a male is forced to endure or witness an incident of harassment. What matters then, as in the case of women targets, is that one incident, however minor, may invoke trauma.

Equally worth noting in light of the seeming consensus among the experts that males are less affected by harassment is that a male's retrospective assessments of experience or his response to an analogue survey may be as fallible as those of females in similar circumstances. If some women tend to deny or diminish harassment, the same is obviously and perhaps more true of males. Yet studies frequently take males' recall and evaluations of their experiences at face value. Researchers would do well to consider Arvey's and Cavanaugh's concern about the extent to which "sexual harassment survey research has to do with the great reliance on self-report methods. . . . Asking respondents to reflect back over thirty-six months or longer . . . leaves open the question of potential memory distortion and bias. . . . Another problem may occur when the events are accurately recalled, but are perceived differently at later points in time."[15] Though focused on harassment of women in the workplace, Fitzgerald's comments on the ambiguity of analogue studies are also insightful.

> With the exception of prevelance surveys, the great majority of sexual harassment research is dominated by analogue studies, most of uncertain generalizability. In particular the research on gender differences in perceptions rests mainly on a base of relatively weak paper and pencil analogue procedures conducted almost exclusively with college students: the emerging work on coping responses appears to be developing in the same vein. This last is particularly problematic, as it is already clear that actual victims behave very differently than research participants report they would behave.[16]

Not only retrospective bur even current accounts and perceptions of sexual harassment must be considered in light of male psychology, which obviously differs considerably from that of females. In *Iron John*, Robert Bly pointed out:

> Geneticists have discovered recently that the genetic difference in DNA between men and women amounts to just over 3 percent. That isn't much. However, the difference exists in every cell of the body. . . .
>
> I think that for this century and this moment it is important to emphasize the 3 percent difference that makes a person masculine, while not losing sight of the 97 percent that men and women have in common. . . .
>
> Some say, "Well, let's just be human, and not talk about masculine or feminine at all." People who say that imagine they are occupying the moral high ground. I say that we have to be a little gentle here, and allow the word *masculine* and the word *feminine* to be spoken, and not be afraid that some moral carpenter will make boxes of those words and imprison us in them.[17]

Recognizing the hazards of placing males and females in gender "boxes," one can nevertheless allow "the word *masculine* . . . to be spoken" in an effort to stimulate interest in the dynamics of sexual harassment as they pertain to male students. A beginning point is observing that male students, traditional and nontraditional, arrive on campus with the same anxieties, aspirations, and needs as their female counterparts. Traditional students are completing the process of transition to the social, psychological, and economic self-sufficiency of adulthood. Older students experience equally pressing concerns; some return to school out of a desire to better themselves economically; others to discover who they are. The point is that, regardless of age or sex, all are vulnerable in that they submit to the rigors of academe because they believe in the promises it offers. They temporarily relinquish power in order to obtain the financial, social, cultural, and emotional rewards that education promises.

Sacrifice of independence and status is especially trying for males, even when they are young. In "Community and Contest: How Women and Men Construct Their Worlds in Conversational Narrative," B. Johnstone concluded that "men live in a world where they see power as coming from an individual acting in opposition to others and to natural forces. For them, life is a contest in which they are constantly tested and must perform, in order to avoid the risk of failure.[18] "This assessment echoes throughout recent studies of males. Popular works like Hazard Adams's *The Hazards of Being Male* and Deborah Tannen's *You Just Don't Understand* chronicle the burdens and misunderstandings that arise when male behaviors and communication styles come into conflict with those of females. Tannen summarized the difference.

> Though all humans need both intimacy and independence, women tend to focus on the first and men on the second. . . . If intimacy says, "We're close and the same," and independence says, "We're separate and different," it is easy to see that intimacy and independence dovetail with connection status. The essential element of connection is symmetry: People are the same feeling equally close to each other. The essential element of status is asymmetry. People are not the same; they are differently placed in a hierarchy. . . . The symmetry of connection is what creates community: if two people are struggling for closeness, they are both struggling for the same thing. And the symmetry of status is what creates contest: Two people can't both have the upper hand, so negotiation for status is inherently adversarial.[19]

The asymmetrical, adversarial worldview of males takes perhaps its greatest toll in the realm of feelings. From childhood, boys learn that the route to center stage lies in winning, exhibiting physical prowess, telling jokes well, and eventually in making sexual conquests. There are few rewards, even today, for expressions of vulnerability or emotion; males discover very early that seeking help from others or admitting to self-limitations negates their quest for independence and status.

K. Druck and J. C. Simmons observed in *The Secrets Men Keep*: "Men deny themselves the right to feel uncertain, fearful, and hurt. This is the most central of men's secrets. Men experience a broad range of emotions, no matter how much they may deny it to others and themselves. Contrary to the reality that big boys cry, men are taught from an early age that 'big boys don't cry'—that is, it is not acceptable for men to show their emotions."[20] Similarly, Marc Fasteau noted in *The Male Machine*: "By five or six, boys know they aren't supposed to cry, ever be afraid, or, and this is the essence of the stereotype, be anything like girls. . . . The strain of trying to pretend that we have no 'feminine' feelings of doubt, disappointment, need for love and tenderness creates fear of these emotions in ourselves and hostility toward women, who symbolize these qualities."[21]

Despite contemporary efforts to free males as well as females from stereotypes, it is probably safe to say that even now the stereotypes exercise great control over who and what most men are. Some would prefer that society work toward androgyny; and others, like Bly, believe it is best for the genders to learn to live "between the opposites. To live between means that we not only recognize opposites, but rejoice that they exist."[22] Regardless of the approach one prefers, the reality, at this moment in history, is that the average male on college campuses exhibits predictable behaviors and values that influence his responses to sexual harassment.

Depending upon the circumstances and the participants, there are at least six types of situations involving male students that merit further consideration and research. These include (1) those who are direct targets of harassment, (2) those who refuse to see the behavior when it is directed at themselves or others, (3) those who identify with perpetrators and regard them as role models, (4) those who blame harassees rather than offenders, (5) those who assume assertive responses with harassers, and (6) those who sympathize with the plight of victims but feel impotent to effect change. There are clearly other ways to categorize male reactions, and individuals may shift from one response to another, but in each case distinct male traits are significant in the sexual harassment dynamic.

MALE TARGETS

As women move into positions of greater power and security in the classroom and administration, the likelihood of males becoming subjects of harassment will increase. Female perpetrators are not the only problem, however, since anecdotal evidence and the limited research on males suggests that they most often suffer harassment by members of their own gender. A study of medical residents, for example, found that 55 percent of perpetrators of male targets were men.[23] If males are unlikely to report harassment by females, it is not difficult to comprehend why they would be even less likely to do so when they are the targets of male perpetrators. Given males' socialization and emphasis on masculinity, unwanted attention from gay men may pose catastrophic menace to self-image.

Recognition, response, and consequences may be as difficult for a male student as for a female. While slower to admit their predicaments than females, males may experience the same complex reactions. Psychological and physical stress may take the same toll; threats to self-esteem and academic/career achievement may seem just as real. However, unlike females, who are accustomed to relying on others when troubled, males generally resist seeking help. This may be one reason their plight has gone unnoticed. If some women resent being labeled victims, men are even more likely to spurn such an identification. Female harassees may complicate their situations by turning to close associates who sympathize but lack expertise. Males exacerbate theirs by silence. Thus, in one of the few examinations of males' response to harassment, Bingham and Scherer noted that "the masculine stereotype that defines men as inexpressive, dominant, independent, and always sexually eager . . . may constrain men from talking with friends and relatives about unwanted sexual attention."[24] It may also color their self-reports of sexual harassment, tainting their accounts and responses with masculine bravado and encouraging them to minimize their experiences.

Predictably, males file harassment suits against institutions very rarely, and when they do so the response to their complaints is often dismissive. This was the case when a thirty-three-year-old male student attending a human sexuality class at California State University at Sacramento claimed to be offended by the female professor's use of sex tales, how-to tips, and close-up slides of women's and adolescent girls' genitalia. He alleged that the professor made derogatory remarks about male genitalia and encouraged her female students to masturbate as a way of freeing themselves from the "hardship" of intercourse with males.[25] When the university refused to take action based upon his complaints that he found the professor's lectures offensive, the student filed a civil suit against the school and the professor, maintaining that he felt "raped" and "trapped" by the professor's pedagogical technique. The lawyer for the professor allegedly dismissed the student's action as "fundamentalist Christian McCarthyism."[26] The attorney for the student responded that "it is unimaginable that a male professor delivering the same lecture while demeaning women wouldn't have been punished."[27] A psychology professor echoed his observation: "[W]e tend to be compassionate to women but there may well be a kind of insensitivity to males."[28]

Powerlessness, perhaps the most destructive of the emotions evoked by sexual harassment, is as damaging to men as it is to women. When it occurs in a male, it may challenge his deepest aspirations toward independence, status, and control. Men have difficulty understanding women's resistance to objectification because they have little or no frame of reference that allows them to comprehend what it is like to be a sex object, so when they are subjected to inappropriate remarks or unwanted sexual attention, some may be even less prepared than their female counterparts to handle the situation. If the student in the California State case was sincerely offended, the institution was obliged to treat his complaint with as much sensitivity and respect as it would that of a female.

DENIAL

Both male targets of and witnesses to sexual harassment may engage in denial. It is an especially destructive response to sexual harassment. Some males, like females, refuse to admit that they or their associates are the objects of undesired sexual or gender attention. Self-deception is as defeating in these instances as in any other. In closing his eyes to his own and to others' discomfort or pain, the male suppresses feelings of anger and anxiety that, if acknowledged, would make him appear unmanly. One student told of being the butt of jokes for several days in a psychology class while the professor was criticizing Freud's theory of penis envy. When asked whether the so-called humor had caused him discomfort, he replied, "Well, I didn't like it, if that's what you mean. But it was no big deal. He was just trying to be funny, I guess." Having internalized the rules by which males live, the student instinctively adopted the "no big deal" and "I can take a joke" approaches to experience. It never occurred to him that it is a very big deal when an educator's store of teaching methods is so depleted that embarrassing students becomes a means of gaining class attention.

Even more than females, males may be drawn to denial because the prospect of complaining about harassment appears so socially unacceptable. Self-deception and avoidance of problems take energy, and when energy is eroded, students, male and female, react in irresponsible ways. They sleep through classes and appointments they want to avoid. They try to alleviate stress by neglecting their schoolwork and, especially if they are "macho," by drinking too much and too often. They get sick, and their grades suffer. A bizarre cycle, set in motion by a self-indulgent professor, continues because few male students have the internal resources and the external support to say, "Enough!" Unwittingly, they cooperate with the offenders.

Denial of harassment has collective as well as individual consequences. When people refuse to acknowledge a problem, it is unlikely to be solved. Institutions cannot discipline perpetrators without specific complaints from students, so male reluctance to recognize harassment and seek help contributes to the paralysis that exists on many campuses. A Catch-22 thus exists for men as well as women because the average male brings with him to college an established value system and behavioral code that discourage him from engaging in the responses to sexual harassment that would be most successful in deterring it.

IDENTIFICATION WITH PERPETRATORS

Equally or perhaps more destructive than denial of the offense is identification with the offender. Little boys, like girls, are taught from their earliest exposure to formal education to "mind" and respect teachers, most of whom are female. Though male children have a harder time accepting discipline, the impact of educators should not be underestimated, especially when male students enter high education and begin to perform at their academic peaks. Poised to enter the "real" world after what may seem an eternity of subjugation in classrooms, the average male student may be presented for the first time with academic role models of his own gender.

Three laboratory studies of sexually harassing behavior by J. B. Pryor and colleagues[29] suggested that social norms and thus role models do indeed influence male tendencies to harass. Having developed the Reliability of the Likelihood to Sexually Harass or LSH scale, which reportedly allows for scientific analysis of the psychological characteristics of potential harassers, Pryor and his associates determined that men high in LSH are likely to harass when social climates make the behavior appear acceptable. In an experiment specifically involving role models, they concluded that "the harassing role model served to define the social norms for behavior in the situation and thus made sexual harassment more socially acceptable for those men who wished to do it."[30]

This is crucial information for institutions if Pryor's experiment is likely to be replicated in the classrooms of perpetrators. Professors dispense information, and "if relations are inherently hierarchical [as men believe], then the one who has more information is framed as higher up on the ladder, by virtue of being more knowledgeable and competent. . . . [Information] is an essential part of the independence that men perceive to be a prerequisite for self-respect."[31] Regardless of male students' personal responses to male professors, they are acutely aware of the independence, power, and status they possess within the confines of academe.

The very presence of predominantly male staff is a novelty for most, whose previous educational experiences are likely to have been mostly with women.

It should come as no surprise, then, when male students view male instructors as role models. This is probably an appropriate choice unless the model also happens to be a sexual harasser. If such an individual appears to flourish professionally without intervention from the institution, a male student can easily assume that his behavior is sanctioned and thus acceptable. He carries that lesson with him during his stay on campus and when he leaves it for the world of work. No one should be surprised at this result, and the burden of blame should not be placed on the student. Reminiscent of Samuel Beckett's Clov in *Endgame*, he sends a provocative message to academe: "I use the words you taught me. If they don't mean anything anymore, teach me others."[32] Professors who dismiss the antics of some of their colleagues as harmless or who refuse, in the name of "academic freedom," to criticize them, need to recognize that professional behaviors teach students as much as books, or more, and that if they genuinely care about creating a just society, educators have an obligation to ensure that their words and actions teach males and females the right messages.

BLAMING THE VICTIM

Ironically, mates who identify with harassers and regard their behaviors as acceptable and those who disapprove of perpetrators' actions often explain harassment in similar ways. They employ a widely recognized defense mechanism of those who are frustrated by their inability to understand a problem or effect change. They blame the victim. This is true even in cases in which they are closely associated with harassees. An architecture student described such a situation: "This prof is bugging my girlfriend like crazy. Every class he makes some little comment about how girls have a hard time when they get out into the world being engineers. Then she goes off on me because she's mad at him, and I try to tell her she doesn't have to take that shit because she's better in math [than I am,] but she won't listen. It pisses me off that she won't do anything to help herself."

In this situation the male refused to understand that the female's way of "handling" the situation may, for the present, simply be to talk it through with him. Sometimes, in recognizing the target's discomfort but focusing on her passivity and refusal to defend herself, the male assuages his own guilt for not acting. By assuming that women who endure crude public jokes and sexist comments without protest "really don't mind" or "like" such behaviors, a male bystander may be relieved of the responsibility of monitoring his own interactions with females. And perhaps academicians, especially those who claim greatest concern about harassment, must accept some degree of culpability for these sorts of uninformed assessments of female behavior. Educational efforts for both students and employees sometimes focus exclusively on the ills of sexual harassment and assume what males may interpret as an accusatory tone. There might be less blaming if there were more effective means of educating college and university communities about the larger issue of gender differences, of encouraging understanding of males' and females' differential responses to sexuality and conflict resolution.

Males may do the most victim-blaming in situations where professors respond sexually to attractive female students, and while only anecdotal evidence supports this theory, it does appear logical. Boys grow to manhood and spend most of their lives in rule-bound endeavors. The games they play as children and enjoy as men are governed by intricate regulations which team players do not violate. The organizations and work environments males have created are hierarchical and rule-laden. Fair play is an enormous concern for them, and they do not look kindly on those who gain power or status by unfair means. A male struggling to maintain an A average in medical school or a C in Freshman English may view a female peer who attracts professorial attention or, worse still, dates a teacher as a competitor who is violating the rules. His masculine instincts may lead him to ignore or misunderstand the predicament of the person who has been singled out for attention and to assume that she is using her sexuality to manipulate the professor and seize the advantage. The female student may or may not be guilty, but if her male counterpart perceives the former to be the case, higher education will have taught him a lesson about women he will not soon forget. He may generalize from this one negative experience and carry with him for years the impression that femininity is a weapon used to acquire control and unfair advantage over males. Thus both male and female students become casualties when educators misuse their positions for personal self-indulgence.

INTERVENTION

Male students may suffer even when they interpret a sexual harassment situation accurately and attempt to intervene. Female students struggling because of inappropriate professorial behavior are not always open to the advice of their well-meaning male peers. Socialized to be less confrontational, less reliant on formal dispute resolution, and more concerned about the effects of their behaviors, women are not comfortable with assertive responses to harassment. Research demonstrates, as noted previously, that while probably 20 percent to 30 percent of females experienced harassment, institutions averaged only 4.3 complaints each year during the 1980s. Hence, the friend of the architectural student defended herself: "I can't make him understand that not everyone is Arnold Schwarzenegger. I'd rather listen to Professor T's craziness than him [her boyfriend] yelling at me to do something when there's no way I can without hurting my grades."

Although there has been no formal research on their experiences, it appears that males who do choose to intervene on behalf of females may encounter censure from friends with locker room mentalities who can't comprehend why a "real guy" would involve himself in a sexual harassment controversy. One freshman clarified this position: "I think Jim is nuts to say he'll talk to the [grievance] committee about Professor N. That guy's the terminator. He'd cut your balls off and not blink an eye. I figure if he thinks he can get it from the girls and nobody's stopping him 'til now, why should any of us act like fags and spill our guts to some committee?"

Males who confront perpetrators appear, at this point in time, relatively rare and report the same anxieties that plague female complainants. "I'm not sorry I went to the hearing with Carol, but I feel like I'll be looking over my shoulder for as long as I'm here," commented one student whose experience taught him that retaliation is a very serious concern for those who agree to take a stand against perpetrators. In some ways the targets of harassment are more protected from the possibility of retaliation than those who support them, and few, if any, institutions have sought to give guidance or encouragement to those willing to support harassees. Institutions are not adverse to monitoring the academic futures of successful complainants, but there are no guarantees for other students—male and female—who may be punished by a resentful harasser or his friends.

This point was illustrated in a letter from a man recalling an experience that occurred twenty years ago.

> I was a graduate student working as a research associate for a center at a university. My job was to supervise a team of work-study students in coding data. The faculty of the center began asking me to send them workers to help them. At first they asked for either of two attractive young women, then for just one of them. I suspected their motive, which was confirmed when I overheard the young woman tell that she was being asked to organize books (over and over) high up on shelves. This required her to stand on a step ladder in the days of extremely short skirts. So when one of the faculty asked for the woman, I sent him a young male worker. Shortly thereafter I was called upon the carpet, charged with not properly overseeing the workers, and I was essentially fired.
>
> I never tried to tell my story, and I don't think I even considered filing a grievance. I was so vulnerable, and I had a fine offer from a famous professor back in the department. I was able to avoid the center's faculty because of my many good faculty supporters/friends. If I had not been an outstanding graduate student, this incident might have sunk my chances for the Ph.D. This incident happened twenty years ago but is clearly burned into my memory.

RECOGNITION AND POWERLESSNESS

Finally, there are the male students who recognize sexual harassment when it occurs but feel powerless to combat it. This is understandable. If Professor Q is publicly pursuing or humiliating Jane Jones and she is unwilling to act on her own behalf, her male classmate, John Smith, cannot be expected to be eager to come to her aid. Actually, what usually happens in such cases is that both the female student and her male peer feel threatened and incapable of exercising control. The only difference is that the negative reactions of female targets have been well documented and analyzed, but almost nothing is known about how observers of sexual harassment fare, especially when they are male.

One possibility is that when a male student witnesses a faculty member's pursuit of a female peer, he engages in a kind of mental combat in which he is doomed to failure. Socialization has taught him to assume that females of his own age and station are, unpalatable though the term may seem, his "territory." When a professor with all the trappings and safeguards of power encroaches on that "territory," the student finds himself in a no-win situation. If females admire and submit to the professor, the student may feel that his own status and masculinity are diminished. If, as has been pointed out, they respond negatively, and he takes the risk of supporting them, he is liable to suffer peer and academic censure, and thus another form of symbolic emasculation.

If a male student believes a female peer wants and needs his help and fear of retaliation deters him from giving it, his most basic nightmares become reality. He flees from confrontation with the professor, thus psychologically failing the woman and humiliating himself. He cannot console himself with recollections of a lost but worthy conflict because he believes he lacked the courage to engage in struggle. Having deserted what he perceives as his masculine responsibility, he may see himself as impotent by his own choice, and once again higher education is in the unenviable position of having helped to promote a distorted and damaging self-image.

Invisibility exacerbates frustration and pain and acts as a deterrent to progress. If the majority of male collegians seem insensitive to the issue of sexual harassment, it is in part because their experience with the problem has been minimized and ignored. If male graduates' understanding of gender issues frequently appears as parochial as that of men denied higher education, it is partially the result of academe's failure to investigate and address their needs.

The predicament of male academicians is equally troubling. Much important leadership and research on sexual harassment has come from males, yet the most pervasive image of the group is that of the lecherous professor. Despite the thousands of pages they have written, presentations they have delivered, and speeches they have made in meetings, the vast majority of male educators have remained silent about sexual harassment. There is little reliable research to indicate how credible they consider it to be as a campus concern, how or whether their perceptions of the problem have changed over time, how the issue has affected their own behavior with students or their attitudes toward and interactions with colleagues who harass. The comment of one English professor may be characteristic: "I'm just trying to survive."

But relations between the genders must be characterized by more than simple survival or "getting by" in a society that demands, as never before, contribution and cooperation from both males and females. It is unfortunate but probable that the numbers of men experiencing sexual harassment will increase as women gain prestige and authority. This is why it is essential that scholars begin now to consider men as crucial a subject of study as women. That is why the campus looms larger than ever as a place for Americans, male and female, to learn to live and work together.

NOTES

1. H-K. Luthar, "The Neglect of Critical Issues in the Sexual Harassment Discussion: Implications for Organizational and Public Policies," *Journal of Individual Employment Rights* 4, no. 4 (1995–96): 261.

2. Ibid., p. 261.

3. Ibid., p. 262.

4. Ibid.

5. "U.S. Merit System Protection Board: Sexual Harassment in the Federal Workplace: An Update" (Washington, D.C.: U.S. Government Printing Office, 1988). This study replicates an earlier study, "U.S. Merit System Protection Board: Is It a Problem?" (Washington, D.C.: U.S. Government Printing Office, 1981).

6. B. Gutek, *Sex and the Workplace: The Impact of Sexual Behavior and Harassment on Women, Men and Organizations* (San Francisco: Jossey-Bass, 1986), p. 49.

7. See L. J. Rubin and S. B. Borgers, "Sexual Harassment in the Universities During the 1980s," *Sex Roles* 23 (1990): 397–41; J. W. Adams, J. L. Kottke, and J. S. Padgitt, "Sexual Harassment of University Students," *Journal of College and Student Personnel* 24 (1983): 494–90; and A. McCormack "The Sexual Harassment of Students by Teachers: The Case of Students in Science," *Sex Roles* 13 (1985): 21–32.

8. See M. Komaromy, A. B. Bindman, R. J. Haber, and M. A. Sande, "Sexual Harassment in Medical Training," *New England Journal of Medicine* 328 (1993): 322–26.

9. See D. C. Baldwin Jr., S. R. Daugherty, and E. J. Eckenfels, "Student Perceptions of Mistreatment and Harassment During Medical School: A Survey of Ten United States Schools," *West Journal of Medicine* 155 (1991): 140–45; D. C. Baldwin Jr., S. R. Daugherty, and E. J. Eckenfels, "Sexual Harassment in Medical Training," *New England Journal of Medicine* 325 (1991): 1803; J. A. Richman, J. A. Flaherty, K. M. Rospenda, and M. L. Christensen, "Mental Health Consequences and Correlates of Reported Medical Student Abuse," *JAMA* 267 (1992): 692–94.

10. Gutek, *Sex and the Workplace*, p. 57.

11. Ibid., p. 58.

12. See E. G. C. Collins and T. B. Blodgett, "Sexual Harassment: Some See It . . . Some Won't," *Harvard Business Review* 59 (1981): 76–95; L. F. Fitzgerald and A. J. Ormerod, "Perceptions of Sexual Harassment: The Influence of Gender and Academic Context," *Psychology of Women Quarterly* 15 (1991): 281–94; S. Kenig, "Sex Differences in Levels of Tolerance and Attribution of Blame for Sexual Harassment on a University Campus," *Sex Roles* 15 (1986): 535–49; B. Lott, M. E. Reilly, and D. R. Howard, "Sexual Assault and Harassment: A Campus Community Case Study," *Signs* 8 (1982): 296–319; M. A. Marks, "Sexual Harassment on Campus: Effects of Professor Gender on Perception of Sexually Harassing Behaviors," *Sex Roles* 28 (1993): 207–17; K. McKinney, "Sexual Harassment of University Faculty by Colleagues and Students," *Sex Roles* 23 (1990): 421–38; P. M. Popovich, "Perceptions of Sexual Harassment as a Function of Sex of Rater and Incident Form and Consequence," *Sex Roles* 27 (1992): 609–25; J. S. Strouse, "Correlates of Attitudes Toward Sexual Harassment among Early Adolescents," *Sex Roles* 31 (1994): 559–77; C. Struckman-Johnson, "College Men's and Women's Reactions to Hypothetical Sexual Touch Varied by Initiator Gender and Coercion Level," *Sex Roles* 29 (1993): 371–85. An exception to these findings is: D. E. Terpstra and D. D. Baker, "A Hierarchy of Sexual Harassment," *Journal of Psychology* 121 (1987): 599–605.

13. See S. G. Bingham, "Factors Associated with Responses to Sexual Harassment and Satisfaction with Outcome," *Sex Roles* 29 (1993): 239–69.

14. N. J. Malovich and J. E. Stake, "Sexual Harassment on Campus: Individual Differences in Attitudes and Beliefs," *Psychology of Women Quarterly* 14 (1990): 79.

15. F. D. Arvey and M. A. Cavanaugh, "Using Surveys to Assess the Prevalence of Sexual Harassment: Some Methodological Problems," *Journal of Social Issues* 51 (1995): 44.

16. L. F. Fitzgerald, "Sexual Harassment: Violence Against Women in the Workplace," *American Psychologist* 48 (1993): 1073.

17. R. Bly, *Iron John: A Book About Men* (Reading, Mass.: Addison-Wesley, 1990), p. 234.

18. B. Johnstone, paraphrased in Deborah Tannen, *You Just Don't Understand* (New York: William Morrow & Co., 1990), p. 178.

19. Tannen, *You Just Don't Understand*, pp. 26, 28–29.

20. K. Druck and J. C. Simmons, *The Secrets Men Keep: Breaking the Silence Barrier* (Garden City, N.Y.: Doubleday, 1985), p. 18.

21. M. F. Fasteau, "The High Price of Macho," *Psychology Today* 9, no. 4 (1975): 60.

22. Bly, *Iron John*, p. 174.

23. See Komaromy et al., "Sexual Harassment in Medical Training."

24. Bingham, "Factors Associated with Responses to Sexual Harassment and Satisfaction with Outcome," p. 260.

25. A. P. Nomani, "Was Prof's Lecture Academic Freedom or Sexual Harassment?: A Male Student in California Irked by 'Male-Bashing' Asserts It Was the Latter," *Wall Street Journal*, March 7, 1995, sec. Al "W," col. 4.

26. Ibid.

27. Ibid.

28. Ibid.

29. See J. B. Pryor, "Sexual Harassment Proclivities in Men," *Sex Roles* 17 (1987): 269–90; J. B. Pryor, C. LaVite, and L. Stoller, "Sexual Harassment Proclivities in Men: A Social Psychological Analysis of Sexual Harassment: The Person/Situation Interaction," *Journal of Vocational Behavior* 42 (1993): 68–83; J. B. Pryor, J. L. Giedd, and K. B. William, "A Social Psychological Model for Predicting Sexual Harassment," *Journal of Social Issues* 51 (1995): 69–84.

30. Pryor, Giedd, and William, "A Social Psychological Model for Predicting Sexual Harassment," p. 79.

31. Tannen, *You Just Don't Understand*, p. 62.

32. S. Beckett, "Endgame," in *Stages of Drama*, 2d ed., ed. Carl H. Klaus, Miriam Gilbert, and Bradford S. Field (New York: St. Martin's Press, 1991), p. 942.

The Workplace

THE DEFINITION
OF SEXUAL HARASSMENT

4

EDMUND WALL

As important as current scientific, legal, and philosophical definitions of sexual harassment are, many of them omit the interpersonal features which define the concept. The view defended in Part I of this essay is that the mental states of the perpetrator and the victim are the essential defining elements. Sexual harassment is described as a form of communication that violates its victim's privacy rights. This interpersonal definition purports to capture the more subtle instances of sexual harassment while circumventing those sexual advances that are not sexually harassing. This proposed definition is contrasted with behavior descriptions of sexual harassment, an approach widely used by sociologists and psychologists. Part II of this essay criticizes definitions formulated in terms of the alleged discriminatory and coercive effects of a sexual advance, and the federal legal definition which omits reference to relevant mental states.

I

There are many types of behavior that may be classified as instances of sexual harassment, and some people, such as Ken-

From *Public Affairs Quarterly* 5, no. 4 (1991): 371–85. Reprinted, with modifications, by permission of the publisher.

neth Cooper, have proposed that managers explain the concept to their employees primarily through descriptions of various behavior patterns. This is no surprise, as numerous sociological and psychological studies which survey people's attitudes toward sexual harassment and which attempt to gauge its frequency also explain sexual harassment primarily or entirely through behavior descriptions. Cooper addresses the sexual harassment of female employees by male managers in an essay that describes what he terms "six levels of sexual harassment." He seems to order these levels according to what he assumes to be two complementary considerations: a third party's ability to identify the perpetrator's behavior as sexually harassing and the severity of the infraction. The categories are presented in ascending order with the first category ostensibly representing the least flagrant type of behavior, the sixth category representing the most flagrant type of behavior. Cooper writes that "obvious and blatant harassment may be decreasing, but borderline harassment behavior has never let up."[1] He takes the first four categories to be accounts of "borderline" cases.

Cooper refers to the first type of behavior as "aesthetic appreciation." This refers to comments which "express a nonaggressive appreciation of physical or sexual features." For example, an alleged perpetrator says to a coworker: "Gee . . . sigh . . . you're looking better every day!"[2] Cooper refers to such examples as the most "innocent" type of sexual harassment, but believes that these examples, nevertheless, constitute sexual harassment. In such cases the harassment is concealed.

Does managerial behavior, which falls under "aesthetic appreciation," necessarily constitute sexual harassment? Cooper argues that "regardless of how harmless these appreciative comments may seem, they are putdowns which lower the group stature of the target." The manager, he tells us, is in a "superior position" from which to judge the employee's physical attributes.[3]

Comments of "aesthetic appreciation" made by male managers to female employees may not be appropriate, but Cooper's argument does not show that all such comments are, as he suggests, instances of sexual harassment. Cooper argues that managerial comments of "aesthetic appreciation" made to employees are sexually harassing because they are "put-downs which lower the group stature of the target." There is a problem here. Cooper has not shown that such comments necessarily reflect a group differential.[4] Of course, the manager is in a "superior position" in relation to his employee, but only with respect to her corporate duties, not to judgments about her physical attributes. The manager may try to use his corporate authority in order to force his employee to listen to his assessment of her physical charms. Furthermore, the employee may feel as though she must submit to the manager's remarks, even if he does not openly attempt to coerce her. However, his sexually harassing behavior need not inherently be an exercise of corporate authority. It could simply be misguided human behavior which utilizes corporate authority.

The second type of behavior which, according to Cooper, constitutes sexual harassment is "active mental groping." Under this heading Cooper places "direct verbal harassment," which evidently includes sexual jokes about the employee, and also the type of staring that may leave employees feeling as though managers are "undressing them with their eyes."[5] This is followed by "social touching." Cooper maintains that, along with the first two categories of behavior, this type of behavior is "borderline," since the offender remains "within normal social touching conventions." In other words, such touching misleadingly appears "totally innocent" to a "third party."[6]

As far as "social touching" is concerned, Cooper distinguishes an innocent "friendly touch" from a "sensual touch." While not providing an example of a "friendly touch," Cooper gives as an example of a "sensual touch" "a caressing hand laid gently on the [employee]," or the movement of the manager's hand up and down his employee's back.[7] Unfortunately, Cooper offers no defense of his distinction between two types of touching. Neither does he clearly relate this distinction to his account of sexual harassment, although he seems to assume that a manager's "friendly touch" does not constitute sexual harassment, whereas his "sensual touch" would. He merely warns managers against any "social touching."

The reason why the distinction between an innocent "friendly touch" and a "sensual touch" makes sense is also the reason why behavior descriptions are not central to the definition of sexual harassment. The basis for the distinction lies in the manager's mental state, not in his behavior. A sincerely "friendly touch" would depend, among other things, upon the manager's motive for touching his employee. Sexual harassment refers to a defect in interpersonal relations. Depending upon the manager's and employee's mental states, it is possible that some examples of managerial behavior which satisfy Cooper's first, most "innocent" category (i.e., "aesthetic appreciation"), would actually be more objectionable than his second and third categories (i.e., "active mental groping" and "social touching," respectively). Indeed, depending upon the manager's and employee's mental states, cases that fall under any of Cooper's first three categories of sexual harassment could be characterized as "innocent."

Consider the case in which a manager finds that one of his employees strikingly resembles his mother. He has managed this employee for three years without incident, and one day in the corporate dining room they begin to discuss their parents. He may tell her of the resemblance between her and his mother. He may stare at her for a long time while (this would constitute "active mental groping" on Cooper's view). He may tell her that her cheekbones are as pretty as those of his mother (an example of "aesthetic appreciation," according to Cooper). Finally, he may put his hand on her shoulder (i.e., an example of friendly "social touching" on Cooper's view) and say "Oh well, I must be getting back to my desk." Given this scenario, it is obvious that at least some employees would take no offense at the manager's behavior. Such a case need not involve sexual harassment, even though mere behavior descriptions would lead us to the opposite conclusion.

Cooper refers to his fourth and final "borderline" category as "foreplay harassment." Unlike "social touching," the touching here is not "innocent in nature and location," although its inappropriateness is still concealed.[8] Examples of "foreplay harassment" include a manager noticing that a button on an employee's blouse is undone. Instead of telling her about it, he buttons it. Another example would be brushing up against her, "as if by accident."[9]

Cooper suggests that the "scope, frequency, and feel" of the touching "shows an obvious intent on the part of the offender to push the limits of decency. . . ."[10] In his description of sexual harassment Cooper alludes to the importance of the manager's motive, but does not make its importance explicit. He does not express it as one of the essential descriptions of sexual harassment. Accidental physical contact between a manager and his employee is not, of course, sexual harassment. When the manager deliberately makes contact with his employee from a certain motive or due to his negligence, then he becomes an offender. Whether or not he makes physical contact, he may still be an offender. Indeed, as Cooper recognizes, an employee could be sexually harassed without *any* physical contact between her and her manager.

Cooper overlooks the possibility that what appears to be "foreplay harassment" of an employee might not be. Even when a manager is sexually "petting" an employee in his office, he is not necessarily sexually harassing her, even though his behavior would be viewed as inappropriate. Consider the case in which a manager and an employee form an uncoerced agreement to engage in such inappropriate office behavior.[11] This is not sexual harassment. The general problem with behavior descriptions of sexual harassment can be seen when we attempt to construct examples of sexual harassment. The application of any of Cooper's four "borderline" categories to our examples may yield false determinations, depending upon the mental states involved.

Cooper's fifth and sixth categories are not "borderline," but involve flagrant sexual advances. They are "sexual abuse" and "ultimate threat," respectively. The latter, which refers to a manager's coercive threats for sexual favors, will be discussed in Part II of this essay. The other category, "sexual abuse," is usually limited to forced sexual contact, but, like "sexual harassment," it may be broader than this.

Probably any behavior which constitutes sexual harassment (i.e., which satisfies certain descriptions of the manager's and employee's mental states) would also constitute sexual abuse—whether physical or verbal. When an individual is maliciously or negligently responsible for unjustified harm to someone, it would seem that he or she has abused that person. Abuse can be subtle; it may include various ways of inflicting psychological harm. In fact, there is a more subtle form of sexual harassment accomplished through stares, gestures, and innuendo. For example, a manager may sexually harass his employee by staring at her and "undressing her with his eyes." *In light of this and the other limitations of behavior descriptions we need a definition of sexual harassment that is capable of capturing all subtle instances of sexual harassment while filtering out (even overt) sexual behavior which is not harassing.*

Where X is the sexual harasser and Y the victim, the following conditions are offered as the definition of sexual harassment:

(1) X does not attempt to obtain Y's consent to communicate to Y, X's or someone else's alleged sexual interest in Y.

(2) X communicates to Y, X's or someone else's alleged sexual interest in Y.

X's motive for communicating this is some perceived benefit that he or she expects to obtain through the communication.

(3) Y does not consent to discuss with X, X's or someone else's alleged sexual interest in Y.

(4) Y feels emotionally distressed because X did not attempt to obtain Y's consent to this discussion and/or because Y objects to what Y takes to be the offensive content of X's sexual comments.

The first condition refers to X's failure to attempt to obtain Y's consent to discuss someone's sexual interest in Y. X's involvement in the sexual harassment is not defined by the type of sexual proposition that X may make to Y. If the first condition was formulated in terms of the content of X's sexual proposition, then the proposed definition would circumvent some of the more subtle cases of sexual harassment. After all, Y may actually agree to a sexual proposition made to her or him by X and still be sexually harassed by X's attempting to discuss it with Y. In some cases Y might not feel that it is the proper time or place to discuss such matters. In any event *sexual harassment primarily involves wrongful communication*. Whether or not X attempts to obtain Y's consent to a certain type of communication is crucial. What is inherently repulsive about sexual harassment is not the possible vulgarity of X's sexual comment or proposal, but X's failure to show respect for Y's rights. It is the obligation that stems from privacy rights that is ignored. Y's personal behavior and aspirations are protected by Y's privacy rights. The intrusion by X into this moral sphere is what is so objectionable about sexual harassment. If X does not attempt to obtain Y's approval to discuss such private matters, then he or she has not shown Y adequate respect.

X's lack of respect for Y's rights is not a sufficient description of sexual harassment, however. X's conduct must constitute a rights violation. Essentially, the second condition refers to the fact that X has acted without concern for Y's right to consent to the communication of sexual matters involving Y. Here X "communicates" to Y that X or someone else is sexually interested in Y. This term includes not only verbal remarks made by X, but any purposeful conveyance such as gestures, noises, stares, etc., that violate its recipient's privacy rights. Such behavior can be every bit as intrusive as verbal remarks.

We need to acknowledge that X can refer to some third party's alleged sexual interest in Y and still sexually harass Y. When X tells Y, without Y's consent, that some third party believes Y is physically desirable, this may be a case of sexual harassment. Y may not approve of X telling him or her this—even if Y and the third party happen to share a mutual sexual interest in each other. This is because X's impropriety lies in the invasive approach to Y. It does not hinge upon the content of what X says to Y. X may, for example, have absolutely no sexual interest in Y, but believes that such remarks would upset Y, thereby affording X perverse enjoyment. Likewise, X's report that some third party is sexually interested in Y may be inaccurate, but this does not absolve X from the duty to respect Y's privacy.

X's specific motive for communicating what he or she does to Y may vary, but it always includes some benefit X may obtain from this illegitimate communication. X might or might not plan to have sexual relations with Y. Indeed, as we have seen, X might not have a sexual interest in Y at all and still obtain what X perceives to be beneficial to himself or herself, perhaps the satisfaction of disturbing Y.[12] Perhaps, as some contemporary psychologists suggest, X's ultimate motive is to mollify his or her feelings of inferiority by controlling Y's feelings, actions, or environment. Yet another possibility is that, if X is male, he might want to conform to what he believes to be parental and/or peer standards for males. The proposed first and second conditions can account for these various motives. The point is that, whatever the perceived benefit, it is the utility of the approach as perceived by X, and not necessarily the content of rs message, that is important to the harasser. Furthermore, the "benefit" that moves X to action might not be obtainable or might not be a genuine benefit, but, nevertheless, in X's attempt to obtain it, X violates Y's rights.

The third condition refers to Y's not consenting to discuss with X, X's or someone else's alleged sexual interest in Y. Someone might argue that the first condition is now unnecessary, that X's failure to obtain Y's consent to the type of discussion outlined in the third condition will suffice; the first condition describing X's failure to *attempt* to obtain Y's consent is, therefore, unnecessary. This objection would be misguided, however. The first condition ensures that some sexual comments will not be unjustly labeled as "harassing." Consider the possibility that the second and third conditions are satisfied. For example, X makes a sexual remark about Y to Y without Y's consent. Now suppose that the first condition is not satisfied, that is, suppose that X *did attempt* to obtain Y's consent to make such remarks. Furthermore, suppose that somewhere the communication between X and Y breaks down and X honestly believes he or she has obtained Y's consent to this discussion, when, in fact, he or she has not. In this case, X's intentions and actions being what they are, X does not sexually harass Y. X has shown respect for Y's privacy. Y may certainly *feel* harassed in this case, but there is no offender here. However, after X sees Y's displeasure at the remarks, it is now X's duty to refrain from such remarks, unless, of course, Y later consents to such a discussion.

The case of the ignorant but well-intentioned X demonstrates the importance of distinguishing between accidents (and merely unfortunate circumstances) and sexual harassment. The remedy for avoiding the former is the encouragement of clear communication between people. Emphasis on clear communication would also facilitate the identification of some offenders, for some offenders would not refrain from making sexual remarks after their targets clearly expressed their objections to those remarks. The above case also reveals the need for people to clearly express their wishes to others. For example, when someone wishes not to discuss an individual's sexual interest in them, it would be foolish for them to make flirting glances at this individual. Such gestures may mislead the individual to conclude that they consent to this communication.

By themselves the first three conditions are not adequate descriptions of sexual harassment. What is missing is a description of the victim's mental state. In sexual harassment cases the wrongful communication must distress Y for a certain reason. Let us say that X has expressed sexual interest in Y without any attempt to obtain Y's consent to such a discussion. Y, in fact, does not consent to it. However, perhaps Y has decided against the discussion because Y finds X too refined and anticipates that X's sexual advances will not interest Y. Perhaps Y welcomes crass discussions about sexual matters. In this case Y might not be sexually harassed by X's remarks. As the fourth condition indicates, Y must be distressed because X did not attempt to ensure that it was permissible to make sexual comments to Y which involve Y, or because the content of X's sexual comments are offensive in Y's view. Yet another possibility is that both the invasiveness of X's approach and the content of what X says causes Y emotional distress. In this example, however, it would appear that Y would neither find the content of X's sexual remarks to be offensive nor would Y object to the fact that X did not attempt to obtain Y's consent to make these remarks to Y. Due to Y's views concerning sexual privacy this case is similar to one in which X does not attempt to obtain Y's consent to discuss with Y how well Y plays tennis, or some other mundane discussion about Y.

II

We have postponed a discussion of the relation of sexual harassment to coercion and discrimination against women. Let us now explore this relation.

The fact that male employers and managers represent the bulk of the reported offenders has caused some legal theorists and philosophers to conclude that sexual harassment necessarily involves discrimination against women as a class. This approach is unacceptable. Sexual harassment is not necessarily tied to discrimination or to coercion.

In an essay titled "Is Sexual Harassment Coercive?" Larry May and John C. Hughes argue that sexual harassment against women workers is "inherently coercive"—whether the harassment takes the form of a threat or an offer. They also maintain that the harm of sexual harassment against women "contributes to a pervasive pattern of discrimination and exploitation based upon sex."[13] May and Hughes begin by defining sexual harassment as "the intimidation of persons in subordinate positions by those holding power and authority over them in order to exact sexual favors that would ordinarily not have been granted."[14]

May and Hughes recognize that male employees might be sexually harassed, but choose to limit their discussion to the typical case in which a male employer or manager sexually harasses a female employee. They choose this paradigm because it represents the "dominant pattern" in society and because they believe that, as a class, women have been conditioned by society to acquiesce "to male initiative."[15] According to May and Hughes, women represent an injured class. The fact that men dominate positions of authority and status in our society renders women vulnerable to sexual harassment. Furthermore, the sexual harassment of female employees by male employers and managers sparks a general increase in the frequency of the crime, since such behavior reinforces male stereotypes of women as sexual objects.[16]

Even if May and Hughes's social assumptions are accepted, that would not entail that their definition of sexual harassment, which includes a power differential between the offender and the victim, is adequate. Unhappily, this circumvents the sexual harassment between employees with equal capabilities and corporate status. Suppose that X and Y are coworkers for some company. X makes frequent comments concerning Y's sexual appeal and repeatedly propositions Y despite Y's refusals. Authority and rank are superfluous here. Y may be sexually harassed regardless of X or Y's corporate status. As argued above in the critique of Cooper's article, the harassment at issue is not an extension of X's corporate authority, nor is the harassment essentially explained by the exercise of his authority. Rather, it is essentially explained by X's lack of respect for Y's right to refuse to discuss sexual matters pertaining to Y. If Y chooses not to enter X's discussion or is upset by X's refusal to recognize Y's privacy rights, then sexual harassment has occurred. The essential element is X and Y's mental state, not an alleged power differential between them.

Of course May and Hughes would also say that society has shaped the "mental states" of men and women in an unhealthy fashion. Women are conditioned to be passive and to expect treatment as sexual objects. According to May and Hughes, the difference in social status between women and men which affords men the opportunity and encouragement to dominate women reflects how sexual harassment is an issue of power. The problem here is that even if such sweeping social assumptions could be verified scientifically, the social conditions referred to in those assumptions would have to play essential roles in the sexual harassment cases in our society—if sexual harassment is to be *defined* in terms of these social conditions. May and Hughes would need to demonstrate that social inequities and issues of power are central to all sexual harassment cases before they could say without qualification that sexual harassment is a form of sex discrimination.

May and Hughes's inaccurate definition of sexual harassment skews their inquiry. Their main objective is to illustrate the coercive nature of sexual harassment; more specifically, the coercive nature of sexual threats and conditional offers made to women employees by male corporate authorities. They focus on the type of sexual advances that are tied to hiring, promotions, or raises.[17] May and Hughes briefly refer to a third type of sexual advance, one that is "merely annoying" and "without demonstrable sanction or reward."[18] However, after introducing this third category the authors circumvent it. This oversight is a serious one. The essence of sexual harassment lies not in the content of the offender's proposal, but in the inappropriateness of his approach to the victim. It lies in the way he violates the victim's privacy. This is the "annoying" aspect of the offender's approach which needs elucidating. May and Hughes could not pursue this third type of sexual advance because they had defined sexual harassment in terms of someone in authority acquiring some sexual favor from his employee. They set themselves the task of proving that sexual harassment is necessarily coercive. Their definition thereby hinged on the alleged coercive effects of the harasser's proposal, rather than on his mental state.

We still need to examine May and Hughes's position that all sexual threats and offers made by male employers or managers to female employees are sexually harassing as well as coercive. They describe a conditional sexual threat from the employer's position: "If you don't provide a sexual benefit, I will punish you by withholding a promotion or raise that would otherwise be due, or ultimately fire you."[19] According to their "baseline" approach to coercion, "sexual threats are coercive because they worsen the objective situation the employee finds herself in." Before the threat the retention of her job only depended upon "standards of efficiency," whereas, after the threat, the performance of sexual favors becomes a condition of employment.[20] Presumably, these same "baseline" considerations also render the threat sexually harassing.

May and Hughes acknowledge their debt to Robert Nozick's "baseline account" of coercive threats. Elsewhere, I have defended an interpersonal description of coercive threats against the "baseline accounts" of Nozick and others.[21] According to my description X issues Y a coercive threat (in his attempt to get Y to do action "A") when X intentionally attempts to create the belief in Y that X will be responsible for harm coming to Y should Y fail to do A. X's coercive threat is described primarily in terms of his intentions. His motive for attempting to create this belief in Y is his desire to bring about a state of affairs in which Y's recognition of this possible harm to himself influences Y to do A. May and Hughes are correct that every conditional sexual threat issued by a male superior to a female subordinate is a coercive threat. (Indeed, a conditional sexual threat issued against anyone is a coercive threat.) The male manager would be trying to create the belief in the female employee that he will be responsible for harm coming to her (i.e., her termination, demotion, etc.) should she fail to comply with his sexual request. He would do this because he wants the prospect of this harm to motivate her to comply. Nevertheless, it is not true that every conditional sexual threat *as May and Hughes describe these threats* would be coercive. If, for example, the employer and the employee are playfully engaging in "banter" when he tells her that without her compliance he will fire her, then she is not being threatened. He does not intend to create the belief in her that harm will come to her. In this scenario she would not be sexually harassed either because the employer has a good faith belief that she consents to this "banter." Therefore, May and Hughes need a more rigorous description of coercive threats which includes the intentions of the person making the threat.

May and Hughes argue that if the employee wants to provide sexual favors to her employer regardless of the employer's demand, she is still coerced. They maintain that her objective baseline situation is still made worse, for now it would be very difficult for her to cease a sexual relationship with her employer should she choose to do so.[22] May and Hughes do not tell us who or what would specifically be making the coercive proposal if the *employee* propositioned the employer. After all, on their view, her offer would worsen her objective situation for the same reason his threat would. Perhaps they would refer to this as a coercive situation, or would find the employer's consent to the sexual relationship to include some sort of a coercive stance, but, nevertheless, their external analysis overlooks the mental state of the individual who is supposedly victimized.

Depending upon her values and personal outlook she may, without reservation, accept her employer's demand as a "career opportunity." By excluding the employee's mental state in their "baseline analysis," May and Hughes overlook the fact that her situation may improve after the demand and that, to her, the prospect of a permanent sexual relationship with her employer is no problem. According to this "baseline account" she would not be coerced or harassed. Unlike May and Hughes's analysis, the proposed interpersonal account of sexual harassment maintains that an employee who receives a sexual threat from her employer is not necessarily sexually harassed. Let us say that he told her she must have sex with him or else be demoted. Still, she may welcome his demand as a "career opportunity." If she is not offended by his demand, then she is not sexually harassed by the threat.

As we have seen, May and Hughes maintain that the sexual harassment of a female employee by a male corporate authority is coercive because it worsens the employee's employment situation. They say that sexual harassment by a male employer makes for an unfair employment condition against women as a class. May and Hughes therefore believe that the discriminatory nature of sexual harassment against female employees is tied to these "coercive" dimensions. They argue that men do not have to endure the maligned "job requirement" foisted upon women, and that when men make sexual threats to their female subordinates they "establish a precedent for employment decisions based upon the stereotype that values women for their sexuality. . . ."[23] Because the sexual harassment of female employees by male employers worsens the employment situation of women as a class, we supposedly have a necessary relation between ("coercive") sexual harassment and sex discrimination.

May and Hughes are not alone in their belief that sexual harassment and discrimination are necessarily related. When they describe their arguments for the coercive-discriminatory effects of a male employer's sexual threat on a female employee, they refer to such a threat as an "instance of discrimination in the workplace."[24] Here they follow federal law by claiming that sexual threats in the workplace fall under the rubric of Title VII of the Civil Rights Act of 1964. They are relying on the fact that in 1980, the Equal Employment Opportunity Commission (EEOC) set a precedent by finding that sexual harassment is a form of sex discrimination.[25]

The view that the sexual harassment of women is a form of sex discrimination is ill-founded. Even if we follow May and Hughes and limit our discussion to the sexual harassment of female employees by male employers—something that the EEOC cannot do—a male employer's sexual threat is not necessarily an "instance" of sex discrimination. For a given sexual harassment case, gender may not be a consideration at all. Picture the bisexual male employer who indiscriminately threatens or propositions the male and female employees in his company. The additional "job requirement" referred to by May and Hughes would, in this case, apply to all employees, male and female. Although the proposed interpersonal account is compatible with the assumptions that sexual harassment against women generally contributes to discrimination against women and that the negative effects of sexual harassment are generally more serious for women than for men, the proposed account does not take sex discrimination to be an essential feature of sexual harassment.

May and Hughes's position must have been influenced by Catharine MacKinnon's book *Sexual Harassment of Working Women: A Case of Sex Discrimination.*[26] MacKinnon has helped to persuade the legal establishment and many social theorists to view the sexual harassment of women as sex discrimination. It appears that May and Hughes's account coincides with that of MacKinnon, except on one major point—MacKinnon acknowledges that the case of the bisexual harasser does not involve sex discrimination (although she says that such cases are rare). At the end of her book she refers to a "bisexual superior who harasses subordinates in a way that shows no gender bias." MacKinnon leaves open the possibility that the bisexual harasser can construct a legal defense sufficient to "negate the claim of sex discrimination."[27]

However, MacKinnon's position on sex discrimination is not clear. Earlier on in her book she says that according to the U.S. Supreme Court's account of sexual harassment—an account she finds inadequate—the case of the bisexual employer is "probably not sex discrimination." In such a case, the Supreme Court would find that the employees are not (mis)treated differently due to gender considerations.[28] Yet, the account of sex discrimination that MacKinnon prefers is not the one offered by the Supreme Court. MacKinnon apparently suggests that one *could* find sex discrimination in the case of the bisexual harasser. This finding would hinge on MacKinnon's view that society has defined the female gender in terms of sexuality and "makes a woman's sexuality a badge of female servitude."[29] MacKinnon refers to the special vulnerability of women and to the "disparate impact" of sexual harassment on women. She argues that even "neutral" employment practices which involve equal *treatment* of female and male employees may still have a disparate *impact* on the employees. Unlike men, women can suffer special negative effects from ostensibly neutral employment practices.[30] Given that society values women primarily for their sexuality, even the harassment of the bisexual supervisor may be seen as reinforcing this type of discrimination.

Does MacKinnon want to say that the case of the bisexual harasser does not involve sex discrimination, thereby qualifying her claim that sexual harassment is sex discrimination, or does she want to say that discrimination is found even in this example because women are disadvantaged in a way that men are not? It seems that there must be at least a few cases involving no special disadvantages, but even if all sexual harassment cases impacted on women in an especially negative way, this would not prove that the special disadvantages render the harassment itself discriminatory. In order to prove this, one would have to overcome the objection that discrimination seems to be more closely tied to an offender's actions and motives rather than to the disadvantageous results of an offender's actions.

Of course, the possibility that federal authority was misdirected when the EEOC set policy for sexual harassment in the workplace, does not entail that the EEOC's definition is incorrect. They maintain that:

> Unwelcome sexual advances, requests for sexual favors, and other verbal or physical conduct of a sexual nature constitute sexual harassment when (1) submission to such conduct is made either explicitly or implicitly a term or condition of an individual's employment, (2) submission to or rejection of such conduct by an individual is used as the basis for employment decisions affecting such an individual, or (3) such conduct has the purpose or effect of unreasonably interfering with an individual's work performance or creating an intimidating, hostile, or offensive working environment.

The EEOC's conditions of sexual harassment appear to include not only sexual threats and offers, but also "annoyances" and other more subtle violations. The EEOC's definition thereby avoids May and Hughes's mistake. Their third condition also allows for sexual harassment between employees, something also lacking in May and Hughes's account. Unfortunately, the EEOC's first two conditions seem to suggest that all sexual threats and offers made by employers to employees are sexually harassing. As argued above, not all sexual threats made by employers to employees need be harassing, their inappropriateness notwithstanding. The EEOC's definition of sexual harassment is too inclusive because it fails to capture precisely the victim's mental state and the way that the victim reacts to the threat. In omitting a description of the victim's mental state the EEOC's definition allows a severely paranoid "victim" to claim sexual harassment against a considerate employer who has merely made some innocent comment or gesture. Moreover, the EEOC makes no provision for the intentions of the employer.

Some states throughout the country maintain that sexually explicit materials which disturb employees are sexually harassing. This stance seems to be in line with the EEOC's definition. According to the EEOC the employer or employee who, for example, displays a sexually explicit poster may exhibit "physical conduct of a sexual nature" that creates an "offensive working environment." This is a difficult example, but it seems that an employee's mere disapproval of such materials does not entail that the employee is being sexually harassed. Even if the disgruntled employee disapproves of the poster's explicit sexual representations, this does not mean that the person displaying the poster is intending to communicate anything to the employee about the employee. Of course, in many cases the poster bearer may be making a subtle statement to the employee about the employee's sexual appeal. For example, the individual may be using the poster in order to communicate a sexual interest in the employee. According to the interpersonal account these cases would involve sexual harassment. If the person is merely displaying the poster for the person's own benefit, however, then this behavior is rude, but not sexually harassing. There is a difference between the disrespect involved in rudeness, which indicates poor taste or a breach of etiquette, and the disrespect involved in sexual harassment. In the latter case the privacy of some specific individual has not been respected.

If May and Hughes's position that all conditional sexual threats by male employers to female employees are sexually harassing and discriminatory in nature has successfully been overturned, their contention that the same considerations also apply to sexual offers collapses. They describe a sexual offer from the male employer's position: "If you provide a sexual benefit, I will reward you with a promotion or a raise that would otherwise not be due."[31] Since the benefit would ostensibly improve the employee's baseline situation, she is made an offer by her employer. Without the offer, she would not get the promotion or raise.

Interestingly, May and Hughes argue that such offers actually worsen the employee's baseline situation and are, therefore, coercive offers. They do not explain how the employee's situation is simultaneously improved and worsened, but perhaps they have the following in mind: the employer's proposal is an offer because it may improve the employee's strategic status, whereas his offer is coercive because of certain social considerations. May and Hughes tell us that the employer's sexual offer changes the work environment so that the employee "is viewed by others, and may come to view herself, less in terms of her work productivity and more in terms of her sexual allure." Moreover, they say that, since women are more "economically vulnerable and socially passive than men," they are inclined to "offset [their] diminished status and to protect against later retaliation" by acquiescing to employer demands. Thus, according to May and Hughes, they are necessarily coerced by a male employer's sexual offer.[32]

May and Hughes argue that there is usually an implicit threat concealed in an employer's sexual offer and that this makes the offer coercive. Of course, here it may be the threat that is coercive and not the offer. What we are interested in is their argument that the employer's sexual offer itself is coercive because it reduces the female employee's self-esteem and also raises the specter of some future threat (should the employee fail to comply or otherwise fall victim to the employer's "bruised" ego). Even if May and Hughes are correct and these are the general social effects of these sexual offers, this does not entail that a sexual offer made by a male employer to a female employee is itself coercive. It would be unreasonable to suggest that every female employee would experience these hardships following a male employer's sexual offer. As mentioned in the discussion of sexual threats, the employee's values and personality contribute to the effects of an employer's presumably coercive proposal. Moreover, May and Hughes's claim about the coercive effects of these sexual offers hinges upon their "baseline account" of coercion (which has been criticized above).

There is a more plausible alternative to a "baseline account" of coercive offers. An interpersonal account is possible. X makes Y a coercive offer when X intends to create the belief in Y that X will not prevent harm from coming to Y unless Y complies with X's request. A genuine offer, on the other hand, would be limited to a mutual exchange of perceived benefits, or it may be a gift. This offer could become coercive if X attempts to cause Y to believe that Y's rejection of X's request will result in some harm to Y. Essentially, the coercive element is that X makes the proposed assistance in preventing this harm conditional upon Y's agreement to X's request. X tries to use Y's belief that harm will occur as a way of controlling Y. Not all offers by male employers to female employees are like this. Thus, on this interpersonal description of offers, a male employer's offer is not coercive by nature.

We still need to address May and Hughes's account of the implications of an employer's sexual offer to an employee. We are told that a noncompliant employee may worry that a disgruntled employer may threaten or harm her at some future date. This is certainly possible. However, such proposals are not coercive unless they involve the relevant intentions. The proposed account does acknowledge that an employer's noncoercive sexual offer might be sexually harassing. As argued above, this depends upon the legitimacy of his approach to the employee and on the employee's wishes. Moreover, the fact that, according to the proposed view, some of these sexual offers are not coercive or sexually harassing does not alter the fact that an employer who is both considerate and prudent would avoid any behavior that could be construed as sexually harassing.[33]

NOTES

1. Kenneth C. Cooper, "The Six Levels of Sexual Harassment," in *Contemporary Moral Controversies in Business*, ed. A. Pablo Iannone (New York: Oxford University Press, 1989), p. 190.

2. Ibid.

3. Ibid.

4. See Part II for a detailed discussion of sexual harassment and discrimination.

5. Cooper, "The Six Levels of Sexual Harassment," p. 191.

6. Ibid.

7. Ibid.

8. Ibid.

9. Ibid., pp. 191–92.

10. Ibid., p. 192.

11. See Part II for a discussion of coercion and sexual harassment.

12. Some sociologists would disagree with me. They believe that the offender must have set himself a "sexual goal" in order for sexual harassment to occur. See K. Wilson and L. Kraus, "Sexual Harassment in the University." This paper was presented at the annual meetings of the American Sociological Association (Toronto, 1981).

13. Larry May and John C. Hughes, "Is Sexual Harassment Coercive?" in *Moral Rights in the Workplace*, ed. Gertrude Ezorsky (Albany: State University of New York Press, 1987), pp. 115–22.

14. Ibid., p. 115.

15. Ibid.

16. Ibid., p. 118.

17. Ibid., pp. 116–17.

18. Ibid., p. 117.

19. Ibid., pp. 116–17.

20. Ibid., pp. 117–18.

21. "Intention and Coercion," *Journal of Applied Philosophy* 5, no. 1 (1988): 75–85.

22. May and Hughes, "Is Sexual Harassment Coercive?" p. 119.

23. Ibid., pp. 118–19.

24. Ibid., p. 118.

25. Equal Employment Opportunity Commission, *Federal Register* 45, no. 74 (1980), p. 677.

26. Catharine A. MacKinnon, *Sexual Harassment of Working Women: A Case of Sex Discrimination* (New Haven, Conn.: Yale University Press, 1979).

27. Ibid., pp. 236–37.

28. Ibid., p. 203.

29. Ibid., p. 189.

30. Ibid., p. 192.

31. May and Hughes, "Is Sexual Harassment Coercive?" p. 117.

32. Ibid., p. 120.

33. I am grateful to Burleigh Wilkins for helpful comments on this paper.

5

SEXUAL HARASSMENT

*Why the Corporate World
Still Doesn't "Get It"*

VAUGHANA MACY FEARY

INTRODUCTION

With the widely publicized charges of sexual harassment brought by neurosurgeon Dr. Frances Conley against Stanford Medical School, the electrifying allegations of Professor Anita Hill against Judge Clarence Thomas, and the sordid Tailhook scandal involving sexual misconduct in the military, the problem of sexual harassment finally exploded into the headlines. As yesterday's silent victims began joining a swelling chorus of protest from today's working women, corporate America suddenly began admitting that sexual harassment is an explosive communication problem. Yet despite all the recent ballyhoo over sexual harassment in the workplace, corporate America still doesn't really "get it" much less understand how to put an end to it.

If sexual harassment in the workplace is to be understood and eliminated, then not only corporate America, but the entire international business community must recognize and discard some old myths about the nature of ethics, and about the relationship between ethics, law, and business, as well as some newer myths about sexual harassment itself. It must recognize

Kluwer Academic Publishers, *Journal of Business Ethics* 13 (1994): 649–62.
With kind permission from Kluwer Academic Publisher.

that sexual harassment in the workplace is not simply a snag in communication resulting from factual ignorance or factual disagreement, or from cultural or gender differences, or from confusions about an especially murky concept. Sexual harassment is not merely a communication problem. It is a moral problem for everyone in the corporate world and, to recognize this, is finally to get to the root of the problem and to understand what measures need to be taken to eliminate it.

SEXUAL HARASSMENT AS A WIDESPREAD MORAL PROBLEM

Why has the business community taken so long to admit that sexual harassment in the workplace is a serious problem? The reason seems to be that it still believes Myth Number One—the tired old joke that business ethics is an oxymoron; business should not really take ethics seriously.

There are numerous statistical studies which show that sexual harassment is an old problem. One of the earliest surveys, conducted by *Redbook* magazine in 1976, found that nine out of ten women responding to the survey had encountered sexual harassment on the job.[1] In 1978, Cornell University found that 70 percent of women workers surveyed reported sexual harassment. In 1981, the National Merit Systems Protection Board conducted the largest study of sexual harassment yet available and found that 42 percent of 23,000 people surveyed believed they had been sexually harassed.[2] In 1981, another study conducted by *Redbook*, in collaboration with *Harvard Business Review*, found that 63 percent of managers responding to the survey reported sexual harassment at their companies.[3] In 1984, Dziech and Weiner reported that 30 percent of undergraduate women experience sexual harassment during their college careers (a staggering 2,000,000 students) and Gutek (1985) reported that 53.1 percent of private-sector workers surveyed believed that they had suffered economic hardship because of refusing to satisfy sexual demands.[4] In 1991, there was little improvement. In October of that year, following the Thomas hearings, a *Time* magazine poll found that 34 percent of the women polled had experienced sexual harassment at work.[5] Such findings corroborated the findings of another recent poll conducted by the National Association for Female Executives which found that 53 percent of the members surveyed had been sexually harassed or knew of someone who had been harassed.[6] A *Working Woman* survey published in June 1992 found that 60 percent of the respondents had been victimized; it attributed this still higher percentage to the fact that the women polled held positions as executives, for "women in managerial and professional positions, as well as those working in male-dominated companies are more likely to experience harassment."[7]

Although studies show that some women are more likely to be harassed than others, they also confirm that no group of women (or men) has remained wholly exempt from sexual harassment.[8] One-tenth of sexual harassment complaints are now being filed by men.[9] Studies also show that workers may be victimized by supervisors or peers, individuals or groups. The most recent June 1992 *Working Woman* study, however, found that 83 percent of the harassers enjoy more powerful positions than the victim.[10]

Finally, no work environment seems to be immune. Sexual harassment is a problem in government, in the military, in corporations, in small businesses, and in academe.

Despite all the evidence indicating that sexual harassment was a major problem in the workplace, the business community remained largely indifferent. Although a 1988 *Working Woman* survey of sexual harassment found that 86 percent of the respondents believed that mandatory training programs would alleviate the problem, only 58 percent yet offered such programs. In 1988, the United States Merit Systems Protection Board also issued an update on sexual harassment with a series of recommendations for employers which included such topics as training, policy statements, enforcement action, complaint and investigation procedures, and additional preventative efforts (e.g., random surveys and follow-up interviews with parties involved in harassment claims).[11] A few companies such as Corning, which began its attempts to combat sexual harassment as early as the 1970s, and DuPont which has long held workshops designed to sensitize managers to the problem, were responsive.[12] Few other companies followed their leadership. It took the Thomas hearings to finally galvanize the business community into recognizing that sexual harassment was rapidly becoming the communication problem of the 1990s.

If the business community had not been as busy repeating the same tired jokes and had taken business ethics seriously, it would not have been caught napping. If business leaders had done their ethics homework, they would have recognized that when women reported being sexually harassed they were not merely supplying factual reports about the conduct of their supervisors or describing the features of their work environment. "Sexual harassment" like the term "rude" is not merely a descriptive term. It is a quasi-moral term. To say "*X* has been sexually harassed" is not merely to imply that certain descriptive conditions have been met, but also to contextually imply that some moral standard has been violated and that the victim disapproves of the action on moral grounds. Moral claims, unlike purely factual claims, are prescriptive in character, which is to say that they are tied to action in ways that purely descriptive claims are not. Thus to say "*X* is being sexually harassed" is also to contextually imply that something ought to be done about it. This explains why business leaders should discard Myth Number One. Moral problems do not fade away in a whimper. As the Thomas hearings indicated, they tend to erupt with a bang.

SEXUAL HARASSMENT IN THE WORKPLACE— A HISTORICAL OVERVIEW

In the wake of the Thomas hearings, the corporate world has been forced to acknowledge that sexual harassment is a serious problem. Unfortunately, however, this epiphany is no harbinger of increased moral sensitivity in corporate America. The source of the change is best explained as a natural outgrowth of Myth Number Two—the belief that the only time moral problems are business problems is when they become legal problems.

Given the business community's allegiance to Myth Number Two, it is understandable that corporations have been lethargic in responding to the problem of sexual harassment. Law has moved very slowly in this area. Although Title VII of the Civil Rights Act of 1964 prohibited discrimination on the basis of sex, it was not until 1972 that an amendment was added to explicitly prohibit sexual harassment. Even then, women were reluctant to complain or sue.[13] When women did sue, they were initially unsuccessful, probably because many judges concurred with the view expressed by Judge Frey who remarked, in finding against the plaintiff in a sexual harassment case, that he was unwilling to set a precedent which would encourage a flood of lawsuits because, "the only way an employer could avoid such charges would be to have employees who were asexual."[14]

It was not until *Barnes* v. *Train* 13 Fair Empl. Prac. Cas. (BNA) 123 (D.D.C) 1974, rev'd sub nom. *Barnes* v. *Costle*, 561 F. 2d 983 (D.C. Cir. 1977) that the court agreed that sexual harassment was prohibited under Title VII. The judge found in favor of the plaintiff who had complained of discrimination on the grounds that she had been belittled, harassed, and ultimately fired because she had refused to have sex with her supervisor.[15] The case was important in finding that what was defined in the EEOC guidelines as "quid pro quo sexual harassment" (cases of "unwelcome sexual conduct" in which "submission to such conduct is made either explicitly or implicitly a term or condition of an individual's employment") was prohibited under Title VII and by establishing some precedent for vicarious employer responsibility for the conduct of a supervisor, at least where the employer was aware of the harassment and took no action.

In most cases, however, the emotional, professional, and financial costs of conducting even a successful suit seemed sufficiently high to insure that few women would even sue, particularly as general compensatory and punitive damages are not available to plaintiffs under Title VII.[16] Despite Judge Frey's assumption that providing legal recognition of sexual harassment would put employers at risk of incurring a flood of suits, in 1980, fully three years after *Barnes*, only seventy-five charges were filed.[17]

It was not until *Meritor Saving Bank* v. *Vinson* 447 U.S. 57 (1986), a case in which the plaintiff alleged that she had been harassed, raped, threatened, and forced to acquiesce to further sexual contacts for fear of losing her job, that the Supreme Court, relying heavily upon the 1980 EEOC guidelines, affirmed that "quid pro quo sexual harassment" AND "environmental harassment" ("unwelcome" sexual conduct that "unreasonably interferes with an individual's job performance" or sustains an "intimidating, hostile, or offensive working environment") both constitute violations of Title VII. *Meritor* was important in reaffirming the decision in *Barnes* that quid pro quo harassment is illegal and in establishing, for the first time, that sexual harassment which creates a hostile work environment (even in the absence of quid pro quo harassment) is sufficient to make such conduct illegal under Title VII. It was also important because it emphasized that the crucial issue in deciding whether conduct constitutes sexual harassment is whether it is "unwelcome," rather than whether it is "voluntary."[18]

Following *Meritor*, subsequent cases continued a trend (begun even before *Meritor*) of expanding the scope of illegal sexual harassment. A series of decisions extended sexual harassment to cover harassment by coworkers, nonemployees (e.g., clients), and third parties (e.g., cases in which employees complain because they are denied benefits accorded to others who acquiesce to sexual harassment).[19] Further decisions extended protection from sexual harassment to homosexuals and to heterosexual men.[20] Other decisions have clarified and extended employer liability. EEOC guidelines, revised in 1988, summarized and incorporated these developments.[21]

Still more significantly, although state and federal antidiscrimination laws were the initial vehicle for legal change vis-à-vis sexual harassment, significant cases have been considered under common law on such grounds as: tort claims based on sexual harassment, worker-compensation statutes, intentional infliction of emotional distress, assault and battery, tortious interference with contracts, invasion of privacy, false imprisonment, wrongful discharge, and even on the peculiar grounds of loss of consortium (the loss of a husband's ability to protect his right to his wife's sexual services).[22] The advantage of claims brought under common law is that they may result in heavy punitive damages for employers.

Finally law began to give recognition to prevention, as well as remediation, and to assess higher punitive damages. As an AP release in the October 18, 1991, *Wall Street Journal* noted, at the time of the allegations against Judge Thomas, Maine had just passed a law requiring employers to educate workers about sexual harassment. The first state law of its kind, it may serve as model for other states. Maine also raised fines for violations of the Maine Human Rights Act to $10,000 for the first offense, to $25,000 for the second, and to $50,000 for a third offense.

Theoretically, given the legal developments just cited, sexual harassment should have become an explosive communication problem in the 1980s. Only two catalysts were missing: power and politics. Despite the much ballyhooed progress of women during the past decades, women still have significantly less political and economic power than men. In 1990, women between the ages of 35–44 (their prime earning years), working full time, only garnered 69 percent of what men earned, and 37 percent of female heads of households had incomes in the bottom fifth of the income distribution.[23] At the time of the Thomas hearings, there were still only two women in the U.S. Senate. Finally, as Susan Faludi (author of *Backlash: The Undeclared War Against American Women*) also pointed out, in a biting article in the *Wall Street Journal* following the Thomas fiasco, Thomas's reign at the EEOC during the Reagan years insured that the issue of sexual harassment, as well as sexual discrimination, would be kept firmly under political wraps.[24]

In the wake of the furor created by the Thomas hearings, the corporate world belatedly recognized that the legal machinery for a full-fledged assault on the problem was now in place and that political winds had shifted. Women still lack economic power and adequate political representation, but in a close election, they will wield considerable political power at the ballot box. Women's issues are likely to be at the forefront of national politics for some time to come.[25]

The lesson to be learned from all this is that Myth Number Two—the idea that moral problems are serious only when they become legal problems—should have been relinquished a long time ago. Morality and legality are not coextensive; only the most harmful forms of immoral conduct are illegal. If corporations are anxious to avoid public relations fiascos and expensive litigation, they must make moral education part of their business.

Legal guidelines which regulate the workplace should emerge, in part, from concern and debate in the business community itself. Simply because sexual harassment has so recently emerged from the shadows of corporate inertia into the glare of judicial scrutiny, it is unlikely that the courts have yet shed any final light upon this matter. Now that sexual harassment has become a subject of public moral and political debate, new cases will be heard, new precedents set, and new laws will be forthcoming. Already punitive damages are soaring. In 1986, an Ohio woman won a $3.1 million verdict against her employer whose quid pro quo offer involved oral sex in order to retain her job.[26] In September 1991, a California court awarded another 3.1 million to two women police officers for being subjected to a hostile work environment.[27] Still more legal problems are emerging because now even alleged perpetrators are suing on the grounds of wrongful discharge. Corporations who have faced, or are facing, such suits include: Polaroid, Newsday, General Motors, AT&T, DuPont, Boeing, and Rockwell International.[28] According to the most recent 1992 *Working Woman* survey, it may cost corporate America more than $1 billion over the next five years to settle existing lawsuits. The business community has paid a high price for its allegiance to outworn myths, not only in punitive damages, but also in marred corporate images. Any lessons learned have been learned at too high a cost.

WHY CORPORATIONS STILL DON'T GET IT

As *Business Week* proclaimed in its 1991 October issue, sexual harassment is finally "Top of the News." Corporations STILL don't get it, but they are trying. Most corporations have adopted the recommendations of the United States Merit Systems Protections Board, enunciated in 1988. As a headline in the *Wall Street Journal* December 2, 1991, points out, "Sexual Harassment Is Topping Agenda in Many Executive Education Programs." According to that article, of 495 companies surveyed, 40.2 percent now provide training programs about sexual harassment. One management consultant in the field estimates that 90 percent of Fortune 500 companies will offer such programs within the year—despite the fact that her package can cost as much as $100,000.[29] Ironically, sexual harassment has now become a thriving business.

Unfortunately, it is doubtful that most of the existing types of sexual harassment education currently being offered by human resource consultants are likely to be very effective because such programs overlook the role of power in organizations and the potential for the abuse of organizational power in today's job market. An effective educational program should result in the reduction and eventual elimination of harassing behaviors without inflicting further damage upon the groups most likely to be victimized, but it is doubtful that even where there is a clearly defined corporate policy about sexual harassment, a formal grievance procedure, and strictly enforced sanctions for noncompliance that incidents of sexual harassment will be fully reported or greatly reduced.

Managers wield enormous power over subordinates through their ability to hire, fire, demote, or promote employees and through their authority (based upon the law of agency) which recognizes and enforces their managerial decisions. As I will show in the concluding sections of this paper, sexual harassment is a flagrant abuse of power because it violates the moral rights of employees. In practice, however, it is very difficult for employees in subordinate positions to insist upon their rights. Sexual harassment is often subtle and difficult to prove. Even if victims do prove their case, they have every reason to fear subtle forms of retaliation in their current positions and subtle forms of discrimination if they attempt to secure other positions. Claims about unfair hiring and promotion decisions are difficult to substantiate, especially in a climate where there are too many equally well qualified applicants for the few positions available. In a recessive economy almost all employees are desperate to retain the jobs they have and to avoid even the semblance of "making waves." Under such conditions, it is almost impossible for those most likely to be victimized to protect themselves without incurring further harms. As a consequence, an effective educational program must focus not only upon educating the potential victim, but also upon the task of deterring the potential victimizers. In sum, it must educate those who hold and exercise the power in the business community about the reasons why sexual harassment is morally wrong and why they have ethical responsibilities to eliminate it.

The kinds of sexual harassment education currently being offered in most corporations are not likely to deter potential victimizers because they are still based on old myths. Myth Number Three—the belief that most moral problems result from ignorance about facts—explains why corporations are hiring consultants to deluge employees with facts about sexual harassment. Of course we need to know the facts, but a lot of this information is old news, and educating people about facts is simply not enough. Moral problems occur not only when there is ignorance or disagreement about facts, but also when there is disagreement about values. There is no logical inconsistency between acknowledging legal and statistical facts about sexual harassment and refusing to take a moral stand. Only moral education can bridge the gap by providing reasons for giving up deeply entrenched ideas that, at best, the issue of sexual harassment is "much ado about nothing" or, at worst, a "legal menace" to which many managers may deeply resent being subjected.

Myth Number Four—the belief that the problem of sexual harassment results primarily from either cultural differences, or from differences in the way men and women feel and communicate—also accounts, in part, for the current influx of psychologists and management consultants into the workplace to conduct trendy little workshops designed to educate people about cultural and gender difference. Thanks to Deborah Tannen et al., we are all supposed to believe that "You Just Don't Understand," and that a little psychodrama will clear up the problem."[30] It won't.

Of course there is some truth in old myths or they wouldn't retain such a tenacious hold on our thinking. There may be cultural differences in attitudes about sex and there may be differences between the way the two genders feel and communicate about sex, and some of these differences may serve to causally explain the incidence of sexual harassment—and probably rape as well.

There may also be considerable truth in all three popular models for understanding sexual harassment According to the natural/biological model, sexual harassment is attributable to biological differences between genders. Men have stronger sexual drives and feel differently about sexual interaction than women do. According to the sociocultural model, sexual harassment is a product of a patriarchal system in which men learn to use and to enjoy the exercise of personal power based on sex. According to the organizational model, sexual harassment results from asymmetrical relationships of power and authority which derive from hierarchical organizational structures.[31]

Taken together, culture and gender-based approaches to sexual harassment do a great deal to causally explain the widespread incidence of sexual harassment. Unfortunately, they do not provide any rational moral reasons which might convince potential victimizers to make any commitment to changing attitudes, beliefs, communication styles, or behavior which perpetuate it.

The almost exclusive emphasis on culture, gender, or communication can also have damagerous side effects. Hiring women consultants to explain facts and to explore differences in feelings and communication styles between the genders can only encourage the notion that sexual harassment is a woman's problem and that all women understand it. It can only reinforce old stereotypes that women form some monolithic group who think and feel alike. This is simply not the case. Moral problems are everyone's problem and everyone, including women, needs to understand their character. Sexual harassment stress syndrome results, in part, from the fact that women, themselves, don't always understand, which is why they lose self-confidence and why they feel worthless and at fault. Some women like feminist attorney Catharine MacKinnon do understand that "objection to sexual harassment is not a neopuritan protest"; other women like revisionist Camille Paglia, who believes "this psychodrama is puritanism reborn," don't understand at all.[32] Analogously, emphasizing cultural differences in communication styles may reinforce old stereotypes, or create new ones encouraging the mistaken idea that all members of ethnic groups supposedly think and behave alike.

The problem of sexual harassment is a moral problem and moral problems do not merely result from differences in feelings or cultural values, nor should human behavior and communication in this area (or any other) properly be understood as mere knee-jerk reactions to biological or cultural drives. Biological drives can be restrained and cultures, including corporate cultures, can be changed. The changes we need are not merely changes in the way people feel and communicate, but rather changes in the way people think about what constitutes appropriate moral conduct.

THE DEFINITION OF SEXUAL HARASSMENT

Undoubtedly one of the biggest obstacles to "getting" sexual harassment is Myth Number Five—the belief that the concept of sexual harassment (like most moral concepts) is "murky." Some people worry that there are such deep cultural and gender-based differences about the topic that no satisfactory definition can ever be provided. It is now fashionable for Europeans to laugh and talk condescendingly about American puritanism, and for people in our own country to act as if the goal of combatting sexual harassment is equivalent to some Machiavellian scheme to "desexualize the workplace" and to deny fellow employees dating and courtship rites.[33] Some people claim to be completely bewildered by what the term means and worry hysterically that a sympathetic hug might be misconstrued as "sexual touching."[34] As one attorney for an employer remarked, "If one woman's interpretation sets the legal standard, then it is virtually up to every woman in the workplace to define if she's been sexually harassed."[35] A great deal of this popular wisdom, however, seems to stem from ignorance about the sophistication of EEOC guidelines, or from deliberate attempts on the part of some members of the political, business, or legal communities to prey on such ignorance and to create a backlash.

Surprisingly, some philosophers have encouraged the supposition that sexual harassment is a murky concept by treating the whole problem of defining it as a complex philosophical problem. Two recent philosophical articles devoted to defining sexual harassment deserve especial comment. Both articles, one would presume, offer definitions which their respective authors believe to be superior to existing EEOC definitions, but although both articles mention EEOC guidelines in passing, neither supply any exhaustive criticism or sustained argument to show why their definitions constitute any improvement.

Susan M. Dodds, Lucy Frost, Robert Pargetter, and Elizabeth W. Prior (1988) and Edmund Wall (1991) represent diametrically opposed views about how sexual harassment should be defined.[36] Dodds et al. propose a behavioral definition, because they believe that sexual harassment can occur even when an individual woman is not offended (e.g., as in cases of women who just shrug off being propositioned). According to Dodds et al., there are no mental states on the part of the victim which are necessary conditions of sexual harassment. They seem to believe that this sharply differentiates their view from the view expressed in EEOC guidelines, and they insist that a behavioral definition is necessary for the administration of public policy.[37]

Wall, by contrast with Dodds et al., believes that the mental states of both the perpetrator and the victim are essential defining elements of sexual harassment.[38] He believes that subjective features are essential in defining sexual harassment because, although a range of behaviors can, on occasion, be identified as sexual harassment, almost any of the behaviors, given different mental states of alleged victimizers and victims, may not qualify as sexual harassment at all. Perhaps a quid pro quo offer was only "banter" or perhaps the alleged victim really welcomed the offer as a "career opportunity."[39] Wall seems very concerned with preventing the much popularized innocent man/paranoid woman scenario.[40] Certainly, his inclusion of the perpetrator's mental states differs from EEOC guidelines which focus on the mental states of a victim, or more accurately, a reasonable victimized person.

Both Dodds et al. and Wall agree, however, that certain features which have been proposed as necessary and sufficient conditions of sexual harassment do not so qualify. Some theorists, such as Larry May and John C. Hughes, as well as EEOC guidelines, hold that sexual harassment always constitutes discrimination.[41] Both Dodds et al. and Wall disagree because, they argue, a bisexual might sexually harass both sexes without the action being discriminatory.[42] This line of argument seems rather silly as an objection to EEOC guidelines and does nothing to establish that sexual harassment is not discriminatory. The whole purpose of Title VII was to prevent invidious discrimination against any employee in the workplace, not merely women. Where sexual issues (gender, sexual preferences, sexual orientation, sexual bias, willingness to succumb to sexual advances, etc.) are used as a basis for making hiring, firing, or promotion decisions, or for any differences in treatment in the workplace, there is invidious discrimination among employees, because sex (in any of the senses just indicated) constitutes a morally inappropriate basis for such decisions.

Dodds et al. and Wall are also in agreement that the presence of coercion and/or negative consequences resulting from harassment are not necessary conditions for the existence of sexual harassment because the victim's personality and values contribute to the effect that a sexual offer will have upon that person. Dodds et al. and Wall are no doubt correct, but they fail to appreciate that the revised EEOC guidelines are compatible with their position. EEOC guidelines do not define sexual harassment in terms of coercion. EEOC guidelines hold that for behavior to constitute sexual harassment, it must be "unwelcome," and decisions about whether a victim found conduct to be unwelcome are to be used upon facts about her conduct.[43] Furthermore, where the victim has submitted to the sexual conduct, the pivotal issue in determining whether the conduct was harassment is whether the conduct was unwelcome; the issue of whether the conduct was voluntary has been ruled to have "no materiality" whatever.

EEOC guidelines do not define sexual harassment in terms of negative consequences for actual victims. The section dealing with "hostile work environment" specifically acknowledges that certain conditions constitute sexual harassment even when "they lead to no tangible or economic job consequences."[44] Emotional consequences are an issue in EEOC guidelines in determining whether certain types of conduct create a hostile work environment, but the responses are not these of the particular victim, but the hypothetical responses of a reasonable person.[45] By contrast, Wall believes that distress on the part of the actual victim is one of the necessary conditions for sexual harassment.[46] Wall simply seems to be wrong here. Women have been conditioned to stoically accept a great deal of sexual behavior which may harm them professionally. Nevertheless, a reasonable person who had not been so conditioned might be quite justifiably distressed. It is the issue of whether it would be rational to be distressed, rather than the issue of actual distress which seems central to defining sexual harassment, and this issue is already accommodated within EEOC guidelines.

If we examine the definitions finally proposed by Dodds et al. and Wall, we will see that neither definition is any improvement over the definition already proposed by the EEOC. Dodds et al. end up defining sexual harassment as:

> behavior which is typically associated with a mental state representing an attitude which seeks sexual ends without any concern for the person from whom those ends are sought, and which typically produces an unwanted and unpleasant response in the person who is the object of that behavior . . . even if the mental states of the harasser or the harassed (or both) are different from those typically associated with such behavior. The behavior constitutes a necessary and sufficient condition for sexual harassment.[47]

The definition proposed by Dodds et al. does (as they claim) possess a number of advantages, but most of those advantages can also be claimed for the EEOC definition which invokes "a reasonable person standard" in deciding whether the victim's response is appropriate, as well as in deciding "the more basic issue of whether challenged conduct is of a sexual nature."[48] Moreover, the EEOC definition has a major advantage that Dodds et al.'s definition does not possess. The EEOC definition, by appealing to the attitudes of the reasonable person (i.e., any reasonable victim) escapes the trap of cultural relativism. Dodds et al., by contrast, provide an account which they acknowledge to be culture relative, for they claim that "it will be a culture-relative kind of behavior that determines sexual harassment." What counts as sexual harassment will vary from society to society and "behavior which may be sexual harassment in one need not be in another."[49] While admittedly the kind of behavior which is recognized as sexual harassment will vary to some extent from culture to culture, and while admittedly employees of multinational corporations should respect the views of those from different cultures who feel harassed, even under conditions under which typically Americans would not feel harassed, there is no reason to think (as Dodds et al. apparently do) that it is the *fact* that the behavior/attitude correlation is typical in a given culture, or any culture, which justifies classifying the behavior as sexual harassment.

The EEOC guidelines which refer to a "reasonable person" standard avoid the trap of both subjective and cultural relativism; what makes behavior count as sexual harassment is not what a particular woman thinks about the behavior, or even what most people think about the behavior, but rather what a *reasonable* victim would think about it. No doubt there are some (perhaps even Dodds et al.)

who might contend that what is regarded as a "reasonable person" is also culture relative, but this is simply not true. Reasonable people employ rational grounds for making moral judgments, and what constitutes a rational ground cannot be decided simply by invoking cultural standards. Behavior is morally wrong, not merely because it is typically regarded as morally wrong in a particular culture, but because there are rational grounds for contending that it violates human rights, inflicts harm, or contributes to social injustice. Morality, as Lawrence Kohlberg and numerous philosophers have pointed out, is not a descriptive term. Pari passu, the same is true of the terms "reasonable person" and "sexual harassment."[50]

Even if sexual harassment were a purely descriptive term, the definition provided by Dodds et al. is too broad, too narrow, and too vague. It is too broad because the definition they provide would apply equally well to selfish sexual behavior on the part of males toward females in many unhappy consensual relationships ranging from affairs to marriages. It also seems too narrow in that it would exclude conduct in which the perpetrator did have some concern for his victim (e.g., he's in love with her for messianic reasons and thinks that she would be better off succumbing to his advances). It also seems too vague to be any improvement on the EEOC definition. What behaviors in our society would be identified as sexual harassment using their definition? Suppose men and women disagree. How is their definition supposed to help? In particular, how is their definition supposed to serve as a basis for proposing uniform guidelines about sexual harassment for multinational corporations?

Wall's proposed definition seems equally unlikely to be an improvement upon that already available in EEOC guidelines. Wall believes that the essence of sexual harassment is wrongful communication which violates the privacy rights of the victim. These rights are violated "not by the content of the offender's proposal, but in the inappropriateness of the approach to the victim."[51]

Wall proposes that:

> Wherein X is the sexual harasser and Y the victim, the following are offered as jointly necessary and sufficient conditions of sexual harassment:
> (1) X does not attempt to obtain Y's consent to communicate to Y, X's or someone else's purported sexual interest in Y.
> (2) X communicates to Y, X's or someone else's purported sexual interest in Y. X's motives for communicating this is some perceived benefit that he expects to obtain through the communication.
> (3) Y does not consent to discuss with X, X's or someone else's purported sexual interest in Y.
> (4) Y feels emotionally distressed because X did not attempt to obtain Y's consent to this discussion and/or because Y objected to the content of X's sexual comments.[52]

There seem to be a number of difficulties with Wall's definition. The worst difficulty is that it is too narrow. It excludes sexist harassment (e.g., demeaning remarks about women in general) and a great deal of environmental harassment (e.g., the display of objectionable sexual objects, discussions of sexual matters unrelated to work, etc.) which most people would want to include. Certainly excluding those elements requires considerably more argument that the perfunctory claim that "girlie" posters probably are better classified as bad taste rather than sexual harassment.[53] Wall's definition does not seem to accord with our basic intuitions. If indeed Judge Thomas did discuss the kinds of topics (e.g., his sexual endowments and prowess, pornographic movies, and the coke can incident) with Professor Hill that she alleges he did, most people would agree that she was certainly being subjected to a hostile work environment, even if he never said that he had an interest in engaging in sex with her or suggested that anyone else had such an interest. This seems to contradict Wall's belief that the content of what is communicated is immaterial.

There could also be cases of even quid pro quo sexual harassment in which few of the four conditions Wall specifies obtain. Wall simply fails to recognize that, in the case of sexual harassment, communication fails, not merely because the message is not communicated in an appropriate manner, but because, given the inequalities in status and income between employees, many employees (most of them women) do not feel at liberty to communicate honestly; few can afford to pay the price of honest communication.[54]

If Dodds et al.'s and Wall's definitions won't do, how should sexual harassment be defined? Don't their difficulties provide still more justification for all the current ballyhoo about the "murkiness" of sexual harassment and the new dangers perfectly well intentioned men and employers may face now that the problem of sexual harassment is being publicly acknowledged? Quite the contrary, defining sexual harassment for the purposes of business ethics is NOT a major philosophical problem. Although, given the difficulty of honest communication, one can hope that the courts will ultimately employ the reasonable person standards in deciding whether conduct is "welcome," the meaning of sexual harassment is reasonably well defined in EEOC guidelines.

Sexual harassment seems to be one of those concepts like the concept "game," to use Wittgenstein's famous example, which form a family.[55] Family members have family resemblances, but there is no shared feature all members of a family necessarily have in common. As a consequence, trying to set out necessary and sufficient conditions for sexual harassment is a thoroughly futile enterprise. The futility of that enterprise, however, does nothing to support the myth that the concept of sexual harassment is hopelessly murky. We are clear enough in paradigm cases about what people mean when they claim they are being sexually harassed. The paradigm cases have already been clearly spelled out by the revised 1985 EEOC guidelines which comprise a twenty-page document incorporating references to cases up to that year. In the absence of some better definition, or in the absence of some sustained philosophical argument for adding or subtracting from the sorts of paradigms those guidelines include, they seem to provide better definitions than those Dodds et al. and Wall have suggested to replace them.

Of course, in addition to paradigmatic cases of sexual harassment identified by law, there are also borderline cases about which corporations, and in some cases the courts, will have to make decisions. As sexual harassment is a quasi-moral term, legal decisions about borderline cases will almost certainly be based upon whether the questionable behavior is sufficiently morally objectionable to count as sexual harassment in the legal sense. All of this suggests that, for the purpose of business ethics, corporations would be well advised not only to educate their employees about EEOC guidelines, but also to educate them about the moral reasons which justify the belief that sexual harassment is genuinely immoral and ought to be legally prohibited. Given that education, employees will be encouraged not only to refrain from sexual harassment in the paradigm sense defined by law, but also to identify the sorts of borderline cases which the courts may find to be illegal in the future, and to refrain from subtle forms of sexual harassment which violate the spirit, if not the letter of existing law.

WHY SEXUAL HARASSMENT IN THE WORKPLACE IS MORALLY WRONG AND WHY IT OUGHT TO BE LEGALLY PROHIBITED

Sexual harassment is not a murky concept, but in the absence of an adequate theory which provides rational grounds for concluding that sexual harassment is morally wrong, many members of the business community will continue to believe that sexual harassment is "much ado about nothing" from the moral point of view. Moreover, given the difficulty of proving the truth of sexual harassment claims, they may believe that courts would have been well advised to treat the problem with benign neglect.

In order to show that the corporate world must make some genuine moral commitment to ending sexual harassment in the workplace, one final myth must be discarded. Myth Number Six (the Neutrality Myth) is the mistaken belief, still widely held by corporate America, that moral beliefs are based upon feelings or cultural values, and therefore one moral theory is as good as any other moral theory and equally deserving of respect. Allegiance to this outworn myth explains why corporations are reluctant to bring in professional philosophers to provide a moral education for their employees. It's all right to bring in business consultants to reach facts and to bring in psychologists to explore feelings, but in a multicultural society, moral education and moral stands are supposedly inappropriate.

The neutrality myth is a piece of outmoded nonsense. Moral education is now a part of the public school curriculum and an essential part of correctional education. Philosophers disagree among themselves about numerous ethical issues, but there is almost universal agreement about the following elementary points of metaethics. A moral theory does not merely express feelings nor is it based merely upon cultural values. A good moral theory provides good moral reasons for actions and beliefs and it must meet certain requirements: (1) *Logical Coherence*—it must be clear and not generate contradictions; (2) *Impartiality*—any moral decision one person makes for himself on the basis of the theory must be a decision that person would be willing for others to make in similar circumstances; (3) *Consistency with*

Basic Moral Intuitions—the use of the theory should not generate consequences any reasonable person would regard as morally objectionable (e.g., increased physical harm and suffering); (4) *Explanatory Adequacy*—the theory should provide reasons for moral judgments and serve as a basis for resolving conflicts; and (5) *Concern for the Facts*—the theory should take into account relevant facts about people, society, and existing circumstances. Inadequate moral theories do not satisfy these requirements, and some moral theories are better than others because they satisfy these requirements better than other theories. People are equally deserving of respect, but their moral views are not equally deserving of respect. The purpose of moral education is to teach people why some moral theories, and a lot of popular wisdom, simply don't hold water.

If we discard the old neutrality myth, and suggest good moral reasons why sexual harassment is NOT "much ado about nothing," corporations will have lost their last excuse for refusing to take a stand about sexual harassment and for failing to provide some moral education about the topic for their employees. What follows is a very brief outline of some good moral reasons for taking the problem of sexual harassment in the workplace seriously, for regarding it as morally objectionable, and for believing that it should be illegal.

First, sexual harassment is morally wrong because it physically and psychologically harms victims, and because environments which permit sexual harassment seem to encourage such harms. Even the most liberal moral theories acknowledge that harm to others is our strongest moral reason for restricting liberty. As the majority of victims in the past have been women, most of the evidence in support of the claim that sexual harassment is harmful is based upon evidence about women, but presumably any group which was habitually so victimized would suffer similar effects.

Some sexual harassment cases associated with "intimidating, hostile, or offensive working environment" involve rape or physical assault. Furthermore, both quid pro quo harassment and environmental harassment can cause sexual harassment trauma syndrome.[56] This syndrome involves both physical and psychological symptoms. According to Peggy Crull, a member of the New York Commission on Human Rights, an analysis of case material gathered from clients of Working Women's Institute's Information, Referral, and Counseling Service showed that 90 percent of the cases experienced psychological stress symptoms (nervousness, fear, and anger) while 63 percent experienced physical symptoms (headaches, nausea, tiredness, etc.).[57] State common-law claims of intentional infliction of emotional distress often accompany suits under Title VII; both require medical and psychiatric testimony to substantiate such claims.[58]

Some sexual touching which qualifies as sexual harassment under EEOC guidelines (even when it is confined to a single severe incident) may not inflict any direct physical harm on women, but permitting unwanted touching may encourage physical violence against women. As feminist philosopher Carole Sheffield has pointed out, America's women live with sexual terrorism.[59] There were 103,000 reported rapes in 1990. As most rapes are unreported, the actual number may have been fifteen times that figure.[60] Every year over one million children are physically abused and the average number of assaults per year is 10.5. The majority of teenage victims are female. The incidence of sexual abuse is difficult to determine, but one survey of women found that 38 percent had experienced intra- or extrafamilial sexual abuse by the time they reached age eighteen.[61] Finally 60 to 70 percent of evening calls to police departments concern domestic violence. One study found that 16 percent of the families surveyed had experienced husband/wife assaults. John Makepeace, in a survey of college students, found that 20 percent of female college students had experienced violence during dating and courtship.[62] Common sense suggests that, as physical violence against women is already a national disgrace, unwanted sexual touching in the workplace should be prohibited by law, and that cultures and institutions which fail to set limits upon unwanted sexual touching (i.e., touching parts of the body associated with sexual response) are encouraging further physical abuse and disrespect for women.

EEOC guidelines also hold that nonphysical conduct (e.g., sexual jokes, sexual conversation, the display of pornographic materials, etc.) in cases where it forms a repeated pattern does qualify as sexual harassment. The courts have been divided about this matter.[63] The 1986 Attorney General's Commission on Pornography did conclude that, although there is no general connection between pornography and violence, exposure to sexually degrading and violent materials does contribute to sexual violence against women.[64] The EEOC guidelines can be justified, in part, on the grounds of preventing physical harm to women.

Second, Wall is quite correct in emphasizing that sexual harassment violates privacy rights. Privacy, like pornography, is a controversial subject. Suffice it to say here that there is a constitutional right to privacy first recognized by the Supreme Court in *Griswold* v. *State of Connecticut* 381 US 479,85 S. Ct. 1678 (1965), a case involving the sale of contraceptives. In that case the Court found that there is a right to privacy emanating from penumbras surrounding the First, Third, Fourth, Fifth, Ninth, and Fourteenth Amendments which create zones of privacy. Presumably unwanted sexual touching would violate zones of privacy emanating from the Third and Fourth Amendments; if our homes cannot be invaded, presumably our bodies should be doubly sacrosanct. There are also moral rights to specific types of privacy in the workplace.[65] William Brenkert, for example, analyzes privacy as a "three-place relationship between a person A, some information X, and another person Z, such that the right to privacy is violated only when Z comes to possess information X and no relationship exists between A and Z which would justify Z's coming to know X."[66] Given this conception of privacy, Brenkert, as well as Joseph DesJardins, argue that the information a person (or institution) is entitled to know about an employee is confined to the sort of information which pertains to the employee's ability to perform his job. Given that sexual matters are irrelevant in assessing an individual's ability to perform a job, privacy rights seem to preclude any inquiries by managers about the sexual lives of their employees outside of the workplace, and to provide a clear moral justification for discouraging sexual conversations within it.

Third, there are certainly historical and causal correlations between sexual harassment and discrimination. It was no accident that the issue was catapulted into national prominence by a black man and a black woman. While sexual harassment is an emotionally charged issue in every community, it is especially charged in those which have suffered from discrimination. Judge Thomas quite justifiably invoked the lynching metaphor to remind his accusers that black men have been victims of vicious sexual stereotypes which have lead to lynchings resulting from wholly unjustified sexual allegations. Professor Hill might equally well have invoked *The Color Purple* to remind skeptics that historically black women have been targets of sexual abuse not only by white men, but also by men of their own race perhaps because, as William Oliver has suggested, black on black sexual violence may be a "function of minority males adopting a 'tough guy, player of women' image in order to deal with the pressure of urban problems."[67] Recent studies verify that women, and especially women of color, are still the group most likely to be victimized by sexual harassment, and that they are usually harassed by men occupying positions of superior authority. Given the complicated connections between discrimination, violence, inequalities in power, and sexual misconduct, corporations have a duty to insist upon sexual propriety in the workplace in order to protect any employee from becoming a victim of further discrimination.

Fourth, sexual harassment violates liberty rights. Many philosophers, like John Rawls, believe that in a just society "Each person is to have an equal right to the most extensive total system of basic liberties compatible with a similar system for all."[68] Sexual harassment restricts liberty. A 1979 Working Women's Institute study found that 24 percent of sexual harassment victims were fired for complaining, while another 42 percent left their jobs. Bailey and Richards (1985) found that 21 percent of women graduate students surveyed reported that they had not enrolled in a course in order to avoid sexual harassment."[69] The Merit Board survey found that between 1983 and 1987 approximately 36,647 employees left their jobs because of sexual harassment. To suggest that women should leave their jobs and deviate from their career tracks when confronted with sexual harassment is only to add injury to injury. Worse yet, it plays into vicious stereotypes that victims of sexual abuse "ask for it."

Fifth, sexual harassment violates rights to fair equality of opportunity. Rawls has argued persuasively that in a just society there should be "roughly equal prospects of culture and achievement for everyone similarly motivated and endowed."[70] There is a wealth of evidence to suggest that women do not enjoy fair equality in the workplace and that sexual harassment is part of the problem. Sexual harassment stress syndrome, resulting from quid pro quo and environmental harassment, impairs job performance. A hostile work environment undermines respect for women making it difficult for them to exercise authority and command respect. Pornography, sexual conversation, sexual and sexist jokes, girlie posters, and the like, are morally objectionable because they violate women's rights to enjoy fair equality of opportunity. They are especially objectionable in any workplace associated with criminal justice; the very life of a woman police or correctional officer may depend upon her ability to command respect from sexually abusive people. To insist that women protest sexual harassment in a public forum, and to fail to institute grievance procedures which protect their privacy only exacerbates the damage already done. It may create resentment among male colleagues, discourage men in positions of authority from serving as mentors to women, irreparably damage victims' prospects from developing warm working relationships with colleagues and for expanding their professional networks, and impair their prospects for securing employment elsewhere.

Sixth, sexual harassment demonstrates the kind of disrespect for persons which is incompatible with Kantian conceptions of the moral point of view. Respect for persons involves respecting every person's rights to be unharmed by others, and to enjoy rights to liberty, privacy, and equality of opportunity.

Seventh, sexual harassment is morally objectionable because it undermines utilitarian justifications for the very free enterprise system upon which the business community depends. The moral justification for such a system is that it supposedly maximizes freedom and efficiency.[71] We have already seen that sexual harassment curtails freedom. It is also inefficient. According to the Merit Board survey sexual harassment cost the federal government at least $267 million in a two-year period. The estimate was based upon conservative conclusions about the costs of job turnover, sick leave, and loss of productivity. The 1985 *Working Woman* survey estimated the cost of harassment for a typical Fortune 400 company of 23,784 employees to be nearly $7 million per year. It also estimated that the costs of permitting sexual harassment were over thirty-one times the initial costs of preventing it.[72] Finally, the traditional argument for insisting that the socioeconomic inequalities of capitalism are morally justifiable consists in claiming that there is fair equality of opportunity and that permitting inequalities ultimately contributes to the benefit of all. Sexual harassment violates rights to fair equality of opportunity and, by doing so, creates inequalities which are disadvantageous to all. Sexual harassment is not merely a woman's problem. It is a problem for the entire business community.

CONCLUSION

Sexual harassment is not merely an abuse of power resulting from ignorance about facts or law. It is not merely a legal problem, a cultural problem, a gender problem, or a communication problem. Sexual harassment is not "murky" and it is not "much ado about nothing."

Sexual harassment is a serious moral problem. To get to the root of the problem, the corporate world must begin to reason critically, to relinquish old myths, to take a strong moral stand, and to provide moral education for employees. It must then assess the effectiveness of that education by conducting anonymous surveys of those groups with the least powerful positions or with the most complaints in the past to determine whether there is a reduction of complaints among those respondents. Until then, sexual harassment will be a potentially explosive communication problem.

NOTES

1. Alba Conte, *Sexual Harassment in the Workplace: Law and Practice* (New York: Wiley Law Publications, John Wiley and Sons, Inc., 1990), p. 2.

2. Michele A. Paludi and Richard B. Barickman, *Academic and Workplace Sexual Harassment: A Resources Manual* (Albany: State University of New York Press, 1991), p. 12.

3. Conte, *Sexual Harassment in the Workplace*, p. 2.

4. Paludi and Barickman, *Academic and Workplace Sexual Harassment*, p. 12.

5. Nancy Gibbs, "Office Crimes," *Time* (October 21, 1991): 52–64.

6. Michele Galen, Joseph Weber, and Alice Cuneo, "Out of the Shadows: The Thomas Hearings Force Business to Confront an Ugly Reality," *Business Week* (October 28, 1991): 30–31.

7. Ronni Sandoff, "Sexual Harassment: The Inside Story" (*Working Woman* Survey), *Working Woman*, June 1992.

8. Conte, *Sexual Harassment in the Workplace*, p. 4.

9. Neal Templin, "As Women Assume More Power, Charges Filed by Men May Rise," *Wall Street Journal*, October 18, 1991, p. B3.

10. Sandoff, "Sexual Harassment," p. 8.

11. Conte, *Sexual Harassment in the Workplace*, pp. 425–26.

12. Troy Segal and Zachary Schiller, "Six Experts Suggest Ways to Negotiate the Minefield," *Business Week* (October 12, 1991): 33.

13. Conte, *Sexual Harassment in the Workplace*, p. 2.

14. Ibid., p. 18.

15. Ibid., pp. 20–23.

16. Ibid., p. 212.

17. Ibid., p. 3.

18. Ibid., pp. 52–61.

19. Ibid., pp. 37–40, 71–74.

20. Ibid., pp. 41, 70; and Templin, "As Women Assume More Power," p. B3.

21. Conte, *Sexual Harassment in the Workplace*, pp. 67–69 and 493–501.

22. Ibid., pp. 261–79.

23. Susan Faludi, "Women Lost Ground in the 1980s and the EEOC Didn't Help," *Wall Street Journal*, October 18, 1991, p. B4.

24. Susan Faludi, *Backlash: The Undeclared War Against American Women* (New York: Crown Publishing Inc., 1991).

25. Priscilla Painton, "Woman Power," *Time* (October 28, 1991): 24–26.

26. Gibbs, "Office Crimes," p. 53.

27. Ted Gest and Amy Saltzman with Betsy Carpenter and Dorian Friedman, *U.S. News & World Report* (October 21, 1991): 38–40.

28. JoAnn Lublin, "As Harassment Charges Rise, More Men Fight Back," *Wall Street Journal*, October 18, 1991, p. B4.

29. JoAnn Lublin, "Sexual Harassment Is Topping Agenda in Many Executive Education Programs," *Wall Street Journal*, December 2, 1991, p. B1.

30. Deborah Tannen, *You Just Don't Understand: Women and Men in Conversation* (New York: Ballantine Books, 1990).

31. Paludi and Barickman, *Academic and Workplace Sexual Harassment*, pp. 61–62.

32. Gest and Saltzman with Carpenter and Freidman, *U.S. News & World Report*, p. 40.

33. John Leo, "Harassment's Murky Edges," *U.S. News & World Report* (October 21, 1991): 26.

34. Cynthia Crossen, "Are You from Another Planet, or What?" *Wall Street Journal,* October 18, 1991, p. B1.

35. Leo, "Harassment's Murky Edges," p. 26.

36. Susan M. Dodds, Lucy Frost, Robert Pargetter, and Elizabeth W. Prior, "Sexual Harassment," in *Moral Issues in Business,* 5th ed., ed. William W. Shaw and Vincent Barry (Belmont, Calif.: Wadsworth Publishing Co., 1992), 464–71; Edmund Wall, "The Definition of Sexual Harassment," *Public Affairs Quarterly* 5, no. 4 (October 1991): 371–85.

37. Dodds et al., "Sexual Harassment," pp. 466–68.

38. Wall, "The Definition of Sexual Harassment," p. 371.

39. Ibid., pp. 380–81.

40. Ibid., pp. 376–78.

41. Larry Hughes and John C. May, "Is Sexual Harassment Coercive?" in *Moral Rights in the Workplace*, ed. Gertrude Ezorsky (New York: State of New York Press, 1982), pp. 115–22.

42. Dodds et al., "Sexual Harassment," p. 466; and Wall, "The Definition of Sexual Harassment," p. 381.

43. Conte, *Sexual Harassment in the Workplace*, p. 446.

44. Ibid., p. 482.

45. Ibid., pp. 489–90.

46. Ibid., p. 374.

47. Dodds et al., "Sexual Harassment," p. 468.

48. Conte, *Sexual Harassment in the Workplace*, p. 490.

49. Dodds et al., "Sexual Harassment," p. 469.

50. Lawrence Kohlberg, "From Ought to Is: How to Commit the Naturalistic Fallacy and Get Away with It in the Study of Moral Development," in *Cognitive Development and Epistemology* (New York: Academic Press, 1971), pp. 131–232.

51. Wall, "The Definition of Sexual Harassment," p. 378.

52. Ibid., p. 374.

53. Ibid., p. 383.

54. Linda Marx, Gail Wescot, Gayle Verner, and Marilyn Balmaci, "The Price of Saying No," *People* (October 28, 1991): 44–49.

55. Ludwig Wittgenstein, *Philosophical Investigations* (New York: MacMillan Co., 1953).

56. Conte, *Sexual Harassment in the Workplace*, p. 9; and Paludi and Barickman, *Academic and Workplace Sexual Harassment*, p. 29.

57. Peggy Crull, "The Stress Effects of Sexual Harassment the Job," in Paludi and Barickman, *Academic and Workplace Sexual Harassment*, 133–44.

58. Conte, *Sexual Harassment in the Workplace*, p. 9.

59. Carole Sheffield, "Sexual Terrorism," in *Feminist Philosophies, Problems, Theories, and Applications*, ed. Janet A. Kourany, James P. Sterba, and Rosemarie Tong (Englewood Cliffs, N.J.: Prentice Hall, 1992), pp. 60–72.

60. Larry J. Siegel, *Criminology*, 4th ed. (St. Paul, Minn.: West Publishing, 1989).

61. Ibid., p. 306.

62. Ibid., p. 308.

63. Conte, *Sexual Harassment in the Workplace*, pp. 491–93.

64. Siegel, *Criminology*, p. 406.

65. George G. Brenkert, "Privacy, Polygraphs and Work," in *Contemporary Issues*

in Business Ethics, ed. Joseph R. DesJardins and John J. McCall (Belmont, Calif.: Wadsworth Publishing, 1985), pp. 227–37; Joseph R. DesJardins, "An Employee's Right to Privacy," in ibid., pp. 221–27; Richard A. Wasserstrom, "Privacy," in *Contemporary Issues in Business Ethics*, 2d ed., ed. Joseph J. DesJardins and John J. McCall (Belmont, Calif.: Wadsworth Publishing, 1990), pp. 196–201.

66. Brenkert, "Privacy, Polygraphs and Work," p. 229.

67. Siegel, *Criminology*, p. 292.

68. John A. Rawls, *Theory of Justice* (Cambridge, Mass.: Harvard University Press, Belknap Press, 1971).

69. Paludi and Barickman, *Academic and Workplace Sexual Harassment*, p. 149.

70. Rawls, *A Theory of Justice*, p. 73.

71. Manuel Velasquez, *Business Ethics: Concepts and Cases*, 2d ed. (Englewood Cliffs, N.J.: Prentice Hall, 1988).

72. Conte, *Sexual Harassment in the Workplace*, pp. 8–9.

Sexual Harassment and Wrongful Communication

6

Edmund Wall

In "Sexual Harassment: Why the Corporate World Still Doesn't 'Get It,' "[1] Vaughana Macy Feary devotes some space to a critique of my paper "The Definition of Sexual Harassment."[2] As I believe that her position shares some fundamental assumptions with feminists such as Catharine MacKinnon, and that these assumptions, which inform Feary's critique, require further analysis, I have constructed a response to her comments in the first section of this essay. As I develop an account of sexual harassment modeled on disrespectful communication, I attempt to show that the model of sexual harassment as sex discrimination, endorsed by feminists such as Feary, is incompatible with fundamental democratic values. But even though I cannot find adequate grounds to revise my definition of sexual harassment in light of Feary's feminist critique, there are other reasons to amend my definition. For it seems that similar criticisms pertaining to freedom can be levied against my own definition. Hence the revised definition in section two.

I

Feary attempts to counter my objection to the view that sexual harassment is a form of sex discrimination. My objection centered on the case of a bisexual manager who harasses both male and female employees. Feary claims this counterexample fails to show that sexual harassment is not inherently discriminatory. She argues that the bisexual manager would still be discriminating against the employees on the basis of sex. Here Feary says that when "sexual issues" such as "gender, sexual preferences, sexual orientation, sexual bias" and "willingness to succumb to sexual advances" are "used as a basis for making employment decisions," this constitutes sex discrimination.[3]

If we examine the context of the debate referred to by Feary, we find that it centered on whether sexual harassment constitutes discrimination against women as a group.[4] My counterexample offered a response to Larry May and John Hughes's position that sexual harassment by male managers necessarily involves sex discrimination against female employees.[5] This view has fueled strong disagreements. Catharine A. MacKinnon's groundbreaking work, *Sexual Harassment of Working Women: A Case of Sex Discrimination*, offered a defense of such a view.[6] The definition of sex discrimination at work in this approach, however, may be too broad. As Feary herself points out, the debate was prompted by the claim that women have suffered a damaging form of indoctrination which encourages their acquiescence to inappropriate sexual advances.[7] Indeed, one of the main contentions of MacKinnon and other feminists is that women have been defined by men as sexual objects.[8] Thus the point of contention appears to pertain to discrimination based on gender and not on "sexual preference," or on "sexual orientation." Certainly these considerations to which Feary refers would constitute irrelevant bases for employment decisions, but that does not offer a reason for defining sex discrimination in terms of "sexual issues."

When a heterosexual manager demands sexual favors from a heterosexual employee is this objectionable because the manager is discriminating against heterosexuals as opposed to homosexuals or bisexuals? This is what Feary would have to say, given her definition of sex discrimination in terms of sexual orientation. However, it is not the alleged discrimination against heterosexuals that makes the manager's behavior morally objectionable. It is morally objectionable because it violates the employee's autonomy rights. When Feary shifts from a gender-based definition of sex discrimination to a broader sexual-issues formulation, "sex discrimination" no longer captures genuinely biased behavior. It no longer characterizes a social injustice against a group.

Feary, MacKinnon, and other feminists argue that sexuality and gender are intimately linked. MacKinnon maintains that gender is a "congealed form of the sexualization of inequality between men and women."[9] According to MacKinnon, gender is not a difference, but a hierarchy of power in which women are dominated by men.[10] We are also told that the abusive treatment of women by men, which, among other things, includes rape, assault, and harassment, is a form of sex for men. Since, in MacKinnon's estimation, whatever is felt as sexual is sexual, such acts of dominance, submission, and violence are all aspects of sex. Men—and women—are said to be sexually aroused by such actions. Given that in our society a violation of the powerless is sexy, and violation of the powerless is central to the very meaning of female and male, gender should not be considered apart from sex and dominance in MacKinnon's estimation.[11]

These background assumptions can explain why Feary is calling for a very broad definition of sex discrimination, a definition that runs the gamut of sexual issues. When MacKinnon and Feary claim that the harassment of women is based on sex, the term "sex" includes a combination of sexuality, power, and gender. Their approach purports to accurately depict social reality rather than to construct a systematic set of abstract principles.[12] All of this may explain why MacKinnon and other feminists talk about sex discrimination in such broad terms, but it does not justify their doing so. If we follow their lead and define gender broadly, we cannot offer a reasonable response to the bisexual harasser counterexample. Even if women have been socially constructed to be the sexual slaves of men, the women harassed by the bisexual perpetrator are not harassed *because* they are women any more than the male victims of the bisexual perpetrator are harassed because they are men. In such cases the issue is not gender, but, rather, a disregard for basic human dignity. To say that someone treats human beings of one gender disrespectfully but not those of the other gender does not seem plausible. We would seriously question whether such an individual could treat *any* human being with genuine respect. Human beings are alike in some fundamental ways. They expect the kind of thoughtful treatment that is compatible with their sense of dignity and worth. These common features of human beings are obfuscated by the emphasis on the male dominance of women.

Now, MacKinnon has argued that the question whether a given case of harassment was based on sex or personal considerations rests on a false dichotomy. She believes that to relegate sexual harassment cases to the category of a "personal episode" is to isolate and further subjugate the victims by stigmatizing them as deviants. In MacKinnon's estimation, the harassment of women is based on sex. It is done because they are women. Here MacKinnon argues that a woman is not only a woman personally, but also socially. She finds that membership in a gender is a part of a woman's individuality.[13]

It would be hard to see how anyone could consider the sexual harassment of female and male employees to be a "personal episode," but let us consider MacKinnon's point that a woman's experiences and very identity are inseparable from her social status and that, therefore, her victimization implies gender discrimination. The response is that the bisexual harasser does not single out women as a group, or men as a group for that matter. The perpetrator's lack of respect is indicative of what he has let *himself* become and not indicative of some social perspective on women *per se*.

Feary's broad definition of sex discrimination, as appealing as it may seem to some feminists, may not advance their attempt to characterize social reality. It focuses on various dichotomies, including the one between heterosexuals and homosexuals, between this and that sexual orientation. It is unclear how this would help to expose the myriad aspects of *gender* inequality in our society, unless someone wanted to identify women with homosexuality and men with heterosexuality. It is obvious, however, that such an identification would do nothing to further an accurate description of social reality. To whatever degree "gender" has been sexualized and tied to the male dominance of women, the bisexual harasser violates both women and men indiscriminately.

The main thrust of Feary's critique centers on her defense of the EEOC's definition of sexual harassment. She argues that "defining sexual harassment for the purposes of business ethics is NOT a major philosophical problem" and that "the meaning of sexual harassment is reasonably well defined in EEOC guidelines"[14] (emphasis in Feary's paper).

Here is the EEOC's definition:

> Unwelcome sexual advances, requests for sexual favors, and other verbal or physical conduct of a sexual nature constitute sexual harassment when (1) submission to such conduct is made either explicitly or implicitly a term or condition of an individual's employment, (2) submission to or rejection of such conduct by an individual is used as the basis for employment decisions affecting such an individual, or (3) such conduct has the purpose or effect of unreasonably interfering with an individual's work performance or creating an intimidating, hostile, or offensive working environment.[15]

In response to Feary, it must be said that the definition of sexual harassment poses an enormous problem for social researchers. Disagreements about the definition as well as differences in survey techniques have prompted many social scientists to throw up their arms at comparisons between studies."[16] Moreover, the project of ensuring reliable research data on sexual harassment cannot be separated from the quest for a philosophically accurate definition. In order to study sexual harassment, we must first be able to identify it.

Of course, Feary's claim is that the definition of sexual harassment is not a major *philosophical* problem, at least for the purposes of business ethics. But here it must be said that the quest for an acceptable definition raises profound philosophical questions pertaining to justice. A democratic society requires a definition that will identify sexual harassment without violating the moral rights of the innocent. The EEOC's definition targets, among other behaviors, "verbal or physical conduct of a sexual nature" which creates an "intimidating, hostile, or offensive working environment." That is too broad.

Suppose that an employee installs a nude painting above his office desk. After doing so, let us say that he never makes a reference to it. The painting has been added solely for the employee's own benefit. Given the volatility of the sexual harassment issue, we surely can envision strong protests by other employees against the painting. In this case, the employee's "physical conduct of a sexual nature" has created a "hostile" working environment. Indeed, the other employees can say, in good faith, that the painting has created a "hostile" working environment. Certainly, the painting may be inappropriate in the workplace, and the other employees may be justified in requesting that it be removed (although even this conclusion is not beyond contention), but should our legal net capture cases such as this? Is the art-loving employee a sexual harasser? Such a judgment seems to be unjustified.

One of Feary's objections is that "Wall seems very concerned with preventing the much popularized innocent man/paranoid woman scenario."[17] My response to this objection is that in constructing a definition of sexual harassment, one ought to be concerned with the requirements of justice. Among other things, a democratic society aspires to protect its citizens against the massive power of the federal government. This fundamental concern anticipates a variety of scenarios, not merely the type involving a paranoid woman. There are quite a few men who have been sexually harassed, and it would be ludicrous to assume that only women can be paranoid.

Not only does the EEOC's definition capture cases that may not involve sexual harassment, it also fails to capture obvious cases of sexual harassment. Suppose a female employee is constantly being stared at in a suggestive way by a male employee. Although this behavior may upset the employee, let us assume that she decides to shrug it off as one of the many drawbacks of the workplace. Let us say that after many long years of enduring similar behavior she has built up psychological defenses against it. Certainly Feary would agree that this must be sexual harassment and that it can be just as objectionable as a case involving verbal harassment. Yet, the EEOC's definition fails to capture cases such as this. After all, "unwelcome sexual advances" or "physical conduct of a sexual nature" are to be labeled as sexual harassment only when one of three conditions are met. The first two conditions require more overt behavior (i.e., quid pro quo sexual harassment) and therefore would not apply to this case. The third condition which seeks to identify hostile environment cases would seem to apply, but comes up short. The unwelcome sexual advances may not have interfered with the employee's work performance, and since she and perhaps the other employees have built up defenses against the inappropriate advances, have not created an "intimidating, hostile, or offensive working environment." Thus it seems that the victimized employee would not have a legal case against the harasser.

Now, it just might be that legal definitions cannot be applied fairly to cases involving leers and prolonged stares. Maybe this is one point in favor of the EEOC's account as a legal definition. However, we are still left with the task of establishing an acceptable philosophical definition, one that can capture all (and only) those cases which involve sexual harassment.

My definition of sexual harassment was formulated as follows:

Wherein X is the sexual harasser and Y the victim, the following are offered as necessary and jointly sufficient conditions of sexual harassment:

(1) X does not attempt to obtain Y's consent to communicate to Y, X's or someone else's purported sexual interest in Y.

(2) X communicates to Y, X's or someone else's purported sexual interest in Y. X's motive for communicating this is some perceived benefit that he expects to obtain through the communication.

(3) Y does not consent to discuss with X, X's or someone else's purported sexual interest in Y.

(4) *Y* feels emotionally distressed because *X* did not attempt to obtain *Y*'s consent to this discussion and/or because *Y* objects to the content of *X*'s sexual comments.[18]

Feary objects to my fourth condition, which requires that a victim experience emotional distress. She endorses a reasonable person standard instead.[19] The proper inquiry, she says, is whether a reasonable person would have felt distressed by the behavior in question. She argues that to focus on the feelings of the actual victim fails to acknowledge that women "have been conditioned to stoically accept" a great deal of harmful sexual behavior.[20] She approvingly points out that the EEOC does not require the actual victim to experience emotional distress.

This position, however, raises questions about individual freedom and autonomy. Sexual harassment is a type of harassment. When an alleged victim is not actually bothered by the behavior in question, we cannot rightfully say that she has been harassed. To design a legal system so that it offers protection against "harassment" to people who may not experience any distress (indeed, who may sincerely believe they have not been harassed) is antidemocratic. The EEOC's definition runs roughshod over basic moral rights. And just who are the beneficiaries of this legal paternalism? On the one hand, we have seen that Feary does not claim that only women need protection from sex discrimination. However, she also has made a case that women have been conditioned throughout the years to accept inappropriate sexual advances. Since she has not made the case that men have been similarly conditioned, she has not provided sufficient assurance that men, also, should be able to claim sexual harassment in the absence of any emotional distress. Basic justice requires such an assurance.

Feary says that the most serious difficulty with my proposed definition of sexual harassment is that it is too narrow. She objects that it fails to capture "sexist harassment" which, for example, may include demeaning comments about women in general.[21] But there is good reason to refer to this as "sexist" harassment. As objectionable as such harassment is, it is still to be distinguished from "sexual" harassment. Feary offers no argument for including gender-based nonsexual communication under the category of sexual harassment.

Feary also objects that my definition would exclude a lot of environmental harassment such as "the display of objectionable sexual objects."[22] She claims that, assuming the charges against Judge Clarence Thomas are true, my definition would fail to capture the sexual harassment of Anita Hill.[23] She argues that even if Judge Thomas never said that he or anyone else "had an interest in engaging in sex with her," she would still have been the victim of sexual harassment. She concludes that this contradicts the belief, which she attributes to me, that "the content of what is communicated is immaterial."[24]

As I pointed out in the first edition of *Sexual Harassment: Confrontations and Decisions*, if the charges against Judge Thomas were true, then it is "clear" that Anita Hill was sexually harassed.[25] But we do not have to look there to find the parameters of my definition. My fourth condition explicitly allows for sexual harassment based on a victim's objection to the content of the sexual communication in question. Here is my fourth condition, again:

(4) Y feels emotionally distressed because X did not attempt to obtain Y's consent to this discussion and/or because Y objects to the content of X's sexual comments.

Feary is mistaken in her judgment that on my definition "the content of what is communicated is immaterial." Moreover, my account does not require, as Feary suggests it does, that a perpetrator verbalize a sexual interest in a victim. A mere gesture will do. And, finally, my account does not require that the sexual interest be limited to the sex act. Any communicated interest of a sexual nature can be captured by my definition.

The genuine disagreement between Feary's view and my own revolves around my requirement that the perpetrator communicate (either verbally or through gestures, stares, etc.) a sexual interest or someone else's sexual interest (whether real or fabricated) in the victim. The Anita Hill case provides no counterexample here, as Judge Thomas clearly did communicate a sexual interest in Hill—provided, of course, that the allegations were bona fide.

For all of the above reasons Feary's critique does not seem to warrant a revision of my definition of sexual harassment. However, there is more that I should have said in my earlier paper about sexual harassment as wrongful communication. Communication cannot be limited to the written or spoken word. Meaning can be conveyed through other symbols, signs, or gestures. When a basketball player collects a rebound and extends an elbow, the player may be communicating a message to opposing players. They can be threatened in this way to avoid trying to steal the ball. Consider that all too often we walk down a street and a stranger will fix a menacing stare on us. This is not a crime. It may not be a violation of our moral rights, either. Nevertheless, these gestures are anything but benign. They communicate disrespect for human beings.

If communication is to be understood broadly, and if disrespectful communication has become commonplace, it is no wonder that sexual harassment is such a pervasive problem. If it is an issue of power and control, then a discussion of it should encompass the pervasive social maladies just described. Low self-esteem, cynicism, and hatred of self and others should be a major focus of the discussion. It is also true, however, that in order to help ensure basic justice, we ought to implement legal remedies fairly. It is, therefore, necessary to distinguish sexual harassment from other disrespectful actions. Unfortunately, since we live in a society in which disrespect is pervasive, it is doubtful that any legal remedy will make a significant difference.

The model of sexual harassment as sex discrimination offers nonconstructive generalizations about women and men. Generally speaking, women have not been conditioned to accept inappropriate sexual advances. Philosophers have correctly denounced this assumption as patronizing.[26] Neither do men, generally speaking, make a practice of demeaning women. Both assumptions lead to a dead end, with a lot of ill feeling along the way. Rather than encouraging respect and healthy relationships between women and men, these assumptions are actually symptoms of the main problem. These are demeaning assumptions about women and men, which is another way of saying that they suggest a disrespect for human beings.

There is no adequate philosophical justification for the view that sexual harassment is a form of sex discrimination. A model of sexual harassment that centers on disrespectful communication seems to be a step in the right direction. Whether it is a menacing stare, unfair criticism of others, the harassment of an employee, etc., the root of the problem is what we think and feel about ourselves. That is the central reason why we have not progressed on this issue. Corporate America will not improve until more people are able to relate to others in a respectful manner.

II

In this part of the essay, I argue for a revised definition of sexual harassment. In their very helpful paper, "Normative Issues in Defining Sexual Harassment," Jaimie Leeser and William O'Donohue find a number of problems with my definition as it stands.[27] They are quite right that my first condition of sexual harassment, which requires that X does not *attempt* to obtain Y's consent to communicate to Y, X's or someone else's purported sexual interest in Y, is problematic. For one thing, the condition may be impossible to satisfy. In order to obtain Y's consent to discuss sexual matters, it would seem that X must first broach the subject. But in doing so, X has already communicated a sexual message to Y without having obtained Y's consent to such a communication. As Leeser and O'Donohue point out, a failure to obtain consent to ask someone out for a date may not even be a breach of etiquette, let alone a moral infraction. For these reasons, it would be wise to drop this first condition.

I should have begun my philosophical definition of sexual harassment with my second condition: X communicates to Y, X's or someone else's purported sexual interest in someone (whether in Y or someone else). "Sexual interest" is meant to capture not only sexual attraction, but also curiosity about another person's sexual behavior or thought processes. The presence of other objectives such as a desire to dominate another person's sexual behavior or thought processes may indicate that X does not have a genuine sexual interest in Y, and thus I make room for this by referring to the "purported" sexual interest in Y. If these other objectives are coupled with the above-mentioned curiosity or with a sexual attraction, which is typical in these cases, then the harasser would have a sexual interest in Y. In any case, the term "sexual interest" is deliberately meant to be broad. Harassers may or may not be sexually attracted to their victims. Thus, on my use of the term, a sexual interest in Y does not imply a sexual attraction to Y, though it certainly could amount to that.

Previously I had required under this second condition that X's motive for communicating his or someone else's purported sexual interest in Y be "some perceived benefit that he expects to obtain through the communication." Given Leeser and O'Donohue's criticism that this is hopelessly broad, this requirement ought to be dropped altogether. Although we want to say that the harasser's objectives can be wide-ranging, the previous provision adds nothing constructive.

No other significant revisions to my original definition would appear to be helpful, except for one major addition, not mentioned by Leeser and O'Donohue. "Harassment" suggests not only that someone has been emotionally upset by someone else's sexual advances, but that the sexual advances are repeated over and against the victim's disapproval. My previous set of conditions acknowledged that a harassment victim is bothered by a perpetrator's advances, but "harassment" suggests that a victim is actually hounded by a perpetrator. A deplorable, onetime sexual advance may violate a victim's moral rights, but it is to be distinguished from repeated and deplorable sexual advances which, due to the repetition, could constitute cases of harassment. Depending on a perpetrator's intentions, the nature of the action, the circumstances, etc., a onetime sexual advance may be more morally repugnant than a series of unacceptable sexual advances, but the onetime offense does not constitute harassment. It may be a full-blown sexual assault, for example, and, as such, it should be legally actionable. But the paradigm of sexual harassment involves a series of less egregious (though disrespectful) sexual advances.

In light of these considerations, I propose the following revised set of necessary and jointly sufficient conditions of sexual harassment:

(1) X successfully communicates to Y, X's or someone else's purported sexual interest in someone (whether in Y or someone else).

(2) Y does not consent to discuss or reconsider such a message about X's or someone else's purported sexual interest in someone.

(3) Disregarding the absence of Y's consent, X repeats a message of this form to Y.

(4) Y feels emotionally distressed because of X's disregard for the absence of Y's consent to discuss or consider such a message and/or because Y objects to the content of X's sexual comments.

When sexual harassment occurs, the perpetrator has engaged in disrespectful communication with the victim. He has successfully communicated some sexual message to the victim, which the victim does not choose to discuss or to consider, and which the perpetrator *continues* to convey to an unwilling victim. The victim, in turn, is bothered by the repeated advances, and thus the harassment.

The second condition requires that the victim does not consent to receive the sexual message put forward by the perpetrator. This lack of consent can take more than one form. The victim may verbally, or by gesturing, convey an objection to the perpetrator in response to the advance, or the victim may maintain a suggestive silence in response to it. Remember, at this point, a perpetrator would have successfully conveyed a sexual message to the victim. If, for example, the perpetrator has not conveyed the message (for example, perhaps the victim did not hear the perpetrator), or if he did convey the message but, for some good reason, believes that he did not do so successfully, then genuine communication has not occurred. The perpetrator has not yet harassed the victim. He is entitled to determine whether or not the victim has received the message. But when the victim has received the message, and the perpetrator has good reason to believe that the victim has received the message, then repeating the message can constitute sexual harassment. Sexual harassment can be either intentional or the result of negligence. With regard to the latter, sometimes an insensitive individual will not realize that he is harassing others, but he is still morally responsible for his disregard of the moral rights of others. The fundamental point here is that the victim does not consent to the communication. In the absence of overriding moral commitments, people ought to be morally sensitive to what others choose to discuss.

It might be said that the proposed conditions could characterize an innocent individual as a harasser. For example, suppose that a member of one culture makes remarks of a sexual nature to a member of another culture, not realizing that the latter would be offended by those remarks. It seems in this case that the so-called perpetrator acted reasonably, given his cultural indoctrination and the information that he had at the time. Is this a genuine counterexample to the proposed conditions? On further reflection, it would seem otherwise. The proposed conditions require that the sexual advances continue even though the recipient of the advances either expresses disapproval or chooses not to take part in the communication. Even if there exist cultures in which individuals are expected to engage in sexual communications of which they disapprove and of which they choose not to engage, it still would seem that this particular practice could be called into question on the grounds of basic respect and autonomy. If a social practice is occurring, that is not adequate reason (or even *a* reason) for concluding that such a practice should occur. Even if disregard for another individual's autonomous choices is prevalent within a culture, we may still criticize it on moral grounds.

Another concern may arise, this time with regard to the third condition which requires that the sexual advances be repeated. One might object that a single, one-hour sexual advance would seem adequate for sexual harassment to occur. However, an hour-long episode actually would involve a *series* of sexual advances and not merely one advance. With regard to yet another line of criticism, it could be said that if Y is genuinely indifferent to X's advances and thereby does not consent to the sexual advances, she might not be harassed. After all, maybe she has not expressed *dissent* to the sexual advance. My response is that such indifference would indicate that the fourth condition would not have been satisfied. The fourth condition requires that Y feel emotionally distressed by X's sexual advances. When each of the four conditions are satisfied, Y feels emotionally distressed about repeated sexual advances to which she does not consent. After all is said and done, the proposed conditions seem to capture cases of sexual harassment.

What about the nature of the moral rights of these victims? How does sexual harassment infringe on those rights, and what rights specifically are violated by perpetrators? In my earlier essay, these rights were identified as privacy rights and autonomy rights. Although I still hold that these are the relevant rights, I believe that my account of how these rights are violated in cases of sexual harassment requires some revision and considerably more clarification.

First of all, in my earlier account of sexual harassment, more attention was given to privacy rights than to autonomy rights. I now believe that more attention should be given to autonomy rights, as they are more fundamental. Moreover, as Leeser and O'Donohue correctly point out, my earlier account of privacy rights wrongly equated such rights with a right to be shielded from all disturbances.[28] My earlier account seemed to suggest that any sexual advance constitutes a privacy-rights violation, provided the perpetrator fails to gain the victim's consent to the communication. Leeser and O'Donohue are correctly concerned that such a broad account of privacy rights may infringe on the rights of free expression. It is, indeed, a mistake to say that any and all sexual advances to which a victim is an unwilling party, constitute an infringement on the victim's privacy rights. Moreover, as the authors suggest, I should have distinguished between a failure to show proper *respect* for a victim's privacy rights and the actual *violation* of a victim's privacy rights. The violation of such rights would involve the actual intrusion into privileged areas (i.e., illegitimate access to privileged information). For these reasons, my previous account of sexual harassment embodied antidemocratic elements. If my objections to Feary's feminist account center on the value of freedom in a democratic society, my revised account should reflect this concern for freedom.

What should be said about moral rights and inappropriate sexual advances? Such advances may not themselves violate an individual's right to privacy, but they are *potential* encroachments on an individual's right to privacy. Such advances seek to elicit some response from the victim. The victim is being encouraged to respond to some sexual advance or to respond to the pressure exerted by the perpetrator, who has repeatedly communicated a message to the victim without regard for the victim's consent to that communication. Such activity constitutes a potential encroachment of a victim's privacy rights, as the victim is being encouraged to discuss sexual matters, despite their objections to doing so. Whether an actual privacy-rights violation occurs is determined by the nature and extent of the pressure exerted by a perpetrator on a victim, and also by just what it is that the victim is being asked to do. If access to privileged information is not involved, then privacy rights would not be violated. The victim's *autonomy* rights would be violated, however.

The fundamental fault with the perpetrator's approach is that he disregards the victim's autonomous choice. The victim does not consent to the sexual advance, and yet the perpetrator persists with more advances. All cases of sexual harassment involve a lack of respect for a victim's autonomy rights. Rather than supporting and promoting autonomous choice, a perpetrator discourages it by showing disrespect for the victim's choice. The perpetrator exhibits more than just disrespect for autonomy rights, however. There is one choice that a victim cannot bring to fruition, one choice that remains ineffectual in the face of the harassment, and that is the choice not to be subjected to the sexual communication. In this way, sexual harassment encroaches on the autonomy of its victims. The victim cannot realize, in the presence of the perpetrator, his reasonable expectations about responsible interpersonal relations. The perpetrator's repeated sexual communication, which imposes obstacles to the realization of the victim's reasonable choices, lies at the root of sexual harassment.

NOTES

This paper benefited considerably from the thoughtful suggestions of Burleigh Wilkins who read an earlier version of it.

1. Vaughana Macy Feary, "Sexual Harassment: Why the Corporate World Still Doesn't 'Get It,' " *Journal of Business Ethics* 13 (1994): 649–62. Reprinted in this edition.

2. Edmund Wall, "The Definition of Sexual Harassment," *Public Affairs Quarterly* 5, no. 4 (1991): 371–85. Reprinted in this edition.

3. Feary, "Sexual Harassment," p. 655.

4. Wall, "The Definition of Sexual Harassment," pp. 377–84.

5. Ibid., p. 381.

6. Selections from MacKinnon's book appear in this anthology.

7. Feary, "Sexual Harassment," pp. 655–56.

8. Wall, "The Definition of Sexual Harassment," pp. 121–36.

9. Catharine A. MacKinnon, *Feminism Unmodified: Discourses on Life and Law* (Cambridge, Mass.: Harvard University Press, 1987), p. 6.

10. Ibid., pp. 3, 37, 39.

11. Ibid., p. 6.

12. Ibid., pp. 40–41.

13. Ibid., pp. 106–107.

14. Feary, "Sexual Harassment," p. 657. As just indicated, Feary defends the EEOC's definition of sexual harassment and argues that sexual harassment is not a major philosophical problem. In the text of this paper, I will offer arguments against the EEOC's definition, but let me point out that another thinker who shares Feary's basic feminist assumptions has argued *against* the EEOC's definition. Here I refer to Anita M. Superson's paper "A Feminist Definition of Harassment," *Journal of Social Philosophy* 24, no. 1 (1993): 46, 49–50, 58–61.

15. Wall, "The Definition of Sexual Harassment," p. 382.

16. There is a plethora of evidence to suggest that the definition of sexual harassment poses a serious problem to social researchers. For a more recent overview of the scope and differences between definitions see, Louise F. Fitzgerald, Suzanne Swan, and Vicki J. Magley, "But Was It Really Sexual Harassment? Legal, Behavioral, and Psychological Definitions of the Workplace Victimization of Women, in *Sexual Harassment: Theory, Research, and Treatment*, ed. William O'Donohue (Boston: Allyn and Bacon, 1997), pp. 5–28. Fitzgerald et al. provide an extensive bibliography as well. In *Sexual Harassment: Confrontations and Decisions*, ed. Edmund Wall (Amherst, N.Y.: Prometheus Books, 1992), p. 19 n. 1, there is a generous list of social research in the 1980s and early 1990s on the problem of defining sexual harassment.

17. Feary, "Sexual Harassment," p. 655.

18. Wall, "The Definition of Sexual Harassment," p. 374.

19. In "Pluralist Myths and Powerless Men: The Ideology of Reasonableness in Sexual Harassment Law," reprinted in *Sexual Harassment*, pp. 229–60, Nancy S. Ehrenreich questions the effectiveness of the reasonable woman standard. Although she believes it to be an improvement on the reasonable man standard, she questions whether our society can adequately construct any equitable social standards, given the fact that women and men, in her estimation, are the victims of their respective social and economic classes.

20. Feary, "Sexual Harassment," pp. 655–56.

21. Ibid., p. 657.

22. Ibid.

23. Ibid.

24. Ibid.

25. Wall, *Sexual Harassment*, p. 12.

26. Ellen Frankel Paul, "Bared Buttocks and Federal Cases," reprinted in this edition of *Sexual Harassment*, pp. 151–57.

27. Jaimie Leeser and William O'Donohue, "Normative Issues in Defining Sexual Harassment," *Sexual Harassment: Theory, Research, and Treatment* (Boston: Allyn and Bacon, 1997), pp. 43–44. On pp. 38–43, Leeser and O'Donohue also critique my definition of coercion, but their objections to that definition do not seem convincing. I have constructed a response to their objections in an unpublished manuscript, "A Theory of Coercion."

28. Leeser and O'Donohue, "Normative Issues in Defining Sexual Harassment," p. 44.

EXPLANATIONS AND CAUSES

Sexual Harassment at Work

Three Explanatory Models

7

Sandra S. Tangri, Martha R. Burt, and Leanor B. Johnson

Several major explanations of sexual harassment have been offered in legal briefs (see Goodman 1981, MacKinnon 1979), in feminist writings, and by the press. However, until recently there has not been a sufficiently large or reliable data base to test these alternative interpretations of this recently "discovered" but long-buried phenomenon (Bularzik 1978). In this [essay] we will describe the three broad models that emerge out of our review of the literature on sexual harassment, and will offer some empirical tests of each. Each model suggests certain predictions regarding: (a) who should be likely victims of sexual harassment, (b) who should be likely harassers, (c) the kinds of acts or behaviors to be expected, (d) how victims should feel and react to those acts, (e) what outcomes and consequences are likely, and (f) what characteristics of the work situation should be associated with greater harassment. For each model, we will first present the general description with citations to the pertinent literature, and then extrapolate to make various predictions. The three models are: (1) the natural or biological model, (2) the organizational model, and (3) the sociocultural model.

Briefly, the first model asserts that sexual harassment is

From the *Journal of Social Issues* 38, no. 4 (1982): 33–54. Reprinted by permission of The Society for the Psychological Study of Social Issues.

simply natural sexual attraction between people. This model has two versions. The first maintains that sexually harassing behavior is not meant as such, but is merely a natural expression of men's stronger sex drive; the second version posits no unequal sex drive, but stresses that any individual may be attracted to any other individual, and may pursue that attraction without intent to harass.

The second, or organizational, model argues that sexual harassment is the result of certain opportunity structures created by organizational climate, hierarchy, and specific authority relations. In various versions it may or may not take into account the differential distribution of men and women within the authority structure.

The third, or sociocultural, model argues that sexual harassment reflects the larger society's differential distribution of power and status between the sexes. It is also seen as a mechanism that functions specifically to maintain male dominance over women within the workplace and within the economy generally. Various versions posit the existence or absence of a conscious collaboration among men toward this end.

We use the term "model" for want of a better one; in many ways these are positions, or preferences for interpreting sexually harassing behavior in particular ways, in the service of particular ends. The "natural model" admits the behavior but denies that the intent is to harass, discriminate, or dominate. Lest anyone think we have only described the natural model in order to shoot it down, we must point out that this model or position has been most vehemently argued in court by corporations seeking to avoid charges of sex discrimination for allowing harassment to exist, and has been the primary interpretation in need of change in the effort to bring sexual harassment under the purview of sex discrimination statutes. The organizational model looks to fairly simple causes and remedies without assuming much in the way of motives or psychological processes contributing to continuing harassment. The cultural model or position views sexual harassment as only one manifestation of a pervasive cultural enforcement of gender inequality. The evidence we report in this [essay] can, at best, negate some premises of these models and support others, rather than "proving" that one or another model is the correct view of the world.

Note that the natural/biological theory is primarily a motivational model; the organizational approach stresses facilitating factors; and the sociocultural model focuses on power differentials of males and females, male motivation to maintain this differential, and female socialization to acquiescence. Thus, the first theory is most sharply differentiated from the second and third by positing positive (i.e., "natural") rather than negative motives for behavior that might appear to be sexual harassment. The organizational and sociocultural models are most similar when the former takes into account the typical differential distribution of women and men in the organizational structure. Therefore, to more clearly differentiate our predictions the organizational model will be treated without this refinement. Finally, we expect that none of these theories will be either totally supported or totally rejected. However, it may be possible to conclude which one yields the greater explanatory power, and which one(s) offers less potential.

THE NATURAL/BIOLOGICAL MODEL

The natural or biological model rests on a number of assumptions about sexual behavior in the workplace, all of which result in a denial that such sexual behavior should be considered illegitimate and discriminatory. One assumption of this model holds that the human sex drive is stronger in men, leading them by biological propensity to aggress sexually against women, but without discriminatory intent (see, e.g., *Bundy* v. *Jackson* 1981, *Dothard* v. *Rawlinson* 1977). That they do this in work settings as well as other situations is neither surprising nor grounds for court action. If this assumption is true, we would expect to see more harassers in the age groups with the highest biological sex drives, and would not expect harassing behavior to vary by organizational position or status.

A second assumption of the natural model maintains that men and women are naturally attracted to each other, that both sexes participate in sexually oriented behavior in the workplace, and that they like it that way (see, e.g., *Corne and DeVane* v. *Bausch and Lomb* 1975, *Miller* v. *Bank of America* 1979, *Vinson* v. *Taylor* 1980). If sexual harassment is simply normal mutual sexual attraction, we would expect it to follow wellestablished patterns for liking and romantic attraction (Berscheid and Walster 1969, Winch 1971). Male-female pairs should be similar in age, race, and other background characteristics, attitudes, and statuses. Further, if asked, both should express interest in and attraction to each other, and no one should want to file a complaint.

A third prong found in the literature by proponents of the natural model attributes sexually harassing behavior to the idiosyncratic ("sick") proclivities of a minority of men (see e.g., *Corne and De Vane* v. *Bausch and Lomb* 1975). While admitting that harassment isn't "nice," this assumption denies any systematic pattern of sexual harassment, or any motive deriving from sex-based discrimination. If this assumption is true, we should see sexually harassing behavior randomly distributed among males of all ages, statuses, and occupational positions (*and* a *low* base-rate of harassers).

The various assumptions of the natural model have the effect of both trivializing sexual harassment (it is normal, idiosyncratic, individual, harmless) and aggrandizing it until all remedies seem hopeless (if it's human nature, change efforts must be futile). All versions of the natural model deny that sexual behavior at work has the intention or the effect of discriminating against women and reducing women's chances to compete successfully in the workplace (see, e.g., *Bundy* v. *Jackson* 1981, *Neely* v. *American Fidelity Assurance Co.* 1978, *Smith* v. *Amoco Chemical Corp.* 1979). This is its critical characteristic. A failure to find any systematic pattern of harassment, or any evidence of harmful effects on women, would support the natural model of sexual harassment.

Predictions Derived from the Natural/Biological Model

Expected Victims

Expected victims should be women or both sexes, and should be similar to their harasser in age, race, and occupational status. If they are truly objects of romantic interest, they should also be unmarried or otherwise "eligible" as continuing partners, and the only person to whom the harasser directs his attention.

Expected Harassers

Harassers should be men or both sexes. If men, they should be young, and if women, middle-aged, to correspond to the times of highest sex drive for males and females, respectively. They should tend to be unmarried, and thus have fewer regular sexual outlets. Harassers should be found in all organizational settings and climates, distributed generally or randomly among the population. Further, incidents should involve only one harasser, since multiple harassers would suggest the sociocultural model rather than the natural one.

Expected Acts

Acts should resemble courtship behavior, and should stop if and when one party indicates disinterest.

Expected Victim Reactions and Behavior

"Victims" should be flattered by the behaviors, or at least not be offended by them. Harassing behaviors should have positive effect or no effect on victims' feelings or work performance or working conditions. Victims would not file any formal complaints or take any other actions to bring the behavior to an end.

Expected Outcomes and Consequences

No negative consequences will happen to the victim.

Work Characteristics

Harassment incidents should not vary by work characteristics or atmosphere, according to the natural model.

THE ORGANIZATIONAL MODEL

The organizational model holds that institutions may provide an opportunity structure that makes sexual harassment possible. Since work organizations are characterized by vertical stratification, individuals can use their power and position to extort sexual gratification from their subordinates. Although typically males harass females, in principle it is possible for females to sexually harass males. It is less likely only because women tend to be employed in occupations subordinate to men (Evans 1978). Minority women, because they usually have the least organizational power, face the greatest economic disadvantage. This asymmetrical relation between superordinate (male) and subordinate (female) deprives subordinates of the material independence and security necessary to resist sexual harassment, and leaves them vulnerable to its economic, psychological, physical, and social consequences (MacKinnon 1979). Economic consequences can be more severe, for all recourses have the potential to affect the subordinate's immediate job and long-term career adversely. When faced with objectionable sexual advances, subordinates' options are to: (a) quit, (b) request a transfer, (c) tolerate, (d) acquiesce, or (e) file a complaint to a superior (Farley 1978, MacKinnon 1979).

Differential power is only one of several organizational characteristics which set the stage for sexual harassment. Martin and Fein[1] and Martin (1978) cite other principal factors: visibility and contact in sex-integrated jobs, the sex ratio, occupational norms, one's job function, and availability of grievance procedures and job alternatives. In *sex-integrated* jobs some employees may work alone, in pairs, or in groups. Some have a work area which is exclusively theirs and others do not. Each working condition allows varying opportunities for sexual harassment. It is possible that the *ratio of males to females* can facilitate or inhibit sexual harassment. The greater visibility of tokens, and "newcomer" status, may make them scapegoats for the dominant group's frustration. If they have colleagues or subordinates who resent their presence, harassment could serve to keep them isolated, humiliated, and uncomfortable enough to resign. *Organizational norms* vary from one occupation to another. As indicated by revealing waitress costumes and the terms "casting couch" and "sexcretary," sexual harassment receives strong informative support in some occupations. Within occupations there may also exist workplace norms that inhibit or facilitate sexual harassment. *Job tasks and requirements*, such as overtime work and business trips, may call into play leisure norms that conflict with work norms. Thus, "kidding around" with the opposite sex may lead to a more "sexy" atmosphere than found during normal working hours. It is possible that subordinates who have access to *informal or formal grievance procedures* and/or alternative jobs are less likely to tolerate or encounter sexual harassment. In sum, the organizational model relates sexual harassment to aspects of the workplace infrastructure that provide opportunities for sexual aggression.

Predictions Derived from the Organizational Model

Expected Victims

The most likely victims are those low in organization power: trainees; temporary or part-time workers; those in low grade or income levels; workers on probation, or newcomers such as token women or men, and low-status workers who are highly dependent on their job.

Expected Harassers

Conversely, the most likely harassers are those higher in organizational power than the victim or those coworkers who, by banding together, can present a powerful front to the victim. Persons who report that they have been accused of sexually harassing others are likely to have a more secure position in the organization.

Expected Acts

The greater the differential power in the organization or the higher the status of the harasser, the more severe and frequent the acts of sexual harassment.

Expected Victim Reactions and Behavior

Negative victim reactions should be greater for (a) the lowest-status workers (see *Expected Victims*) and (b) those who do not see themselves as having any formal or informal recourse.

Expected Outcomes and Consequences

The organizational model says that sexual harassment is a way to intimidate and control subordinates by using organizational authority to extort sexual favors. The use of such organizational authority should be seen in the loss of occupational mobility as the price of resisting such demands. It would therefore predict that various negative economic consequences for the victim should be part of the sexual harassment experience.

Work Characteristics

Sexual harassment is more likely in work organizations that (a) are highly structured and stratified, (b) discourage redress on work-related concerns, (c) have options or requirements for weekend or overtime work, (d) have skewed sex ratios, and (e) have expectations for "sexy" behavior within the workplace. Furthermore, the severity of sexual harassment should be a function of both the degree of privacy in the work space and the work group size: (f) more severe forms of sexual harassment are most likely in organizations with large work groups and private or semiprivate offices, and (g) less severe forms of harassment are most likely when semi- or private work space is *not* provided and the work groups are small.

THE SOCIOCULTURAL MODEL

According to the sociocultural model, sexual harassment is one manifestation of the larger patriarchal system in which men rule and social beliefs legitimize their rule (Farley 1978, MacKinnon 1979, 1981). According to this model, male dominance is maintained by cultural patterns of male-female interaction as well as by economic and political superordinancy. Society rewards males for aggressive and domineering sexual behaviors and females for passivity and acquiescence. Members of each sex are socialized to play their respective and complementary roles. Because women, more than men, are taught to seek their self-worth in the evaluation of others, particularly of men (Bardwick 1971), they are predisposed to try to interpret male attention as flattery, making them less likely to define unwanted attention as harassment. Their training to be sexually attractive, to be social facilitators and avoid conflict, to not trust their own judgment about what happens to them, and to feel responsible for their own victimization contributes to their vulnerability to sexual harassment. According to this model, the function of sexual harassment is to manage ongoing male-female interactions according to accepted sex status norms, and to maintain male dominance occupationally and therefore economically, by intimidating, discouraging, or precipitating removal of women from work.

Predictions Derived from the Sociocultural Model

Expected Victims

The sociocultural model would predict that gender is a better predictor of who is victimized than organizational position and that women are more often victims than men. It would also predict that a given harasser is likely to bother several victims. Women who are breaking into traditional male turf occupationally are also more likely to be harassed than other women.

Expected Harassers

As was the case for expected victims, the model predicts that gender is a better predictor of who will harass than organizational position, and that men are more often harassers than are women.

Expected Acts

The model does not suggest that certain forms of sexual harassment will be more common than others since all forms serve the same purpose. However, we would expect that women more than men would experience the "do it, or else" types of sexual harassment.

Expected Victim Reactions and Behavior

The sociocultural model predicts that female victims would react as powerless persons do, with damaged feelings about themselves and their work. It would also predict that it would have similar effects on other women, and that the emotional consequences would be worse for those victims with fewer options and a greater need for the job.

Because of their relative powerlessness and sex-role socialization, women victims are not likely, according to this model, to take interpersonally assertive action or to act on an expectation that the organization will help them solve their problem. The theory would also predict that women are correct in not expecting management to help them.

Expected Outcomes and Consequences

The sociocultural model says that the function of sexual harassment is to keep women economically dependent and generally subordinate. It would therefore predict that various negative economic consequences for the victim would be a part of the harassment experience.

Work Characteristics

Sexual harassment should occur more frequently, according to this model, when the sex-ratio in the work group is highly skewed either way, although for different reasons. The singular or heavily outnumbered women would be targeted as intruders invading male territory and without sufficient numbers to support each other. The female-dominated workplace is likely to be a traditionally feminine job with low status, several rungs below a male supervisor. These women are likely to have little job security, and traditional sex-role socialization.

A SURVEY OF FEDERAL EMPLOYEES

The data presented here were collected by the U.S. Merit Systems Protection Board, to which the authors served as consultants on the design of the study. The U.S. Merit Systems Protection Board (USMSPB) is a federal agency headquartered in Washington whose mission is to protect the merit system in federal employment practices. Data were collected in May 1980 from a stratified random sample of federal employees listed in the Central Personnel Data File of the Office of Personnel Management. The sample excluded: (a) persons working outside the continental United States, Alaska, or Hawaii; (b) military personnel; (c) persons employed by the FBI, CIA, Federal Election Commission, U.S. Postal Service and Postal Rate Commission, National Security Agency, Federal Reserve Board, White House Office, and Tennessee Valley Authority Agency; and (d) persons whose file lacked legitimate values for any of the stratification variables. The sample was stratified by sex (male, female), minority status (minority, nonminority), salary (five ordered categories), and organization (Department of Defense, Veteran's Administration, all others) in order to assure adequate representation from all parts of the federal workforce, and particularly those segments which, though small in number, might be disproportionately subject to harassment. For instance, low-income minority women constitute a very small portion of the federal workforce, but might on theoretical grounds be expected to experience a disproportionate amount of harassment. An equal number of cases were drawn from each of the 60 cells (2×2×5×3). All data presented here have been weighted by the appropriate sampling ratios. Anonymous, confidential, and usable questionnaires were returned from 83.8 percent of the 23,964 persons who received the questionnaire. The response rates from the various cells ranged from a low of 67.6 percent for low-income minority men in the Veteran's Administration, to a high of 93.6 percent for medium-low-income minority women in the Defense Department. The final sample size is 20,083 (10,644 women and 9,439 men).

"Victims" are persons who indicated that they had experienced one or more forms of sexual harassment on the job during the previous twenty-four months. All others are termed "nonvictims." Most of the figures presented here are contained in the MSPB's final report (USMSPB 1981) to the president and Congress.

PARTIAL TESTS OF THE MODELS USING SURVEY RESULTS

We cannot test all derivations from the three models with the data available, but even though incomplete, the tests we can make are instructive. Some conclusions are very clear. Models Two and Three receive more support than Model One. Male and female victims have different experiences, and men and women have different views about sexual behavior at work. The survey results are presented in relation to the questions asked of each model in the first part of the paper.

Who Are the Victims?

Men and women are not equally likely to experience sexual harassment. Forty-two percent of the women and only 15 percent of the men report having been sexually harassed at work within the preceding twenty-four months. Also, a higher percentage of female victims than of male victims experienced the most severe form of sexual harassment (3.1 percent vs. 1.7 percent). The "normal sexual attraction" version of Model One would suggest attention focused on only one person at a time, rather than indiscriminately spread over whoever is an easy target. Yet only a small minority (3 percent of the women and 8 percent of the men) report that they are unique in suffering the attentions of their harasser (a majority of each sex doesn't know whether there are other victims, but 43 percent of the women and 31 percent of the men report that there are other victims).

Single and divorced women are more likely to be victims (53 percent and 49 percent, respectively) than married women (37 percent). The incidence rate for widows is somewhat lower (31 percent) than for married women, but this may be associated with age as well. The same pattern holds for men even more strongly.

Neither the findings on sex of victim nor multiplicity of victims per harasser unequivocally support Model One's interpretation of sexual harassment. However, the relationship to marital status certainly does.

The evidence for more victimization of organizationally vulnerable workers is mixed. Women trainees report more harassment (51 percent) than other workers, but otherwise there is no relationship between job categories (Blue Collar, Clerical, Professional, Administration/Management) and harassment for either women or men. For men there is a clear negative relationship between GS level and incidence of harassment, which ranges from 9 percent of the GS 16's and above to 19 percent for GS 1 to GS 4. But for women, only being in the very highest GS levels somewhat reduces the probability of harassment (36 percent vs. 41–43 percent), while being in an ungraded or "Other" slot increases it somewhat. For both sexes, being a supervisor and not being on probation somewhat reduces one's risk of being harassed (46 percent and 54 percent, respectively). There is no clear relationship between income and incidence of sexual harassment, and education is *positively* related to incidence of harassment. Persons with less than a high school diploma report the least harassment while those with some graduate education report the most. This may reflect differences in awareness, differences in work situation (sex-ratio of one's work group, nontraditionally of one's job), or other factors.

Two measures of *personal* vulnerability, on the other hand, are strongly related to sexual harassment for both sexes. Younger workers report more harassment than older workers, and dependence on the job ("at the time of this experience, how much did you need this job?") dramatically increases the incidence of harassment (over 60 percent of the victims report "great" dependence on that job), a result that correlates with frequency of harassment and with duration of harassment for women.

We also find that women pioneers are more likely to be victims (53 percent) than nonpioneers (41 percent). But the same is true of men pioneers (20 percent) vs. nonpioneers (14 percent). The findings on education fit Model Three better than they fit Model Two, but the findings on GS level and income (which are highly correlated) support neither. Perhaps any single monotonic relationship is wiped out because both—opposite—forces are at work.

Who Are the Harassers?

The preponderance of harassers are male (78 percent of the victims were harassed by males only; 95 percent of female victims and 22 percent of male victims). Most victims (about 80 percent) were harassed by only one person but about a fifth were harassed by more than one person. While most women were harassed by married persons (67 percent), men were somewhat more likely to be harassed by single persons than by married persons.

It is difficult to test the similarity of victim and harasser on demographic variables because the data are imprecise or absent. With respect to age we only know whether the harasser was younger, older, or the same age, but we do not know how much older or younger. We do not know the harasser's level of education, income, or religion. With respect to ethnicity, we do know whether it is the same as or different from the victim's. Most victims were harassed by a person of the same ethnicity as themselves (63 percent of female victims, 68 percent of male victims), although women were more likely to be victimized by someone of a different ethnicity (26 percent) than men were (17 percent). But most women's harassers are older than themselves (68 percent) while men's harassers, in contrast, are most likely to be younger (38 percent), less than half as likely as women's harassers to be older (29 percent), and somewhat more likely to be the same age (18 percent). These findings provide some support for Model One in the similarity of ethnicity, but not for age or marital status.

The pattern of organizational relationships is also somewhat different for male and female victims. Although coworkers are the most common harassers for both sexes (65 percent for female victims, 76 percent for male victims), supervisors are two and a half times more common as harassers of women (37 percent) than as harassers of men (14 percent). For female but not male victims, subordinates are the least common harassers (4 percent and 16 percent, respectively). Thus the power differential component of sexual harassment, though not typical, is more common for women victims than men victims. Coworker harassment, although not usually a direct abuse of organizational power, still may be a power move by one or more coworkers trying to invoke the victim's sexual rather than work status in a work setting. Also, when organizational hierarchies fail to prohibit coworker harassment, the situation becomes one in which official power implicitly condones and supports harassment.

Thus, women's harassers are most likely to be older married men, while men's harassers are most likely to be younger, single women. While both sexes are most likely to be harassed by a coworker, more women than men are harassed by a superior and more men than women are harassed by subordinates. These differences suggest that the male's harasser might be more attractive to him than the female's harasser would be to her.

This pattern of difference, together with findings presented later on attitudinal differences and with other findings on the nature and outcome of the harassment, suggests that sexual harassment of women conforms more to a model suggesting intimidation while that of men conforms more to a model suggesting attraction (whether or not this is reciprocated).

What Took Place?

One percent of the female workforce reported actual or attempted rape or sexual assault, as did .03 percent of the male workforce. This corresponds to 3 percent of the female victims and almost 2 percent of the male victims reporting on the USMSPB survey. Almost three times as many men as women report that this happened to them more than once (56 percent vs. 20 percent). Less serious forms of harassment (sexual remarks, suggestive looks, deliberate touching) occurred more frequently than more serious forms of harassment (pressure for dates or sexual favors, letters or phone calls, rape or assault).

The quid pro quo type of harassment (in which victims fear retaliation if they do not cooperate) was somewhat more common among female victims than male victims, and was even reported by victims harassed by coworkers as well as superiors. For each type of penalty (worse assignments, unable to get promotions, losing one's job, etc.), a slightly higher proportion of women than men victims thought this would happen if they did not go along with the harasser. However, the differences are only a few percentage points. Oddly enough, men victims were equally or more likely than women victims to think there would be benefits if they *did* go along. Again, however, most of the differences are very small.

How Did the Victim Respond?

The data on female victims' response to sexual harassment [are] perhaps the most damaging to the view that harassment is an expression of attraction which the perpetrator presumably expects or would like to have reciprocated. Only a very small number of female victims go along with the overtures of the harasser (8 percent). But fully one-fourth of male victims do report "going along." Even these figures may overrepresent the number of true romance among these incidents, since some of these individuals may have gone along out of fear of retaliation as Models Two and Three would predict. Furthermore, 23 percent of these female victims and 21 percent of the male victims also said that doing so made things worse.

As shown before, a majority of victims harassed by their immediate supervisor did think something bad would happen if they did not go along with the supervisor (56 percent of both sexes); and a substantial minority of victims of other harassers also expected negative consequences (20 to 60 percent). Yet less than 5 percent of male and female victims took any formal action against the harasser, and most but not all of these did not see any need to report the behavior (61 percent females, 71 percent males).

Rather than it making victims feel good, the harassment worsened their emotional or physical condition (33 percent of the women and 21 percent of the men), worsened their ability to work with others on the job (15 percent and 15 percent), and worsened their feelings about work (36 percent and 19 percent).

The evidence for feelings of powerlessness among these victims is also mixed. Less than 10 percent of the victims felt that there is very little that either employees or management can do to reduce sexual harassment. At the same time, however, only slightly more than 10 percent felt that any formal action they took would be effective in stopping sexual harassment. Almost half the women and two-fifths of the men responded by avoiding the person who was harassing them. Another 60-plus percent ignored the behavior or did nothing. Such indirect and nonthreatening behavioral responses may reflect feelings of powerlessness or may reflect victim's feelings that the behavior is not a problem for them. Supportive of the latter interpretation is the finding that 61 percent of the women and 71 percent of the men said they "saw no need to report it."

More women than men did nothing because they were embarrassed (15 percent and 10 percent), because they did not think anything would be done (33 percent and 17 percent), because they thought it would be held against them (23 percent and 11 percent), or because they didn't know what action to take (15 percent and 7 percent).

What Outcomes or Consequences Ensued?

The vast majority of victims reported no actual changes in their job situation (81 percent of the women and 87 percent of the men) with respect to assignments, promotions, etc. One percent or fewer reported that some aspect of their work situation became better. Less than 10 percent reported that their working conditions or assignments worsened or that they experienced other negative job changes (denial of promotion, step increase, good performance rating, or reference; being reassigned or fired; quitting without another job; transferring or quitting to another job). Although the differences are small (1–4 percentage points), more female than male victims did experience negative job consequences.

Other kinds of negative consequences were more common. Over a third of the female victims (36 percent) and almost a fifth of the male victims (19 percent) reported that their "feelings about work became worse"; similar numbers reported that their "emotional or physical condition became worse" (33 percent women, 21 percent men); and eight to fifteen percent reported deterioration in their ability to work with others on the job, in their time and attendance at work, and in the quantity or quality of their work. These kinds of consequences are likely to have negative effects of some magnitude on one's ability to and likelihood of advancing in the job market. One should also remember that even though the percentages of each sex reporting a given outcome are similar, the actual numbers of women and men being affected are very different since there are three-fourths again as many women victims as men victims (294,000 to 168,000 in the federal workforce as a whole, extrapolating from survey data).

Part of Model Three is the assumption that the maintenance of dominance relations does not require that every woman be a victim, nor that every victim suffer all possible consequences. As with rape, the widespread knowledge that such things can and do happen serves to keep many women in the psychological condition of being wary—of being potential victims. Thus data on what victims *expected* to happen are also important in evaluating this model. Many more victims expected negative consequences than actually experienced such outcomes, especially when the harasser was a supervisor. More than half expected some kind of negative job-related consequences if they did not go along with their immediate boss. The figures are somewhat lower for the perceived penalty of not going along with a superior above their immediate boss. Moreover, 30 percent of the female victims (and 26 percent of the male victims) expected penalties if they did not go along with a coworker who was harassing them. On the other hand, 12 to 29 percent of the women (and 20 to 35 percent of the men) thought they would obtain some job advantage if they did go along with a supervisor. Even going along with a coworker or some other nonsupervisory worker was perceived as having some potential payoffs by some workers (2 to 9 percent of the victims of each sex).

Model Three would also predict that, beyond the abuse of power by an individual as predicted by Model Two, the organizations themselves—as male-dominated entities—would tacitly tolerate (or even encourage) sexual harassment of women as a way of perpetuating that dominance. This prediction is not generally supported: Only 4 percent of the women but 16 percent of the men victims reported that their organization was hostile or took action against them while 6 percent of the women and less than .1 percent of the men report that their organization did nothing. In fact, taking some kind of formal action was more effective in remedying the situation than was generally expected by the sample as a whole, and was generally more effective than informal actions. Of the organizational variables, only sex ratio, climate, and management responsiveness show a relationship to incidence of sexual harassment. For both sexes, likelihood of experiencing sexual harassment is associated with working in a group where the opposite sex predominates. This finding is most consistent with Models Two and Three. Victims of both sexes are more likely to report working in a sexy climate than nonvictims, and less likely to report working under a management that is responsive to their concerns. Neither size of work group, privacy of work space, nor work schedule show any relationship to incidence of sexual harassment.

Attitudes: How Do Men and Women View Sexually Harassing Behaviors?

Although the models as presented do not include predictions about people's *consciousness* regarding sexual harassment, it is instructive to examine the data available to us on this question. The first section of the questionnaire presented a series of attitudinal items . . . regarding various aspects of sexual behavior at work, and the second section asked respondents to indicate which specific sexual behaviors (by a supervisor or a coworker) would bother them and which they would consider sexual harassment. The attitudinal items contained statements representing each of the three models, i.e., some items reflect a view of sexual harassment as natural and nonserious, some reflect the perspective that it is based on organizational power rather than gender, and some that it is a part of a large power structure based on gender.

Of the six attitudinal items that reflect a view of sexual behavior at work as natural, nonthreatening, and even legitimately useful, only one receives the support of a majority of respondents: "People can usually stop unwanted sexual attention by telling the offender to stop." There is least agreement with using sex to get ahead: Less than 5 percent of both men and women felt this was all right for either sex to do. Greater differences between the male and female respondents are found on the remaining three items, and in each case more men than women agreed. Less than one-fourth of the women, but over 40 percent of the men, agreed that, "The issue of sexual harassment has been exaggerated—most incidents are simply normal sexual attraction between people." More than a third of the women (36 percent) agreed with the statement, "People shouldn't be so quick to take offense when someone expresses a sexual interest in them," but this is still fewer than the percentage of men agreeing with it (48 percent). And finally, 17 percent of the women and 26 percent of the men think that "It's all right for people to have sexual affairs with people they work with." Thus most of the respondents do not endorse items consistent with a natural/biological view of sexual harassment, although more men than women do so. However, while they do not strongly endorse this view, many respondents (more men than women) downplay the seriousness of the behavior and exaggerate the ease with which victims are expected to handle it.

Only one item directly reflects the organizational view of sexual harassment, namely that it is simply one expression of the abuse of power that comes with a hierarchical structure, and persons of either sex having that power are equally likely to abuse it. Half of the men and two-fifths of the women agreed that, "Women in positions of power are just as likely as men in such positions to sexually bother the people who work for them."

Only one item directly expresses the view that sexual harassment is essentially a power play which is not necessarily dependent on, or related to, organizational position: "Those who sexually bother others are usually seeking power over those they bother." Interestingly, while women endorsed this item at about the same rate as they did the "organizational" item (43 percent and 41 percent, respectively), men were less likely to endorse this item than the previous one (33 percent vs. 50 percent). In fact, this is the only attitude item which women endorsed at a higher rate than men did.

Two other items discredit the concept of sexual harassment as "uninvited and unwanted sexual attention" by either blaming the victim or discrediting the victim's claims. Endorsement of either item reflects a view which is contrary to both Models Two and Three. Only a minority of either sex endorsed these items, although again more men than women did so. Less than a third of the men and a fourth of the women agreed that, "People who receive annoying sexual attention have usually asked for it." Thirteen percent of the men and 7 percent of the women agreed that "When people say they've been sexually harassed, they're usually trying to get the person they accuse into trouble."

In sum, most respondents strongly reject the attitudinal derivatives of Model One, but do not strongly reject those of Models Two and Three. More men than women hold views consistent with the biological/natural model, while more women than men hold views consistent with the cultural model.

For all of the specific sexual behaviors presented, a majority of men and women say they would be bothered if a coworker or supervisor did these, and would call it sexual harassment in either case. There was one exception. Fewer than half the men said that they would consider sexual teasing, jokes, remarks, or questions from a coworker to be sexual harassment. Consistent with the sex differences on attitudes, more women than men said that each kind of behavior from each source (supervisor or coworker) would bother them, and would be sexual harassment. Both sexes consider such behaviors from supervisors more serious than from coworkers (more persons would be bothered by these behaviors and call it sexual harassment); and both sexes rank the behaviors similarly.

Thus, although women and men appear to apply the same criteria for using the term "sexual harassment," women's threshold is lower, and they are more bothered by it.

CONCLUSIONS

The most striking thing about these findings is not some clear-cut support for one model or the other, but rather that no clear pattern emerges. Certainly one conclusion to be drawn from these data is that sexual harassment is not a unitary phenomenon, especially across the sexes, but even within those incidents reported by women. Some sexual harassment may indeed be clumsy or insensitive expressions of attraction, while some is the classic abuse of organizational power. Our data suggest that men are more likely than women to be victims of the former, while women are more likely than men to be victims of the latter. Most clear is that the victim experiences the most adverse effect in the latter case, and in almost no case does sexual harassment have beneficial outcomes. Women, who are four times as likely to be victims as men, also view sexual harassment more negatively, and in general are more likely to feel that sexual behavior and work don't mix.

These are actually important findings to document, since the data set on which they rest is the first random sample available for analysis in which nonself-selected individuals were asked about sexual harassment, with that specific label attached to behaviors many people experience. In the past, self-selected samples (all female) have reported much more homogeneous harassment experiences which more directly fit the quid pro quo ("do it or else") type of harassment. The three theoretical models posited in this [essay] were derived from the literature, court cases, and legal defenses describing these more homogeneous situations. Now that we have data reflecting a broader range of experience among a valid sample of respondents, what conclusions can we draw?

The consistent negative reactions of female victims to incidents they consider harassing, plus the tendency of individuals with greater degrees of personal vulnerability and dependence on their job to experience more harassment constitute the strongest evidence available in these data against the natural model. Nevertheless, given the relatively simple hypotheses with which we began, each model receives some support from these data. An important area for further analysis would be to separate coworker harassment from superior-subordinate harassment, with further splits by sex of victim and seriousness of harassment, and look for differential patterns, of causes and consequences within the different types thus created. This would best be done not as tests of three models, but rather as a multivatiate analysis exploring the interactive role of demographic, organizational, and cultural factors on incidence and consequences.

Even with the type of analysis just described, however, we now have some doubt about the predictability of harassment incidents themselves. If sexual harassment is as widespread as the results of the MSPB survey indicate, it may approximate a random event in women's working lives—something which is highly likely to happen at some time, with just when, where, and how being so multidetermined that prediction is difficult. This very fact supports the cultural model in some ways, but it also implies that finding empirical support for the cultural model will not be easy, if only because few, if any, circumstances exist where the dominant culture does not exert its influence. Even within the minds of the survey respondents, what they call sexual harassment and how they respond to it will already be determined by the cultural context. For instance, most respondents who experienced sexual harassment did not report it to anyone, and did not see reporting it as an appropriate response. As researchers, we must interpret this finding, but have little basis in the survey results for doing so. Do respondents believe any appeal to organizational authority would be ineffective? Since most of the incidents involve coworkers, do respondents view these as not organizationally threatening enough to warrant formal action? Are respondents caught up in the cultural mandate, based on the natural model, that they should be able to handle such incidents themselves? If thinking about the acceptability of sexual harassment changes, would we be likely to see more formal action and more anger at employers for permitting harassment to continue? We cannot answer these questions, and therefore cannot finally decide which model best reflects what "is." In no small part, this inability arises because what "is" is changing, respondents are themselves at different points along an ideological continuum, and thus what they report and how they see it will be full of contradictions for some time to come.

A survey of the USMSPB type is useful for documenting incidence and prevalence, and certain general patterns of sexual harassment at single points in time. As such, it provides an invaluable snapshot not heretofore available. Nevertheless, such data, on such a large sample, can only scratch the surface of understanding the intrapersonal and interpersonal dynamics of sexual harassment. If at all possible, future research should use these data and the types of harassment derivable from them to structure more in-depth explorations of how victims see sexual harassment and their options when confronted with it. In particular, creative thought must be given to ways to explore the cultural assumptions underlying harassment, since survey methods may not be able to discover enough variance to make that particular mode of analysis meaningful. A similar in-depth analysis of consequences would need to explore victims' reduced expectations and aspirations for a satisfying work environment, changed perceptions of self, changes in self-confidence, and productivity factors which are easily denied in a survey research format.

Note

1. S. Martin and S. Fein. Sexual Harassment in the Workplace: A Problem Whose Time Has Come, Paper presented at the annual meeting of the Society for the Study of Social Problems, September 2, 1978.

REFERENCES

Bardwick, J. *The Psychology of Women.* New York: Harper and Row, 1971.

Berscheid, E., and E. Walster. *Interpersonal Attraction.* Reading, Mass.: Addison-Wesley, 1969.

Bularzik, M. "Sexual Harassment at the Workplace: Historical Notes." In F. Brodhead et al., eds., *Radical America* 12, no. 4 (1978).

Bundy v. *Jackson.* D.C. Action No. 77-1359 (D.C. Cir., January 12, 1981).

Corne and DeVane v. *Bausch and Lomb, Inc.* 390 F. Suppl. 161 (D. Ariz. 1975). Reversed and remanded on other grounds, 562 F. 2n 55 (9th Cir. 1977).

Dothard v. *Rawlinson,* 433 U.S. 321 (1977).

Evans, L. J. "Sexual Harassment: Women's Hidden Occupational Hazard." In *The Victimization of Women*, edited by J. Roberts Chapman and M. Gates, pp. 203–23. Beverly Hills, Calif.: Sage Publications, 1978.

Farley, L. *Sexual Shakedown: The Sexual Harassment of Women on the Job.* New York: McGraw Hill, 1978.

Goodman, J. "Sexual Harassment: Some Observations of the Distance Traveled and the Distance Yet to Go." *Capital Universal Law Review* 10, no. 3 (1978): 445–70.

MacKinnon, C. A. Introduction. *Capital University Law Review* 10, no. 3 (1981): i–viii.

———. *Sexual Harassment of Working Women.* New Haven, Conn.: Yale University Press, 1979.

Martin, S. "Sexual Politics in the Workplace: The Interactional World of Policewomen." *Symbolic Interaction* 1, no. 2 (1978): 44–60.

Miller v. *Bank of America.* 418 F. Supp. 233 (N.D. Cal. 1976), (Rev'd 600 F. 2d 211 C.D.C. Cir. 1979) Appeal Pending.

Neely v. *American Fidelity Assurance Co.*, 17 F.E.P. 482 (W.D. Okla. 1978).

Smith v. *Amoco Chemical Corp.*, 20 F.E.P. 724 (S.D. Texas 1979).

U.S. Merit Systems Protection Board. *Sexual Harassment in the Federal Workplace: Is It a Problem?* Washington, D.C.: U.S. Government Printing Office, 1981.

Vinson v. *Taylor,* 23 F.E.P. 37 (D.D.C. 1980).

Winch, R. F. *The Modern Family,* 3d. ed. New York: Holt, Rinehart and Winston, 1971.

SEXUAL AGGRESSION AND NATURE

8

CAMILLE PAGLIA

In the beginning was nature. The background from which and against which our ideas of God were formed, nature remains the supreme moral problem. We cannot hope to understand sex and gender until we clarify our attitude toward nature. Sex is a subset to nature. Sex is the natural in man.

Society is an artificial construction, a defense against nature's power. Without society, we would be storm-tossed on the barbarous sea that is nature. Society is a system of inherited forms reducing our humiliating passivity to nature. We may alter these forms, slowly or suddenly, but no change in society will change nature. Human beings are not nature's favorites. We are merely one of a multitude of species on which nature indiscriminately exerts its force. Nature has a master agenda we can only dimly know.

Human life began in flight and fear. Religion rose from rituals of propitiation, spells to lull the punishing elements. To this day, communities are few in regions scorched by heat or shackled by ice. Civilized man conceals from himself the extent of his subordination to nature. The grandeur of culture, the consolation of religion absorb his attention and win his faith. But

From *Sexual Personae: Art and Decadence from Nefertiti to Emily Dickinson* (New Haven, Conn.: Yale University Press, 1990), pp. 1–5, 7–10, 19, 20, 30–33. Copyright © 1990 by Camille Paglia. Reprinted by permission of the publisher and the author.

let nature shrug, and all is in ruin. Fire, flood, lightning, tornado, hurricane, volcano, earthquake—anywhere at any time. Disaster falls upon the good and bad. Civilized life requires a state of illusion. The idea of the ultimate benevolence of nature and God is the most potent of man's survival mechanisms. Without it, culture would revert to fear and despair.

Sexuality and eroticism are the intricate intersection of nature and culture. Feminists grossly oversimplify the problem of sex when they reduce it to a matter of social convention: readjust society, eliminate sexual inequality, purify sex roles, and happiness and harmony will reign. Here feminism, like all liberal movements of the past two hundred years, is heir to Rousseau. *The Social Contract* (1762) begins: "Man is born free, and everywhere he is in chains." Pitting benign Romantic nature against corrupt society, Rousseau produced the progressivist strain in nineteenth-century culture, for which social reform was the means to achieve paradise on earth. The bubble of these hopes was burst by the catastrophes of two world wars. But Rousseauism was reborn in the postwar generation of the sixties, from which contemporary feminism developed.

Rousseau rejects original sin, Christianity's pessimistic view of man born unclean, with a propensity for evil. Rousseau's idea, derived from Locke, of man's innate goodness led to social environmentalism, now the dominant ethic of American human services, penal codes, and behaviorist therapies. It assumes that aggression, violence, and crime come from social deprivation—a poor neighborhood, a bad home. Thus feminism blames rape on pornography. . . . But rape . . . [has] been evident throughout history and, at some moment, in all cultures.

This . . . [selection] takes the point of view of Sade, the most unread major writer in Western literature. Sade's work is a comprehensive satiric critique of Rousseau, written in the decade after the first failed Rousseauist experiment, the French Revolution, which ended not in political paradise but in the hell of the Reign of Terror. Sade follows Hobbes rather than Locke. Aggression comes from nature; it is what Nietzsche is to call the will-to-power. For Sade, getting back to nature (the Romantic imperative that still permeates our culture from sex counseling to cereal commercials) would be to give free reign to violence and lust. I agree. Society is not the criminal but the force which keeps crime in check. When social controls weaken, man's innate cruelty bursts forth. The rapist is created not by bad social influences but by a failure of social conditioning. Feminists, seeking to drive power relations out of sex, have set themselves against nature. Sex *is* power. Identity is power. In Western culture, there are no nonexploitative relationships. Everyone has killed in order to live. Nature's universal law of creation from destruction operates in mind as in matter. As Freud, Nietzsche's heir, asserts, identity is conflict. Each generation drives its plow over the bones of the dead.

Modern liberalism suffers unresolved contradictions. It exalts individualism and freedom and, on its radical wing, condemns social orders as oppressive. On the other hand, it expects government to provide materially for all, a feat manageable only by an expansion of authority and a swollen bureaucracy. In other words, liberalism defines government as tyrant father but demands it behave as nurturant mother. Feminism has inherited these contradictions. It sees every hierarchy as repressive, a social fiction; every negative about woman is a male lie designed to keep her in her place. Feminism has exceeded its proper mission of seeking political equality for women and has ended by rejecting contingency, that is, human limitation by nature or fate.

Sexual freedom, sexual liberation. A modern delusion. We are hierarchical animals. Sweep one hierarchy away, and another will take its place, perhaps less palatable than the first. There are hierarchies in nature and alternate hierarchies in society. In nature, brute force is the law, a survival of the fittest. In society, there are protections for the weak. Society is our frail barrier against nature. When the prestige of state and religion is low, men are free, but they find freedom intolerable and seek new ways to enslave themselves, through drugs or depression. My theory is that whenever sexual freedom is sought or achieved, sadomasochism will not be far behind. Romanticism always turns into decadence. Nature is a hard taskmaster. It is the hammer and the anvil, crushing individuality. Perfect freedom would be to die by earth, air, water, and fire.

Sex is a far darker power than feminism has admitted. Behaviorist sex therapies believe guiltless, no-fault sex is possible. But sex has always been girt around with taboo, irrespective of culture. Sex is the point of contact between man and nature, where morality and good intentions fall to primitive urges. I called it an intersection. This intersection is the uncanny crossroads of Hecate, where all things return in the night. Eroticism is a realm stalked by ghosts. It is the place beyond the pale, both cursed and enchanted.

. . . Integration of man's body and mind is a profound problem that is not about to be solved by recreational sex or an expansion of women's civil rights. Incarnation, the limitation of mind by matter, is an outrage to imagination. Equally outrageous is gender, which we have not chosen but which nature has imposed upon us. Our physicality is torment, our body the tree of nature on which Blake sees us crucified.

Sex is daemonic. This term, current in Romantic studies of the past twenty-five years, derived from the Greek *daimon*, meaning a spirit of lower divinity than the Olympian gods (hence my pronunciation "daimonic"). The outcast Oedipus becomes a daemon at Colonus. The word came to mean a man's guardian shadow. Christianity turned the daemonic into the demonic. The Greek daemons were not evil—or rather they were both good and evil, like nature itself, in which they dwelled. Freud's unconscious is a daemonic realm. In the day we are social creatures, but at night we descend to the dream world where nature reigns, where there is no law but sex, cruelty, and metamorphosis. Day itself is invaded by daemonic night. Moment by moment, night flickers in the imagination, in eroticism, subverting our strivings for virtue and order, giving an uncanny aura to objects and persons revealed to us through the eyes of the artist.

The ghost-ridden character of sex is implicit in Freud's brilliant theory of "family romance." We each have an incestuous constellation of sexual personae that we carry from childhood to the grave and that determines whom and how we love or hate. Every encounter with friend or foe, every clash with or submission to authority bears the perverse traces of family romance. Love is a crowded theater, for as Harold Bloom remarks, "We can never embrace (sexually or otherwise) a single person, but embrace the whole of her or his family romance."[1] We still know next to nothing of the mystery of cathexis, the investment of libido in certain people or things. The element of free will in sex and emotion is slight. As poets know, falling in love is irrational.

Like art, sex is fraught with symbols. Family romance means that adult sex is always representation, ritualistic acting out of vanished realities. A perfectly humane eroticism may be impossible. Somewhere in every family romance is hostility and aggression, the homicidal wishes of the unconscious. Children are monsters of unbridled egotism and will, for they spring directly from nature, hostile limitations of immorality. We carry that daemonic will within us forever. Most people conceal it with acquired ethical precepts and meet it only in their dreams, which they hastily forget upon waking. The will-to-power is innate, but the sexual scripts of family romance are learned. Human beings are the only creatures in whom consciousness is so entangled with animal instinct. In Western culture, there can never be a purely physical or anxiety-free sexual encounter. Every attraction, every pattern of touch, every orgasm is shaped by psychic shadows. . . .

Sex cannot be understood because nature cannot be understood. Science is a method of logical analysis of nature's operations. It has lessened human anxiety about the cosmos by demonstrating the materiality of nature's forces, and their frequent predictability. But science is always playing catch-up ball. Nature breaks its own rules whenever it wants. Science cannot avert a single thunderbolt. Western science is a product of the Apollonian mind: its hope is that by naming and classification, by the cold light of intellect, archaic night can be pushed back and defeated. . . .

The westerner knows by seeing. Perceptual relations are at the heart of our culture, and they have produced our titanic contributions to art. Walking in nature, we see, identify, name, *recognize*. This recognition is our apotropaion, that is, our warding off of fear. Recognition is ritual cognition, a repetition-compulsion. We say that nature is beautiful. But this esthetic judgment, which not all peoples have shared, is another defense formation, woefully inadequate for encompassing nature's totality. What is pretty in nature is confined to the thin skin of the globe upon which we huddle. Scratch that skin, and nature's daemonic ugliness will erupt. . . .

. . . The identification of woman with nature was universal in prehistory. In hunting or agrarian societies dependent upon nature, femaleness was honored as an immanent principle of fertility. As culture progressed, crafts and commerce supplied a concentration of resources freeing men from the caprices of weather or the handicap of geography. With nature at one remove, femaleness receded in importance.

Buddhist cultures retained the ancient meanings of femaleness long after the West renounced them. Male and female, the Chinese yang and yin, are balanced and interpenetrating powers in man and nature, to which society is subordinate. This code of passive acceptance has its roots in India, a land of sudden extremes where a monsoon can wipe out 50,000 people overnight. The femaleness of fertility religions is always double-edged. The Indian nature-goddess Kali is creator *and* destroyer, granting boons with one set of arms while cutting throats with the other. She is the lady ringed with skulls. The moral ambivalence of the great mother goddesses has been conveniently forgotten by those American feminists who have resurrected them. We cannot grasp nature's bare blade without shedding our own blood.

Western culture from the start has swerved from femaleness. The last major Western society to worship female powers was Minoan Crete. And significantly, that fell and did not rise again. The immediate cause of its collapse—quake, plague, or invasion—is beside the point. The lesson is that cultic femaleness is no guarantee of cultural strength or viability. What did survive, what did vanquish circumstance and stamp its mindset on Europe was Mycenaean warrior culture, descending to us through Homer. The male will-to-power: Mycenaeans from the south and Dorians from the north would fuse to form Apollonian Athens, from which came the Greco-Roman line of Western history.

Both the Apollonian and Judeo-Christian traditions are transcendental. That is, they seek to surmount or transcend nature. . . . Judeo-Christianity, like Greek worship of the Olympian gods, is a sky-cult. It is an advanced stage in the history of religion, which everywhere began as earth-cult, veneration of fruitful nature.

The evolution from earth-cult to sky-cult shifts woman into the nether realm. Her mysterious procreative powers and the resemblance of her rounded breasts, belly, and hips to earth's contours put her at the center of early symbolism. . . .

. . . From the beginning of time, woman has seemed an uncanny being. Man honored but feared her. She was the black maw that had spat him forth and would devour him anew. Men, bonding together, invented culture as a defense against female nature. Sky-cult was the most sophisticated step in this process, for its switch of the creative locus from earth to sky is a shift from belly-magic to head-magic. And from this defensive head-magic has come the spectacular glory of male civilization, which has lifted woman with it. The very language and logic modern woman uses to assail patriarchal culture were the invention of men.

Hence the sexes are caught in a comedy of historical indebtedness. Man, repelled by his debt to a physical mother, created an alternate reality, a heterocosm to give him the illusion of freedom. Woman, at first content to accept man's protections but now inflamed with desire for her own illusory freedom, invades man's systems and suppresses her indebtedness to him as she steals them. By headmagic she will deny there ever was a problem of sex and nature. He has inherited the anxiety of influence.

The identification of woman with nature is the most troubled and troubling term in this historical argument. Was it ever true? Can it still be true? Many feminist readers will disagree, but I think this identification not myth but reality. All the genres of philosophy, science, high art, athletics, and politics were invented by men. But by the Promethean law of conflict and capture, woman has a right to seize what she will and to vie with man on his own terms. Yet there is a limit to what she can alter in herself and in man's relation to her. Every human being must wrestle with nature. But nature's burden falls more heavily on one sex. With luck, this will not limit woman's achievement, that is, her action in male-created social space. But it must limit eroticism, that is, our imaginative lives in sexual space, which may overlap social space but is not identical with it.

Nature's cycles are woman's cycles. Biologic femaleness is a sequence of circular returns, beginning and ending at the same point. Woman's centrality gives her a stability of identity. She does not have to become but only to be. Her centrality is a great obstacle to man, whose quest for identity she blocks. He must transform himself into an independent being, that is, a being free of her. If he does not, he will simply fall back into her. Reunion with the mother is a siren call haunting our imagination. Once there was bliss, and now there is struggle. Dim memories of life before the traumatic separation of birth may be the source of Arcadian fantasies of a lost golden age. The Western idea of history as a propulsive movement into the future, a progressive or providential design climaxing in the revelation of a Second Coming, is a male formulation. No woman, I submit, could have coined such an idea, since it is a strategy of evasion of woman's own cyclic nature, in which man dreads being caught. Evolutionary or apocalyptic history is a male wish list with a happy ending, a phallic peak. . . .

What has nature given man to defend himself against woman? Here we come to the source of man's cultural achievements, which follow so directly from his singular anatomy. Our lives as physical beings give rise to basic metaphors of apprehension, which vary greatly between the sexes. Here there can be no equality. Man is sexually compartmentalized. Genitally, he is condemned to a perpetual pattern of linearity, focus, aim, directedness. He must learn to aim. Without aim, urination and ejaculation end in infantile soiling of self or surroundings. Woman's eroticism is diffused throughout her body. Her desire for foreplay remains a notorious area of miscommunication between the sexes. Man's genital concentration is a reduction but also an intensification. He is a victim of unruly ups and downs. Male sexuality is inherently manic-depressive. Estrogen [i.e., the female hormone] tranquilizes, but androgen [i.e., the male hormone] agitates. Men are in a constant state of sexual anxiety, living on the pins and needles of their hormones. In sex as in life they are driven *beyond*—beyond the self, beyond the body. Even in the womb this rule applies. Every fetus becomes female unless it is steeped in male hormones, produced by a signal from the testes. Before birth, therefore, a male is already beyond the female. But to be beyond is to be exiled from the center of life. Men know they are sexual exiles. They wander the earth seeking satisfaction, craving and despising, never content. There is nothing in that anguished motion for women to envy.

The male genital metaphor is concentration and projection. Nature gives concentration to man to help him overcome his fear. Man approaches woman in bursts of spasmodic concentration. This gives him the delusion of temporary control of the archetypal mysteries that brought him forth. It gives him the courage to return. Sex is metaphysical for men, as it is not for women. Women have no problem to solve by sex. Physically and psychologically, they are serenely self-contained. They may choose to achieve, but they do not need it. They are not thrust into the beyond by their own fractious bodies. But men are out of balance. They must quest, pursue, court, or seize. Pigeons on the grass, alas: in such parkside rituals we may savor the comic pathos of sex. How often one spots a male pigeon making desperate, self-inflating sallies toward the female, as again and again she turns her back on him and nonchalantly marches away. But by concentration and insistence he may carry the day. Nature has blessed him with obviousness to his own absurdity. His purposiveness is both a gift and a burden. In human beings, sexual concentration is the male's instrument for gathering together and forcibly fixing the dangerous chthonian* superflux of emotion and energy that I identify with woman and nature. In sex, man is driven into the very abyss which he flees. He makes a voyage to nonbeing and back.

Through concentration to projection into the beyond. The male projection of erection and ejaculation is the paradigm for all cultural projection and conceptualization—from art and philosophy to fantasy, hallucination, and obsession. Women have conceptualized less in history not because men have kept them from doing so but because women do not need to conceptualize in order to exist. I leave open the question of brain differences. Conceptualization and sexual mania may issue from the same part of the male brain. Fetishism, for instance, a practice which like most of the sex perversions is confined to men, is clearly a conceptualizing or symbol-making activity. Man's vastly greater commercial patronage of pornography is analogous.

An erection is *a thought* and the orgasm an act of imagination. The male has to will his sexual authority before the woman who is a shadow of his mother and of all women. Failure and humiliation constantly wait in the wings. No woman has to prove herself a woman in the grim way a man has to prove himself a man. He must perform, or the show does not go on. Social convention is irrelevant. A flop is a flop. Ironically, sexual success always ends in sagging fortunes anyhow. Every male projection is transient and must be anxiously, endlessly renewed. Men enter in triumph but withdraw in decrepitude. The sex act cruelly mimics history's decline and fall. Male bonding is a self-preservation society, collegial reaffirmation through larger, fabricated frames of reference. Culture is man's iron reinforcement of his ever-imperiled private projections. . . .

. . . Man's focus, directedness, concentration, and projection, which I identified with urination and ejaculation, are his tools of sexual survival, but they have never given him a final victory. The anxiety in sexual experience remains as strong as ever. This man attempts to correct by the cult of female beauty. He is erotically fixated on woman's "shapeliness," those spongy material fat deposits of breast, hip, and buttock which are ironically the wateriest and least stable parts of her anatomy. Woman's billowy body reflects the surging sea of chthonian nature. By focusing on the shapely, by making woman a sex-object, man has struggled to fix and stabilize nature's dreadful flux. Objectification is conceptualization, the highest human faculty. Turning people into sex objects is one of the specialties of our species. It will never disappear, since it is intertwined with the art-impulse and may be identical to it. A sex object is ritual form imposed on nature. It is a totem of our perverse imagination. . . .

---

*Paglia defines "chthonian" as " 'of the earth'—but earth's bowels, not its surface." (*Ed.*)

Man, the sexual conceptualizer and projector, has ruled art because art is his Apollonian response toward and away from woman. A sex object is something to aim at. The eye is Apollo's arrow following the arc of transcendence I saw in male urination and ejaculation. The Western eye is a projectile into the *beyond*, that wilderness of the male condition. . . .

Western culture has a roving eye. Male sex is hunting and scanning: boys hang yelping from honking cars, acting like jerks over strolling girls; men lunching on girders go through the primitive book of wolf whistles and animal clucks. Everywhere, the beautiful woman is scrutinized and harassed. She is the ultimate symbol of human desire. The feminine is that-which-is-sought; it recedes beyond our grasp. Hence there is always a feminine element in the beautiful young man of male homosexuality. The feminine is ever-elusive, a silver shimmer on the horizon. We follow this image with longing eyes: maybe this one, maybe this time. The pursuit of sex may conceal a dream of being freed from sex. Sex, knowledge, and power are deeply tangled; we cannot get one without the other. Islam is wise to drape women in black, for the eye is the avenue of eros. Western culture's hard, defined personalities suffer from inflammation of the eye. They are so numerous that they have never been catalogued, except in our magnificent portrait art. Western sexual personae are nodes of power, but they have made a torment of eroticism. From this torment has come our grand tradition of literature and art. Unfortunately, there is no way to separate the whistling ass on his girder from the rapt visionary at his easel. In accepting the gifts of culture, women may have to take the worm with the apple. . . .

NOTE

1. *The Anxiety of Influence: A Theory of Poetry* (New York, 1973), p. 94.

THE SOCIAL CAUSES OF SEXUAL HARASSMENT

9

CATHARINE A. MACKINNON

According to Catharine MacKinnon, society believes that being male or female is a biological given when, in fact, the meaning and consequences of such categories are primarily determined by society itself. Society has attributed submission and sexuality to the female role, thereby defining women as sexual objects. Women are therefore subordinated, or treated as if they are not equal to men in dignity and worth.

MacKinnon believes that society's discrimination against women manifests itself in various ways. One way is through unwanted sexual advances in contexts of unequal power (i.e., sexual harassment). But women are also subordinated to men in many other ways—through acts of violence as well as through social mechanisms that deny women the social and economic opportunities and resources available to men. Thus, MacKinnon views sexual harassment against the background of a society systematically shaped by beliefs, attitudes, and practices which devalue, degrade, and disadvantage women on the basis of their sex. Although she takes sexual harassment to be one of the products of a society that discriminates against women, MacKinnon recognizes that "discrimination based upon sex" is often not a simple notion.

Much is riding on the view that sexual harassment is sex

From *Sexual Harassment of Working Women: A Case of Sex Discrimination* by Catharine A. MacKinnon (New Haven, Conn.: Yale University Press, 1979). Copyright © 1979. Reprinted by permission of the publisher and the author.

discrimination. Legal actions in sexual harassment law are usually brought under Title VII of the Civil Rights Act of 1964. This outlaws discriminatory employment practices, whether these practices are based upon race, color, religion, national origin—or sex. Among other things, this legislation enables the Equal Employment Opportunity Commission to initiate action on behalf of plaintiffs in sexual harassment cases. [Ed.]

NATURAL/BIOLOGICAL

With a tone of "you can't change *that*," the cases rejecting sexual harassment claims repeatedly excuse the incidents as "biological" or "natural." In the *Miller* case, Judge Williams, denying relief, stated with astonishing equanimity and/or candor: "The attraction of males to females and females to males is a natural sex phenomenon and it is probable that this attraction plays at least a subtle part in most personnel decisions."[1] One wonders what this factor has to do with merit and whether subtle racial revulsion is equally permissible. The brief for Bausch and Lomb was similarly explicit in its appeal to nature to exonerate the perpetrator: "Obviously, certain biological differences exist between male and female. . . . [I]t would appear that in the foreseeable future that the attraction of males to females and females to males will not soon disappear."[2] The *Tomkins* district court also referred to "this natural sex attraction," stating, in a breathtaking but indecisive midsentence reversal, "while sexual desire animated the parties, or at least one of them. . . ."[3]

. . . In the biological view, sexual expression seems presumed to derive from a biological need or genital drive or to be deeply rooted in a natural order that connects biological differences with expressions of mutual attraction. The idea is that biology cannot be questioned or changed, and is legitimate, while society can be, and may be "artificial." Perhaps this presumption underlies the clear doctrinal necessity, if sexual harassment is to be considered sex discrimination under existing conceptions, to establish sexual harassment as less a question of "sexuality" than of gender status: an implicit legal presupposition that sexuality is buried in nature, while gender status is at least in part a social construct. In the above quotations, in an attempt to justify legal nonintervention, sexual harassment is implicitly argued to be an inevitable and integral part of the naturally given, not socially contingent or potentially changeable, sexual relations between women and men.

Upon closer scrutiny, these presumptions about sex have little to do with the occurrence of sexual harassment. Women possess a physical sex drive equal to or greater than that of men,[4] yet do not systematically harass men sexually. Some men, who have nothing wrong with them sexually, seem able to control their behavior. Not all women experience sexual attraction to all men, nor all men to all women. These factors suggest that something beyond pure biology is implicated. Usually, the last thing wanted in these incidents is species reproduction, which removes any connection with a natural drive in that direction. Moreover, not everything deemed natural by defining all sexual behavior as biological is thereby made socially acceptable. If economically coerced intercourse is biological, rape must be also, but it is not legally allowed for that reason.

The image of codetermination in sexual matters by men and women is scrupulously maintained in these cases. But for the unwilling woman, no "attraction" is involved, and little power. Even if the "attractiveness of the sexes for one another" were inevitable, that would not make its expression indiscriminate. Calling sex "natural" means here, in effect, that women are to be allowed no choice of with whom and under what conditions to have sexual relations. In these cases, we are dealing with a male who is allegedly exercising his power as an employer, his power over a woman's material survival, and his sexual prerogatives as a man, to subject a woman sexually. One would have to argue that sexual power is by nature asymmetrical, and hence that it is biological for males to threaten, force, blackmail, coerce, subject, exploit, and oppress women sexually, to conclude that sexual harassment is natural. . . .

WHAT IS SEX?

The legal interpretation of the term *sex*, as illustrated by the foregoing, has centered upon the gender difference between women and men, which the law views as a biological given. "Gender per se" is considered to refer to an obvious biological fact with a fixed content. Factors "other than gender per se," but correlated with it, may also ground a discrimination claim. These factors are treated in legal discourse accretions—some biological, some social—upon the biological foundation. These presuppositions about sex and gender have been so widely assumed that it has seldom been considered whether they are appropriate foundations for a social policy directed toward women's equality, or even whether they are, to the best of our current knowledge, true.

One major contradiction within the legal conception of sex as gender was posed by the *Gilbert* analysis.* The plaintiff argued that pregnancy was a gender distinction per se because only women become pregnant. The majority of the Supreme Court argued that pregnancy was other than gender per se, in part because it is voluntary, while gender is not; in part because not all women become pregnant, so it is not a characteristic of the sex; and in part because no men become pregnant, so women and men were not being *treated* discriminatorily, they merely *are* different. Defining sex with reference to gender was inadequate to resolve the issue of whether, in order for a classification such as pregnancy to be considered sex-based, all women must be actually or potentially so classified, or whether it is sufficient that all those so classified are women, with no men even potentially included, or whether the fact that no men can be so affected means that the exclusion *cannot* discriminate against women.

To generalize beyond the explicit terms of the Supreme Court's holding, its

---

*Gilbert v. General Electric, 429 U.S. (1976). (Ed.)

resolution of this issue could be stated as follows: for differential treatment of the sexes to be considered sex-based, it must occur, or potentially occur, to all members of a group defined by biological gender, but not for reasons unique to that biology. That is, to be sex-based, a treatment (or classification or factor) must be universal to women but not unique to women. It must affect all women and, in some sense, not only women. Pregnancy was considered both not universal to women and unique to women, thus not a gender classification. . . .

Several empirical presumptions are implicit in this approach. It is assumed that a solid physical underpinning exists for the sex difference and that sex is dimorphic. The sexes are understood in terms of their differences and these differences are considered physical and bipolar. It is assumed that a clear, known line can be drawn between those attributes of gender which are biological and those which are other than biological. The relevant referent for the legal meaning of sex is supposed to be primarily in biology rather than society.

The particular place of "sexuality" as one index to maleness or femaleness has never been firmly located in this legal scheme of sex as gender and gender as biology. Other than in the few sexual harassment cases, the question has rarely been posed. One recent EEOC [Equal Employment Opportunity Commission] case, justifying the lack of protection for homosexuals under Title VII, distinguished "sexual practice" from "gender as such," the latter defined as "an immutable characteristic with which a person is born."[5] Sexuality, or at least homosexuality, seemed to mean something one does, gender something one is. Similarly, the *Harvard Law Review* implicitly distinguished between sexuality and sex as gender under Title VII as follows: "Although jobs which require sex appeal may exploit their occupants as sex objects, [Title VII] was not designed to change *other* views that society holds about sexuality"[6] (emphasis added). A series of interconnected propositions emerges: "sex" in the legal sense is primarily a matter of gender status; gender status is a matter of innate biological differences; homosexuality is a "practice," not a matter of gender status, hence not within the ambit of sex discrimination. But what exactly is heterosexuality? What is its relationship to the gender difference? How do gender and heterosexuality interrelate in what discrimination law means by "sex"?

The relationship of sexuality to gender is the critical link in the argument that sexual harassment is sex discrimination. Empirically, gender is not monolithic. Three dimensions can be distinguished: physical characteristics, gender identification, and sex-role behavior. Contrary to legal presumptions, current research shows that none of these dimensions is perfectly intercorrelated with, nor strictly predetermines, any other. Gender, then, is not as simple as the biological difference between women and men, nor is that difference itself purely or even substantially a biological one. Sexuality as a complex interaction of (at least) all three is even less simply biologically determinate. It is neither simply a matter of gender status nor a practice without reference to biological differences. Perhaps most significantly, social and cultural factors, including attitudes, beliefs, and traditional practices—quite proper targets for legal change, compared with biological facts—are found to have a substantially broader and more powerful impact upon gender, even upon its biological aspects, than legal thinking on the sex difference has recognized.

Physical characteristics which provide indices of gender include internal and external reproductive organs and genitalia, gonads, hormone balance, and genetic and chromosomal makeup.[7] Strictly speaking, in several of these physical senses gender is not immutable, merely highly tenacious. A transsexual operation, with hormone therapy, can largely transform gender on the physical level, with the major exception of reproductive capacity. But then many born males and females do not possess reproductive capacity for a variety of biological and social reasons. Aside from these characteristics, some evidence of physical differences between the sexes in the aggregate exists in the following areas: body shape, height and weight, muscularity, physical endurance, possibly metabolic rate, possibly some forms of sensory sensitivity, rate of maturation, longevity, susceptibility to certain physical disorders, and some behaviors at birth (irritability, type of movement, and responsiveness to touch).[8] The scientific research stresses the wide, if not complete, mutability of even these differences by social factors such as psychological reinforcements, type of customary physical activity, and career patterns.[9] Moreover, on the biological level, the sex difference is not a polar opposition, but a continuum of characteristics with different averages by sex grouping. . . .

Most sexual behaviors which differ by sex or within sex groupings have been found to lack any known biological basis. Choice of sexual object in terms of sex preference for the same or opposite sex is one; intensity of sexual desires and needs is another. Masters and Johnson's research has decisively established that women's sexual requirements are no less potent or urgent than those of men.[10] "There is little factual basis for the belief that males need sex more than do females. It is more likely that men do not exercise [as] much control over sexual behavior. Male sexual behavior is condoned, even encouraged, whereas females are taught restraint in sexual expression."[11] Social factors rather than biological differences are seen to shape observed differences in sexual needs and patterns of their expression.[12] For example, in spite of physiological differences between women and men, there is no physiological basis for male aggressiveness and female passivity in sexual initiation. Without changing biology, "a woman can be aggressively receptive and a man be motivationally passive in the sexual act."[13] Some scholars locate sexual excitement itself more in society than in nature. "The very experience of sexual excitement that seems to originate from hidden internal sources is in fact a learned process and it is only our insistence on the myths of naturalness that hides these social components from us."[14] Sexual feeling and expression are seen as a form of "scripted" behavior[15] which is as powerfully determined by sexism as by sex.[16] Gagnon and Simon note that "many women's . . . participation in sexual activity, has often—historically, possibly more often than not—had little to do with their own sense of the erotic."[17] The social facts of sexual inequality increasingly appear to define this fact of the meaning of sex, rather than the facts of sex differences providing an irrefutable argument against their existence.

Nor is gender *identity* primarily determined by physical attributes, according to current thought and research. Gender identification, defined as the sense one has of being a man or a woman and the presentation of self and acceptance by others as such, is neither a fact nor a sense "with which one is born." Rather, it is assigned and learned. John Money's innovative experiments on hermaphrodites[18] show that gender identity need not correspond to internal organs, external genitalia, hormones, or chromosomes. In cases where, because of external genital ambiguity or deformity, a child's sex is misidentified (in the sense of later proving to be at odds with the body), children after age six persist immovably in the gender identity originally assigned; resistance to change survives even surgical conformity of external genitalia with internal sex organs. Sexual behavior in such cases is socially appropriate to the learned gender rather than to the physical one. Irrespective of sexual biology, the sex socially assigned a child, through deep and early psychological imprinting, becomes the gender identification of the adult. "One is confronted with the conclusion, perhaps surprising to some, that there is no primary genetic or other innate mechanism to preordain the masculinity or femininity of psychosexual differentiation." Money concludes that his research shows "a complete overriding of the sex-chromosomal constitution and of gonadal status in the establishment of gender role and identity."[19]

The importance of Money's research is not that one cannot tell a man from a woman, although there are difficulties at times; rather, it is that the element of sex that is made up of a basic gender identification as a man or a woman is not primarily determined by physiological factors. It is secondarily determined by the body, of course, in the social sense. Genital anatomy tends under usual circumstances to determine which gender parents assign a baby, to shape gender-specific social responses, and to elicit reinforcing behavior considered appropriate to each sex. But social factors aside, a female sexual identity does not feel intrinsically out of place in a biologically male body and vice versa. To the extent that one "is" a man or a woman because one takes oneself to be so, sexual biology does not predetermine gender.

The effect of biology on the behavior of the sexes, so often accepted as primary, has been found to be largely secondary. In its place, a vast body of research documents the powerful and pervasive impact of social sex roles on attitudes and behavior, including sexual ones. A "sex role" is a widely held, learned, acted upon, and socially enforced definition of behaviors, attitudes, or pursuits as intrinsically more appropriate or seemly for one sex than for the other. It refers to the cultural practice of allocating social roles according to gender. Socialization is the process by which men and women are socially created to correspond to each society's definition of its "masculine" and "feminine" sex roles. Although scholars differ in their views and evaluations of the origins, social functions, exact transmission processes, contents, and impact upon individual personality of sex roles, the existence of strongly sex-typed social patterns within most cultures is barely disputed.

Choice of occupation, activities, goals, and feelings are strongly associated with masculine or feminine roles in virtually all cultures. The content of these categories varies sufficiently across cultures to suggest that the institutionalization of specific sex-role conceptions derives from the specific history and development of each society, rather than from anything intrinsic to the sex difference—even including dimorphism itself.[20] Some societies, for example, have more than two genders.[21] On the whole, sex roles reproduce themselves and tend to describe sex groups in the aggregate, which is not surprising, since people have been modeled in their image. As with biology, however, individual characteristics vary as much within sex groups as between them, and sex groups overlap to a considerable extent.[22]

What hermaphrodism does to the concept of biological gender, transsexuality does to the concept of sex roles. The rigid exclusivity of each sex of the other is undercut in the clear presence of some of both. Transsexuals experience a sense of sex identity cruelly trapped in a nonconforming body. Whatever the cause of this sense, it cannot be biological gender, since sex identity stands opposed to the body; nor can it be the sex-role conditioning alone, since sex identity is also opposed to that. The source of such a thorough rejection of standard sex-role conditioning as well as physiology is obscure. But it is testimony to the power of the social correlation of sexual identity with physiology that, in order to pursue the desired behavior patterns fully, transsexuals consider it necessary to alter their *bodies* to accord with their gender identity. A final observation captures both meanings: first, gender identification may be better understood as a social definition of biology than as a biological definition of society, and, second, the power of that definition. Commenting upon the justice of a proposed chromosome test for determining the femaleness of the transsexual tennis player Dr. Renee Richards, one woman observed: "I think nature is not always correct. . . . She looks like a woman, plays like a woman. She *is* a woman. Chromosomes make things scientific, but nature is not always a hundred percent correct."[23]

Socially as well as biologically, gender is not as rigidly dimorphic as it is commonly supposed to be in legal discussions of equality. It is, instead, a range of overlapping distributions with different median points. The majority of men and women are located in the area of overlap. If for most characteristics the majority of women and men fall in the area where the sexes overlap, to premise legal approaches to the sexes on their differences requires the exclusion of those persons whose characteristics overlap with the other sex—that is, most people. The extremes, the tails of both curves, which apply only to exceptional women and men, are implicitly used as guidelines for sex specificity. They become norms, ideals for emulation, and standards for judgment when they are not even statistically representative.

There is a real question whether it makes sense of the evidence to conceptualize the reality of sex in terms of differences at all, except in the socially constructed sense—which social construction is what the law is attempting to address as the *problem*. To require that a given characteristic, in order to be considered a sex characteristic, be universal to the sex grouping is to require something that is not uniformly true even of most of the primary indices of gender. To then require (as the *Gilbert* approach does) that that same characteristic be comparable to, while remaining different from, the corresponding characteristic of the opposite sex, tends to exclude those few characteristics that approach being truly generic to a sex group.

While the biological sex difference has been both exaggerated and used to justify different treatment, sex inequality as a social force has been reflected in the substantive content of sex roles. Sex roles shape the behavior and express the relative position of the sexes. Although social differences between the sexes are far more pronounced than biological differences, to the extent they have been seen as differences they have not been seen as inequalities. It is not at all a distortion of the evidence to characterize the *social* situation of the sexes as largely dimorphic. In fact, the sexes are, and have been, far more dimorphic socially than they are, or have been, biologically. Much of the specific content of sex roles in American culture are those stereotypes that the law prohibits as overt job qualifications: women are weak, good with their fingers, bad at numbers, unable to stand long hours, too emotional for high seriousness. Male sex roles encourage men to be strong, aggressive, tough, dominant, and competitive. These values, which come to be considered "male," do describe conforming and common male behavior in many spheres, including the sexual.[24] Interpreting sexual behavior in sex-role terms, Diana Russell argues that rape should be viewed not as deviance but as overconformity to the male sex role.[25] In support, one recent study found that convicted rapists were "sexually and psychologically normal" according to male social norms.[26] Another study quotes a parole officer who worked with rapists in prison facilities: "Those men were the most normal men there. They had a lot of hangups, but they were the same hang-ups as men walking out on the street."[27] Although intending to exonerate men as a sex rather than to criticize male sex roles as socially defined, Lionel Tiger makes a corroborative observation that implicitly links rape findings to sexual harassment: "[It] is relatively 'normal' for males to seek sexual access to females who are their subordinates."[28]

As the examples suggest, such behaviors are almost never observed in women. Powerful social conditioning of women to passivity, gentleness, submissiveness, and receptivity to male initiation, particularly in sexual contact, tends effectively to constrain women from expressing aggression (or even assertion) sexually, or sexuality assertively, although there probably is no biological barrier to either. The constraints appear linked to women's relative social position.

> [It is] males who are supposed to initiate sexual activity with females. Females who make "advances" are considered improper, forward, aggressive, brassy, or otherwise "unladylike." By initiating intimacy they have stepped out of their place and usurped a status prerogative.[29]

> Women are considered synonymous with sex, yet female sexuality is seen as valid only under certain conditions, such as marriage. Even in more permissive ages like our own, there are still limits. One of these is the point where a female can be labeled promiscuous. Another is the point where she attempts to exercise any power: women who initiate and direct sexual activity with male partners find that they have gone too far and are feared and rejected as "castrators."[30]

Implicit in these observations is the view that sexual expression shaped by sex roles prescribes appropriate male and female conduct, defines normalcy, designs sexual rituals, and allocates power in the interest of men and to the detriment of women. In this respect, there definitely is a "difference" between the sexes:

> The value of such a prerogative [to initiate intimacy] is that it is a form of power. Between the sexes, as in other human interaction, the one who has the right to initiate greater intimacy has more control over the relationship. Superior status brings with it not only greater prestige and greater privileges, but greater power.[31]

> [The] fantasy world that veils [women's] experience is the world of sex as seen through male eyes. It is a world where eroticism is defined in terms of female powerlessness, dependency, and submission.[32]

The substance of the meaning of sex roles, in sexuality as in other areas, just as with the social roles allocated to the races, is not symmetrical between women and men. Rather, male and female sex roles complement each other in the sense that one function of the female sex role is to reinforce the impression, and create the social actuality, of male dominance and female subordination. Ellen Morgan describes this asymmetry in sexual relationships as one means through which gender in equality is expressed and maintained in American society:

> We have a sexual situation in which the humanity and personhood of the woman, which make her seek autonomy and action and expression and self-respect, are at odds with her socially organized sexuality. We have a situation in which the dominant male sexual culture aggrandizes the male ego whereas the subordinate female style damages the female ego. Sex means different things to women and men by this time.[33]

. . . The implications of these roles for interpersonal behavior on the one hand and systemic powerlessness on the other are drawn in the following quotation:

> The "trivia" of everyday life—using "sir" or first name, touching others, dropping the eyes, smiling, interrupting, and so on . . . are commonly understood as facilitators of social intercourse but are not recognized as defenders of the status quo—of the state, the wealthy, of authority, of those whose power may not be challenged. Nevertheless, these minutiae find their place on a continuum of social control which extends from internalized socialization (the colonization of the mind) . . . to sheer physical force (guns, clubs, incarceration).[34]

This examination suggests that the legally relevant content of the term *sex*, understood as gender difference, should focus upon its *social meaning* more than upon any biological givens. The most salient determinants of sexuality, much like those of work, are organized in society, not fixed in "nature." As might be expected, sex-role learning, inseparably conjoined with economic necessity when the sexual aggressor is both a man and an employer, tends to inhibit women's effective resistance to "normal" male intrusions and claims upon women's sexuality, whether they come as a look or a rape. In this perspective, sexual harassment expresses one social meaning that sex roles create in the sex difference: gender distributes power as it divides labor, enforcing that division by sexual means. . . .

SEXUALITY

. . . The behaviors to which women are subjected in sexual harassment are behaviors specifically defined and directed toward the characteristics which define women's sexuality: Secondary sex characteristics and sex-role behavior. It is no accident that the English language uses the term *sex* ambiguously to refer both to gender status (as in "the female sex") and to the activity of intercourse (as in "to have sex"). The term *sexual* is used in both senses. Further study of the language reveals that references to sexuality have a pejorative connotation for woman as a gender that is not comparable for men.

> Words indicating the station, relationship, or occupation of men have remained untainted over the years. Those identifying women have repeatedly suffered the indignity of degeneration, many of them becoming sexually abusive. It is clearly not the women themselves who have coined and used these terms as epithets for each other. One sees today that it is men who describe women in sexual terms and insult them with sexual slurs, and the wealth of derogatory terms for women reveals something of their hostility. . . . [T]he largest category of words designating humans in sexual terms are those for women—especially for loose women. I have located roughly a thousand words and phrases describing women in sexually derogatory ways. There is nothing approaching this multitude for describing men.[35]

As a critical convergence of the physiological, psychological, social, economic, cultural and aesthetic, and political forces, sexuality is overburdened with determinants. Gender itself is largely defined in terms of sexuality in that heterosexuality is closely bound up with the social conceptions of maleness and femaleness.

Woman's sexuality is a major medium through which gender identity and gender status are socially expressed and experienced. An attack upon sexuality is an attack upon womanhood. A deprivation in employment worked through women's sexuality is a deprivation in employment because one is a woman, through one of the closest referents by which women are socially identified as such, by themselves and by men. Only women, and (as is not the case with pregnancy) all women possess female sexuality,* the focus, occasion, and vehicle for this form of employment deprivation. Few men would maintain that they would have found a given woman just as ready or appropriate a target for sexual advances if she had been sexually male. Indeed, the close association between sexuality and gender identity makes it hard to imagine that a woman would be sexually the same if male. If any practice could be said to happen to a woman because she is a woman, sexual harassment should be one of the more straightforward examples of it. . . .

---

*Transsexuals and transvestites would probably be considered legally female for this purpose.

NOTES

1. [*Miller* v. *Bank of America*] 418 F. Supp. 233, 236 (N.D. Cal. 1976).

2. Answering Brief for Defendants—Appellees, at 32–33.

3. 422 F. Supp 553, 556 (D.N.J. 1976).

4. "It can hardly be claimed any longer that men have greater 'sex drives' and therefore, a lesser expression of sex must be attributed to an inhibition on the part of women to display sexual interest in this manner." Nancy Henley, "Power, Sex and Non-verbal Communication," in *Language and Sex: Difference and Dominance*, ed. Barrie Thorne and Nancy Henley (Rowley, Mass.: Newbury House, Publishers, 1975), p. 193. G. Schmidt and V. Sigusch in a study entitled "Women's Sexual Arousal" reported little gender difference in physiological or self-ratings of sexual arousal in response to erotic stimuli, in J. Zubin and J. Money, *Contemporary Sexual Behavior: Critical Issues in the 1970s* (Baltimore: Johns Hopkins University Press, 1973), pp. 117–43. Such differences are widely attributed to cultural factors. See, for example, W. J. Gadpaille, "Innate Masculine-Feminine Differences," *Medical Aspects of Human Sexuality* (1973): 141–57.

5. 2 Empl. Prac. Guide (CCH) Par. 6493 (1976).

6. *Harvard Law Review* 84 (1971); 1109, 1184 (emphasis added). . . .

7. John Money, "Developmental Differentiation of Femininity and Masculinity Compared," in *The Potential of Woman*, ed. Seymour M. Farber and Roger H. L. Wilson (New York: McGraw-Hill, 1963), p. 56; John Money and Patricia Tucker, *Sexual Signatures: On Being a Man or a Woman* (Boston: Little, Brown, 1975); R. Stoller, *Sex and Gender: On the Development of Masculinity and Femininity* (London: Hogarth, 1968); R. Green and J. Money, *Transsexualism and Sex Reassignment* (Baltimore: Johns Hopkins University Press, 1969); Edward S. David, "The Law and Transsexualism: A Faltering Response to a Conceptual Dilemma," *Connecticut Law Review* 7 (1975): 288; J. Money and A. Erhardt, *Man and Woman, Boy and Girl* (Baltimore: Johns Hopkins University Press, 1972); J. Money, *Sex Errors of the Body* (Baltimore: Johns Hopkins University Press, 1968); Note, "Transsexuals in Limbo," *Maryland Law Review* 31 (1971): 236.

8. Ashton Barfield, "Biological Influences on Sex Differences in Behavior," in *Sex Differences: Social and Biological Perspectives*, ed. M. Tietelbaum (Garden City, N.Y.: Anchor Press, Doubleday, 1976), p. 107. Bibliography of research supporting this summary, ibid., pp. 110–21.

9. Eleanor F. Maccoby, ed., *The Development of Sex Differences* (Stanford, Calif.: Stanford University Press, 1966).

10. Robert Masters and Virginia Johnson, *Human Sexual Response* (Boston: Little, Brown, 1966).

11. R. Staples, "Male-Female Sexual Variations: Functions of Biology or Culture," *Journal of Sexual Response* 9 (1973): 11–20.

12. A. C. Kinsey et al., *Sexual Behavior in the Human Male* (Philadelphia: W. B. Saunders, 1948). Kinsey's famous studies of sexual arousal in women and men in the 1930s and 1940s seemed to confirm that the sexes differed substantially in this respect. Culturally, his results were used to endow men with animal lust, women with demure passionlessness. (Demonstrating that obscure ability of racism to survive evidence, the stereotype of the black woman as sex-crazed was never apparently confronted by these findings purporting to represent the sexuality of all biological females.) A recent replication of Kinsey's studies suggests that cultural repression of women's sexuality largely accounts for his findings. Sigusch and Schmidt conclude that sexual arousability "is as strongly and quite similarly structured for both women and men." They explain the difference between their results and Kinsey's as follows:

His findings cannot serve as evidence for a lesser capacity for women to become sexually aroused by pictoral and narrative stimuli. They reflect one aspect of the cultural desexualization of women in western societies which 20 to 30 years ago, when Kinsey collected his data, was more extensive than today.

V. Sigusch and G. Schmidt, "Women's Sexual Arousal," in Zubin and Money, *Contemporary Sexual Behavior*, pp. 118–19.

13. J. Marmor, "Women in Medicine: The Importance of the Formative Years," *Journal of American Medical Women's Association* (July 1968): 621.

14. John H. Gagnon and William Simon, *Sexual Conduct: The Social Sources of Human Sexuality* (Chicago: Aldine Publishing Company, 1973), p. 9.

15. Ibid., pp. 19–26.

16. See Judith Long Laws and Pepper Schwartz, *Sexual Scripts: The Social Construction of Female Sexuality* (Hinsdale, Ill.: Dryden Press, 1977), who apply Gagnon and Simon's concept to women's sexuality specifically.

17. John H. Gagnon and William Simon, eds., *The Sexual Scene* (Chicago: Aldine Publishing Company, 1970), p. 4.

18. See note 6.

19. John Money, in Farber and Wilson, *The Potential of Woman*, p. 56.

20. Margaret Mead, *Sex and Temperament in Three Primitive Societies* (New York: Dell, 1935); Margaret Mead, *Male and Female: A Study of the Sexes in a Changing World* (New York: William Morrow & Co., 1975), pp. 7–8; Michele Rosaldo and Louise Lamphere, eds., *Woman, Culture and Society* (Palo Alto, Calif.: Stanford University Press, 1974); Rayna R. Reiter, ed., *Toward an Anthropology of Women* (New York: Monthly Review Press, 1975).

21. See Anna S. Meigs, "Male Pregnancy and the Reduction of Sexual Opposition in a New Guinea Highlands Society," *Ethnology: An International Journal of Cultural and Social Anthropology* 15, no. 4 (October 1976): 393–407; C. S. Ford and F. Beach, *Patterns of Sexual Behavior* (New York: Harper, 1951) provides background and several illustrative examples.

22. There are numerous excellent reviews and collections of sex-role research. A classic in the field is Eleanor E. Maccoby, ed., *The Development of Sex Differences* (Stanford, Calif.: Stanford University Press, 1966). A bibliography of research conducted from 1973 to 1974 can be found in *Women's Work and Women's Studies, 1973–4, A Bibliography* (Barnard College Women's Center, 1975), pp. 285–32, and a list of bibliographies on the subject at ibid., pp. 321–22. Recent books on varying levels include Carol Tavris and Carole Offir, *The Longest War: Sex Differences in Perspective* (New York: Harcourt, Brace Jovanovich, 1977); Nancy Reeves, *Womankind: Beyond the Stereotypes* (Chicago: Aldine Publishing Company, 1977); Shirley Weitz, *Sex Roles: Biological, Psychological and Social Foundation* (Oxford University Press, 1977). For a political perspective on sex roles in terms of power, see, e.g., Nancy Hartsock, "Political Change: Two Perspectives on Power," *Quest: A Feminist Quarterly* (Summer 1974): 10–25. An application to the law is Barbara Kirk Cavanagh, "A Little Dearer Than His Horse: Legal Stereotypes and the Feminine Personality," *Harvard Civil Rights-Civil Liberties Law Review* 6 (1970): 260–87.

23. *New York Times*, August 22, 1976, Sports Section, p. 3. See also the discussion by Germaine Greer of transsexual April Ashley, *The Female Eunuch* (New York: McGraw Hill, 1970), pp. 54–55, but cf. the legal decision in the same case, *Corbett* v. *Corbett*, [1971], p. 83 (P. P. Div'l Ct.) (England).

24. A very different approach to analyzing sexuality for legal purposes can be found

in the psychoanalytic interpretations collected in Ralph Slovenko, *Sexual Behavior and the Law* (Springfield, Ill.: Charles C. Thomas, 1965).

25. Diana E. H. Russell, *The Politics of Rape* (New York: Stein & Day, 1975), p. 260.

26. Andrea Medea and Kathleen Thompson, *Against Rape* (New York: Farrar, Straus & Giroux, 1974), pp. 29–30.

27. Susan Griffin, "Rape: The All-American Crime," *Ramparts* 10 (September 1971): 25–35, reprinted in *Women: A Feminist Perspective*, ed. Jo Freeman (Palo Alto, Calif.: Mayfield Publishing Co., 1975), p. 26.

28. Lionel Tiger, *Men in Groups* (New York: Random House, 1969), p. 271. Lynn Wehrli, "Sexual Harassment at the Workplace: A Feminist Analysis and Strategy for Social Change," (M.A. Thesis, Massachusetts Institute of Technology, December 1976) makes the same connection, p. 86.

29. Nancy Henley and Jo Freeman, "The Sexual Politics of Interpersonal Behavior," in *Women: A Feminist Perspective*, ed. Freeman (Palo Alto, Calif.: Mayfield Publishing, 1975), pp. 393–94.

30. Linda Phelps, "Female Sexual Alienation," in Freeman, *Women: A Feminist Perspective*, p. 20.

31. Henley and Freeman, in Freeman, *Women: A Feminist Perspective*, pp. 393–94.

32. Phelps, in Freeman, *Women: A Feminist Perspective*, p. 19.

33. Ellen Morgan, "The Erotization of Male Dominance/Female Subordination," University of Michigan, *Papers in Women's Studies* 2 (1975): 112–45, reprint by Know, Inc., p. 20. See also Nancy M. Henley, *Body Politics: Power, Sex and Nonverbal Communication* (Englewood Cliffs, N.J.: Prentice-Hall, 1977), pp. 94–123.

34. Henley, "Power, Sex and Nonverbal Communication," in Thorne and Henley, *Language and Sex*, p. 184.

35. D. Schulz, "The Semantic Derogation of Women," in Thorne and Henley, *Language and Sex*, pp. 67, 71.

PART 3

LEGAL RESPONSES

The Civil Rights Act

SEXUAL HARASSMENT AS SEX DISCRIMINATION

10

CATHARINE A. MACKINNON

TORT LAW

W omen's bodies, particularly the conditions and consequences of men's sexual access to them, are not a novel subject for the law. . . . The law of torts, or private harms, historically provided civil redress for sexual invasions at a time when social morality was less ambiguous in defining a woman's sexuality as intrinsic to her virtue, and her virtue as partially constitutive of her value, hence as capable of compensable damage. Perhaps with this tradition in mind, several recent sexual harassment cases have suggested—usually as a reason for holding sexual harassment not to be sex discrimination—that sexual harassment should be considered tortious. The federal court in *Tomkins*, implicitly finding that since sexual harassment is a tort it is not discrimination, stated that Title VII "is not intended to provide a federal tort remedy for what amounts to physical attack motivated by sexual desire on the part of a supervisor and which happened to occur in a corporate corridor rather than a back alley."[1] One appellate judge, concurring in the judgment in *Barnes* that sexual harassment is sex discrimination, observed, "An act of sexual harassment which caused the victim, because of her rejection of such advances, to be damaged in her job, would constitute a tort."[2] Which tort is not specified, although "[t]here is no necessity whatever that a tort must have a name."[3] It is, however, necessary that the definition of the legal wrong fit the conceptual framework of tort law. Brief examination of traditional tort views of sexual wrongs against women illustrates that tort law is not simply wrong, and is partially helpful, but is fundamentally insufficient as a legal approach to sexual harassment.

Sexual touching that women do not want has historically been considered tortious under a variety of doctrines, usually battery, assault, or, if exclusively emotional damage is done, as the intentional infliction of emotional distress. A battery is a harmful or offensive contact which is intentionally caused. While contact must be intentional, hostile intent, or intent to cause all the damages that resulted from the contact, is not necessary. Variously formulated, "taking indecent liberties with a woman without her consent,"[4] "putting hands upon a female with a view to violate her person,"[5] or "intentional touching of a woman by a man without excuse or justification"[6] have been considered battery. Battery is said to include instances in which a compliment is intended, "as where an unappreciative woman is kissed without her consent."[7]

Battery, the actual touching, is often combined with assault, the fear of such a touching. The tort of assault consists in placing a person in *fear* of an immediate harmful or offensive contact. It is "a touching of the mind, if not of the body."[8] The invasion is mental. The defendant must have intended at least to arouse apprehension, and actually have done so. The fear-producing event must be more than words alone, but words can clarify an otherwise equivocal act. Defenses include consent, but only to those acts consented to; consent to a kiss, for example, does not extend to anything further. Nor are provocative words a defense.

Kissing a woman without her consent has been considered actionable under a combination (or confusion) of assault and battery doctrines. In 1899, a husband and wife recovered $700 for assault on the wife for forcibly hugging and kissing "against her wish and by force."[9] In 1921, a railroad was found responsible for the embarrassment and humiliation of a woman passenger caused when a drunken man, of whose boisterous conduct and inebriated condition the railroad was aware, fell down on top of her and kissed her on the cheek.[10] In 1895 in Wisconsin, a twenty-year-old schoolteacher recovered $1,000 from the employer of a railroad conductor who grabbed and kissed her several times despite her clear attempts to discourage and repel him.[11]

Other early cases finding sexual incursions actionable reveal that little has changed men's sexual behavior, although something seems to have changed in the social and legal standards by which it is evaluated. In a case in 1915, a woman recovered damages for assault and battery against a man who squeezed her breast and laid his hand on her face. The defendant denied the whole incident, then characterized the touching as "nothing more than a harmless caress."[12] In a similar case in 1921, a woman recovered for the mental anguish arising from an indecent assault, defined as "the act of a male person taking indecent liberties with the person of a female, or fondling her in a lewd and lascivious manner without her consent and against her will." The judge found it unnecessary for the assault to be made in an angry or insolent manner: "Indecent assaults are not made in that way."[13] Sexual assault—whether or not it was done with bad feeling—is still assault.

Contemporary sexual mores make it difficult to imagine such cases in court. Women are, it seems, supposed to consider acts in this tradition harmless, and litigation in this area is now relatively uncommon. . . .

One common rejoinder to charges of sexual harassment is that the individual woman is unduly and overly sensitive to these advances, raising the question of the standards by which an at least partly subjective injury is to be evaluated. Unless the defendant has reason to believe that the individual would permit more or less contact, the tort standard in battery cases prohibits contact that would be "offensive to an ordinary person not unduly sensitive as to his dignity."[14] However, even "innocuous and generally permitted contacts may become tortious if they are inflicted with knowledge that the individual plaintiff objects to them and refuses to permit them."[15] For assault, in which the fear of contact constitutes the injury, the test is what the defendant's conduct "denote[d] at the time to the party assaulted."[16] The standard treatment of the hypersensitive individual is to find liability if the conduct would have been offensive to the person of ordinary sensibilities. If it would have been, the perpetrator is liable for all the damages caused *this* individual, whether she is unduly sensitive or not.

The standard of recovery in the strictly emotional area is particularly instructive. The tort of intentional infliction of emotional distress, codified by the second *Restatement of Torts*, allows recovery for purely emotional disturbance.[17] The conduct must be extreme and outrageous to a person of ordinary sensibilities. The departure here is that the perpetrator is liable for the emotional distress alone, and for the bodily harm that results from it, without requiring a physical act or invasion. The tort conception of "parasitic damages," in which a tortfeasor is liable for all the consequences of his acts (for example, loss of employment) once he is liable for the tort, raises the possibility of covering the entire range of consequences of sexual harassment in sufficiently aggravated circumstances.

Sexual propositions in themselves have not generally been considered torts where there is no physical incursion upon or trespass against the person, or no physical injury. In Magruder's famous formulation: "Women have occasionally sought damages for mental distress and humiliation on account of being addressed by a proposal of illicit intercourse. This is peculiarly a situation where circumstances alter cases. If there has been no incidental assault or battery, or perhaps trespass to land, recovery is generally denied, the view being apparently, that there is no harm in asking."[18] Expressing attitudes toward women's assertions of sexual injury which have remained largely unchanged to the present day, the court in one case of solicitation of sexual intercourse found the injury of a sexual proposition "generally considered more sentimental than substantial . . . vague and shadowy" and "easily simulated and impossible to disprove." Without physical "impact," the injury of a sexual proposition is considered "remote" and to have a "metaphysical character."[19] It is not an injury *in itself.*[20]

Sexual harassment that consisted solely in propositions as a condition of work apparently would not be tortious unless it became outrageous enough to constitute intentional infliction of emotional distress. One recently filed tort case, *Fuller* v. *Williames*,[21] makes just such allegations, pleading as intentional infliction of emotional distress a "condition of work" type situation of sexual harassment. The plaintiff complained that the defendants on several occasions, in the presence of others, "unlawfully, wilfully, maliciously, outrageously and contemptuously [did] insult, demean and humiliate plaintiff by making crude remarks of an explicit sexual nature including remarks deprecating to women in general," knowing that this conduct was likely to cause severe emotional distress. She allegedly

> became upset, embarrassed, humiliated, nervous and depressed; suffered frequent tension headaches, had difficulty sleeping, suffered stress in her marriage, and was unable to concentrate on her photographic work and public school and photographic teaching; suffered mental anguish and humiliation and damage to her reputation as a dignified self-respecting woman and impairment of her earning capacity.[22]

Damages included "unpaid wages due." In another case which also pled sexual harassment as sex discrimination, one count complained of intentional infliction of emotional stress through acts of sexual harassment wherein the defendant "disturbed and disquieted the plaintiff by soliciting her to be his sex object if she wished to continue to be employed." The plaintiff "regarded such proposals . . . [as] repugnant, abhorrent, and a shock to her moral sensitivities and ideals of decency and propriety," took steps to end his sexual advances, but they continued until her discharge.[23] The results in these cases may help to clarify the potential of this approach.

Torts prohibiting interference with family relations by sexual means—seduction, enticement, criminal conversation, alienation of affections, loss of consortium, and the like—have blended the enforcement of moral standards with protections for men's possessory interests, whether by design or pattern of administration. Civil recovery usually went to men for loss of consortium, a "relational injury" which included loss of "conjugal affection." Blackstone explains why husbands have recovered for this loss far more often than wives:

> We may observe that in these relative injuries notice is only taken of the wrong done to the superior of the parties related . . . while the loss of the inferior by such injuries is totally unregarded. One reason for which may be this; that the inferior hath no kind of property in the company, care or assistance of the superior, as the superior is held to have in those of the inferior, and therefore the inferior can suffer no loss or injury.[24]

·   ·   ·

Most actions for interference with domestic relations "which carry an accusation of sexual misbehavior" have been abolished by statute. The reasons, as summarized by William Prosser, are instructive on social attitudes toward women's accusations of sexual injury as these attitudes have been reflected in tort law:

> It is notorious that [such actions] have afforded a fertile field for blackmail and extortion by means of manufactured suits in which the threat of publicity is used to force a settlement. There is good reason to believe that even genuine actions of this type are brought more frequently than not with purely mercenary or vindictive motives; that it is impossible to compensate for such damage with what has derisively been called "heart balm"; and that no preventive purpose is served, since such torts seldom are committed with deliberate plan. Added to this is perhaps an increasing notion of personal or even sexual freedom on the part of women.[25]

The essence of the first objection is that women lie about sex for money. As to the second, one wonders why bad motives for bringing good suits is not a more common reason for eliminating many other causes of action. Further, money does not adequately compensate for most injuries (for example, wrongful death), yet the cause of action is not eliminated. Then, the sophisticated calculus so basic to tort that distinguishes negligent from intentional harm is abandoned in favor of the proposition that a tort committed without "deliberate plan" is not a tort at all. Money damages are required to serve a deterrent function in these cases, while it suffices for other torts that deterrence is merely a desirable by-product of the point of damages: to help make the victim whole for the injury. These inconsistencies lend themselves to the interpretation that society has increasingly come to view such incidents as not very damaging.

    . . . This reference to women's increasing "personal or even sexual freedom" inadequately criticizes the premise common to all these causes of action: that a man's wife's sexuality belonged to him, in the sense that another man was liable to him in damages for sexual acts with her, even with her consent. This attitude may be no less prevalent although it is no longer legally enforceable in this way. The point is not that these common law* torts should be revived, but that their statutory abolition for these reasons reveals attitudes toward women's sexuality which can be expected to arise in connection with attempts to impose sanctions upon men's sexual violation of women in employment as well. . . .

    Most broadly considered, tort is conceptually inadequate to the problem of sexual harassment to the extent that it rips injuries to women's sexuality out of the context of women's social circumstances as a whole. In particular, short of developing a new tort for sexual harassment as such, the tort approach misses the nexus between women's sexuality and women's employment, the system of reciprocal sanctions which, to women as a gender, become cumulative. In tort perspective, the injury of sexual harassment would be seen as an injury to the individual person, to personal sexual integrity, with damages extending to the job. Alternatively, sexual harassment could be seen as an injury to an individual interest in employment, with damages extending to the emotional harm attendant

---

*The "common law" refers to legal principles that evolved over time through judicial opinions. (*Ed.*)

to the sexual invasion as well as to the loss of employment. The approach tends to pose the necessity to decide whether sexual harassment is essentially an injury to the person, to sexual integrity and feelings, with pendent damages to the job, or whether it is essentially an injury to the job, with damages extending to the person. Since it is both, either one omits the social dynamics that systematically place women in these positions, that may coerce consent, that interpenetrate sexuality and employment to women's detriment because they are women.

Unsituated in a recognition of the context that keeps women secondary and powerless, sexual injuries appear as incidental or deviant aberrations which arise in one-to-one relationships gone wrong. The essential purpose of tort law, although it has policy assumptions and implications, is to compensate individuals one at a time for mischief which befalls them as a consequence of the one-time ineptitude or nastiness of other individuals. The occurrence of such events is viewed more or less with resignation, as an inevitability of social proximity, a fallout of order which can be confronted only probabilistically. Sexual harassment as [it should be] understood is not merely a parade of interconnected consequences with the potential for discrete repetition by other individuals, so that a precedent will suffice. Rather, it is a group-defined injury which occurs to many different individuals regardless of unique qualities or circumstances, in ways that connect with other deprivations of the same individuals, among all of whom a single characteristic—female sex—is shared. Such an injury is *in essence* a group injury. The context which makes the impact of gender cumulative—in fact, the context that makes it injurious—is lost when sexual harassment is approached as an individual injury, however wide the net of damages is cast. Tort law compensates individuals for injuries while spreading their costs and perhaps setting examples for foresightful perpetrators; the purpose of discrimination law is to change the society so that this kind of injury need not and does not recur. Tort law considers individual and compensable something which is fundamentally social and should be eliminated.

A related defect in the vision underlying the sexual tort cases, from the standpoint of their usefulness as a solution to sexual harassment, is their disabling (and cloying) moralism. The aura of the pedestal, more rightly understood as the foundation of the cage, permeates them. In one case, the judge opined, "Every woman has a right to assume that a passenger car is not a brothel and that when she travels in it, she will meet nothing, see nothing, hear nothing, to wound her delicacy or insult her womanhood."[26] Another case reveals an underlying reason for age limits on women's capacity to consent to sex. The ability fully to appreciate the consequences of sex outside of marriage is essential for an act which "when discovered ostracizes her from good society."[27] When it becomes clear that such protections of delicacy and purity have worked women's exclusion from the decisive arenas of social life, while the same society that morally approves economically punishes the sexually independent (that is, noncompliant) woman, more moralism looks like more of the problem. Just as women are tired of being commended rather than paid, they are tired of being considered sexually virtuous rather than hired or promoted—a choice men must seldom confront and a currency of compensation men must seldom settle for. Prohibitions on sexual harassment as acts conceived as moral violations emerge as repressive impositions of state morality. Inventing special rules of morality for the workplace would institutionalize new taboos rather than confront the fact that it is *women* who are systematically disadvantaged by the old ones. Resistance to sexual harassment can be misconstrued as a revival of moral delicacy only until it is grasped that sexual harassment is less an issue of right and wrong than an issue of power. Women are in no *position* to refuse, which is what makes refusal so moral an act and surrenders so unfairly the price of survival.

All of this is not to say that sexual harassment is not both wrong and a personal injury, merely that it is a social wrong and a social injury that occurs on a personal level. To treat it as a tort is less simply incorrect than inadequate. The law recognizes that individual acts of racism could be torts in recognizing that the dignitary harm of racist insults can be compensated like any other personal injury.[28] This does not preclude a finding that the same acts of racial invective on the job are race discrimination.[29] Although racial insults impact upon blacks on a personal level, they are systematically connected to the "living insult" of segregation.[30] Although reparations may be due,[31] the stigma is not eradicable by money damages to one black person at a time. As with sexual harassment, the reason these acts can occur and recur, and the source of their sting, is not the breaking of a code of good conduct, but the relegation to inferiority for which they stand.

To see sexual harassment as an injury to morality is to turn it into an extreme case of bad manners, when the point is that it is the kind of bad manners almost exclusively visited upon women by men with the power to get away with it. One can see the social invisibility of blacks as white rudeness, but it makes more sense to see it as racism. The major difference between the tort approach and the discrimination approach, then, is that tort sees sexual harassment as an illicit act, a moral infraction, an outrage to the individual's sensibilities and the society's cherished but unlived values. Discrimination law casts the same acts as economic coercion, in which material survival is held hostage to sexual submission. . . .

Notes

1. *Tomkins* v. *Public Service Electric & Gas Co.*, 422 F. Supp. 553, 556 (D.N.J. 1976), rev'd, 568 F.2d 1044 (3d Cir. 1977).

2. *Barnes* v. *Costle*, 561 F.2d 983, 995 (D.C. Cir. 1977) (MacKinnon, J., concurring).

3. W. Prosser, *The Law of Torts*, 3.

4. Ibid., p. 36.

5. *Hough* v. *Iderhoff*, 69 Or. 568, 139 P. 931, 932 (1914).

6. *Gates* v. *State*, 110 Ga. App. 303, 138 So.2d 473, 474 (1964). This was a criminal battery, the quotation taken from another criminal battery case, *Goodrum* v. *State*, 60 Ga. 509 (1878). "If to put the arm, though tenderly, about the neck of another man's wife, against her will, is not an assault and battery, what is it? . . . There was nothing to excite rapture or provoke enthusiasm. Why should he embrace her? Why persist in caressing her? . . . He took the risk of not meeting with a responsive feeling in her, and must abide

all the consequences of disappointment," ibid., at 510, 511. On the question of what is and is not a sexual touching, see *People* v. *Thomas*, 91 Misc. 2d 724 (1977).

7. Prosser, *The Law of Torts,* note 62, at 36, n. 85.

8. *Kline* v. *Kline*, 158 Ind. 602, 64 N.E. 9, 10 (1902), cited in Prosser, *The Law of Torts*, note 62, at 38.

9. *Ragsdale* v. *Ezell*, 20 Ky. 1567, 49 S.W. 775, 776 (1899).

10. *Liljegren* v. *United Rys. Co. of St. Louis*, 227 S.W. 925 (Mo. Ct. App. 1921). She was awarded $500, which corrected for inflation is $1,684 in 1977. Similarly corrected for inflation to 1977, the damage awards for sexual harassment tort cases, infra, are as follows. The actual awards are in parentheses. *Skousen* (1961), $7,350 ($3,500) actual, $3,015 ($1,500) punitive, for $10,065 ($5,000) total damages; *Hatchett* (1915), $2,969 ($500); *Martin* (1920), $1,354 ($450); *Kurpgeweit* (1910), $9,670 ($1,500); *Ragsdale* (1899), $5,051 ($700); *Craker* (1895), $7,220 ($1,000); *Davis* (1905), $26,740 ($4,000) (note that the *Davis* jury award was overruled).

11. In a situation familiar to sexually harassed women, the perpetrator simply did not believe her when she told him she wanted him to leave her alone. Their dialogue reportedly ended as follows: " 'Look me in the eye, and tell me if you are mad.' I said, 'I am mad.' " *Craker* v. *The Chicago and Northwestern Railway Company*, 36 Wis. 657, 659, 17 Am. Rep. 504 (1895). She apparently was. Her report precipitated his immediate firing; she proceeded criminally (for criminal assault and battery) and won, and then sued the employer for civil damages. The *Craker* decision is notable in several respects. The treatment of the size of the damage awarded—which amounts to an inquiry into how much this woman's bodily integrity and sexual feelings are worth—is incisive and sympathetic: "who can be found to say that such an amount would be in excess of compensation to his own or his neighbor's wife or sister or daughter?" 36 Wis., at 679. The judge's refusal to separate the woman's sense of wrong at the injustice done her from her mental suffering and pain, holding both proper objects of *compensatory* damages, would be considered pathbreaking had it been more widely followed:

> And it is difficult to see how these are to be distinguished from the sense of wrong and insult arising from injustice and intention to vex and degrade. The appearance of malicious intent may indeed add to the sense of wrong; and equally, whether such intent be really there or not. But that goes to mental suffering, and mental suffering to compensation. . . . What human creature can penetrate the mysteries of his own sensations, and parcel out separately his mental suffering and his sense of wrong—so much for compensatory, so much for vindictive damages? 36 Wis., at 678.

The decision further held the employer responsible for this intentional tort by the employee, an unusual departure. The standard view is that employers are only responsible for employee negligence.

> One employing another . . . would be as little likely to authorize negligence as malice. . . . [T]he true distinction ought to rest—on the condition whether or not the act of the servant be in the course of his employment. . . . If we owe bread to another and appoint an agent to furnish it, and the agent of malice furnish a stone instead, the principal is responsible for the stone and its consequences. In such cases, negligence is malice. 36 Wis., at 688–69.

12. *Hatchett* v. *Blacketer*, 162 Ky. 266, 172 S.W. 533 (1915).

13. *Martin* v. *Jensen*, 113 Wash. 290, 193 P. 674 (1920). By analogy with the law of trespass to property, recovery for mental anguish alone was allowed where suffering "is the result of a wanton or intentional trespass on the person of a woman." 193 P., at 676.

14. Prosser, *The Law of Torts*, note 62, at 37.

15. Ibid., p. 37.

16. Ibid., p. 41.

17. Restatement (Second) of Torts § 46 (1965).

18. Magruder, "Mental and Emotional Disturbance in the Law of Torts," *Harvard Law Review* 49 (1936): 1033, 1055. It is interesting that the cases commonly cited in support of Magruder's proposition do not squarely support it. Some hold that the facts were improperly pleaded. *Prince* v. *Ridge* states that an attempt by words of persuasion to induce a female to have sexual intercourse does not constitute an assault, but finds that the instant case presents sufficient acts for a battery, an assault, or both. 32 Misc. 666, 66 N.Y.S. 454, 455 (Sup. Ct. 1900). It would seem usual that more than simply asking would be involved.

Other cases referenced to support the formulation require that a physical injury, not merely an act, must be alleged to make out an assault. As is often the case where sex is involved, this requirement confuses the basic doctrine. The doctrine of assault requires only an act, not an injury. An example of a correct application of assault doctrine requiring physical acts, not physical injuries, is one 1880 Vermont case, in which a blind traveling music teacher, sleeping overnight in the defendant's house, was propositioned. "During the night he stealthily entered her room, sat on her bed, leaned over her person, and made repeated solicitation to her for sexual intimacy, which she repelled." *Newell* v. *Witcher*, 53 Vt. 589 (1880), quoted in *Reed* v. *Maley*, 115 Ky. 816, 74 S.W. 1079, 1081 (1903). The defendant was found liable for trespass and assault on the person for sitting on the bed and leaning over her. (Although it was the defendant's property, the sleeping room was considered exclusively the plaintiffs for the night.) The assault finding meant that the plaintiff was found in fear of sexual touching from the proposition; the cited physical acts were sufficient to ground actionable assault, while the proposition alone would not.

Davis v. *Richardson*, 76 Ark, 348, 89 S.W. 318 (1905), by contrast, required physical injury. In this case, a fifteen-year-old girl was seized and embraced "in a rude and indecent manner" by a man who kissed her with "violent and indecent familiarity" and "acted like he was going to do something else." The damage award of $4,000 ($26,740 in 1977) was overturned because an instruction allowed the jury to conclude that the mere proposal was actionable, although acts sufficient for both assault and battery were evidenced. *Bennett* v. *McIntire*, 121 Ind. 231, 23 N.E. 78 (1889) similarly took the approach of requiring some physical invasion of itself actionable before any recovery could he allowed for sexual propositions. In a case for seduction and debauching of his wife, the plaintiff pleaded a cause of action in trespass. Defendant was argued to have gained permission to come upon plaintiff's property by fraud, then seducing his wife. It was held that since he was on the property by permission, albeit fraudulent, no damages were recoverable. Trespass was the only cause of action apparently considered, with seduction as aggravation of damages.

Similarly, in *Reed* v. *Maley*, 115 Ky. 818, 74 S.W. 1079 (1903), in which a man solicited a woman to have sexual intercourse, no cause of action was held to exist.

19. 74 S.W., at 1080 (referring to several other cases).

20. The judge posed a reverse familiar to readers of the early sexual harassment cases:

Suppose a bawd should solicit a man upon a public street to have sexual intimacy with her; he certainly could not maintain a civil action against her. If an action could be maintained by a woman against a man for such solicitation, the same right to maintain one would exist in his favor. Whilst he might not suffer the same anguish and humiliation on account of such solicitation as the woman, yet the right of recovery would be the same. The amount of it would only be determined by reason of the difference in effect such a solicitation would have upon one or the other. 74 S.W. at 1081.

Although a proposition would have a different impact upon the sexes, it is nevertheless argued that because a man "certainly could not maintain a civil action" for a proposition by a woman (why not is not considered), a woman should be similarly precluded.

The dissenting judge in this case urged that a sexual proposition should be actionable as solicitation to commit adultery, It should be prohibited not because it preys upon women, but because "if unsuccessful, it is liable to lead to violence and bloodshed at the hands of the [one supposes male] relatives of the woman; and if successful it defeats the end for which marriage is intended, and destroys the woman." 74 S.W. 1079, 1083. He thought punitive damages appropriate for reasons that combined solicitude for the woman's shattered virtue with an eye toward her undone housework: "The purity of woman and the sanctity of the marriage relation lie at the basis of our whole social fabric.
. . . The natural effect of an indecent proposal of this character to a virtuous woman would be to upset her nerves and unfit her for discharging for the time her domestic duties." 74 S.W. 1074, 1083–1084.

21. No. A7703–04001 (Or. Cir. Ct. 1977).

22. First Amended Complaint, *Fuller* v. *Williames et al.*

23. Complaint, *Morgenheim* v. *Hiber and Midnight Sun Broadca*sters (Alaska Superior Court, filed December 29, 1975).

24. 3 *W. Blackstone Commentaries*, pp. 142–43, quoted and discussed by Leo Kanowitz, *Women and the Law: The Unfinished Revolution* (Albuquerque: University of New Mexico Press, 1969), p. 82.

25. Prosser, *The Law of Torts*, note 3, at 887.

26. *Craker* v. *The Chicago and Northwestern Railway Co.*, 36 Wis. 657, 674, 17 Am. Rep. 504 (1895).

27. *Hough* v. *Iderhoff*, 69 Or. 568, 139 P. 931 (1914).

28. See, for example, *Alcorn* v. *Ambro Engineering, Inc.*, 468 P. 2d 216, 36 Cal. Rptr. 216 (Sup. Ct. 1970); *Wiggs* v. *Coursin*, 355 F. Supp. 206 (S.D. Fla. 1973); *Gray* v. *Serruto Builders*, 110 N.J. Sup. 297, 265 A. 2d 404 (1970).

29. See EEOC cases discussed at 210, infra.

30. *Brunson* v. *Board of Trustees*, 429 F. 2d 820, 826 (1970).

31. See Boris Bittker, *The Case for Black Reparations* (New York: Random House, 1973).

BARED BUTTOCKS AND FEDERAL CASES

11

ELLEN FRANKEL PAUL

W omen in American society are victims of sexual harassment in alarming proportions. Sexual harassment is an inevitable corollary to class exploitation; as capitalists exploit workers, so do males in positions of authority exploit their female subordinates. Male professors, supervisors, and apartment managers in ever increasing numbers take advantage of the financial dependence and vulnerability of women to extract sexual concessions.

These are the assertions that commonly begin discussions of sexual harassment. For reasons that will be adumbrated below, dissent from the prevailing view is long overdue. Three recent episodes will serve to frame this disagreement.

Valerie Craig, an employee of Y & Y Snacks, Inc., joined several coworkers and her supervisor for drinks after work one day in July of 1978. Her supervisor drove her home and proposed that they become more intimately acquainted. She refused his invitation for sexual relations, whereupon he said that he would "get even" with her. Ten days after the incident she was fired from her job. She soon filed a complaint of sexual harassment with the Equal Employment Opportunity Commission (EEOC), and the case wound its way through the courts.

Craig prevailed, the company was held liable for damages, and she received back pay, reinstatement, and an order prohibiting Y & Y from taking reprisals against her in the future.

Carol Zabowicz, one of only two female forklift operators in a West Bend Co. warehouse, charged that her coworkers over a four-year period from 1978–1982 sexually harassed her by such acts as: asking her whether she was wearing a bra; two of the men exposing their buttocks between ten and twenty times; a male coworker grabbing his crotch and making obscene suggestions of growling; subjecting her to offensive and abusive language; and exhibiting obscene drawings with her initials on them. Zabowicz began to show symptoms of physical and psychological stress, necessitating several medical leaves, and she filed a sexual harassment complaint with the EEOC. The district court judge remarked that "The sustained, malicious, and brutal harassment meted out . . . was more than merely unreasonable; it was malevolent and outrageous." The company knew of the harassment and took corrective action only after the employee filed a complaint with the EEOC. The company was, therefore, held liable, and Zabowicz was awarded back pay for the period of her medical absence, and a judgment that her rights were violated under the Civil Rights Act of 1964.

On September 17, 1990, Lisa Olson, a sports reporter for the *Boston Herald*, charged five football players of the just-defeated New England Patriots with sexual harassment for making sexually suggestive and offensive remarks to her when she entered their locker room to conduct a postgame interview. The incident amounted to nothing short of "mind rape," according to Olson. After vociferous lamentations in the media, the National Football League fined the team and its players $25,000 each. The National Organization of Women called for a boycott of Remington electric shavers because the owner of the company, Victor Kiam, also owns the Patriots and allegedly displayed insufficient sensitivity at the time when the episode occurred.

All these incidents are indisputably disturbing. In an ideal world—one needless to say far different from the one that we inhabit or are ever likely to inhabit—women would not be subjected to such treatment in the course of their work. Women, and men as well, would be accorded respect by coworkers and supervisors, their feelings would be taken into account, and their dignity would be left intact. For women to expect reverential treatment in the workplace is utopian, yet they should not have to tolerate outrageous, offensive sexual overtures and threats as they go about earning a living.

One question that needs to be pondered is: What kinds of undesired sexual behavior women should be protected against by law? That is, what kind of actions are deemed so outrageous and violate a woman's rights to such [an] extent that the law should intervene, and what actions should be considered inconveniences of life, to be morally condemned but not adjudicated? A subsidiary question concerns the type of legal remedy appropriate for the wrongs that do require redress. Before directly addressing these questions, it might be useful to diffuse some of the hyperbole adhering to the sexual harassment issue.

Surveys are one source of this hyperbole. If their results are accepted at face value, they lead to the conclusion that women are disproportionately victims of legions of sexual harassers. A poll by the *Albuquerque Tribune* found that nearly 80 percent of the respondents reported that they or someone they knew had been victims of sexual harassment. The Merit Systems Protection Board determined that 42 percent of the women (and 14 percent of men) working for the federal government had experienced some form of unwanted sexual attention between 1985 and 1987, with unwanted "sexual teasing" identified as the most prevalent form. A Defense Department survey found that 64 percent of women in the military (and 17 percent of the men) suffered "uninvited and unwanted sexual attention" within the previous year. The United Methodist Church established that 7 percent of its clergywomen experienced incidents of sexual harassment, with 41 percent of these naming a pastor or colleague as the perpetrator, and 31 percent mentioning church social functions as the setting.

A few caveats concerning polls in general, and these sorts of polls in particular, are worth considering. Pollsters looking for a particular social ill tend to find it, usually in gargantuan proportions. (What fate would lie in store for a pollster who concluded that child abuse, or wife beating, or mistreatment of the elderly had dwindled to the point of negligibility!) Sexual harassment is a notoriously ill-defined and almost infinitely expandable concept, including everything from rape to unwelcome neck massaging, discomfiture upon witnessing sexual overtures directed at others, yelling at and blowing smoke in the ears of female subordinates, and displays of pornographic pictures in the workplace. Defining sexual harassment, as the United Methodists did, as "any sexually related behavior that is unwelcome, offensive, or which fails to respect the rights of others," the concept is broad enough to include everything from "unsolicited suggestive looks or leers [or] pressures for dates" to "actual sexual assaults or rapes." Categorizing everything from rape to "looks" as sexual harassment makes us all victims, a state of affairs satisfying to radical feminists, but not very useful for distinguishing serious injuries from the merely trivial.

Yet, even if the surveys exaggerate the extent of sexual harassment, however defined, what they do reflect is a great deal of tension between the sexes. As women in ever increasing numbers entered the workplace in the last two decades, as the women's movement challenged alleged male hegemony and exploitation with ever greater intemperance, and as women entered previously all-male preserves from the boardrooms to the coal pits, it is lamentable, but should not be surprising, that this tension sometimes takes sexual form. Not that sexual harassment on the job, in the university, and in other settings is a trivial or insignificant matter, but a sense of proportion needs to be restored and, even more importantly, distinctions need to be made, In other words, sexual harassment must be de-ideologized. Statements that paint nearly all women as victims and all men and their patriarchal, capitalist system as perpetrators, are ideological fantasy. Ideology blurs the distinction between being injured—being a genuine victim—and merely being offended. An example is this statement by Catharine A. MacKinnon, a law professor and feminist activist:

Sexual harassment perpetuates the interlocked structure by which women have been kept sexually in thrall to men and at the bottom of the labor market. Two forces of American society converge: men's control over women's sexuality and capital control over employees' work lives. Women historically have been required to exchange sexual services for material survival, in one form or another. Prostitution and marriage as well as sexual harassment in different ways institutionalize this arrangement.

Such hyperbole needs to be diffused and distinctions need to be drawn. Rape, a nonconsensual invasion of a person's body, is a crime clear and simple. It is a violation of the right to the physical integrity of the body (the right to life, as John Locke or Thomas Jefferson would have put it). Criminal law should and does prohibit rape. Whether it is useful to call rape "sexual harassment" is doubtful, for it makes the latter concept overly broad while trivializing the former.

Intimidation in the workplace of the kind that befell Valerie Craig—that is, extortion of sexual favors by a supervisor from a subordinate by threatening to penalize, fire, or fail to reward—is what the courts term *quid pro quo* sexual harassment. Since the mid-1970s, the federal courts have treated this type of sexual harassment as a form of sex discrimination in employment proscribed under Title VII of the Civil Rights Act of 1964. A plaintiff who prevails against an employer may receive such equitable remedies as reinstatement and back pay, and the court can order the company to prepare and disseminate a policy against sexual harassment. Current law places principal liability on the company, not the harassing supervisor, even when higher management is unaware of the harassment and, thus, cannot take any steps to prevent it.

Quid pro quo sexual harassment is morally objectionable and analogous to extortion: the harasser extorts property (i.e., use of the woman's body) through the leverage of fear for her job. The victim of such behavior should have legal recourse, but serious reservations can be held about rectifying these injustices through the blunt instrument of Title VII. In [outrageous] cases the victim is left less than whole (for back pay will not compensate for her ancillary losses), and no prospect for punitive damages are offered to deter would-be harassers. Even more distressing about Title VII is the fact that the primary target of litigation is not the actual harasser, but rather the employer. This places a double burden on a company. The employer is swindled by the supervisor because he spent his time pursuing sexual gratification and thereby impairing the efficiency of the workplace by mismanaging his subordinates, and the employer must endure lengthy and expensive litigation, pay damages, and suffer loss to its reputation. It would be fairer to both the company and the victim to treat sexual harassment as a tort—that is, as a private wrong or injury for which the court can assess damages. Employers should be held vicariously liable only when they know of an employee's behavior and do not try to redress it.

As for the workplace harassment endured by Carol Zabowicz—the bared buttocks, obscene portraits, etc.—that too should be legally redressable. Presently, such incidents also fall under the umbrella of Title VII, and are termed hostile environment sexual harassment, a category accepted later than quid pro quo and with some judicial reluctance. The main problem with this category is that it has proven too elastic: cases have reached the courts based on everything from off-color jokes to unwanted, persistent sexual advances by coworkers. A new tort of sexual harassment would handle these cases better. Only instances above a certain threshold of egregiousness or outrageousness would be actionable. In other words, the behavior that the plaintiff found offensive would also have to be offensive to the proverbial "reasonable man" of the tort law. That is, the behavior would have to be objectively injurious rather than merely subjectively offensive. The defendant would be the actual harasser, not the company, unless it knew about the problem and failed to act. Victims of scatological jokes, leers, unwanted offers of dates, and other sexual annoyances would no longer have their day in court.

A distinction must be restored between morally offensive behavior and behavior that causes serious harm. Only the latter should fall under the jurisdiction of criminal or tort law. Do we really want legislators and judges delving into our most intimate private lives, deciding when a look is a leer, and when a leer is a Civil Rights Act offense? Do we really want courts deciding, as one recently did, whether a school principal's disparaging remarks about a female school district administrator was sexual harassment and, hence, a breach of Title VII, or merely the act of a spurned and vengeful lover? Do we want judges settling disputes such as the one that arose at a car dealership after a female employee turned down a male coworker's offer of a date and his colleagues retaliated by calling her offensive names and embarrassing her in front of customers? Or another case in which a female shipyard worker complained of an "offensive working environment" because of the prevalence of pornographic material on the docks? Do we want the state to prevent or compensate us for any behavior that someone might find offensive? Should people have a legally enforceable right not to be offended by others? At some point, the price for such protection is the loss of both liberty and privacy rights.

Workplaces are breeding grounds of envy, personal grudges, infatuation, and jilted loves, and beneath a fairly high threshold of outrageousness, these travails should be either suffered in silence, complained of to higher management, or left behind as one seeks other employment. No one, female or male, can expect to enjoy a working environment that is perfectly stress-free, or to be treated always and by everyone with kindness and respect. To the extent that sympathetic judges have encouraged women to seek monetary compensation for slights and annoyances, they have not done them a great service. Women need to develop a thick skin in order to survive and prosper in the workforce. It is patronizing to think that they need to be recompensed by male judges for seeing a few pornographic pictures on a wall. By their efforts to extend sexual harassment charges to even the most trivial behavior, the radical feminists send a message that women are not resilient enough to ignore the run-of-the-mill, churlish provocation from male coworkers. It is difficult to imagine a suit by a longshoreman complaining of mental stress due to the display of nude male centerfolds by female co-workers. Women cannot expect to have it both ways: equality where convenient, but special dispensations when the going gets rough. Equality has its price and

that price may include unwelcome sexual advances, irritating and even intimidating sexual jests, and lewd and obnoxious colleagues.

[Outrageous] acts—sexual harassment per se—must be legally redressable.
Lesser but not trivial offenses, whether at the workplace or in other more social
settings, should be considered moral lapses for which the offending party
receives opprobrium, disciplinary warnings, or penalties, depending on the setting and the severity. Trivial offenses, dirty jokes, sexual overtures, and sexual
innuendoes do make many women feel intensely discomfited, but, unless they
become outrageous through persistence or content, these too should be taken as
part of life's annoyances. The perpetrators should be either endured, ignored,
rebuked, or avoided, as circumstances and personal inclination dictate. Whether
Lisa Olson's experience in the locker room of the Boston Patriots falls into the
second or third category is debatable. The media circus triggered by the incident
was certainly out of proportion to the event.

As the presence of women on road gangs, construction crews, and oil rigs
becomes a fact of life, the animosities and tensions of this transition period are
likely to abate gradually. Meanwhile, women should "lighten up," and even dispense a few risqué barbs of their own, a sure way of taking the fun out of it for
offensive male bores.

Legal Theories of Sexual Harassment

12

Alba Conte

Sexual harassment law, while unsettled, has evolved into a significant facet of the employment discrimination bar. Early claims of sexual harassment found little acceptance by judges who were unwilling to deem the "personal proclivit[ies]" of supervisors sexual harassment (*Corne* v. *Bausch & Lomb, Inc.*, 1975), and even those who were sympathetic to the concept that such conduct was discrimination had trouble integrating that notion into existing law. In the mid-1970s more enlightened opinions began to surface in the federal circuit courts, but the disparity in judicial construction lingered. Sexual harassment takes on many forms, but it usually falls into one or both of two categories: quid pro quo or hostile environment harassment. *Quid pro quo*, or sexual harassment for tangible benefit, involves the exchange of employment benefits by a supervisor or employer for sexual favors from a subordinate employee. *Hostile environment harassment* consists of verbal or physical conduct that unreasonably interferes with one's work or creates an intimidating, hostile, or offensive working environment. Although most victims of sexual harassment are women, men have also charged female superiors with sexual harassment, and a number of cases have involved harassment by members of the same sex. Not until 1986 did the U.S. Supreme Court rule in

From William O'Donohue, ed., *Sexual Harassment: Theory, Research and Treatment*. Copyright © 1997 by Allyn & Bacon. Reprinted by permission.

Meritor Savings Bank v. *Vinson* that, "without question," sexual harassment is a form of sex discrimination and that hostile environment as well as quid pro quo harassment violates Title VII of the Civil Rights Act of 1964. Unresolved questions regarding scope, employer liability, and evidentiary issues remain, however, to concern employers, employees, supervisors, unions, personnel staffs, and employment attorneys. Nevertheless, in this decision the Supreme Court took an important step toward legitimizing this elusive area of law for complainants and putting employers and harassers on notice that unwelcome sexual conduct will not be tolerated in the workplace. In *Harris* v. *Forklift Systems, Inc.* (1993) the Court addressed the issue of hostile environment again, holding that a plaintiff need not demonstrate psychological injury to prove sexual harassment. This chapter addresses the evolution of sexual harassment law generally and the range of legal theories and remedies available to the victim of sexual harassment.

TYPES OF SEXUAL HARASSMENT

Quid Pro Quo

Quid pro quo is the most obvious form of sexual harassment, involving the conditioning of employment benefits on sexual favors. As in traditional Title VII sex discrimination suits, the plaintiff must demonstrate that she was otherwise qualified to receive the relevant job benefit and that the job benefit was actually withheld or altered because of sexual harassment. The harassment may take several forms. Benefits may be withheld until a subordinate complies with sexual demands, a superior may retaliate against a subordinate for refusing to acquiesce, or a subordinate may comply with sexual demands and not receive a promised job benefit. Noncompliance has resulted in termination, transfer, denial or delay in receiving job benefits, and negative performance reviews. Underlying sexual harassment and other sexual discrimination claims is the requirement that, but for the sex of the complainant, the offending conduct would not have occurred (*Boyd* v. *James S. Hayes Living Health Care Agency*, 1987).

A plaintiff charging quid pro quo sexual harassment must prove by a preponderance of the evidence that she was denied an employment benefit because she refused to grant sexual favors (*Bundy* v. *Jackson*, 1981). In response an employer must show some legitimate motive for the adverse employment action, such as poor work performance, excessive absenteeism, lack of credentials, insubordination, dishonesty, personality conflicts, violation of company policy, or lack of work. If the employer adequately supports its argument, the plaintiff must then demonstrate by a preponderance of the evidence that the proffered explanation was not the real reason for the employment decision (*Texas Dep't. of Community Affairs* v. *Burdine*, 1981). There are a number of ways in which a plaintiff may rebut the defendant's case, such as the employer failed to warn the plaintiff of poor work performance, failed to uncover the basis for the deterioration of work performance, or did not follow company policy in making the employment decision.

Unlike hostile environment harassment, a quid pro quo harassment claim may be based on a single incident. Almost all lower federal courts have held employers strictly liable for the quid pro quo sexual harassment of an employee by a supervisor, based on the agency doctrine of respondeat superior. An employer is generally liable for the torts committed by its employees who are acting within the scope of their employment. The doctrine breaks down in this context when sexual harassment occurs outside the scope of employment. Although the dynamics and potential for coercion remain outside the workplace or without delegated functions, courts have found employer liability in such situations. A policy prohibiting sexual harassment cannot insulate an employer from liability in quid pro quo cases, particularly when the complainant must report any grievances to her supervisor, the alleged offender, in order to invoke internal procedures.

Evidence of sexual advances made to other employees may be admitted on the issue of motive, intent, or plan in making the sexual advances toward the plaintiff.

Hostile Environment

The concept of hostile environment sexual harassment has challenged courts to broaden their notions of sexual discrimination and offensive conduct. Hostile environment claims challenge workplace practices, rather than tangible job benefits, and consist of "verbal or physical conduct of a sexual nature" that unreasonably interferes with the employee's work or creates an "intimidating, hostile or offensive working environment" (EEOC Guidelines, 1993, §1604.11 [a][3]). In *Meritor* the Supreme Court noted that the requirement that "a man or woman run a gauntlet of sexual abuse in return for the privilege of being allowed to work and make a living can be as demeaning and disconcerting as the harshest of racial epithets," and that requiring a victim of sexual harassment to demonstrate the loss of a tangible economic benefit would undermine the purpose of Title VII, which was to prevent discrimination against an employee with respect to "terms, conditions or privileges of employment." This type of harassment is both more pervasive and more elusive. Courts have acknowledged its debilitating emotional consequences:

> Victims of sexual harassment suffer stress effects from the harassment. Stress as a result of sexual harassment is recognized as a specific, diagnosable problem by the American Psychiatric Association. . . . Among the stress effect suffered is "work performance stress," which includes distraction from tasks, dread of work, and an inability to work. . . . Another form is "emotional stress," which covers a range of responses, including anger, fear of physical safety, anxiety, depression, guilt, humiliation, and embarrassment. . . . Physical stress also results from sexual harassment; it may manifest itself as sleeping problems, headaches, weight changes, and other physical ailments. . . . A study by the Working Women's Institute found that 96 percent of sexual harassment victims experience emotional stress, 45 percent suffered work performance stress, and 35 percent were afflicted with physical stress problems.

Sexual harassment has a cumulative, eroding effect on the victim's well-

being. . . . When women feel a need to maintain vigilance against the next incident of harassment, the stress is increased tremendously. . . . When women feel
that their individual complaints will not change the work environment materially, the ensuing sense of despair further compounds the stress. (*Robinson* v.
Jacksonville Shipyards, Inc., 1991, pp. 1506–1507)

Conduct Constituting a Hostile Environment

Hostile environment harassment takes many forms, including repeated requests
for sexual favors, demeaning sexual inquiries and vulgarities, offensive language, and other verbal or physical conduct of a sexual or degrading nature.
Offensive conduct need not be sexual to contribute to a hostile environment. The
First Amendment does not protect sexually harassing language in a hostile environment case. The regulation of such conduct in the workplace "constitutes
nothing more than a time, place, and manner regulation of speech" (*Robinson* v.
Jacksonville Shipyards, Inc., 1991, p. 1535). In Robinson the court held that the
First Amendment guarantee of freedom of speech did not impede the remedy of
injunctive relief for verbal harassment and the pervasive use of pinups. The court
noted that (1) the defendant disavowed that it sought to express itself through the
sexually oriented pictures or the verbal harassment of its employees, (2) the pictures and verbal harassment were regulable because the eradication of workplace
discrimination is a compelling governmental interest, (3) female workers are a
captive audience in relation to the speech that constituted the hostile environment, and (4) the cleansing of the workplace of impediments to the equality of
women is a compelling interest that permits the regulation of the speech and the
regulation is narrowly drawn to serve this interest.

The physical work environment can be offensive when sexually offensive
explicit or sexist signs, cartoons, calendars, literature, or photographs are displayed in plain view. In *Robinson* a female welder successfully asserted sexual
harassment claims stemming from the extensive, pervasive posting of pictures
depicting nude women and from sexual conduct by male coworkers. In *Sanchez*
v. *City of Miami Beach* (1989) a district court concluded that a sexually harassing
work environment was created by male police officers who subjected a female
patrol officer to verbal abuse, "a plethora of sexually offensive posters, pictures,
graffiti, and pinups placed on the walls throughout the Police Department"
(*Sanchez*, p. 977).

Offensive graffiti may demean and intimidate an employee to the point that
it affects her job performance. In *Danna* v. *New York Telephone Co.* (1990), graffiti and vulgar comments on workplace walls were at least partially responsible
for the plaintiff seeking a demotion. The plaintiff's failure clearly to adduce specific harm did not relieve the defendant from liability when the graffiti remained
on the walls for at least two years and the plaintiff was advised to not make "a
stink about it" (*Danna*, p. 609).

An employer or supervisor also can alter working conditions by, for
example, denigrating the employee in front of other workers, constantly picking
on her, monitoring the plaintiff's work more closely than others', threatening her

job security, or giving the employee different work assignments or less desirable physical facilities.

Whether the sexual conduct complained of is sufficiently pervasive to create a hostile or offensive work environment must be determined by a totality of the circumstances (*Vinson* v. *Meritor Savings Bank*, 1986; *Harris* v. *Forklift Systems, Inc.*, 1994). In *Ross* v. *Double Diamond, Inc.* (1987) the District Court for the Northern District of Texas noted that a short duration of sexual harassment does not obviate a Title VII claim if the harassment is frequent and/or intensely offensive, finding that it would be inconsistent with this new awakening to allege that someone who has been intensely sexually harassed at the workplace does not have a claim under Title VII because he or she did not stay on the job for a longer period of time and subject himself or herself to further degradation.

Incidents of sexual harassment directed at employees other than the plaintiff may be used to establish a hostile work environment, and the alleged offensive conduct need not be purely sexual.

African American women face unique patterns of harassment. In *Hicks* v. *Gates Rubber Co.* (1987), for example, the Tenth Circuit held that although the employer's work environment was not openly hostile to African Americans, evidence of racial treatment could be combined with that of sexual harassment to establish a hostile work environment toward an African American woman employee. "[A]n employer who singles out black females for less favorable treatment does not defeat plaintiff's case by showing that white females or black males are not so unfavorably treated" (*Graham* v. *Bendix Corp.*, 1984, p. 1047).

Liability

While quid pro quo sexual harassment can only be committed by someone with authority to change the employee's job status, employers, supervisors, coworkers, customers, or clients can create a hostile work environment. Generally, employers are liable for the conduct of their employees in hostile environment cases only when they knew or should have known of the offensive behavior. Actual knowledge may be obtained through firsthand observations, an internal complaint to other management employees, or a formal complaint of discrimination. Evidence of the pervasiveness of the conduct may establish constructive knowledge. The Supreme Court in *Meritor* declined to issue a definitive rule on employer liability, noting that the record was insufficient to decide the issue, but it concluded that the court of appeals erroneously applied a strict liability standard to employers whose supervisors have created a hostile environment. Rejecting the views of both the EEOC guidelines and the court of appeals, the Court stated that it was "wrong to entirely disregard agency principles and impose strict liability on employers for the acts of their supervisors, regardless of the circumstances of the particular case." The Court felt that in defining "employer" under Title VII to include any "agent" of the employer, Congress intended to limit the scope of employer liability (*Meritor*, p. 73).

Unlike quid pro quo sexual harassment cases, in which a supervisor has actual or apparent authority to affect the employee's job status, the creation of a sexually hostile environment is less clear-cut in terms of whether a supervisor is acting within the scope of his or her employment. In quid pro quo cases, employers are strictly liable because agency principles impute notice of supervisory harassment to the employer. In a typical hostile environment action the harassers may be coworkers who do not act as the employer's agents, and thus the employer should not be liable without notice and an opportunity to remedy the situation. But the power enjoyed by supervisors over employees would seem to leave no room for a liability distinction between quid pro quo and hostile environment cases. The legal relationship between an employer and a supervisor should be such that an employer is on notice of liability for all of its supervisors' actions. In his concurrence, Justice Marshall noted that a supervisor's responsibilities do not begin and end with the power to hire, fire, and discipline employees, or with the power to recommend such actions; rather, a supervisor is charged with the day-to-day supervision of the work environment and with ensuring a safe, productive workplace, and there was no reason why abuse of the latter authority should have different consequences than abuse of the former.

Although the majority in *Meritor* rejected the notion of strict liability in hostile environment cases, it recognized that agency principles "may not be transferable in all their particulars to Title VII" and appeared to reject an absolute requirement of notice as well, stating that "absence of notice to an employer does not necessarily insulate that employer from liability" (*Meritor*, 1986, p. 72). Nor does the existence of a grievance procedure and a policy against discrimination preclude a finding of liability.

CONDUCT MUST BE UNWELCOME

"The gravamen of any sexual harassment claims is that the alleged sexual advances were 'unwelcome'" (*Meritor*, 1986, p. 68). The plaintiff must show she was actually offended by the conduct and suffered some injury from it. A number of courts have focused on the plaintiff's participation in allegedly offensive conduct or other workplace behavior. In *Meritor* the Supreme Court held that the court of appeals erred in concluding that testimony regarding the plaintiff's "provocative dress and publicly expressed fantasies" had no place in the litigation (*Meritor*, 1986, p. 69). The Court rejected the bank's contention that it could not be held liable for the alleged sexual conduct because Vinson participated in the acts voluntarily, concluding that the district court had improperly focused on Vinson's compliance. The correct inquiry was whether Vinson by her conduct indicated that the alleged sexual advances were unwelcome, not whether her actual participation was voluntary, and that evidence such as dress and fantasies was "obviously relevant" in determining whether sexual harassment occurred (*Meritor*, 1986, p. 69). So, although voluntary participation is not an absolute defense to a claim of sexual harassment, it is a factor in deciding whether sexual advances were unwelcome. Because the alleged harasser maintained that the alleged sexual incidents never occurred, not that the plaintiff welcomed his advances, the Court could have declined to consider whether the plaintiff's fantasies and clothing supported a finding that the sexual advances were welcome. By admitting such evidence, courts turn the plaintiff into the accused and shift the focus from the conduct of the harasser to the nature of the harassed. While employers still should be able to argue that the plaintiff welcomed sexual advances, such a showing should be made without introducing highly charged and subjective evidence. Courts may now feel compelled to consider this type of evidence whether or not they consider it appropriate to do so. For example, in *Jones* v. *Wesco* (1988) the Eighth Circuit stated that a court must consider any provocative speech or dress of the plaintiff in a sexual harassment case and observed from the record that the plaintiff "wore nonprovocative clothing." In *Weiss* v. *Amoco Oil Co.* (1992), a wrongful termination action by a male employee fired for sexual harassment, the plaintiff sought to engage in discovery concerning the alleged victim's sexual history. According to the plaintiff, the alleged victim had cards pinned up at her workstation that were of a sexual nature, sent another male employee a birthday card that showed the torso of an adult female wearing a bikini, made sexual jokes with other employees, and discussed her sexual activities while at work. The court held that the alleged victim, a non-party witness, failed to meet her burden of showing that information concerning her sexual history was irrelevant and not reasonably calculated to lead to discovery of admissible evidence. The court noted that the material sought was relevant in assessing the thoroughness of Amoco's investigation into Streebin's complaint of sexual harassment. Weiss alleged that he and Streebin were social friends who dated occasionally, and that Streebin dated other fellow employees. Weiss alleges that a thorough investigation into Streebin's complaint against him would have disclosed these facts, facts that would be necessary in any analysis of Streebin's sexual harassment complaint against Weiss.

The fact that the plaintiff had a consensual relationship with her alleged harasser does not welcome harassment that occurs after the relationship ends. In *Shrout* v. *Black Clawson* (1988) a consensual relationship of three years between the plaintiff and the defendant was followed by four years of sexual advances and comments and refusals to give the plaintiff pay raises and performance evaluations because she refused to continue the relationship. The court concluded that the plaintiff had been subjected to quid pro quo as well as hostile environment sexual harassment. In *Babcock* v. *Frank* (1990), allegations that the plaintiff's supervisor begged her to love him again, along with his subsequent issuance of a disciplinary letter against her, were more than sufficient to raise an inference in a reasonable person that the defendant used his supervisory authority to blackmail the plaintiff into accepting his sexual advances. After ending the relationship, the plaintiff had the right, like any other worker, to be free from a sexually abusive environment and to reject sexual advances without the threat of punishment. Some courts, however, have refused to find sexual harassment in cases involving prior consensual relationships because of the requirement that the plaintiff must have been discriminated against because of membership in a particular class. In *Huebschen* v. *Department of Health and Social Services* (1983) the Seventh Circuit reversed the trial court's finding of sexual harassment when there was no evidence that a female supervisor who had started insulting the plaintiff after they had had a "one-night stand" intentionally discriminated against the plaintiff because he was a man or that she had attempted to discriminate against other men in the workplace. In *Keppler* v. *Hinsdale Township High School District 86* (1989) the court construed Huebschen to preclude quid pro quo claims by plaintiffs who had had consensual relationships with their alleged harassers and distinguished the type of quid pro quo claims stemming from the conditioning of job benefits on the receipt of sexual favors from those stemming from retaliatory conduct, concluding that retaliatory claims create a presumption against a finding of sexual harassment. The court noted that an employee who chooses to become involved in an intimate affair with her employer removes an element of her employment relationship from the workplace, and in the realm of private affairs, people have the right to react to rejection, jealousy, and other emotions that Title VII says have no place in the employment setting.

Victims of sexual harassment often tolerate offensive conduct in fear of retribution. Failure to report incidents of harassment, however, may suggest to the court that the conduct was not so severe or pervasive as to alter the plaintiffs condition of employment. Courts almost always consider whether the plaintiff complained of the challenged conduct in making a determination of hostile environment.

PSYCHOLOGICAL IMPACT OF HARASSMENT

In *Harris* v. *Forklift Systems* (1993), in which the plaintiff alleged that she was constructively discharged from her manager position because of a sexually hostile environment created by the company president, the trial court found that although the plaintiff "was the object of a continuing pattern of sex-based derogatory conduct from Hardy," including sexual innuendos about clothing worn by the plaintiff and other female employees; throwing things on the ground in front of the plaintiff and other female employees and asking them to pick them up; asking the plaintiff and other female employees to retrieve coins from his front pockets; stating to the plaintiff, "Let's go to the Holiday Inn and negotiate your raise. . . . You're a woman, what do you know," "You're a dumb-ass woman," and "We need a man as the rental manager," the plaintiff was not able to prove that the president's conduct was so severe as to create a hostile work environment when the court found that the alleged harasser's comments could not be characterized as much more than annoying and insensitive. The trial court did not believe that the plaintiff was subjectively so offended that she suffered injury, when she repeatedly testified that she loved her job, she and her husband socialized with Hardy and his wife, and she herself drank beer and socialized with Hardy and her coworkers.

In a unanimous opinion the Supreme Court rejected the standard adopted by the lower courts and held that psychological harm is one factor among many that the courts may weigh in a sexual harassment case. Federal law "comes into play before the harassing conduct leads to a nervous breakdown." Writing for the Court, Justice O'Connor stated that Title VII as applied to sexual harassment is violated when, for any of a variety of reasons, "the environment would be perceived, and is perceived, as hostile or abusive" and that "no single factor is required."

> As we made clear in *Meritor Savings Bank* v. *Vinson*, (1986), [Title VII's] language "is not limited to 'economic' or 'tangible' discrimination. The phrase 'terms, conditions, or privileges of employment' evinces a Congressional intent 'to strike at the entire spectrum of disparate treatment of men and women' in employment," which includes requiring people to work in a discriminatorily hostile or abusive environment. When the workplace is permeated with "discriminatory intimidation, ridicule, and insult" that is "sufficiently severe or pervasive to alter the conditions of the victim's employment and create an abusive working environment," Title VII is violated,
>
> This standard, which we reaffirm today, takes a middle path between making actionable any conduct that is merely offensive and requiring the conduct to cause a tangible psychological injury. As we pointed out in *Meritor*, "mere utterance of an . . . epithet which engenders offensive feelings in an employee" does not sufficiently affect the conditions of employment to implicate Title VII. Conduct that is not severe or pervasive enough to create an objectively hostile or abusive work environment, an environment that a reasonable person would find hostile or abusive, is beyond Title VII's purview. Likewise, if the victim does not subjectively perceive the environment to be abusive, the conduct has not actually altered the conditions of the victim's employment, and there is no Title VII violation.
>
> But Title VII comes into play before the harassing conduct leads to a nervous breakdown. A discriminatorily abusive work environment, even one that does not seriously affect employees' psychological well-being, can and often will detract from employees' job performance, discourage employees from remaining on the job, or keep them from advancing in their careers. Moreover, even without regard to these tangible effects, the very fact that the discriminatory conduct was so severe or pervasive that it created a work environment abusive to employees because of their race, gender, religion, or national origin offends Title VII's broad rule of workplace equality. The appalling conduct alleged in *Meritor*, and the reference in that case to environments " 'so heavily polluted with discrimination as to destroy completely the emotional and psychological stability of minority group workers,' " merely present some especially egregious examples of harassment. They do not mark the boundary of what is actionable.
>
> We therefore believe the District Court erred in relying on whether the conduct "seriously affect(ed) plaintiffs psychological well-being" or led her to "suffe(r) injury." Such an inquiry may needlessly focus the factfinder's attention on concrete psychological harm, an element Title VII does not require. Certainly Title VII bars conduct that would seriously affect a reasonable person's psychological well-being, but the statute is not limited to such conduct. So long as the environment would reasonably be perceived, and is perceived, as hostile or abusive, there is no need for it also to be psychologically injurious.
>
> This is not, and by its nature cannot be, a mathematically precise test. We need not answer today all the potential questions it raises, nor specifically address

the E.E.O.C.'s new regulations on this subject. But we can say that whether an environment is "hostile" or "abusive" can be determined only by looking at all the circumstances. These may include the frequency of the discriminatory conduct; its severity; whether it is physically threatening or humiliating, or a mere offensive utterance; and whether it unreasonably interferes with an employee's work performance. The effect on the employee's psychological well-being is, of course, relevant to determining whether the plaintiff actually found the environment abusive. But while psychological harm, like any other relevant factor, may be taken into account, no single factor is required. (*Harris*, pp. 370–71)

Justice Ginsburg concurred, stating that Title VII's critical issue is whether members of one sex are exposed to disadvantageous terms or conditions of employment to which members of the other sex are not exposed, and that, as the EEOC as amici curiae emphasized, "the adjudicator's inquiry should center, dominantly, on whether the discriminatory conduct has unreasonably interfered with the plaintiff's work performance" (*Harris*, p. 372), and that to show such interference, the plaintiff need not prove that her or his tangible productivity has declined as a result of the harassment but only that the harassment so altered working conditions as to make it more difficult to do the job.

Justice Scalia concurred as well, noting that although he knew of no alternative to the course taken by the Court, he was concerned that the term "abusive" did not seem to be a very clear standard and that clarity was not increased by adding the adverb "objectively" or by appealing to a "reasonable person's" notion of what the "vague" word means:

> Today's opinion does list a number of factors that contribute to abusiveness, but since it neither says how much of each is necessary (an impossible task) nor identifies any single factor as determinative, it thereby adds little certitude. As a practical matter, today's holding lets virtually unguided juries decide whether sex-related conduct engaged in (or permitted by) an employer is egregious enough to warrant an award of damages.
>
> One might say that what constitutes "negligence" (a traditional jury question) is not much more clear and certain than what constitutes "abusiveness." Perhaps so. But the class of plaintiffs seeking to recover for negligence is limited to those who have suffered harm, whereas under this statute "abusiveness" is to be the test of whether legal harm has been suffered, opening more expansive vistas of litigation. (*Harris*, p. 372)

THE REASONABLE WOMAN STANDARD

Robinson v. *Jacksonville Shipyards* (1991) was the first case to delve into the issue of whether sexually harassing conduct should be measured by its impact on a reasonable woman, rather than a reasonable person or victim. The Ninth Circuit advanced the reasonable woman standard in *Ellison* v. *Brady* (1991) to determine whether conduct is sufficiently pervasive to alter the conditions of employment and create a hostile working environment. A female revenue agent for the

IRS had alleged that a male coworker's amorous attention frightened her, and even though he was subsequently transferred, he returned to her office and wrote her another love letter. The court held that it is the harasser's conduct that must be pervasive or severe, not the alteration in the conditions of employment, and that in evaluating the severity and pervasiveness of sexual harassment, a court should focus on the perspective of the victim. The court adopted the perspective of a reasonable woman primarily because it believed that a sex-blind reasonable person standard tends to be male-biased and to systematically ignore the experiences of women. If courts only examined whether a reasonable person would engage in allegedly harassing conduct, they would run the risk of reinforcing the prevailing level of discrimination. Harassers could continue to harass merely because a particular discriminatory practice was common, and victims of harassment would have no remedy. A thorough understanding of the victim's view requires, among other things, an analysis of the different perspectives of men and women. For example, because women are disproportionately victims of rape and sexual assault, women have a stronger incentive to be concerned with sexual behavior. Women who are victims of mild forms of sexual harassment may understandably worry whether a harasser's conduct is merely a prelude to violent sexual assault. Men, who are rarely victims of sexual assault, may see sexual conduct in a vacuum without a full understanding of the social setting or the underlying threat of violence that a woman may perceive.

The court noted that in order to shield employers from having to accommodate the idiosyncratic concerns of the rare hypersensitive employee, it would hold that a female plaintiff states a prima facie case of hostile environment sexual harassment when she alleges conduct that a reasonable woman would consider sufficiently severe or pervasive to alter the conditions of employment and to create an abusive working environment.

In *Andrews* v. *City of Philadelphia* (1990), in which the plaintiff police officers alleged a hostile work environment created by abusive language, sexually explicit pictures at the workplace, the destruction of the plaintiffs' private property and work product, physical injury, and anonymous telephone calls at home, the court of appeals reversed the trial court's ruling against the plaintiffs and held that to prove a hostile environment, a plaintiff must demonstrate that the discrimination would detrimentally affect a reasonable person of the same sex in that position, thus protecting the employer from an oversensitive employee but still serving the goal of equal opportunity by removing the walls of discrimination that deprive women of self-respecting employment. The court noted that men and women have different perspectives on obscene language and pornography: "Although men may find these actions harmless and innocent, it is highly possible that women may feel otherwise" (*Andrews*, p. 1486).

In *Austin* v. *State of Hawaii et al.* (1991) the district court cited *Ellison* with approval in ruling in favor of the plaintiff English professor in an action alleging sexual harassment by the male chair of the English department, noting that the chair referred to her in ways that reasonable women consider to be typical of males who consider women inferior.

The court certified a class of women employees alleging sex discrimination including sexual harassment in *Jenson* v. *Eveleth Taconite Co.* (1991), noting that the common question of law was not how an individual class member reacted, but whether a reasonable woman would find the work environment hostile.

Several state courts have also applied the reasonable woman standard. In *Lehmann* v. *Toys 'R' Us, Inc.* (1993), the New Jersey Supreme Court carefully considered the basis for such a test, noting that an objective reasonableness standard better focuses the court's attention on the nature and legality of the conduct rather than on the reaction of the individual plaintiff, which is more relevant to damages, and that as community standards evolve, the standard of what a reasonable woman would consider harassment will also evolve. In *Radtke* v. *Everett* (1991), however, in which the plaintiff alleged that her employer forcibly held her down, caressed and attempted to kiss her, the Supreme Court addressed the elements of a prima facie case of a hostile work environment under the Michigan Civil Rights Act and held that the reasonable woman standard violated the legislative intent of the act, concluding that if the legislature intended a departure from that standard, it would have explicitly mandated that alteration, and that the reasonable person standard should be utilized because it is sufficiently flexible to incorporate gender differences.

THIRD-PARTY EMPLOYEES

Quid Pro Quo

Otherwise qualified employees who lose employment opportunities because job benefits went to those who submitted to sexual harassment may have discrimination claims under Title VII. Both men and women may be entitled to bring such a claim. A qualified male may lose a potential job benefit on the basis of sex, or a qualified woman who was not approached sexually by a supervisor may lose a job benefit to a less qualified woman who submitted unwillingly to sexual advances. In *Broderick* v. *Ruder* (1988) a female attorney who refused to participate in workplace sexual conduct successfully challenged a work environment in which compliance with sexual advances brought career advancement and other employment benefits to other employees.

Although romantic relationships between a supervisor and an employee sometimes result in the woman subordinate's enjoying certain unique job benefits, some courts have held that such preferential treatment is not gender-based discrimination (*Miller* v. *Aluminum Co. of Am.*, 1988). But in *Piech* v. *Arthur Andersen & Co.* (1994) the plaintiff asserted a claim that a less qualified, single female coworker was promoted to manager instead of her because of the "favored" female's knowledge of inappropriate male partner sexual conduct and her amorous relationship with a partner in the decision-making process, but did not allege that she suffered an adverse employment decision because of her sex. The plaintiff did allege that it was generally necessary for women to grant sexual favors to decision makers for professional advances and that because she did not grant sexual favors she was denied a promotion, fitting the classic definition of quid pro quo harassment. Plaintiff's allegations "regarding the favored female coworker who received a promotion while involved romantically with a decision maker may be considered simply circumstantial evidence that her employer conditioned employment benefits on the granting of sexual favors" (*Piech*, pp. 442–43). And in *Dirksen* v. *City of Springfield* (1994) a demoted female secretary for the city police department claimed that a police officer made numerous nonconsensual sexual advances toward her that included attempts to kiss and touch her body; offensive placement of his hands on her body; forcing the placement of her hands on his body; attempted sexual assault, during which the alleged harasser stated that if the plaintiff wanted to be promoted to his personal secretary, she had to submit to sexual intercourse with him; and that when she went on medical leave, she was replaced by a worker who was having sexual relations with him. The complainant stated a claim for quid pro quo sexual harassment, despite the defendant's argument that the plaintiff was not discriminated against on the basis of sex but because her boss allegedly favored his paramour. This was not a single instance of favoritism; plaintiff alleges that it was generally necessary for *women* to grant sexual favors to the officer to obtain professional advancement.

When such romantic involvement and its job-related implications are a matter of common knowledge, however, the work atmosphere may be tainted in violation of Title VII, and thus a hostile environment claim may be appropriate.

Hostile Environment

A hostile work environment is most likely experienced by other employees besides the complainant. Even a woman who was never herself the object of harassment might have a Title VII claim if she were forced to work in an atmosphere in which such harassment was pervasive. This type of harassment includes situations in which male supervisors have romantic relationships with female subordinates and afford them job benefits to the detriment of other employees. In *Broderick* v. *Ruder* (1988) an attorney for the Securities and Exchange Commission was awarded $120,000 in back pay and interest and previously denied promotions for proving that her office supervisors created a hostile work environment by engaging in sexually offensive conduct. Such conduct included rewarding employees who complied with sexual advances with promotions and other employment benefits to the detriment of Broderick, who had refused such requests. Despite the fact that few of the alleged incidents of harassment had been directed at Broderick herself, the environment "poisoned any possibility of plaintiffs having the proper professional respect for her supervisors and, without any question, affected her motivation and her peformance of her job responsibilities" (*Broderick*, p. 1273). Although Broderick had complained to higher management, no one was ever disciplined for conduct that was common knowledge, and management made no serious effort to enforce guidelines prohibiting sex discrimination.

Broderick clearly established a violation of Title VII through her testimony and that of coworkers. Not only were her working conditions "poisoned" to the extent that she suffered psychologically, but she was denied tangible work benefits as a result of her supervisors' flagrant sexual conduct. The hybrid nature of Broderick's hostile environment claim, which included allegations that employment benefits were bestowed upon compliant employees to Broderick's detriment, gave the case that quid pro quo element that courts have embraced. However, it is unclear how far the courts will take Title VII.

Preferential treatment not only undermines an employee's motivation and work performance but also deprives her of job opportunities. Some courts have argued that because women and men are in the same position with respect to lost employment opportunities, such conduct cannot form the basis of a sex discrimination charge (*Miller* v. *Aluminum Co. of Am.*, 1988). While it is true that women and men both may suffer the loss of similar benefits, the bases for their respective charges differ. Because the qualified man is an unlikely candidate for an office romance with a presumably heterosexual supervisor, he relinquishes a job opportunity to the less qualified but involved woman on the basis of his sex, and thus he may bring an employment discrimination action. The qualified woman who loses job benefits to a less qualified but involved woman or who is exposed to male supervisors having affairs with subordinates and showering them with attention is undermined. She is made to feel that, among other things, merit and hard work by women are irrelevant, women get ahead by sleeping with their superiors, sexual objectification is a by-product of employment, and women have no control over their professional destinies short of submitting to sexual advances. This sense of loss of control may be enhanced when the plaintiff is also subjected to sexual advances or fears physical violence. Clearly, these elements create a hostile work environment in violation of Title VII.

An employee who protests the sexual harassment of other employees may bring a retaliation action if adverse personnel actions are taken in response to such complaints. For such a claim to survive judicial scrutiny, the plaintiff must give the employer a fair opportunity to remedy the situation.

CONSTRUCTIVE DISCHARGE

An employee is constructively discharged when the employer deliberately makes that employee's working conditions so onerous that a reasonable person would find them intolerable. In *EEOC* v. *Gurnee Inn Corp.* (1988), for example, the decision of a female employee to quit her job amounted to a constructive discharge when in addition to rebuffing a supervisor's advances, she was forced to observe sexual conduct in her workplace and watch employees who tolerated it receive better treatment by the supervisor. She was unable to help her subordinates avoid the supervisor's advances because management refused to take action.

Sexual harassment may force a person to quit her job, giving rise to a separate constructive discharge claim in addition to claims of sexual harassment, although someone who leaves a position need not prove constructive discharge in order to obtain relief for sexual harassment under Title VII. Intent may be inferred from circumstantial evidence, including a failure to act in the face of known intolerable conditions. Either type of harassment, quid pro quo or hostile environment, may form the basis for a constructive discharge claim. Constructive discharge will not be established, however, merely by demonstrating that sexual harassment occurred. Nor will constructive discharge be established if the incidents of harassment are too remote in time from the resignation. Constructive discharge also will not be found if resignation occurred for reasons other than alleged sexual harassment, or if the employer did not receive actual or constructive notice of the alleged harassment or was not given sufficient time to remedy the situation. The Sixth Circuit has required some inquiry into the employer's intent and the reasonably foreseeable impact of its conduct on the employee. A reasonable woman standard should be applied to determine whether the harassed employee quit because of sexual harassment. In *Radtke* v. *Everett* (1991) the Michigan Court of Appeal held that the constructive discharge claim of a female veterinary technician who was caressed and kissed by her supervisor during a break and who subsequently ended her employment and sought counseling should have survived summary judgment. A single incident of sexual harassment could be sufficiently severe under some circumstances to support a finding that a reasonable woman's employment was substantially affected or that a hostile environment was created. In some cases the mere presence of a harasser may create a hostile environment. The proper perspective to view the offensive conduct from was that of a reasonable woman. Most courts have applied a reasonable person standard, and the reasonable person "in the plaintiff's position" test may imply a reasonable woman standard.

Coworkers and nonemployees as well as supervisors may create conditions giving rise to a constructive discharge claim. The failure by supervisors to take immediate remedial action after notice of harassment by coworkers may constitute constructive discharge.

An employee need not quit her job to raise a claim of constructive discharge. For example, forced medical leave without pay may be deemed a constructive discharge for purposes of back pay liability. Nor does an employee have to resign immediately after the harassing conduct has occurred in order to plead constructive discharge.

RETALIATION

Title VII prohibits discrimination against an employee who has either opposed an employment practice made unlawful under Title VII or made a charge or participated in any manner in an investigation, procedure, or hearing under Title VII. To determine whether an action is protected by Title VII, the court must consider whether the employee's conduct was reasonable in light of the circumstances. The trial court also should balance the employer's right to run a business with the right of employees to express their grievances.

Sexual harassment complaints often include claims of retaliation, and such claims may succeed despite a finding that no violation of Title VII has occurred. A prima facie case of retaliation is established by proof that (1) the plaintiff engaged in statutorily protected opposition or participation, (2) an adverse employment action occurred, and (3) there was a causal link between the opposition or participation and the adverse employment action.

The opposition clause of Title VII protects a variety of forms of expression. In addition to the filing of charges, protected activity includes resisting advances; registering internal complaints of sexual harassment; testifying on behalf or supporting the claims of another employee; picketing; or, when appropriate, notifying law-enforcement authorities.

The most common form of retaliatory action is dismissal. Other adverse employment actions may include demotion, transfer, negative evaluation, and verbal misconduct. Temporary transfers or demotions that reduce an employee's duties and responsibilities but maintain salary and benefits may not constitute adverse employment actions.

The causal link element requires only that the plaintiff establish that the protected activity and the adverse action "were not wholly unrelated" (*Petrosky* v. *Washington-Greene County Branch Pa. Assoc. for the Blind*, 1987, p. 825). "Essential to a causal link is evidence that the employer was aware that the plaintiff had engaged in the protected activity" (*Miller* v. *Aluminum Co. of Am.*, 1988, p. 504). A plaintiff may establish this link when only a short period of time has passed between the protected activity and the adverse personnel action, as well as by circumstantial evidence. For example, the employee may have received favorable evaluations before engaging in the protected activity but negative evaluations afterward.

An employee may not use her right to oppose unlawful activity to undermine legitimate interests of the employer. In *Jones* v. *Flagship International* (1986) the court of appeals affirmed the district court's decision that a former equal employment opportunity manager who encouraged other employees to file discrimination charges and who sought to maintain a class action clearly engaged in protected activity when she filed a discrimination charge with the EEOC. Her subsequent suspension and termination were adverse employment actions, but she failed to establish the causal link between the two. The district court found that the defendant suspended the plaintiff to avoid the "conflict of interest inherent in Jones's representation of Flagship before the agency to whom she made the complaint" and because she planned to initiate a class-action suit against the company. The court considered the evidence of Jones's solicitation of other employees to sue or join the class suit and concluded that Jones's actions "not only rendered her ineffective in the position for which she was employed, but critically harmed Flagship's posture in the defense of discrimination suits brought against the company."

As in disparate-treatment cases, the plaintiff meets the initial burden by establishing facts sufficient to permit an inference of retaliatory motive. Once this burden is met, the defendant must articulate a legitimate, nondiscriminatory reason for the personnel action. The employer must show by clear and convincing evidence that the plaintiff would not have been treated differently if she had not opposed the harassment. The reason for this different rule in sexual harassment cases is that once a plaintiff establishes that she was harassed, it is difficult to see how an employer can justify the harassment. The plaintiff will prevail if she then demonstrates by a preponderance of the evidence that the proffered reason was but a pretext for retaliation or by persuading the court that the desire to retaliate more likely motivated the employer.

EMPLOYER RESPONSE TO COMPLAINTS OF SEXUAL HARASSMENT

An employer's liability for sexual harassment often turns on the response to complaints of sexual harassment. The response must be reasonably calculated to prevent further harassment (*Juarez* v. *Ameritech Mobile Communications*, 1990). In *Robinson* v. *Jacksonville Shipyards, Inc.* (1991) the court measured the effectiveness of employer response in two ways. First, the total response may be evaluated on the basis of the circumstances as then existed. It is ineffective if the employer delayed unduly and the action taken, however promptly, was not reasonably likely to prevent the harassment from recurring. Second, an employer can show that the conduct brought to the company's attention was not repeated after the employer took action. In *Watts* v. *New York Police Department* (1989) the court held that Title VII imposes an affirmative duty on the employer to investigate charges, even if the harassment stops after the complaint is made. Here a probationary police officer who filed a sexual harassment charge against her instructor was subsequently subjected to further harassment in the form of verbal attacks and ostracism by her coworkers and supervisors, but not her instructor. The court concluded that the employer has an obligation to investigate whether acts conducive to the creation of an atmosphere of hostility do in fact occur, and, if so, it must attempt to dispel workplace hostility by taking prompt remedial steps. For that reason, the fact that the plaintiff, after apprising the police department of concerns about harassment by one officer, instead became the victim of harassment by another did not provide the department with a shield against its duty to take reasonable measures to enforce the federal policy that sexual harassment will not be tolerated in the workplace.

The prompt investigation of a sexual harassment complaint followed by appropriate action will usually prevent a finding of liability against the employer. In *Carmon* v. *Lubrizol Corp.* (1994) the district court determined that an employer took prompt and remedial action in response to a female employee's two sexual harassment complaints when the employer sprang into action immediately: met with the plaintiff on the same day as her first complaint, questioned the alleged harasser, interviewed six witnesses, found that the alleged harasser and the plaintiff had used foul language, reprimanded the alleged harasser, and transferred him to another shift. A similar investigation was conducted the next year following another complaint of sexual harassment. Similarly, in *Saxton* v. *American Tel. & Tel. Co.* (1993), the employer took appropriate corrective action upon notice of sexual harassment when the department head promptly began a thorough investigation of the employee's charges, interviewing principals as well as witnesses; recommended the separation of the parties; began the process of transferring the supervisor after learning that the employee did not want a transfer; and allowed the employee to work at home during the entire process.

Allegations of harassment that are investigated only to the extent that the alleged harasser denies the charges may be insufficient (*Mays* v. *Williamson & Sons, Janitorial Servs.*, 1985). In *Heelan* v. *Johns-Manville Corp.* (1978), management's response to complaints of sexual harassment by a supervisor consisted only of calling the accused harasser on the phone for verification or denial and hardly satisfied the company's obligation under Title VII. And in *Hansel* v. *Public Service Co.* (1991), merely discussing the issue with four of the perpetrators was insufficient to stop harassment of female machine operators that had been occurring over an eight-year period when, although physical harassment ceased, other forms continued. The court noted that a hostile environment "is like a disease. It can have many symptoms, some of which change over time, but all of which stem from the same root" (*Hansel*, p. 1132). The court went so far as to hold that Title VII imposes an affirmative duty on employers to seek out and eradicate a hostile work environment. "An employer simply cannot sit back and wait for complaints. The very nature of sexual harassment inhibits its victims from coming forward because of fear of retaliation" (*Hansel*, p. 1133).

Termination of an alleged harasser usually is not required; other forms of discipline such as suspension, demotion, or transfer may be appropriate. A warning may suffice in certain cases if more severe discipline is imposed for subsequent misconduct (*Bigoni* v. *Pay 'n Pak Stores*, 1990), but one court has held that an employer's knowledge of previous sexual harassment could render the employer liable for the harasser's subsequent conduct (*Paroline* v. *Unisys Corp.*, 1989). The transfer of the complainant is usually not appropriate, but in *Nash* v. *Electrospace System, Inc.* (1993) the defendant employer adequately responded to an employee's claim of sexual harassment by a supervisor, thus precluding liability under Title VII, when the employer immediately began an investigation of the supervisor, and, when the charges could not be corroborated because the supervisor denied them and coworkers had not experienced offensive behavior by him, the plaintiff was transferred to another department with no loss of pay or benefits. The investigation and transfer occurred within a week of the plaintiff's first complaint, and the record indicated that the transfer was successful as the plaintiff got along well with her new boss and soon was eligible for a raise.

The existence of an effective grievance procedure and the enforcement of a sexual harassment policy can help an employer avoid liability.

FEDERAL REMEDIES FOR SEXUAL HARASSMENT

Title VII

Most sexual harassment suits are brought under Title VII of the Civil Rights Act of 1964. Title VII provides in part:

> It shall be an unlawful employment practice for an employer (1) to fail or refuse to hire or to discharge any individual, or otherwise to discriminate against any individual with respect to [her or] his compensation, terms, conditions, or privileges of employment, because of such individual's ... sex ... ; or (2) to limit, segregate, or classify [her or] his employees or applicants for employment in any way which would deprive or tend to deprive any individual of employment opportunities or otherwise adversely affect [her or] his status as an employee, because of such individual's ... sex. (Title VII, Civil Rights Act §2000e-2[a])

Title VII was passed to provide equal opportunity through the removal of artificial barriers to employment. To accomplish the congressional purpose of giving an effective voice to victims of employment discrimination, Title VII also prohibits employers from retaliating against employees who initiate complaints. In 1972, Congress extended the protections of Title VII to federal employees. With little legislative history available to assist the courts, judicial interpretation of the prohibition against sex discrimination has been largely a self-guided process. Indeed, the addition of the provision prohibiting sex discrimination apparently was a last-minute attempt to defeat Title VII's passage. However, the 1972 amendments to Title VII indicate a clear congressional intent to eliminate sex discrimination.

Title VII has been broadly construed. In *Sprogis* v. *United Airlines, Inc.* (1971) the Seventh Circuit stated that Congress intended to strike at the entire spectrum of disparate treatment of men and women resulting from sex stereotypes. Ten years after the enactment of Title VII, sexual harassment claims became an important part of the discrimination spectrum.

The Civil Rights Act of 1991

In the aftermath of the Clarence Thomas hearings, former President Bush signed the Civil Rights Act of 1991 on November 21, 1991, thus ending a two-year political battle. The act amends Title VII of the Civil Rights Act of 1964, section 1981 of the Civil Rights Act of 1866, the Attorney's Fees Awards Act of 1976, the Age Discrimination in Employment Act of 1967 (ADEA), and the Americans with Disabilities Act of 1990 (ADA). The act has a significant impact on sexual harassment cases by providing damage awards in federal court as well as expert-witness fees and jury trials. The act is particularly beneficial to sexual harassment plaintiffs who live in states where damages for such conduct are not available under state law or in jurisdictions unsympathetic to such claims. Under prior law, damages were available only to victims of intentional racial or ethnic discrimination. The Civil Rights Act of 1991 (CRA) corrects the inadequate remedial provisions of Title VII by extending compensatory and punitive damages to victims of employment discrimination based on sex, religion, and disability as well as race under Title VII, the ADA, and the Rehabilitation Act of 1973. Compensatory damages are available from private employers and federal, state, and local governments. Punitive damages, however, may only be recovered from private employers when the employer acted with malice or with reckless indifference to the rights of the victim. Under the 1991 law, punitive damages are capped at $50,000 for companies of 100 or fewer workers and at $100,000 for companies with 101 to 200 employees, $200,000 for employers with 201 to 500 employees, and $300,000 for employers of over 500 employees. Sexual harassment plaintiffs who sought monetary relief for their injuries previously had to resort to state court or append state law claims to their federal claims. Federal courts must agree to assert jurisdiction over the pendent state law claims. A major deterrent to the litigation of sexual harassment claims has been the financial investment necessary to obtain elusive remedies. Reinstatement is often not an option, as the victim of sexual harassment may be unwilling to return to a hostile environment or has found other employment during what can be years of litigation. An injunction provides only prospective relief, and back pay may be offset by subsequent earnings in a new job. Under the Civil Rights Act of 1991, victims of sexual harassment can recover compensatory damages for medical bills or psychiatric treatment necessary as a result of harassment. Compensatory damages include future pecuniary losses, emotional pain, suffering, inconvenience, mental anguish, loss of enjoyment of life, and other nonpecuniary losses. Punitive damages may be recovered when the plaintiff can demonstrate that the employer acted with malice or with reckless indifference to the individual's federally protected rights.

The number of state court actions or pendent state claims for damages may diminish as a result of an enhanced federal law. Courts will not allow double recovery. In *Bristow* v. *Drake Street* (1992) the court declined to award compensatory damages to a sexually harassed female employee when a jury awarded her $30,000 for intentional infliction of emotional distress and to award compensatory damages would be to issue duplicative judgments.

Experts play an important role in sexual harassment cases. In *Robinson* v. *Jacksonville Shipyards, Inc.* (1991), as well as a number of other cases, the court relied on the testimony of expert witnesses on sexual harassment and sexual stereotyping to conclude that pinups of nude and partially nude women, demeaning sexual remarks, and other harassment created a hostile working environment. The Civil Rights Act reversed the Supreme Court decision in *West Virginia University Hospitals, Inc.* v. *Casey* (1991), in which the Court held that expert-witness fees were not part of the "reasonable" attorney fees awarded under the Civil Rights Attorneys Fees Awards Act or Title VII and thus recovery for such fees was limited to $30.00 per day. Under the act, prevailing parties should be able to recover fees for expert consultation throughout the course of litigation, as the act provides for "expert fees," not only expert-witness fees.

Jury trials are seldom allowed under Title VII. Under the 1991 act, any party to a discrimination action may demand a jury trial when compensatory or punitive damages are sought. In addition, the court may not inform the jury about the cap on damages.

Section 1983

Section 1983 has formed the basis for many sexual harassment claims against government bodies, both alone and in conjunction with a Title VII claim. To establish liability under §1983, a plaintiff must demonstrate that the defendant's actions deprived her of the rights, privileges, or immunities granted by the Constitution and that the defendant acted under color of state law (*Gomez* v. *Toledo*, 1980). In contrast to Title VII, "section 1983 is not a statute with any substantive content but merely the conduit through which individuals may obtain redress for violations to rights protected by the federal constitution or by federal law" (*Monell* v. *Department of Social Servs.*, 1978, pp. 690–91). Section 1983 may not be used to sustain an action for violation to Title VII only, however. Similarly, a plaintiff may not bring a §1983 action based on Title VII against a defendant who could not be sued directly under Title VII.

Any injured person may sue under §1983, and any person who acts under color of state law may be sued. The "person" who acts under color of state law has been broadly construed, and includes cities, counties, and other local governmental entities. Private persons may be liable under §1983 if the nexus between the action and the state is close enough to satisfy the state action requirement of the Fourteenth Amendment. Section 1983 covers actions of federal officials done under color of state law, but not actions under color of federal law.

The Eleventh Amendment bars a suit against the state unless the state expressly waives sovereign immunity or injunctive relief is sought.

Supervisors are not vicariously liable for the §1983 violations of their subordinates unless the supervisor knew or should have known of the misconduct and could have prevented future harm but did not. Furthermore, municipalities and other local government entities may not be sued for the acts of their employees unless the unconstitutional conduct stems from governmental "custom" or a "policy statement, ordinance, regulation, or decision officially adopted and promulgated by the body's officers," and the government entity has notice of the custom or policy.

A plaintiff need not exhaust state administrative procedures before bringing a §1983 action, but if the plaintiff has sought a state administrative review, the findings of fact are binding in the federal action.

A plaintiff in a §1993 action for damages is entitled to a jury trial. No such entitlement exists when the plaintiff seeks only equitable relief. If both damages and equitable relief are sought, a jury will decide the damages claim initially and the court alone will hear the claim for equitable relief.

The plaintiff asserting a §1983 claim must prove its elements by a preponderance of the evidence. In proving a violation of equal protection under the

Fourteenth Amendment, the plaintiff must demonstrate intentional discrimination based on a class characteristic.

A prevailing plaintiff suing for violations of §1983 may recover a court award of reasonable attorneys' fees under 42 U.S.C. §1988, the Civil Rights Attorney's Fees Awards Act, payable by the losing defendant. Such fees generally are awarded to prevailing plaintiffs unless such an award would be unjust.

Section 1985(3)

Section 1985(3) of 42 U.S.C. provides that if two or more persons conspire to deprive another person of equal protection, the victim of the conspiracy may recover damages against any one or more of the conspirators. In order to succeed in a §1985(3) claim, a sexual harassment plaintiff must demonstrate that a conspiracy existed to deprive her of her rights to equal treatment with members of the opposite sex. She is not required to allege that the discriminatory treatment was classwide in its application by the defendant. A plaintiff may demonstrate that the employer and/or supervisors were aware of her grievance, discussed it among themselves, and either did nothing or themselves participated in the harassment.

Title IX

Title IX of the 1964 Civil Rights Act prohibits sex discrimination in any educational program receiving federal financial assistance. Several courts have applied the standards governing Title VII to Title IX cases, at least when the action involved employment discrimination, but few sexual harassment victims have sought relief under this statute. In *Alexander* v. *Yale University* (1977) a district court held that quid pro quo harassment was a justifiable claim under Title IX but that a claim based only on allegations of a hostile environment was not viable. The Second Circuit affirmed without addressing the issue of hostile environment when it determined that the issue was moot. In *Moire* v. *Temple University* (1986) the court recognized the hostile environment claim but did not find such an environment in the case before it.

The First Circuit addressed the issue in *Lipsett* v. *University of Puerto Rico* (1988). Following the reasoning in *Meritor*, the court held that an educational institution is liable for hostile environment sexual harassment by its supervisors or coworkers upon employees if an institutional official knew, or should have known, of the harassment, unless the official can show that he or she took appropriate steps to halt it. In this action by a female surgical resident the constant attack by male residents on the capabilities of the plaintiff and other female residents and frequent sexual comments created a hostile environment so blatant that it put the defendants on constructive notice that sex discrimination permeated the residency program. In *Duron* v. *Hancock* (1993) the former owners of an unincorporated hairstyling school could be found directly liable for a supervisor's alleged sexual harassment of an instructor in a Title IX action when the former owners delegated authority to the supervisor to run the school and could fire or promote the plaintiff.

RICO Actions

The Racketeer Influenced and Corrupt Organizations Act (RICO), 18 U.S.C. §§1961–1968, provides a private civil action to recover treble damages for injury to a person in her or his business or property for a violation of §1962. That section prohibits the use of income derived from a "pattern of racketeering activity" (RICO, 18 U.S.C. §19612) to acquire an interest in, establish, or operate an enterprise engaged in or affecting interstate commerce; the acquisition or maintenance of any interest in an enterprise through a pattern of racketeering activity; conducting or participating in the conduct of an enterprise through a pattern of racketeering activity; and conspiring to violate any of these provisions. Allegations of a prolonged pattern and practice of sexual harassment may be sufficient to demonstrate a pattern of racketeering activity. In *Hunt* v. *Weatherbee* (1986), allegations regarding the union shop steward's use of sexual harassment to coerce a female journeyman carpenter into purchasing raffle tickets for a union "political action fund" and of a pattern of sexual harassment against the plaintiff and other female union members gave rise to a RICO claim when the union business agent allegedly condoned and ratified the harassing conduct.

STATE REMEDIES FOR SEXUAL HARASSMENT

State Fair Employment Practice Laws

Most states have employment statutes that prohibit discrimination based on race, color, sex, religion, national origin, age, or handicap. Some states have distinct provisions related to sexual harassment, and such provisions may provide the exclusive statutory remedy. In *Bergeson* v. *Franchi* (1992) a former employee who was subjected to conduct by her employer including sexual advances; touching; threats; attempts to kiss her; discussion of rape and infidelity; begging her to fly to Florida with him and stay at his house there; and attempts to bribe her to accept his advances with a raise, a fur coat, money to finance her restaurant business, and medical expenses could not bring an independent cause of action under both the Massachusetts civil rights act and the Massachusetts discrimination statute based on a claim for sexual harassment when to permit such duplication of remedies would allow claimants to bypass the procedural prerequisites defined by the legislature, crippling the effectiveness of this specific statutory remedy.

State antidiscrimination statutes generally are similar to Title VII, but differences in coverage, exhaustion of jurisdictional requirements, applicable statutes of limitation, the range of possible remedies, or the availability of attorneys' fees may render one or the other preferable in a particular situation. Those statutes that parallel the prohibitions of Title VII have been interpreted similarly (*Gallagher* v. *Witton Enterprises*, 1992).

Although most statutes cover public and private employers, some apply to state workers only. A number of statutes follow Title VII in requiring that the defendant employ at least fifteen people before the antidiscrimination statute applies. However, many have no such minimum requirement and in others the minimum number of employees ranges from two to twelve.

Exhaustion of administrative requirements is required by almost half of the state antidiscrimination statutes. Like Title VII, some state antidiscrimination statutes also prohibit retaliation against persons who have asserted their rights under the relevant law.

A jury trial is available under almost half the state statutes. A number of state antidiscrimination statutes provide for a range of relief beyond Title VII's provisions, including actual damages; incidental damages for pain and suffering; compensatory damages; treble damages; damages for pain, humiliation, mental anguish, and embarrassment; and punitive damages. Some limit damage awards to $1,000 to $6,000.

More than half of the state antidiscrimination statutes provide for an award of attorneys' fees, at least to prevailing plaintiffs. In some states, prevailing defendants are entitled to fees if the action was brought in bad faith or if the complaint was frivolous. Attorneys' fee awards are available under Title VII. In the absence of a fee provision in the state statute, a contingent fee arrangement is possible if damages are available under the state statute.

State Equal Rights Amendments

"The equal protection guaranty and a fortiori an equal rights amendment condemn discrimination on grounds of sex" (*Attorney General* v. *Massachusetts Interscholastic Athletic Ass'n*, 1979, p. 351). In *O'Connell* v. *Chasdi* (1987) the Massachusetts Supreme Court construed the state equal rights amendment to prohibit sexual harassment in the workplace. State equal rights amendments seldom are asserted as grounds for a sexual harassment suit, perhaps because of the success of state and federal antidiscrimination laws and the availability of damages under state common law. Courts have also attempted to resolve state statutory and/or common law issues without addressing constitutional claims.

Pendent or Supplemental Jurisdiction

Pendent state claims often are included in Title VII sexual harassment complaints. Courts may assert supplemental jurisdiction over pendent claims that arise out of "a common nucleus of operative fact" with the Title VII action (*United Mine Workers* v. *Gibbs*, 1966, p. 725). Tort theories that have been asserted include intentional infliction of emotional distress, assault and battery, tortious interference with an employment contract, false imprisonment, and negligence.

In *United Mine Workers* v. *Gibbs* (1966) the Supreme Court established a two-pronged standard for pendent state claims. A court must first determine whether it has jurisdiction over the state law claims, and then it must decide whether it should hear them. Jurisdiction may be asserted over state claims if (1) there exists a federal claim with substance sufficient to confer subject matter jurisdiction on the court, (2) the state and federal claims derive from a common nucleus of operative fact, and (3) the claims are such that the plaintiff would ordinarily be expected to try them all in one proceeding. Gibbs set out a number of factors that courts have considered in deciding whether to exercise jurisdiction over pendent state claims:

1. Judicial economy, convenience, and fairness to the litigants
2. Whether the pendent state claims present unsettled questions of state law
3. Whether state issues predominate in terms of proof, scope of issues raised, or comprehensiveness of remedies sought
4. Whether the existence of divergent state and federal claims and theories would confuse a jury

Courts have declined to exercise pendent jurisdiction over related state claims when the only substantial federal claim arose under Title VII (*Bouchet* v. *National Urban League, Inc.*, 1984), when state law claims invoke undecided issues of state law (*Guzman Robles* v. *Cruz*, 1987), or when the defendant would be unduly prejudiced if the claims were tried in one proceeding (*Swanson* v. *Elmhurst Chrysler/Plymouth, Inc.*, 1987).

Plaintiffs may also plead state civil rights claims under state human rights or fair employment acts. In *Bridges* v. *Eastman Kodak Co.* (1992) the court exercised pendent jurisdiction over the plaintiff's state human rights act claims despite the defendants' contention that both jury confusion and predomination of state issues were likely to result because of the disparity in damages awarded under state and federal laws and different standards of employer liability. The CRA provides that the jury not be informed of damages limitations, and juries are instructed regularly on different theories of relief, even when only federal claims are present. "The mere existence of one difference in legal theory does not create a sufficient likelihood of jury confusion to justify dismissing plaintiffs' HRL claims" (*Bridges*, p. 1179).

A court may refuse to hear state law claims if doing so would complicate the trial and result in the predominance of state issues. Jury confusion may result if state law standards for proving sex discrimination are stricter or broader than under Title VII. If the federal claims are dismissed before trial, state claims may be dismissed as well. "The district court, of course, has the discretion to determine whether its investment of judicial energy justifies retention of jurisdiction . . . or if it should more properly dismiss the claims without prejudice" (*Otto* v. *Heckler*, 1986, p. 338).

Liability under Common Law Theories

Under common law theories applicable to sexual harassment an employer may be directly or indirectly liable for its own conduct or that of its employees. The doctrine of respondeat superior extends liability to the employer for acts of its agent when the agent's act is expressly authorized by the principal, when the act is committed within the scope of employment and in furtherance of the principal's business, or when the act is ratified by the principal (*Restatement [Second] of Agency*, 1958). Obviously, sexual harassment is seldom officially authorized by the employer or committed in furtherance of the principal's business, except perhaps in cases involving revealing dress requirements. Conduct is implicitly ratified when it involves quid pro quo sexual harassment. In *Lehmann* v. *Toys 'R' Us, Inc.* (1993) the New Jersey Supreme Court noted that in cases of quid pro quo sexual harassment the employer is strictly liable for all equitable damages and relief, including hiring or reinstating the victim, disciplining, transferring or firing the harasser, proving back or front pay, and taking preventative and remedial measures at work. In cases of hostile environment sexual harassment, employers are vicariously liable if the supervisor acted within the scope of his or her employment, and, if the supervisor acted outside the scope of employment, the employer will be vicariously liable if the employer contributed to the harm through its negligence, intent, or apparent authorization of the harassing conduct, or if the supervisor was aided in the commission of the harassment by the agency relationship. The employer may be vicariously liable for compensatory damages stemming from a supervisor's creation of a hostile work environment if the employer grants the supervisor the authority to control the working environment and the supervisor abuses that authority to create a hostile environment. An employer may also be held vicariously liable for compensatory damages for supervisory sexual harassment occurring outside the scope of the supervisor's authority if the employer had actual or constructive notice of the harassment, or even if the employer did not have actual or constructive notice, if the employer negligently or recklessly failed to have an explicit policy that bans sexual harassment and that provides an effective procedure for the prompt investigation and remediation of such claims.

The employer may be liable for punitive damages only in the event of actual participation or willful indifference. In *Monge* v. *Superior Court* (1989) the plaintiff pleaded facts sufficient to demonstrate oppression and malice for purposes of punitive damages when she alleged that corporate officers conspired to display the message "How about a little head?" on her computer terminal, then retaliated against her when she complained.

Tort Claims Based on Sexual Harassment

In *Kerans* v. *Porter Paint Co.* (1991) the Ohio Supreme Court created a common law tort remedy for sexual harassment, holding that workplace sexual harassment could be a tort in and of itself for which the victim could file suit not only against the offending employee, but also against the employer. To hold the employer liable, the plaintiff must prove that the alleged harasser had a past of sexually harassing behavior and the employer knew or should have known about it. In *Kerans* a store employee was molested by a supervisor five separate times in one day. As a result of this conduct, the plaintiff suffered severe emotional injury, including nightmares, flashbacks, and stomach cramps, and was in psychiatric care for at least two years. The employer took no immediate action when she finally complained, even though the alleged harasser had engaged in similar conduct on at least eight other occasions with five other female employees and the employer knew or should have known about these incidents. The company had responded to other complaints with a "boys will be boys" attitude.

The state supreme court concluded that at least a genuine issue of fact existed for a jury as to whether employer liability could be imposed in this case when the employer had put the alleged harasser in a supervisory position where he could exert control over the victim and cause her to believe that she would have to endure the harassment to keep her job. The court also held liability may be imposed for sexual harassment for failing to take appropriate action against an offending employee when the employer knows or has reason to know that the alleged harasser poses an unreasonable risk of harm to other employees.

Tort law has been recognized repeatedly as a proper remedy for the sexual harassment victim. Actions have been brought under the theories of assault and battery, intentional infliction of emotional distress, invasion of privacy, tortious interference with contractual relations, and others. However, because sexual harassment does not fit neatly into the traditional grounds for relief, and because the courts are unclear about what sexual harassment is, the application of these theories has been inconsistent. Although it is clear that the standards for tortious conduct are connected to the relative authority of the parties, courts are sometimes unwilling to find liability for the abuse of authority if there is no physical injury or loss of a tangible work benefit. Others acknowledge the unique economic coercion inherent in workplace sexual harassment in sustaining claims for intentional infliction of emotional distress. Conceptual distinctions based on the unique character of the relationship between superior and subordinate are proper and necessary. Economic considerations affect coworker relationships as well. Although a coworker harasser may not have the means to alter the victim's work status, her economic dependence on her job may limit her options.

Workers' Compensation Statutes

State workers' compensation statutes generally provide an exclusive remedy for workplace injuries. Many states, however, have developed exceptions to the exclusivity provision of these laws. In *Gantt* v. *Sentry Insurance* (1992) the court declined the invitation to retreat from its long-held view that employees discharged in violation of fundamental public policy may bring a tort action against their employers and held that the exclusive remedy provisions of the state workers' compensation act did not preempt the plaintiff's wrongful discharge claim in an action charging that the plaintiff was constructively discharged in retaliation for supporting a coworker's claim of sexual harassment. The court rejected the defendant's contention that there was something anomalous in restricting the recovery of an employee who incurs a standard industrial injury, while extending a tort remedy to one who suffers similar injuries from sexual or racial discrimination.

Although the scope of injuries covered by state workers' compensation laws varies, most courts have held that common law tort claims arising from sexual harassment are not barred by the statutes. Some courts have found sexual harassment to fall within the willful physical assault or intentional wrong exceptions to exclusivity provisions. Under the doctrine of ratification an employee who was harassed by a supervisor or coworker may state a sexual harassment claim against an employer by alleging that the employer knew of the conduct but did nothing to discipline the offender. Even if a claim is barred against the employer by the state workers' compensation law, a plaintiff may still be able to assert claims against individual harassers. In *Dickert* v. *Metropolitan Life Ins. Co.* (1993) the state workers' compensation act provided the exclusive remedy in a sexual harassment claim against an employer, but a coworker could be held individually liable for an intentional tort committed while acting within the scope of employment.

One point of contention in these cases is whether sexual harassment arises out of employment for purposes of workers' compensation statutes, as illustrated by cases under Missouri law. In *Pryor* v. *United States Gypsum Co.* (1984), an assault and battery action, the District Court for the Western District of Missouri could not conclude that as a matter of law the plaintiff's injuries from sexual harassment arose out of her employment, even though the alleged incidents occurred in the workplace during normal working hours. "The court is simply not prepared to say that a female who goes to work in what is apparently a predominately male workplace should reasonably expect sexual harassment as part of her job, so as to bring any such injuries under the Workers' Compensation Law." However, in *Miller* v. *Lindenwood Female College* (1985), an action charging intentional infliction of emotional distress, the District Court for the Eastern District of Missouri noted that it would be inconsistent to deem sexual harassment by a supervisor as outside the course of employment for purposes of the workers' compensation law but within the course of employment when establishing vicarious liability against the employer for the wrongful acts of its agent. The Eastern District also held that the workers' compensation law barred an action for assault and battery and intentional infliction of emotional distress arising from sexual harassment in *Harrison* v. *Reed Rubber Co.* (1985), when the alleged injuries occurred at the place of employment and arose out of, and in the scope of, the plaintiff's employment. The Missouri State Court of Appeals held in *Hollrah* v. *Freidrich* (1982) that an employee could properly assert tort claims against her employer and a coworker when the record did not indicate that the conduct arose in the course of, and out of, the employment.

In *Cox* v. *Chino Mines/Phelps Dodge* (1993) an employee's injury from three instances of sexual harassment in the workplace did not arise out of employment for purposes of workers' compensation. The incidents included being accosted on the job twice by a coworker who attempted to hug and kiss her and stated that he wanted to take her to bed and hearing a comment by a coworker to several other coworkers that another employee had obtained a job "because he sucked cock." All three incidents were reported, and the coworker who accosted her was threatened with discharge after the second incident. The claimant subsequently saw a psychiatrist and complained of anxiety, gastric pain, depression, sleeplessness, lack of energy, crying spells, and feelings of despair, all due to the incidents of sexual harassment. Her subsequent workers' compensation claim was dismissed, and the court of appeal affirmed, noting that the plaintiff admitted in her testimony that she had experienced no incidents of sexual harassment in approximately nine years of previous employment with her employer and that she was unaware of any other female employee who had previously been sexually harassed at this workplace.

Some courts frame the issue in terms of whether the conduct was employment-related or "personal." In *Fernandez* v. *Ramsey County* (1993), an action by a county employee against supervisors and the county alleging sexually motivated assault and battery stemming from acts including the touching of breasts, massaging of shoulders and neck, dropping paper clips down her blouse, fluffing her hair, and standing so close as to touch her body, the court of appeals held that whether such a common law action arising from employment was barred by the exclusivity provisions of the workers' compensation statute turned on whether the alleged intent to injure was for personal reasons or directed against the employee as an employee; summary judgment was not appropriate when fact issues existed as to whether the alleged acts were for personal reasons or directed against the plaintiff as an employee.

Intentional Infliction of Emotional Distress

The tort of intentional infliction of emotional distress is the most widely asserted state common law claim in sexual harassment actions. A full range of tort remedies, including punitive damages, is available for successful claims of intentional infliction of emotional distress. The potential for significant damages has steered many victims of sexual harassment toward this remedy. Damages are available under Title VII, but plaintiffs may still prefer to bring suit in state court or find a pendent tort action against a particular party viable. In most states, in order to prove intentional infliction of emotional distress, a plaintiff must demonstrate that:

1. The defendant acted outrageously.
2. The defendant intentionally caused or should have known that his conduct would cause plaintiff's emotional distress.
3. The defendant actually and proximately caused plaintiff's severe or extreme emotional distress.
4. The plaintiff suffered severe or extreme emotional distress. (*Restatement [Second] of Torts* §46, 1965; *Fletcher* v. *Western Nat'l Life Ins. Co.*, 1970)

Because the relative nature of the parties' power creates the potential for abuse, the tort of intentional infliction of emotional distress clearly applies to sexual harassment cases. The power of sexual harassment is staggering and often affects not only the victim's job, but her health, relationships, and mental stability. Although many states have heard claims for intentional inflictions of emotional distress, the standard for "outrageous" conduct is unclear. The *Restatement (Second) of Torts* (1965) offers this circular explanation:

> Liability has been found only where the conduct has been so outrageous in nature, and so extreme in degree, as to go beyond all possible bounds of decency and to be regarded as atrocious, and utterly intolerable in a civilized community. Generally, the case is one in which the recitation of the facts to an average member of the community would arouse [her or] his resentment against the actor, and lead [her or] him to exclaim, "Outrageous!" (*Restatement [Second]* §46 comment d)

The notion that women may be more offended by or sensitive to certain behavior may work in the plaintiff's favor in a determination of outrageousness but may be based on an antiquated notion of women's roles. Although the plaintiff failed to show that a cartoon drawn by a coworker in which she was depicted in a "sexually compromising" position with a male coworker was gender-oriented or that the posting of the cartoon created a hostile environment in *Linebaugh* v. *Sheraton Michigan Corp.* (1993), the trial court erred in granting summary disposition to the defendant coworker with respect to the claim of intentional infliction of emotional distress.

> Once having viewed the cartoon at issue, a reasonable factfinder could conclude that the depiction of plaintiff engaged in a sexual act with a coworker constitutes conduct so outrageous in character and so extreme in degree that it goes beyond all bounds of common decency in a civilized society. We note that a number of plaintiff's coworkers testified that the cartoon was offensive. Furthermore, Herring's creation of the cartoon and his delivery of it to Shorkey may well constitute reckless behavior. (*Linebaugh*, pp. 588–89)

The *Restatement* also notes that the distress must be "so severe that no reasonable man could be expected to endure it. The intensity and the duration of the distress are factors to be considered in determining its severity" (*Restatement [Second]* §46 comment j), as well as the response by management to complaints of harassment. In *Laughinghouse* v. *Risser* (1992) the plaintiff proved that her supervisor's conduct was extreme and outrageous for purposes of her outrage claim when during the eighteen months following the plaintiff's refusal of her supervisor's sexual advance, he was constantly critical, cursed, called the plaintiff "stupid," attacked her personal life, threatened to fire her, screamed, threw things, constantly engaged in sexual overtones, and said that he tried to "squeeze" employees until they "popped" if he wanted employees to leave. In *Bustamento* v. *Tucker* (1992) a female employee was harassed almost daily over a two-year period by a coworker who cursed at her; made sexual comments, innuendos, and advances; invaded her privacy by asking her about her marital affairs and sexual relationship with her husband; and threatened her with physical violence, including rape, running her out of the plant, and running her over with his fork-lift. He also used his forklift to terrorize her by driving it at her, attempting to run her over and pinning her against the walls of the plant. The Supreme Court held that in an action for intentional infliction of emotional distress resulting from sexual harassment, when the acts or conduct are continuous on an almost daily basis, by the same action, of the same nature, and the conduct becomes tortious and actionable because of its continuous, cumulative, synergistic nature, a one-year prescription does not commence until the last act occurs or the conduct is abated. But in *Hendrix v. Phillips* (1993) the state court properly held that conduct by an employee, including showing the plaintiff a hole in the crotch of his pants and asking her in the presence of coworkers if she would like to staple the hole closed, showing her a drawing he made depicting fecal matter moving through a colon, a lewd gesture referring to sexual activity he supposed she engaged in with her husband on a vacation trip, a verbal confrontation during which he cursed her, and a series of complaints he filed against her with her supervisor, was "tasteless and rude social conduct" but did not rise to the level necessary to inflict emotional distress. The trial court could grant summary judgment without first ruling on the sufficiency of affidavits from the plaintiff's treating psychiatrist and psychologist tending to show that she suffered severe depression and anxiety as a result of the harassment when the plaintiff failed to establish a prima facie case of liability.

The court should consider the context in which the acts were committed as well as the severity of the acts themselves. In *Dias v. Sky Chefs* (1990) the jury properly found for the plaintiff on her intentional infliction of emotional distress claim. The plaintiff's injury was distinguishable from ordinary employment abuses because it was carried out in the context of an allegedly sexually abusive work environment intentionally established by Sky Chef's local general man-ager; the jury was entitled to consider that context and look behind the manager's specific acts in its determination of outrageousness.

In *Underwood v. Washington Post Credit Union*, an action alleging sexual harassment and intentional infliction of emotional distress by a female credit union employee who had broken off an affair with the chair of the board of the credit union and was subsequently subjected to hostile treatment, a district court held that a finding by the jury that the plaintiff had not been sexually harassed did not mean that the employer and its chair could not be found liable for intentional infliction of emotional distress, despite the defendants' argument that sexual harassment has a lower threshold than intentional infliction of emotional distress. Jury verdicts may be inconsistent, and because the elements of sexual harassment and intentional affliction of emotional distress differ somewhat, it was at least theoretically possible on the facts of this case for the jury to have reached different verdicts on the two claims. The court noted that while general mental distress was not a covered injury, when the emotional distress has as its consequence physical disability, the adminis-trative agency and the courts have both ruled that the injury is a covered one.

Other courts have held that a claim for intentional infliction of emotional distress requires more than what is required for sexual harassment. In *Piech* v. *Arthur Andersen & Co.* (1994) the court noted that the plaintiff's most extreme allegation was that she was subjected to one isolated proposition or advance over four years, and other allegations included being subjected to sexual humor, references to female anatomy, and general discriminatory conduct; such allegations lacked the required elements of being systematic and intentional actions designed to humiliate the plaintiff.

The testimony of treating physicians or psychiatrists may play an important role. In *Benavides* v. *Moore* (1993) the plaintiff did not state a claim for intentional infliction of emotional distress when, although she testified that she felt stress and anguish from her termination because her income decreased and she did not know why she was fired, she admitted that she consulted no psychologists or psychiatrists and had no plans to do so and offered no evidence that directly showed the severity of her distress. Severity of distress is an element of a cause of action for intentional infliction of emotional distress, not only of damages. But in *Hackney* v. *Woodring* (1993), an action by a female employee against her employer alleging assault, battery, false imprisonment, and intentional infliction of emotional distress stemming from acts including touching, fondling, spanking and holding her down in his lap, threatening her life while ripping off her clothes and exposing himself, the court of common pleas improperly granted the employer's motion for judgment notwithstanding the verdict in favor of the plaintiff for the intentional infliction of emotional distress claim and for $15,000 in compensatory damages on the ground that the plaintiff, by failing to introduce expert medical testimony, had not sustained her burden of proof as to damages. The court concluded that expert testimony was not necessary to explain the issues in this case and would have only served the purpose of buttressing plaintiff's credibility, thus usurping the province of the jury.

Because employment status entitles a person to greater protection from insult and outrage, sexual harassment in employment, as defined under Title VII and state antidiscrimination statutes, should be deemed outrageous per se. In *Retherford* v. *AT&T Communications* (1992), a sexual harassment and retaliation action by a former employee against her employer, supervisors, and coworkers, allegations that after she complained about sexual harassment, coworkers followed her around and intimidated her with threatening comments and looks and manipulated circumstances at her work in ways that made her job markedly more stressful were sufficient to satisfy the objective conduct requirement of the tort of intentional infliction of emotional distress. The court noted that any other conclusion would amount to an intolerable refusal to recognize that our society has ceased seeing sexual harassment in the workplace as a playful inevitability that should be taken cheerfully and has awakened to the fact that sexual harassment has a corrosive effect on those who engage in it as well as those who are subjected to it, and that such harassment has far more to do with power than it does with sex.

The per se approach has found acceptance in some state courts. In *Howard University* v. *Best* (1984) the District of Columbia Court of Appeals rejected the notion that appears to form the basis for much of the disparity in sexual harassment decisions and recognized that women suffer sexual harassment in the workplace based on outmoded sexual stereotypes and male domination of subordinate female employees. The court thus rejected the view, articulated by the trial court, that, as a matter of law, the degrading and humiliating behavior in this case was at worse a "social impropriety" that did not amount to the intentional infliction of emotional distress.

Although in most states a plaintiff need not have suffered a physical injury to recover for intentional infliction of emotional distress, some courts seem to distinguish between verbal harassment and conduct that includes physical contact. In *Class* v. *New Jersey Life Insurance Co.* (1990) the court held that the conduct of a male supervisor would not have been sufficiently outrageous had it remained verbal, even though he subjected the plaintiff to an eight-week period consisting of daily sexual jokes, personal stories of group sex, invitations to visit his home, asking if she swallowed during oral sex, describing the size of his penis, and commenting that he enjoyed anal sex with women. What made the difference for the court was that the alleged harasser retaliated against the plaintiff for complaining about his conduct. The Restatement supports a distinction between verbal and physical conduct. One court has held that verbal harassment alone is not outrageous conduct unless tangible work benefits are at stake. Another deemed the absence of overt propositions determinative. In *Kinnally* v. *Bell of Pennsylvania* (1990) a phone company engineer was subjected to a "regime of misogynous comments"; one defendant made "vulgar and suggestive comments in her presence, some of which were directed toward plaintiff, and showed a videotape of rabbits mating at a meeting where she was the only female present" (*Kinnally*, p. 1138). Another defendant unnecessarily singled her out as a woman on a memorandum recording attendance rates and repeated to the plaintiff comments made by the defendant and others regarding the ability of women to work as engineers. After a history of superior work performance the plaintiff received an unjustifiably poor work evaluation from one defendant. Plaintiff subsequently suffered a mental breakdown. "However disturbing" the allegations were, "the regime of derision and intimidation" fell short of the state prescription for intentional infliction of emotional distress. "Plaintiff does not claim to be either the recipient or the victim of any overt propositions. Accordingly, her claim of intentional infliction of emotional distress must be dismissed" (*Kinnally*, p. 1145). Several courts have found at least a stated claim for intentional infliction of emotional distress when the challenged conduct included unwelcome touching. When appropriate, an accompanying claim for assault and battery may bolster an emotional distress claim. Allegations of retaliation also may support such a claim. In *Pommier* v. *James L. Edelstein Enterprises* (1993) a female former employee stated a claim for intentional infliction of emotional distress when the plaintiff alleged repeated acts of sexual harassment and a pattern of retaliation in response to her internal complaint of sexual harassment—the defendants allegedly withheld information necessary to perform her job, sabotaged programs she had implemented to ensure she would fail, and interfered with her customer contacts in order to ruin her professional reputation and credibility.

Employment has been considered a property right, and both tangible and hostile environment harassment interfere with the enjoyment of that right. The notion that in the absence of accompanying trespass or assault there was "no harm in asking" (Magruder, 1936) has given way to a heightened societal sensitivity regarding the "bounds of decency." Although the injuries generated by a threat to job security or retaliatory conduct may appear to present a clearer case of intentional infliction of emotional distress, harassment engendered by words, looks, and gestures may in fact be more emotionally debilitating. In the tangible harassment situation an employee may feel wronged and angry because the nature of the injury is straightforward. An employee who is subjected to a hostile work environment and whose job is not directly threatened, however, may be more likely to live with the degradation longer and suffer more far-reaching consequences. Physical symptoms are common; sexual harassment victims experience a range of stress-related ailments including high blood pressure, nausea, chest pains, nervous tics, weakness, insomnia, and headaches.

As in the federal sexual harassment context, courts should analyze the facts from the perspective of a reasonable woman in an employment situation because only this standard can capture the essence of sexual harassment. Some courts have not agreed. In *Garcia* v. *Andrews* (1993) a Texas court rejected the plaintiff's attempt to use the reasonable woman standard to determine what constituted conduct that was extreme and outrageous in cases of intentional infliction of emotional distress, concluding that existing policy is concerned not only with safeguarding freedom of expression, but also with the even-handed disposition of all claims without regard to whether the plaintiff is a woman or a man, is young or old, or is a member of any one of numerous and varied subgroups in our society, each, possibly, with its own standard of decency.

A claim of intentional infliction of emotional distress may be brought against an employer, a supervisor, or a coworker. An employer may be responsible for failing to respond to complaints of sexual harassment by a supervisor or coworker. A showing of intent may not be necessary in this situation; a reckless disregard of the harassing conduct may be sufficient. Generally, the more attenuated the employment relationship between the parties, the greater the injury must be to establish a claim.

Assault and Battery

Assault occurs when a person "acts intending to cause a harmful or offensive contact with the person of the other or a third person or an imminent apprehension of such conduct and . . . the other is thereby put in such imminent apprehension" (*Restatement [Second] of Torts* §21, 1965, §31). Verbal harassment alone without a threat of physical harm thus may not constitute assault. This threat may be in the form of a gesture or movement toward the plaintiff. Liability for battery results from intentional unwelcome physical contact, which may include touching, kissing, embracing, or rubbing up against the body of the plaintiff. In *Waltman* v. *International Paper Co.* (1988) an employee stated claim for battery when she alleged subjection to unwelcome touching and pinching of breasts and thighs and placing of an air hose between her legs. Damages have been awarded for assault and battery based on sexual advances and unwelcome touching. In *Troutt* v. *Charcoal Steak House, Inc.* (1993) an award of $50,000 as punitive damages for sexual battery was made in an action for sexual harassment and assault against a former employer. After the plaintiff's first month at work as a waitress, her supervisor began to make sexually suggestive remarks that escalated into physical contact including putting his hands on her waist and breast, grabbing her buttocks, kissing her on the neck, reaching under her skirt, and grabbing her crotch. The supervisor's conduct caused the plaintiff to suffer extreme emotional distress, sleeplessness, and depression, and she quit her job.

Although touching need not be of sexual areas to be actionable, the plaintiff usually must show that the touching incident itself, apart from previous harassment, caused an injury. Mental suffering is an injury for which damages may be awarded. Evidence of repeated physical contact, however, is more likely to sustain a claim of battery.

Damages available for assault and battery include those for humiliation and fright.

Tortious Interference with Contracts

A plaintiff may recover compensatory and punitive damages from a defendant who "intentionally acts to deprive another of an economic benefit" (*Kyriazi* v. *Western Elec. Co.*, 1978, p. 950). Under this theory, a victim of sexual harassment may recover damages directly from the person who harassed her. In order to state a claim for tortious interference with an employment contract, a plaintiff must prove that:

1. A valid contract existed at the time of the harassment.
2. The defendant, who was not a party to the contract, had knowledge of the contractual relationship.
3. The defendant intentionally interfered with the contract for an improper purpose or by an improper means.
4. The plaintiff suffered damages as a result of the interference. (*Restatement [Second] of Torts* §§766–767, 1979)

Many state courts have recognized actions brought under this theory even when the employment involved is at will. Because the action may not be brought against a party to the employment contract and the plaintiff must demonstrate the loss of an economic benefit, this theory may have limited value. However, it may be useful when supervisors or coworkers force an employee to quit by making her work environment intolerable, or when a supervisor or coworker retaliates against an employee who has rejected his advances by maligning that employee to his superior, who discharges the harassed employee or otherwise alters her employment status. For example, in *Favors* v. *Alco Mfg. Co.* (1988) the plaintiff alleged that her supervisor tortiously interfered with her employment contract when he facilitated her discharge after she rejected his sexual advances. In *Lewis* v. *Oregon Beauty Supply Co.* (1987), punitive damages were warranted when a male coworker's threats, insults, and intimidation forced the plaintiff to leave her job. In *Fisher* v. *San Pedro Peninsula Hospital* (1989), however, a plaintiff nurse did not prove that a doctor's sexual harassment of other nurses negatively affected her employment relationship with the hospital when the court found no evidence that the doctor intended to disrupt the plaintiff's employment relationship through the sexual harassment of others.

A female former employee who alleged, in *Gruver* v. *Ezon Products* (1991), that during the course of her employment she was subjected to various forms of sexual harassment by her supervisor that though reported went unpunished could not argue that, by allowing the harassment to go unpunished, the defendant breached a provision of an employment contract established by the antiharassment terms of the employee handbook. Common law requires that for a policy to become part of an employment contract, it must be part of the offer of employment—an inducement to join the company—and nowhere in the complaint did the plaintiff state that she accepted employment by the defendant because of the antiharassment section of the handbook or that the definite terms of the policy were made known to her prior to her acceptance.

When the employer is the alleged harasser, a breach of contract action may be appropriate. A supervisor cannot be liable for intentional interference with an employment contract if he is acting within the legitimate scope of authority, so a plaintiff must argue that the defendant acted out of improper personal reasons.

In order to establish a claim for intentional interference with an employment contract, the plaintiff must show that the alleged harasser acted intentionally, but a finding of malice is not required for liability. Proof of an interference claim also may require that "the interference either be in pursuit of an improper or wrongful motive or involve the use of an improper or wrongful means" *Lewis* v. *Oregon Beauty Supply Co.*, 1987, p. 434). The motives or means may be defined as improper in a statute or other regulation or a recognized rule of common law, but it is unnecessary to prove all the elements of another tort.

A range of remedies, including punitive damages, is available for intentional interference with an employment relationship.

DEFAMATION, LIBEL, AND SLANDER

A sexual harassment plaintiff may sue for defamation when the employer makes false statements about the employee to coworkers or to a prospective employer. A plaintiff must establish that:

1. The defendant made a false or defamatory statement.
2. The defendant made that statement in an unprivileged communication to a third party.

3. The defendant was at least negligent in communicating the statement.
4. The communication either proximately caused plaintiff special harm or was actionable irrespective of special harm or proximately. (*Restatement [Second] of Torts*, 1977)

Written defamatory matter has traditionally been considered libel, while oral defamation constitutes slander. An individual may prove libel without any proof of special harm. In *Linebaugh* v. *Sheraton Michigan Corp.* (1993), although the plaintiff failed to show that a cartoon drawn by a coworker in which she was depicted in a "sexually compromising" position with a male coworker was gender-oriented or that the posting of the cartoon created a hostile environment, the drawing of the cartoon was actionable as libel irrespective of special harm because the cartoon could be interpreted as depicting the plaintiff in a sexual act with a man other than her husband, thus imputing want of chastity to the plaintiff. Proof of actual damage is required in slander cases unless the slander involves the plaintiff's business, trade, or profession; the commission of a crime by the plaintiff, the contraction of a "loathsome" disease; or the unchasteness of a female plaintiff. In *Garcia* v. *Williams*, 704 F. Supp. 984 (N.D. Cal. 1988) the plaintiff sustained a slander claim when she alleged that her former employer, a judge, had told other people that she was romantically interested in him. In *Chamberlin* v. *101 Realty* (1985) the plaintiff who was discharged for allegedly resisting her employer's sexual advances stated a claim for defamation when the employer made statements implying that the plaintiff had improperly removed property from the employer's office.

Invasion of Privacy

There are several different types of torts under the general heading of invasion of privacy. Applicable to sexual harassment are intrusion, public disclosure of private facts, and false light publicity.

Intrusion

Sexual harassment may constitute the tortious invasion of privacy called intrusion when, for example, an alleged harasser badgers an employee by following her into her office, telephoning her in her office or at home, making sexually related inquiries, or putting her in fear of sexual contact. Under the *Restatement (Second) of Torts* a plaintiff usually can establish intrusion by showing that:

1. The defendant committed an intentional intrusion, physical or otherwise, upon the solitude or seclusion of the employee's private affairs or concerns.
2. This intrusion would be highly offensive to a reasonable person.
3. The plaintiff suffered damages as a result of this intrusion. (*Restatement [Second] of Torts*, 1977)

In the employment context, intrusion usually involves an invasion by the employer or supervisor into an area in which the employee had a reasonable expectation of privacy to elicit personal information from the employee. This tort "is directed to protecting the integrity and sanctity of physical areas a person would naturally consider private and off limits to uninvited, unwelcomed, prying persons" (*Cummings* v. *Walsh Constr. Co.*, 1983, p. 884). Although in some instances physical location may be a factor in determining whether the alleged intrusion is actionable, the challenged conduct may be so offensive that it would be actionable no matter where it occurred. The actions of the defendant must be unwanted, uninvited, and unwarranted. Sexual touching and propositions may support a claim of intrusion. In *Waltman* v. *International Paper Co.* (1988) the plaintiff stated a claim for invasion of privacy when the plaintiff alleged that a coworker placed a high-pressure air hose between her legs.

The right to privacy may be waived by discussing the relevant issues in the workplace. In *Moffett* v. *Gene B. Glick Co.* (1985) the plaintiff's open discussions about her interracial relationship waived a privacy claim based on racial comments and threats by supervisory personnel. Privacy rights may also be waived by acquiescing to the challenged conduct. In *Cummings* v. *Walsh Construction* (1983) the court held that a plaintiff waived her right to privacy when she yielded to her supervisor's sexual advances.

Public Disclosure of Private Facts

Generally, there are four elements to a claim of unauthorized disclosure of private facts:

1. The defendant publicized a private matter about the plaintiff.
2. The publicity would be highly offensive to a reasonable person.
3. The disclosed matter was not of legitimate concern to the public.
4. The plaintiff suffered injury from the publicity. (*Restatement [Second] of Torts*, 1977, §652D)

A plaintiff may negate the effect of a challenged publication by communicating the events herself to third persons.

False Light Publicity

A sexual harassment plaintiff may recover damages for publicity that places her in a false light in the public eye. Publicity requires "communicati[on] to the public at large, or to so many persons that the matter must be regarded as substantially certain to become one of public knowledge" (*Restatement*, 1977, §652D comment a). The false light must be objectionable to a reasonable person, but need not be defamatory. For example, in *Tornson* v. *Stephan* (1988) a federal district court held that a female employee could seek damages for injuries arising from her employer's failure to keep the terms of a sexual harassment settlement confidential by discussing it at a news conference and declaring the lawsuit "without merit" and "totally unfounded."

False Imprisonment

Acts of sexual harassment often include conduct that falls within the parameters of the tort of false imprisonment. False imprisonment involves an act by a person who intends to confine another person "within the boundaries fixed by the act" that results in a confinement of which the confined person is aware. A plaintiff may state a cause of action for false imprisonment when one party restrains another's freedom of movement, such as when a supervisor calls an employee into an office and subsequently blocks the entrance or locks the door. In *Priest* v. *Rotary* (1986) a restaurant owner was guilty of false imprisonment when he picked up a waitress and carried her across the room and later trapped her while he fondled her. Employees who have been forced to remain in supervisors' hotel rooms while on business also may claim false imprisonment. Physical force is not necessary as long as the plaintiff demonstrates unwelcome restraint. Despite the physical nature of the tort, the injury is in large part a mental one, and a successful plaintiff may recover damages for injuries including mental suffering and humiliation.

Loss of Consortium by Partner of Victim

The spouse of a person alleging sexual harassment may bring an accompanying claim for loss of consortium. In several reported opinions, courts have heard loss of consortium claims from husbands whose wives became nervous, depressed, and withdrawn and suffered physical symptoms as a result of sexual harassment at work. Although an injury need not be physically disabling to form the basis of a loss of consortium claim, plaintiffs have suffered physical injuries that gave rise to assault and battery charges or physical symptoms of emotional stress, such as headaches and nausea. In *Bowersox* v. *P. H. Glatfelter Co.* (1988) the court noted that the manifestations of sexual harassment, including depression, severe emotional distress, headaches, and nausea, clearly may result in the deprivation of society and companionship.

Wrongful Discharge

Historically, courts generally considered employment contracts to be "at will" unless otherwise specified, making them terminable with or without cause by either party at any time. Over the years, however, construction of this doctrine has narrowed, and employees have enjoyed an increasing number of implied rights notwithstanding the absence of a formal contract. In a wrongful discharge action a victim of sex discrimination may argue that she has an implied right to be free from conduct that violates public policy, or that the employer has an implied good faith duty to refrain from acting maliciously or arbitrarily when discharging employees. In *Monge* v. *Beebe Rubber Co.* (1974), for example, the New Hampshire Supreme Court ruled in favor of a female employee who was given different duties and ultimately discharged when she refused to submit to her supervisor's sexual advances, noting that "a termination by the employer of a contract of employment at will which is motivated by bad faith or malice or based on retaliation is not in the best interest of the economic system or the public good and constitutes a breach of the employment contract" (*Monge*, p. 551). In *Chamberlin* v. *101 Realty, Inc.* (1985) the district court of New Hampshire noted that the state supreme court had narrowed the scope of *Monge* somewhat by requiring the plaintiff in a wrongful discharge action to show that the defendant was motivated by bad faith, malice, or retaliation and that he or she was discharged for performing an act that public policy would encourage or for refusing to do something that public policy would condemn. The court was convinced, however, that public policy would condemn the endurance of sexual harassment as a means of retaining employment. Evidence that conduct violates Title VII or state antidiscrimination law supports a finding that the conduct was in contravention of an express public policy,

A wrongful discharge action must stem from conduct by a party who has authority to participate in personnel actions against the plaintiff.

In states whose courts have held that the state employment discrimination statute is the exclusive remedy for those claims predicated on the policies or provisions of the state law a wrongful discharge claim may not be viable.

Negligent Hiring, Retention, and Supervision

A number of sexual harassment cases have asserted claims of negligent hiring, retention, and/or supervision. To find negligent hiring or retention, the court generally must find that the employer knew or should have known of the employee's offensive conduct. In *Geise* v. *Phoenix Company of Chicago, Inc.* (1993) the district court improperly dismissed the plaintiff's claims for the negligent hiring and retention of a manager who was sexually harassing her by attempting to kiss and touch her body, placing his hands on her body and objects down the front of her dress. The court recognized a duty on the part of the employer to make a prehiring inquiry into an applicant's history of workplace harassment, given the serious harm that sexual harassment has been legislatively deemed to constitute, the foreseeable hazard of that harm's occurring upon hiring a new manager of a staff comprised primarily of persons not of the manager's gender, the plaintiff's allegation that the employer could have but failed to learn through investigation that the manager had a predisposition to female coworkers, and the plaintiff's allegation of her proximate injuries from the employer's failure to act. The judgment fell short of a declaration of a specific duty to investigate and fully learn potential management employees' sexual harassment history; the court's conclusion was merely that the plaintiff's pleadings support her cause of action, considering the Illinois courts' long-held view that an employer has a duty to exercise ordinary and reasonable care in the employment and selection of careful and skillful co-employees and to discharge that duty with care commensurate with the perils and hazards likely to be encountered in the employee's performance of her job.

> With reference to the serious concern now afforded the issue of sexual harassment in the workplace, we find that the plaintiff sufficiently pleaded a cause of action based on whether the company negligently breached its duty of diligent and cautious hiring in consideration of coworkers. . . . In our judgment, that duty can comprise a need to make the sort of investigation urged by the plaintiff here, and even with that inclusion, it imposes no inappropriate administrative or economic burden for employers. . . . We also find that in being sufficiently broad to address the harm of sexual harassment, that duty serves a prophylactic role in the interest of today's ethical or moral thinking and in the general interest of justice. (*Geise*, p. 1185)

The plaintiff properly stated a claim for negligent retention when she alleged that she suffered proximate injury after she repeatedly informed the company of the manager's sexually harassing conduct toward her and that the company took no action. The plaintiff's complaint was not rendered insufficient by her acknowledgment that the manager's sexual harassment ended after the company verified her complaints; the complaint alleged that before the harassing conduct ended, she complained of it to the company and that the company took no responsive action.

Some courts have held that the tort of negligent supervision or retention requires a showing of bodily injury. In *Laughinghouse* v. *Risser* (1992) the physical harm requirement for emotional distress damages in a negligent retention suit against the employer was satisfied by evidence that the employee suffered life-threatening hives, high blood pressure, angina, fatigue, depression, and post-traumatic stress disorder as a result of her supervisor's harassment.

The exclusivity provisions of state workers' compensation laws may bar negligent hiring, supervision, or retention claims. In *Byrd* v. *Richardson-Greenshields Securities* (1989), however, the Florida Supreme Court held that workers' compensation laws were never intended to address acts of sexual harassment and thus declined to apply the exclusivity provisions to claims of negligent hiring and retention, noting that state and federal policies are strongly committed to eliminating sex discrimination in employment.

CONCLUSION AND FUTURE TRENDS

Although the Supreme Court's recent ruling in *Harris* played an important role in the refinement of sexual harassment law by holding that a plaintiff need not show psychological injury to prove sexual harassment, the court left a number of questions unanswered. Unsettled is whether the objective standard in sexual harassment cases should be the reasonable person or the reasonable woman or victim. While all the opining justices used the reasonable person language, the Court did not explicitly reject the reasonable woman standard.

Because of the availability of damages in Title VII cases under the Civil Rights

Act of 1991, more sexual harassment cases may be litigated in federal court. The *Harris* court did not address how compensatory damages, available under the Civil Rights Act of 1991, can be measured and awarded in light of its decision that proof of psychological injury is not required to prove sexual harassment.

Finally, also in dispute is the scope of employer liability in hostile environment cases. The issue was not relevant in *Harris*, but in *Kauffman* v. *Allied Signal* (1992) the Supreme Court refused to review a decision by the Sixth Circuit holding that the proper standard for determining employer liability for a supervisor's actions is whether the supervisor's conduct was foreseeable and within the scope of employment.

References

Alexander v. *Yale University*, 459 F. Supp. 1 (D. Conn. 1977), *aff'd*, 631 F.2d 178 (2d Cir. 1980).

Andrews v. *City of Philadelphia*, 895 F.2d 1469 (3d Cir. 1990).

Attorney General v. *Massachusetts Interscholastic Athletic Ass'n*, 378 Mass. 343, 393 N.E.2d 284 (1979).

Austin v. *State of Hawaii et al*, 759 F. Supp. 612 (D. Haw. 1991), *aff'd*, 967 F.2d 583 (9th Cir. 1992).

Babcock v. *Frank*, 729 F. Supp. 279 (S.D.N.Y. 1990).

Benavides v. *Moore*, 848 S.W.2d 190 (Tex. Ct. App. 1993).

Bergeson v. *Franchi*, 783 F. Supp. 713 (Tex. Ct. App. 1992).

Bigoni v. *Pay 'n Pak Stores*, 746 F. Supp. 1 (D. Or. 1990).

Bouchet v. *National Urban League, Inc.*, 730 F.2d 799 (D.C. Cir. 1984).

Bowersox v. *P. H. Glatfelter Co.*, 677 F. Supp. 307 (M.D. Pa. 1988).

Boyd v. *James S. Hayes Living Health Care Agency*, 671 F. Supp. 1155, 1165 (W.D. Tenn. 1987).

Bridges v. *Eastman Kodak Co.*, 800 F. Supp. 1172 (S.D.N.Y. 1992).

Bristow v. *Drake Street*, 57 Fair Empl. Prac. Cas. (BNA) 1367 (N.D. Ill. 1992).

Broderick v. *Ruder*, 685 F. Supp. 1269 (D.D.C. 1988).

Bundy v. *Jackson*, 641 F.2d 934 (D.C. Cir. 1981).

Bustamento v. *Tucker*, 607 So.2d 532 (La. 1992).

Byrd v. *Richardson-Greenshields Securities*, 552 So.2d 1099 (Fla. 1989).

Canada v. *Board Group, Inc.*, 1992 WL 387581 (D. Nev. Oct. 27, 1992).

Carmon v. *Lubrizol Corp.*, 64 Fair Empl. Prac. Cas. (BNA) 481 (5th Cir. 1994).

Chamberlin v. *101 Realty, Inc.*, 626 F. Supp. 865 (D.N.H. 1985).

The Civil Rights Act of 1964, 42 U.S.C. § 1983.

The Civil Rights Act of 1964, Title VII, 42 U.S.C. §2000e *et. seq.*

The Civil Rights Act of 1964, §42 U.S.C. 1985.

Civil Rights Attorney's Fees Awards Act, 42 U.S.C. §1988.

Class v. *New Jersey Life Insurance Co.*, 746 F. Supp. 776 (N.D. Ill. 1990).

Corne v. *Bausch & Lomb, Inc.*, 390 F. Supp. 161 (D. Ariz. 1975), *vacated*, 562 F.2d 55 (9th Cir. 1977).

Cox v. *Chino Mines/Phelps Dodge*, 850 P.2d 1038 (N.M. Ct. App. 1993).

Cummings v. *Walsh Constr. Co.*, 561 F. Supp. 872 (S.D. Ga. 1983).

Danna v. *New York Telephone Co.*, 752 F. Supp. 594 (S.D.N.Y. 1990).

Dias v. *Sky Chefs*, 919 F.2d 1370 (9th Cir. 1990), *vacated on other grounds*, 111 S. Ct. 532, *on remand*, 948 F.2d 532 (9th Cir. 1991), *cert. denied*, 112 S. Ct. 1294 (1992).

Dickert v. *Metropolitan Life Ins. Co.*, 428 S.E.2d 700 (S.C. 1993).

Dirksen v. *City of Springfield*, 64 Fair Empl. Prac. Cas. (BNA) 116 (C.D. Ill. 1994).

Drinkwater v. *Union Carbide Corp.*, 904 F.2d 853 (3d Cir. 1990).

Duron v. *Hancock*, 64 Fair Empl. Prac. Cas. (BNA) 81 (D. Kan. 1993).

EEOC v. *Gurnee Inn Corp.*, 48 Fair Empl. Prac. Cas. (BNA) 871 (N.D. Ill. 1988), *aff'd*, 914 F.2d 815 (7th Cir. 1990).

Ellison v. *Brady*, 924 F.2d 872 (9th Cir. 1991).

Equal Employment Opportunity Guidelines on Discrimination Because of Sex, 29 C.F.R. § 1604.11 (1993).

Favors v. *Alco Mfg. Co.*, 186 Ga. App. 480, 367 S.E.2d 328 (1988).

Fernandez v. *Ramsey County*, 495 N.W.2d 859 (Minn. Ct. App. 1993).

Fisher v. *San Pedro Peninsula Hospital*, 214 Cal. App. 3d 590, 262 Cal. Rptr. 842 (1989).

Fletcher v. *Western Nat'l Life Ins. Co.*, 10 Cal. App. 3d 376, 89 Cal. Rptr. 78 (1970).

Gallagher v. *Witton Enterprises*, 59 Fair Empl. Prac. Cas. (BNA) 1251 (1st Cir. 1992).

Gantt v. *Sentry Insurance*, 1 Cal. 4th 1083, 4 Cal. Rptr.2d 874, 824 P.2d 680 (Cal. 1992).

Garcia v. *Andrews*, 867 S.W.2d 409 (Tex. Ct. App. 1993).

Geise v. *Phoenix Company of Chicago, Inc.*, 615 N.E.2d 1179 (Ill. Ct. App. 1993).

Gomez v. *Toledo*, 446 U.S. 635 (1980).

Graham v. *Bendix Corp.* 585 F. Supp. 1036 (N.D. Ind. 1984).

Greenland v. *Fairtron Corp.*, 500 N.W.2d 36 (Iowa 1993).

Gruver v. *Ezon Products*, 64 Fair Empl. Prac. Cas. (BNA) 270 (M.D. Pa. 1991).

Guzman Robles v. *Cruz*, 670 F. Supp. 54 (D.P.R. 1987).

Hackney v. *Woodring*, 622 A.2d 286 (Pa. Super. Ct. 1993).

Hansel v. *Public Service Co.*, 778 F. Supp. 1126 (D. Colo. 1991).

Harris v. *Forklift Systems, Inc.*, 114 S. Ct. 367 (1993).

Harrison v. *Chance*, 797 P.2d 200 (Mont. 1990).

Harrison v. *Reed Rubber Co.*, 603 F. Supp. 1457 (E.D. Mo. 1985).

Heelan v. *Johns-Manville Corp.*, 451 F. Supp. 1382 (D. Colo. 1978).

Hendrix v. *Phillips*, 207 Ga. App. 394, 428 S.E.2d 91 (Ga. Ct. App. 1993).

Henson v. *Dundee*, 682 F.2d 897 (11th Cir. 1982).

Hicks v. *Gates Rubber Co.*, 833 F.2d 1406 (10th Cir. 1987).

Hollrah v. *Freidrich*, 634 S.W.2d 221 (Mo. Ct. App. 1982).

Howard University v. *Best*, 484 A.2d 958 (D.C. 1984).

Huebschen v. *Department of Health and Social Services*, 716 F.2d 1167 (7th Cir. 1983).

Hunt v. *Weatherbee*, 626 F. Supp. 1097 (D. Mass. 1986).

Jenson v. *Eveleth Taconite Co.*, 139 F.R.D. 657 (D. Minn. 1991).

Jones v. *Flagship International*, 793 F.2d 714 (5th Cir. 1986), *cert. denied*, 479 U.S. 1065 (1987).

Jones v. *Wesco*, 846 F.2d 1154 (8th Cir. 1988).

Juarez v. *Ameritech Mobile Communications*, 746 F. Supp. 798 (N.D. Ill. 1990).

Kauffman v. *Allied Signal*, 970 F.2d 178 (6th Cir. 1992), *cert. denied*, 113 S. Ct. 831 (1992).

Keppler v. *Hinsdale Township High School District 86*, 715 F. Supp. 862 (N.D. Ill. 1989).

Kerans v. *Porter Paint Co.*, 575 N.E.2d 428 (Ohio 1991).

Kinnally v. *Bell of Pennsylvania*, 748 F. Supp. 1136 (E.D. Pa. 1990).

Kyriazi v. *Western Elec. Co.*, 461 F. Supp. 894 (D.N.J. 1978), *modified*, 473 F. Supp. 786 (D.N.J. 1979), *aff'd*, 647 F.2d 388 (3d Cir. 1981).

Laughinghouse v. *Risser*, 786 F. Supp. 920 (D. Kan. 1992).

Lehmann v. *Toys 'R' Us, Inc.*, 133 N.J. 587, 626 A.2d 445 (N.J. 1993) (Garibaldi, J.).

Lewis v. *Oregon Beauty Supply Co.*, 302 Or. 616, 733 P.2d 430 (1987).

Linebaugh v. *Sheraton Michigan Corp.*, 198 Mich. App. 335, 497 N.W.2d 585 (1993).

Lipsett v. *University of Puerto Rico*, 864 F.2d 881 (1st Cir. 1988).

Magruder, C. (1936). "Mental and Emotional Disturbance in the Law of Torts." *Harvard Law Review* 49: 1033, 1055.

Mays v. *Williamson & Sons, Janitorial Servs.*, 591 F. Supp. 1518 (E.D. Ark. 1984), *aff'd*, 775 F.2d 258 (8th Cir. 1985).

Meritor Savings Bank v. *Vinson*, 477 U.S. 57 (1986).

Miller v. *Aluminum Co. of Am.*, 679 F. Supp. 495, 502 (W.D. Pa.), *aff'd*, 856 F.2d 184 (3d Cir. 1988).

Miller v. *Lindenwood Female College*, 616 F. Supp. 860 (E.D.Mo. 1985).

Moffett v. *Gene B. Glick Co.*, 621 F. Supp. 244 (N.D. Ind. 1985).

Moire v. *Temple University*, 613 F. Supp. 1360 (E.D. Pa. 1983), *aff'd*, 800 F.2d 1136 (3d Cir. 1986).

Monell v. *Department of Social Servs.*, 436 U.S. 658 (1978).

Monge v. *Beebe Rubber Co.*, 114 N.H. 130, 316 A.2d 549 (1974).

Monge v. *Superior Court*, 176 Cal. App.3d 503, 222 Cal. Rptr. 842, 860 (1989).

Nash v. *Electrospace System, Inc.*, 9 F.3d 401 (5th Cir. 1993).

O'Connell v. *Chasdi*, 400 Mass. 686, 511 N.E.2d 349 (1987).

Otto v. *Heckler*, 802 F.2d 337 (9th Cir. 1986).

Paroline v. *Unisys Corp.*, 879 F.2d 100 (4th Cir. 1989).

Petrosky v. *Washington-Greene County Branch Pa. Assoc. for the Blind*, 663 F. Supp. 821 (1987).

Piech v. *Arthur Andersen & Co.*, 64 Fair Empl. Prac. Cas. (BNA) 439 (N.D. Ill. 1994).

Pommier v. *James L. Edelstein Enterprises*, 816 F. Supp. 476 (N.D. Ill. 1993).

Priest v. *Rotary*, 634 F. Supp. 571 (N.D. Cal 1986).

Pryor v. *United States Gypsum Co.*, 47 Fair Empl. Prac. Cas. (BNA) 159 (W.D. Mo. 1984).

Racketeer Influenced and Corrupt Organizations Act. Ct. 1138 (1991). (RICO), 18 U.S.C. §1961–1968.

Radtke v. *Everett*, 56 Fair Empl. Prac. Cas. (BNA) 923 (Mich. Ct. App. 1991).

Restatement (Second) of Torts (1977).

Restatement (Second) of Torts (1965).

Restatement (Second) of Agency (1958).

Retherford v. *AT&T Communications*, 844 P.2d 949 (Utah 1992).

Robinson v. *Jacksonville Shipyards, Inc.*, 760 F. Supp. 1486 (M.D. Fla. 1991).

Ross v. *Double Diamond, Inc.*, 672 F. Supp. 261 (N.D. Tex. 1987).

Sanchez v. *City of Miami Beach*, 720 F. Supp. 974 (S.D. Fla. 1989).

Saxton v. *American Tel. & Tel. Co.*, 785 F. Supp. 760 (N.D. Ill. 1992), *aff'd*, 10 F.3d 526 (7th Cir. 1993).

Shrout v. *Black Clawson*, 689 F. Supp. 774 (S.D. Ohio 1988).

Sprogis v. *United Airlines, Inc.*, 444 F.2d 1194 (7th Cir.), *cert. denied*, 404 U.S. 991 (1971).

Swanson v. *Elmhurst Chrysler/Plymouth, Inc.*, 43 Fair Empl. Prac. Cas. (BNA) 399 (N.D. Ill. 1987).

Texas Dep't. of Community Affairs v. *Burdine*, 450 U.S. 248 (1981).

Tomson v. *Stephan*, 696 F. Supp. 1407 (D. Kan. 1988).

Troutt v. *Charcoal Steak House, Inc.*, 835 F. Supp. 899 (W.D. Va. 1993).

Underwood v. *Washington Post Credit Union*, 59 Fair Empl. Prac. Cas. (BNA) 952 (D.C. Sup. Ct. 1992).

United Mine Workers v. *Gibbs*, 383 U.S. 715 (1966).

Waltman v. *International Paper Co.*, 47 Fair Empl. Prac. Cas. (BNA) 671 (W.D. La. 1988), *rev'd on other grounds*, 875 F.2d 468 (5th Cir. 1989).

Watts v. *New York Police Department*, 724 F. Supp. 99 (S.D.N.Y. 1989).

Weiss v. *Amoco Oil Co.*, 142 F.R.D. 311 (S.D. Iowa 1992).

West Virginia University Hospitals, Inc. v. *Casey*, 111 S. Ct. 1138 (1991).

13 VINSON V. TAYLOR

(APPELLATE COURT DECISION, 1985)

Spottswood W. Robinson, III, Chief Judge:

This appeal presents principally the question whether a corporate employer is accountable under Title VII of the Civil Rights Act of 1964, as amended by the Equal Employment Opportunity Act of 1972, for its supervisor's sexual harassment of a woman employee notwithstanding the employer's lack of actual knowledge thereof. The District Court answered in the negative.[1] We conclude that this holding is inconsistent with the intent of Title VII, and accordingly reverse.

I

We launch our review with a summary of the pertinent facts, as they were accepted by the District Court. In 1974, appellant Mechele Vinson met appellee Sidney L. Taylor, who was a vice president of appellee Capital City Federal Savings and Loan Association and the manager of its northeast branch. At Vinson's request, Taylor gave her an application for employment which

Federal Reporter 753, 2d Series. Mechele VINSON, Appellant v. Sidney L. TAYLOR, et al. United States Court of Appeals, District of Columbia Circuit. Argued February 16, 1982. Decided January 25, 1985. Rehearing En Banc Denied May 14, 1985. "En banc" refers to the full court (*Ed.*).

she completed and returned, and promptly thereafter she was hired by Capital City. With Taylor as her supervisor, Vinson began her employment as a teller-trainee, and thereafter was promoted successively to teller, head teller, and finally to assistant branch manager. It is undisputed, and the District Court expressly found, that Vinson's advancement was achieved on merit alone. Vinson worked at the northeast branch for four years, when she took indefinite sick leave, and was discharged two months later for excessive use of that leave.

[1] Vinson brought an action under Title VII against Taylor and Capital City, alleging that she had been victimized by sex discrimination in the form of sexual harassment by Taylor. At trial, the evidence bearing on Taylor's behavior during Vinson's employment was conflicting. Vinson testified that Taylor asked her to have sexual relations with him, claiming that she "owed him" because he had obtained the job for her; that after initially declining his invitation she ultimately yielded, but only because she was afraid that continued refusal would jeopardize her employment. She further testified that thereafter she was forced to submit to sexual advances by Taylor at the northeast branch both during and after business hours, and that often Taylor assaulted or raped her. In addition, she avowed, Taylor caressed her on the job, followed her into the ladies' room when she was there alone, and at times exposed himself to her. . . .

[2] Taylor denied Vinson's accusations of sexual activity and contended that Vinson aired them in retaliation for a business-related dispute. Capital City also controverted Vinson's story, and asserted that any sexual harassment by Taylor was unknown to and unauthorized by it. The District Court rendered judgment for Taylor and Capital City on the grounds that Vinson had not been subjected to sexual harassment or discrimination, and that in any event Capital City would not be accountable. Our interpretation of Title VII leads us to disagree.

II

We first address the District Court's holding that Vinson did make out a case of sex discrimination, even against Taylor. Given due deference to the court's findings of fact, we believe that in critical respects they fatally undermine the legal conclusion that Vinson did not suffer a violation of Title VII.

[3] The District Court found that Vinson "was not required to grant Taylor or any other member of Capital sexual favors as a condition of either her employment or in order to obtain promotion." That finding would have significance had Vinson been confined to a theory of discrimination based on an imposition of sex-oriented conditions of her employment status. An infringement of Title VII is not, however, necessarily dependent upon the victim's loss of employment or promotion.[2]

Depending upon the particular facts, at least two separate avenues may be open to a Title VII plaintiff for a demonstration of unlawful sex discrimination. The first was recognized in *Barnes* v. *Costle*,[3] where we held that abolition of the job of a female employee because she spurned her male superior's sexual advances was an infringement of Title VII.[4] The second approach is illustrated by *Bundy* v. *Jackson*,[5] decided after the District Court's judgment herein, where we sustained a Title VII cause of action in favor of a woman employee seeking relief simply for pervasive on-the-job sexual harassment by her superiors.[6]

[4, 5] Vinson's grievance was clearly of the latter type and, accordingly, her cause counseled an inquiry as to whether Taylor "created or condoned a substantially discriminatory work *environment*, regardless of whether the complaining employees lost any tangible job benefits as a result of the discrimination."[7] The District Court did not undertake a determination on whether a Title VII violation of this nature had occurred. It follows that we must remand [i.e., order the case back to the District Court] in order that the court may ascertain whether, as in *Bundy*, Vinson was subjected to "sexually stereotyped insults" or "demeaning propositions" that illegally poisoned the "psychological and emotional work environment."

> The District Court further found that [i]f [Vinson] and Taylor did engage in an intimate or sexual relationship during the time of [Vinson's] employment with Capital, that relationship was a voluntary one by [Vinson] having nothing to do with her continued employment at Capital or her advancement or promotions at that institution.

This finding leaves us uncertain as to precisely what the court meant. It could reflect the view that there was no Title VII violation because Vinson's employment status was not affected, an error to which we already have spoken. Alternatively, the finding could indicate that because the relationship was voluntary there was no sexual harassment—no "[u]nwelcome sexual advances, requests for sexual favors, or other verbal or physical conduct of a sexual nature . . . ha[ving] the purpose or effect of unreasonably interfering with an individual's work performance or creating an intimidating, hostile, or offensive working environment." If, however, the evidence warranted a finding of sexual harassment by that standard, Vinson's "voluntar[iness]" had no materiality whatsoever.[8]

[6] *Bundy* held that a woman employee need not prove resistance to sexual overtures in order to establish a Title VII claim of sexual harassment. From that point we take what is hardly a major step by recognizing that a victim's capitulation to on-the-job sexual advances cannot work a forfeiture of her opportunity for redress. If capitulation were dispositive, the "cruel trilemma" identified in *Bundy*— in which a victim must choose among acquiescence in the harassment, opposition to it, or resignation from her job—would be an even more hideous quadrilemma featuring a fourth option—to yield and thereby lose all hope of legal redress for being put in this intolerable position in the first place. We cannot ascribe to Congress a willingness to visit such an unenviable quandary upon an employee. A

victim's "voluntary" submission to unlawful discrimination of this sort can have no bearing on the pertinent inquiry: whether Taylor made Vinson's toleration of sexual harassment a condition of her employment.

[7] Another matter, an evidentiary ruling, prompts brief discussion. The District Court refused to allow Vinson to elicit, from other women under Taylor's supervision during her tenure, testimony that assertedly would have established that Taylor sexually harassed them also. Some testimony of this kind was admitted on the issue of notice to Capital City of Taylor's behavior, but Vinson was not permitted to use it in her case-in-chief for other purposes. *Bundy* makes clear that evidence tending to show Taylor's harassment of other women working alongside Vinson is directly relevant to the question whether he created an environment violative of Title VII.[9] Even a woman who was never herself the object of harassment might have a Title VII claim if she were forced to work in an atmosphere in which such harassment was pervasive.[10] The District Court erred when it denied Vinson the opportunity to demonstrate that Taylor had directed his advances toward other women also.

III

The District Court also ruled that Vinson's employer, Capital City, could not be held responsible for any infringements of Title VII by Taylor because it had no notice of the offensive conduct charged to him. To the court, "it seem[ed] reasonable that an employer should not be liable in these unusual cases of sexual harassment where notice to the employer must depend upon the actual perpetrator and when there is nothing else to place the employer on notice."[11] We cannot accept this conclusion or its rationale.

So much as this court has heretofore decided runs counter to the District Court's holding. Nothing before us in *Barnes* suggested that the employer, a federal agency, was aware of the activity of the superior involved, yet we adverted to the general rule that "an employer is chargeable with Title VII violations occasioned by discriminatory practices of supervisory personnel,"[12] and rejected the notion that the superior's conduct insulated the employer merely "because it was a general escapade rather than an agency project." And in *Bundy*, we reaffirmed our continuing allegiance to the proposition that an employer is answerable for discriminatory acts committed by supervisory personnel, though we were not required there to apply that principle to employers without notice, since those having control over personnel practices had full knowledge of the harassment and did virtually nothing to stop it.

Today, however, we are confronted by the question that was not directly and actively litigated in *Barnes* or *Bundy*: Whether Title VII imposes upon an employer without specific notice of sexual harassment by supervisory personnel responsibility for that species of discrimination. We hold that it does.

With exceptions not relevant here, Title VII provides in pertinent part that

[it] shall be an unlawful employment practice for an employer . . . to discriminate against any individual with respect to . . . terms, conditions, or privileges
of employment, because of such individual's . . . sex. . . .

"Employer" is defined as "a person engaged in an industry affecting commerce"
with a workforce of specified size, "and any agent of such a person . . . ," and
"person" includes "associations." Taken literally, then, Title VII as much outlaws
sex discrimination by an "agent" of an association as by the association itself; put
another way, such discrimination by an "agent" of Capital City is as much an
affront to Title VII as it would be if engaged in by Capital City as an entity. It is
clear that Taylor, as manager of Capital City's Northeast Branch, was Capital
City's "agent" with respect to other employees of that branch, and equally clear
that the sexual harassment charged to Taylor was forbidden sex discrimination.

We have encountered nothing impugning our reading of the statutory text as
meaning that infractions of Title VII by agents are unlawful employment practices attributable to their employers. The legislative history of Title VII is virtually barren of indications, one way or the other, of a vicarious responsibility* for
employers. . . .

What the legislative history does not provide can be gleaned, however, from
other persuasive indicators of congressional intent. To begin with, the Equal
Employment Opportunity Commission (EEOC), has promulgated guidelines
which, as "administrative interpretation[s] of the Act by the enforcing agency,"
are "entitled to great deference," especially when they are supported by the
statute and not inconsistent with its legislative history; and EEOC's *Guidelines
on Discrimination Because of Sex* are unambiguous on the subject:

> Applying general Title VII principles, an employer . . . is responsible for its acts
> and those of its agents and supervisory employees with respect to sexual harass-
> ment regardless of whether the specific acts complained of were authorized or
> even forbidden by the employer and regardless of whether the employer knew
> or should have known of their occurrence.

We attach considerable weight to this interpretation, and we agree that treatment of supervisory personnel as "agents" is in conformity with "general Title
VII principles." Our cases have established, as the cornerstone of present
analysis, that sexual harassment is a violation of Title VII. Neither the statutory
language nor its legislative history suggests that, as a trespass on Title VII, it
should be treated any differently from transgressions arising out of racial or religious discrimination. And the caselaw in these latter areas establishes beyond
cavil that "an employer is chargeable with Title VII violations occasioned by discriminatory practices of supervisory personnel."

[8, 9] We have no difficulty in concluding that an employer may be held
accountable for discrimination accomplished through sexual harassment[13] by any

---

*In this case, "vicarious responsibility" refers to the employer's legal liability for the actions of
his corporate agents. (*Ed.*)

supervisory employee with authority to hire, to promote, or to fire. An employer's delegation of this much authority vests in the supervisor such extreme power over the victimized employee that the supervisor's stature as an "agent" of the employer cannot be doubted. We do not believe, however, that vicarious responsibility is limited to discrimination by supervisors so richly endowed. The mere existence—or even the appearance—of a significant degree of influence in vital job decisions gives any supervisor the opportunity to impose upon employees. That opportunity is not dependent solely upon the supervisor's authority to make personnel decisions; the ability to direct employees in their work, to evaluate their performances, and to recommend personnel actions carries attendant power to coerce, intimidate, and harass. For this reason, we think employers must answer for sexual harassment of any subordinate by any supervising superior. . . .

. . . Confining liability, as the common law* would, to situations in which a supervisor acted within the scope of his authority conceivably could lead to the ludicrous result that employers would become accountable only if they explicitly require or consciously allow their supervisors to molest women employees. While modern courts seem more inclined to treat intentional misconduct on the job as arising out of and in the course of the employment . . . there simply is no need to confine either the analysis or the solution where Title VII applies.

To hold that an employer cannot be reached for Title VII violations unknown to him is, too, to open the door to circumvention of Title VII by the simple expedient of looking the other way, even as signs of discriminatory practice begin to gather on the horizon. As the Ninth Circuit has said, "[s]uch a rule would create an enormous loophole in the statutes," one we think the courts should strive to seal. Instead of providing a reason for employers to remain oblivious to conditions in the workplace, we think the enlightened purpose of Title VII calls for an interpretation cultivating an incentive for employers to take a more active role in warranting to each employee that he or she will enjoy a working environment free from illegal sex discrimination. . . .

Employer responsiveness to on-the-job discrimination at the supervisory level is an essential aspect of the remedial scheme embodied in Title VII. It is the employer alone who is able promptly and effectively to halt discriminatory practices by supervisory personnel, and only the employer can provide reinstatement, back pay, or other remedial relief contemplated by the Act. Much of the promise of Title VII will become empty if victims of unlawful discrimination cannot secure redress from the only source capable of providing it. . . .

In sum, we hold that Vinson alleged facts sufficient to state a claim of sex discrimination cognizable under Title VII, and that any discriminatory activity by Taylor is attributable to Capital City. Vinson is entitled to an adjudication of that claim on the evidence, considered in light of the legal principles applicable. To that end, we reverse the judgment appealed from and remand the case to the District Court for proceedings consistent with this opinion.

So ordered.

---

*The "common law" refers to legal principles, not necessarily mentioned in written laws and statutes, that have evolved over time through judicial opinions. (*Ed.*)

NOTES

1. *Vinson* v. *Taylor*, 23 Fair Empl. Prac. Cas. (BNA) 37,42 (D.D.C. 1980).

2. *Bundy* v. *Jackson*, 205 U.S. App. D.C. 444, 456, 641 F.2d 934, 946 (1981).

3. 183 U.S. App. D.C. 90, 561 F.2d 983 (1977).

4. Ibid. at 99, 561 F.2d at 992.

5. *Bundy* v. *Jackson*.

6. 205 U.S. App. D.C. at 453–44, 641 F.2d at 943–44.

7. *Bundy* v. *Jackson*, 205 U.S. App. D.C. at 453–44, 641 F.2d at 943–944 (emphasis in original).

8. The District Court did not elaborate on its basis for the finding of voluntariness, but it may have considered the voluminous testimony regarding Vinson's dress and personal fantasies. . . . Since, under *Bundy*, a woman does not waive her Title VII rights by her sartorial or whimsical proclivities, *Bundy* v. *Jackson*, 205 U.S. App. D.C. at 454, 455–456, 641 F.2d at 944, 945–946, that testimony had no place in this litigation.

9. Such evidence could be critical to a plaintiff's case, for a claim of harassment cannot be established without a showing of more than isolated indicia of a discriminatory environment. *Bundy* v. *Jackson*, 205 U.S. App. D.C. at 453, n. 9, 641 F.2d at 943 n. 9.

10. Cf. *EEOC Decision No. 71-909*, Fair Empl. Prac. Cas. (BNA) at 269–70 (maintenance of working environment in which racial insults against blacks are habitual also violation of white employees' statutory rights).

11. *Vinson* v. *Taylor*, 23 Fair Empl. Prac. Cas. (BNA) at 42. Capital City had a grievance procedure whereby a complaint was first to be made to the aggrieved employee's supervisor, and thereafter the grievance was to be resolved by the division head or the president. . . . Vinson contended that management had been notified of Taylor's alleged harassing conduct by various means, but the District Court found that the employer had no knowledge of it. . . . The court held that notice to Taylor would not constitute notice to Capital City. . . .

12. *Barnes* v. *Costle*, 183 U.S. App. D.C. at 100, 561 F.2d at 993.

13. In determining the appropriateness of attribution, enough specificity must be imparted to "harassment" to filter out personal relationships that are not products of employment-related intimidation. For purposes of this case, we are well served by the criteria reflected in the EEOC *Guidelines*. See 29 C.F.R. § 1604.11(a) (1984). . . . The touchstone of these criteria is that sexual advances must be unwelcome, and must in some way amount to an explicit or implicit term or condition of employment in the sense either of job status or work environment.

VINSON V. TAYLOR

14

(DISSENTING OPINION)

Appellees' suggestion for hearing *en banc* has been transmitted to the full Court. A majority of the judges of the Court in regular active service have not voted in favor thereof. Upon consideration of the foregoing, it is ordered, by the Court *en banc*, that the suggestion is denied.

A dissenting opinion filed by Circuit Judge Bork is attached and is joined by Circuit Judges Scalia and Starr.

Bork, Circuit Judge, with whom Circuit Judges Scalia and Starr join, dissenting from the denial of rehearing en banc:

This case should be heard en banc. It involves important issues of antidiscrimination law, at least two of which are wrongly decided. The panel's resolutions of the various issues before it, taken in combination, produce an unacceptable result. According to the panel opinion, when an employee charges sexual harassment in the workplace, the supervisor charged may not prove that the sexual behavior, far from constituting harassment, was voluntarily engaged in by the other person, nor may the supervisor show that the charging person's conduct was in

Federal Reporter 753, 2d Series. Mechele VINSON, Appellant v. Sidney L. TAYLOR, et al. United States Court of Appeals, District of Columbia Circuit. May 14, 1985.

fact a solicitation of sexual advances. These rulings seem plainly wrong. By depriving the charged person of any defenses, they mean that sexual dalliance, however voluntarily engaged in, becomes harassment whenever an employee sees fit, after the fact, so to characterize it.

The panel opinion explicitly states that a plaintiff's voluntariness in participating in a sexual relationship with her supervisor "can have no bearing on the pertinent inquiry" in a sexual harassment suit brought under Title VII. *Vinson* v. *Taylor*, 753 F.2d 141, 146 (D.C. Cir. 1985). The panel finds legally insignificant the following factual finding by the district court:

> if [Vinson] and Taylor did engage in an intimate or sexual relationship during
> the time of [Vinson's] employment with Capital, that relationship was a volun-
> tary one by [Vinson] having nothing to do with her continued employment at
> Capital or her advancement or promotions at that institution.

. . . This finding may have been irrelevant to environmental, as opposed to quid pro quo, harassment because it speaks of continued employment and advancement. But the panel did not rest on that distinction and rejected voluntariness as a defense in any kind of case. The panel's reasoning on this point is entirely circular. The opinion states that to allow proof of voluntariness on the part of a woman employee would expose her to what the panel sees fit to characterize as a "hideous quadrilemma"—the victim must acquiesce in the harassment, oppose it, resign, or yield and lose all hope of legal redress. . . . Passing the point that yielding and acquiescing would seem to be the same thing, the argument succeeds only because the defendant is denied the right to prove that the "victim" is not that but a willing participant. The rules of evidence are rigged so that dalliance is automatically harassment because no one is allowed to deny it.

The harmfulness of the panel decision is augmented by additional rulings on what evidence is to be admissible in Title VII sexual harassment cases. On the one hand, the panel holds that plaintiffs must be allowed to introduce evidence of their supervisor's behavior toward other employees in an effort to establish a pattern or practice of sexual harassment. . . . On the other hand, the panel also holds that a supervisor must not be allowed to introduce similar evidence of an employee's dress or behavior in an effort to prove that any sexual advances were solicited or welcomed. . . . In this case, evidence was introduced suggesting that the plaintiff wore provocative clothing, suffered from bizarre sexual fantasies, and often volunteered intimate details of her sex life to other employees at the bank. While hardly determinative, this evidence is relevant to the question of whether any sexual advances by her supervisor were solicited or voluntarily engaged in. Obviously, such evidence must be evaluated critically and in the light of all the other evidence in the case, but it is astonishing that it should be held inadmissible.[1] Added to the elimination of any voluntariness defense, these rulings make certain that to be charged is to be guilty.

But it is not the supervisor alone who is deprived of essential defenses. The panel decision makes the employer vicariously liable for the acts of the supervisor even though those facts were wholly unknown to the employer and were directly contrary to his instructions.[2] Of course, the employer is also prohibited from demonstrating that the alleged harassment was instead voluntary participation or that advances made were solicited. The result is that the employer is virtually converted into an insurer that all relationships between supervisors and employees are entirely asexual. Though the employer has no way of preventing sexual relationships, he is defenseless and must pay if they occur and are then claimed to be harassment.[3]

The Supreme Court has never addressed the question of an employer's vicarious liability under Title VII. I would, however, not suggest that we sit en banc to decide that issue were it not clear that the evidentiary rulings already discussed should be reconsidered en banc. That being so, we ought to take up the difficult and important question of an employer's vicarious liability under Title VII for conduct he knows nothing of and has done all he reasonably can to prevent. In doing this, we cannot necessarily import wholesale notions of vicarious liability which are evolving in lower court Title VII cases involving racial discrimination. We have previously recognized that various Title VII doctrines may require some modification before they can be applied in sexual harassment cases.[4] *Bundy* v. *Jackson* 641 F.2d 934, 951 (D.C. Cir. 1981). The doctrine of vicarious liability may be one such doctrine since it is extremely unlikely that a supervisor would harass an employee for the purpose of furthering his employer's business. Indeed, supervisors engaging in such harassment (whether or not in violation of an explicit company policy) would ordinarily be aware that their employer disapproved of their actions.

Therefore, whatever the proper rule in cases involving racial discrimination, it would be appropriate for the en banc court to reexamine the vicarious liability issue in the unique context presented by sexual harassment claims. The panel's rule is at odds with traditional practice which was not to hold employers liable at all for their employee's intentional torts involving sexual escapades. In addition, the panel's rule is at odds with, or is at least a substantial extension of, the prior case law in this circuit. The two prior decisions of this court upon which the panel relied were both cases where the employer was fully aware of the acts of sexual harassment perpetrated by its supervisory employees. *Bundy* v. *Jackson*, 641 F.2d at 943; *Barnes* v. *Costle*, 561 F.2d 983, 1001 (D.C. Cir. 1977) (MacKinnon, J., concurring). Indeed, we qualified our holdings in both cases by indicating that if "a supervisor contravene[s] employer policy without the employer's knowledge and the consequences are rectified when discovered, the employer may be relieved from responsibility under Title VII." *Barnes*, 561 F.2d at 993; *Bundy*, 641 F.2d at 943. Accordingly, the panel in the present case has apparently gone well beyond *Barnes* and *Bundy* in holding this employer vicariously liable for its supervisor's alleged sexual harassment when the employer was not even made aware of and given the chance to rectify the consequences of the harassment alleged. . . .

Perhaps some of the doctrinal difficulty in this area is due to the awkwardness of classifying sexual advances as "discrimination." Harassment is reprehensible, but Title VII was passed to outlaw discriminatory behavior and not simply behavior of which we strongly disapprove. The artificiality of the approach we have taken appears from the decisions in this circuit. It is "discrimination" if a man makes unwanted sexual overtures to a woman, a woman to a man, a man to another man, or a woman to another woman. But this court has twice stated that Title VII does not prohibit sexual harassment by a "bisexual superior [because] the insistence upon sexual favors would . . . apply to male and female employees alike." *Barnes* v. *Costle*, 561 F.2d at 990 n. 55; *Bundy* v. *Jackson*, 641 F.2d at 942 n. 7. Thus, this court holds that only the differentiating libido runs afoul of Title VII, and bisexual harassment, however blatant and however offensive and disturbing, is legally permissible. Had Congress been aiming at sexual harassment, it seems unlikely that a woman would be protected from unwelcome heterosexual or lesbian advances but left unprotected when a bisexual attacks. That bizarre result suggests that Congress was not thinking of individual harassment at all but of discrimination in conditions of employment because of gender. If it is proper to classify harassment as discrimination for Title VII purposes, that decision at least demands adjustments in subsidiary doctrines. See, e.g., *Bundy* v. *Jackson*, 641 F.2d at 951.

NOTES

1. The panel cited no evidentiary rules or authorities in defense of its statement that this evidence should be suppressed. The sole reason given for excluding the evidence was that "under *Bundy* [v. *Jackson*, 641 F.2d 934 (D.C. Cir. 1981)], a woman does not waive her Title VII rights by her sartorial or whimsical proclivities" [chapter 13, n. 8]. I am not aware of anything in Title VII or the Federal Rules of Evidence that authorizes a court to suppress evidence that may be relevant to the presence of discriminatory intent. The panel has thus failed to perform the analysis required before relevant evidence may be excluded.

2. In this case, employer Capital City had an official policy of nondiscrimination. *Vinson* v. *Taylor*, 23 Fair Empl. Prac. Cas. (BNA) 37, 43 (findings of fact Par. 15) (D.D.C. 1980). Accordingly, any acts of harassment by supervisor Taylor were unauthorized and against company policy.

3. In this case, the employer could not have done more to avoid liability without actually monitoring or policing his employees' voluntary sexual relationships. Aside from the very outrageousness of such policing, it would be a very high-cost way, undoubtedly the highest-cost way, of solving the problem. But cf. *Horn* v. *Duke Homes*, 755 F.2d 599 mem. op. (7th Cir. 1985) (Swygert, J.) (holding employer strictly liable in Title VII sexual harassment case in part because "the employer is a more efficient cost avoider than is the injured employee").

4. We recognized in *Bundy* v. *Jackson*, 641 F.2d 934 (D.C. Cir. 1981), for example, that the "literal" *McDonnell-Douglas* test, see *McDonnell Douglas Corp.* v. *Green*, 411 U.S. 792, 802, 805, 93 S. Ct. 1817, 1824, 1825, 36 L.Ed.2d 668 (1973), which normally governs Title VII actions, does not apply "precisely" to Title VII sexual harassment claims. As we explained in *Bundy*, this is because

the *McDonnell* formula presumes the standard situation where the alleged discrimination is due to the bare fact of the claimant's membership in a disadvantaged group. It therefore . . . fails to fit with precision the very unusual, perhaps unique, situation of sexual harassment, where the alleged basis of discrimination is not the employee's gender *per se*, but her refusal to submit to sexual advances which she suffered in large part because of her gender.

641 F.2d at 951 (emphasis in original). Accordingly, it was necessary to modify the *McDonnell* test in *Bundy* so that it would fit the unique situation of the sexual harassment claim.

SEXUAL HARASSMENT LAW IN THE AFTERMATH OF THE HILL-THOMAS HEARINGS

15

SUSAN DELLER ROSS

Anita Hill once said that she hoped history would view her as a catalyst for change. Obviously she has been, and in many ways. As the 1992 elections demonstrated, she inspired many women to run for the Senate and the House, and many other women to change their party registration or their vote. Indeed, notwithstanding the 1994 elections, it is safe to say the Congress will never be the same again. But the impact of her courageous stand has extended to other arenas as well.

Let's consider Professor Hill's impact on sexual harassment law. At the time Hill testified, a woman who had endured sexual harassment had incomplete legal remedies at best. If the harasser had acted blatantly, by firing her or demoting her for rejecting his advances, she could only recover her lost wages and get a court order against future harassment. If she had not lost her job or any pay—if she was someone in Anita Hill's position, that is—she could merely get the court order. Title VII provided no monetary damages to a woman in either situation to compensate her for the pain and humiliation she had suffered, or to punish and deter the man and provide the employer with an incentive to take effective action against harassment.

When the Hill-Thomas hearings began, Congress was considering a civil rights bill that would award monetary damages to victims of sexual harassment for the first time. But President Bush had already vetoed the bill the previous year, veto threats were circulating again, and the proponents of the legislation were convinced it was going nowhere. Then came the hearings. The air was filled, first with the sound of senators proclaiming their aversion to sexual harassment, and then with the sound of senators and Bush administration officials verbally assaulting the actual victim of sexual harassment who had come to testify. Thomas was confirmed. But in the wake of the confirmation, suddenly the veto threats evaporated and the bill became law as the Senate and the president faced the need to convince the women of the country that they were serious about taking action against sexual harassment. Now, under the new law, victims of sexual harassment *can* sue for damages—in amounts up to $300,000 per complainant, depending on the size of the employer.[1]

Lawyers in the field reported that the law quickly made a significant difference. Employers became much more willing to settle claims and began inundating groups like the Women's Legal Defense Fund for help in training employees to recognize and prevent sexual harassment. I believe that without Anita Hill's courageous appearance before the Senate Judiciary Committee we would not now have this remedy.

Another significant development enlarging the remedies for sexual harassment came from the Supreme Court itself. A high school student named Christine Franklin had sued her school under Title IX of the Education Amendments of 1972.[2] She claimed that starting in the tenth grade, one of her teachers had subjected her to continuing sexual harassment. She said that he

> engaged her in sexually oriented conversations in which he asked about her sexual experiences with her boyfriend and whether she would consider having sexual intercourse with an older man, . . . that [he] forcibly kissed her on the mouth in the school parking lot, . . . that he telephoned her at her home and asked if she would meet him socially . . . and that, on three occasions in her junior year, [he] interrupted a class, requested that the teacher excuse Franklin, and took her to a private office where he subjected her to coercive intercourse.[3]

She also claimed that the school took no action to halt the harassment. The federal trial court had dismissed her action, saying she could not sue for damages. The case was appealed all the way to the Supreme Court and was argued shortly after Justice Thomas joined the bench.

Lawyers practicing sexual harassment law on behalf of women plaintiffs were nervous. The Bush administration's Justice Department had filed an amicus brief taking the position that Christine Franklin could not get damages under Title IX, and the Court was now solidly conservative. But in February 1992, when the decision was handed down, all nine justices ruled that Christine could sue for damages (although Justice Scalia, joined by Thomas and Rehnquist, issued a narrower opinion concurring in the judgment). And *these* damages were not even limited by the size of the institution, as were those available under the new civil rights law. Christine's lawyers and supporters were astounded but delighted. Is it not possible that the Court feared the impression that would be created if it ruled *against* a victim of sexual harassment so soon after Professor Hill's testimony? If so, we have Professor Hill to thank for this new protection for women and girls who work or study in the federally funded education programs covered by Title IX. And this full-damages remedy has wrought a sea change in the attention paid to sexual harassment issues in the education world.

Just two years after Professor Hill's testimony, the Court issued yet another unanimous sexual harassment decision, this time rejecting a narrow interpretation of what constitutes a "hostile environment." This term of art is used to distinguish sexual harassment in which a woman loses a job because she rejects sexual advances ("quid pro quo" harassment) from harassment that she endures at work (hence, "hostile environment") but that does not cost her a job opportunity.

The Court's 1993 decision concerned Teresa Harris, a woman who—like Anita Hill—was not fired or demoted for rejecting unwelcome sexual innuendo, but who eventually found the environment so unpleasant that she left. As Justice Sandra Day O'Connor described the facts:

> Teresa Harris worked as a manager at Forklift Systems, Inc., an equipment rental company, from April 1985 until October 1987. Charles Hardy was Forklift's president.
>
> The Magistrate found that, throughout Harris's time at Forklift, Hardy often insulted her because of her gender and often made her the target of unwanted sexual innuendos. Hardy told Harris on several occasions, in the presence of other employees, "You're a woman, what do you know" and "We need a man as the rental manager"; at least once, he told her she was "a dumb-ass woman." Again in front of others, he suggested that the two of them "go to the Holiday Inn to negotiate [Harris's] raise." Hardy occasionally asked Harris and other female employees to get coins from his front pants pocket. He threw objects on the ground in front of Harris and other women, and asked them to pick the objects up. He made sexual innuendos about Harris's and other women's clothing.
>
> In mid-August 1987, Harris complained to Hardy about his conduct. Hardy said he was surprised that Harris was offended, claimed he was only joking, and apologized. He also promised he would stop, and based on this assurance Harris stayed on the job. But in early September, Hardy began anew: While Harris was arranging a deal with one of Forklift's customers, he asked her, again in front of other employees, "What did you do, promise the guy . . . some [bugger][4] Saturday night?" On October 1, Harris collected her paycheck and quit.[5]

Harris then sued Forklift and lost, but pursued her case to the Supreme Court. The lower courts found that she was offended by Hardy's conduct, and that reasonable women managers would likewise be offended. Under the guidelines of the Equal Employment Opportunity Commission (EEOC), that should have been enough for Harris to win her case initially, for the federal agency had ruled that

> unwelcome sexual advances, requests for sexual favors, and other verbal or physical conduct of a sexual nature constitute sexual harassment when . . . such conduct has the purpose or effect of unreasonably interfering with an indi-

vidual's work performance *or creating an intimidating, hostile, or offensive working environment.*[6]

But the lower courts ruled that even when such unwelcome behavior was directed only against women employees, and even when the behavior was offensive to Harris and would be so to other reasonable women managers, that was not enough to win a hostile environment sexual harassment case. Naturally, Charles Hardy agreed. He argued to the Court that Teresa Harris had failed to prove her job performance suffered, and had failed to prove that she was psychologically injured by his offensive behavior. Without either psychological injury or an effect on job performance, he concluded, no woman should be able to sue an employer over "merely" offensive, hostile, or intimidating sexual harassment, as the EEOC guidelines allowed. In essence, he was arguing that because Teresa Harris was a strong woman who could keep working despite his behavior, *he* had not violated Title VII.

The Court rejected this argument out of hand. It ruled that "no single factor is required" to prove a sexual harassment claim. Thus, victims of harassment do not have to prove that they became mental basket cases or stopped being productive employees in order to prevail, although evidence of either effect would obviously be relevant to their case. Justice O'Connor explained the Court's rationale:

> Title VII comes into play before the harassing conduct leads to a nervous breakdown. A discriminatorily abusive work environment, even one that does not seriously affect employees' psychological well-being, can and often will detract from employees' job performance, discourage employees from remaining on the job, or keep them from advancing in their careers. Moreover, even without regard to these tangible effects, the very fact that the discriminatory conduct was so severe or pervasive that it created a work environment abusive to employees because of their . . . gender . . . offends Title VII's broad rule of workplace equality.[7]

Harris was thus another decisive victory for working women, one that significantly strengthened the definition of illegal "hostile environment" sexual harassment.

Another change in the field of sexual harassment law is simply the volume of new cases. Despite initial fears that Professor Hill's experience would scare women out of coming forward, many women instead were inspired by her example. The EEOC reported a 60 percent increase in the volume of sexual harassment charges during the first nine months after the hearings; three years after the hearings, the number of women filing complaints was still growing.[8] Women's groups, too, reported being flooded with calls for help.

With the new attention to the issue, lawyers have tried innovative approaches to litigating sexual harassment cases. When Lori Peterson, a young attorney fresh out of law school, represented female bottlers and machinists who sued Stroh's Brewery for sexual harassment, she pointed to the role of Stroh's advertising in encouraging sexual harassment.[9] As Ronald K. L. Collins described the case in the *Los Angeles Times,*

> What the company voice says outside of the office carries into it as well. That's part of what the St. Paul women were saying when they filed a lawsuit against their employer, Stroh Brewing Co. In Stroh's "It Does Not Get Better" television ad, bikini-clad young Swedish women parachute into a male campsite bearing six-packs of beer. (Tellingly, the "Swedish bikini team" will be featured on the cover of the January issue of *Playboy* magazine.) Buxom women convey the same message in the company's promotional posters. The advertising fantasy is that men can have both the beer and the "broads."[10]

Peterson thus provoked discussion of the media's role in promoting the sexual objectification of women.

Some women miners made history by bringing the first class-action suit charging hostile-environment sexual harassment, and the judge agreed they could proceed as a class.[11] After trial, the court found that Eveleth Mines discriminated against the entire class of its women employees by "maintaining an environment sexually hostile to women." The judge relied on evidence of multiple forms of unwanted sexual innuendo and physical contact, including graffiti, photos, and cartoons that visually referred "to sex and to women as sexual objects," "verbal statements and language reflecting a sexualized, male-oriented, and antifemale atmosphere," and "physical acts that reflect a sexual motive or concern." While the judge found that both men and women sometimes cursed, he also found that only men went further and referred "to women generally in terms of their body parts." Men also made "comments to or about specific women and their sex lives, including proposing sexual relationships and discussing sexual exploits." Other examples of male behavior included pretending "to perform oral sex on a sleeping woman coworker," touching a woman "in an objectionable manner," and presenting women with "various dildos, one of which was named 'Big Red.' " The judge concluded:

> In work places which have been traditionally male and where females constitute a small minority of the employees, employers may have an increased obligation to create environments which are safe for all employees. Whatever an employer's responsibility may be in that situation, it cannot close its eyes when confronted with sexual harassment; it has the obligation to determine the scope of the problem and take steps to alleviate it.[12]

State legislators have also been trying out new approaches. Alaska, California, Connecticut, Illinois, Minnesota, Tennessee, Vermont, and Washington have enacted "water cooler" legislation requiring employers to post in prominent and accessible locations notices informing employees that sexual harassment is illegal and telling them what to do if they are harassed.[13] California, Vermont, and Wisconsin have passed laws further defining existing prohibitions on sexual harassment; Illinois has required all businesses contracting with the state to have written sexual harassment policies; and Iowa has enacted a comprehensive prohibition covering state employees, people in the care or custody of the state, and students.[14] In another approach, employers have been required to conduct training sessions on sexual harassment and how to prevent it. California, Connecticut, Illinois, Tennessee, and Vermont have all enacted such initiatives.[15] In a sign of the impact of Christine Franklin's case, a number of other states—California, Connecticut, Iowa, Minnesota, New Hampshire, Tennessee, and Washington—have required state educational institutions to take various steps against harassment, such as adopting policies and disciplinary procedures on the subject.[16]

Anita Hill's experience has also prompted legal theorists to confront the doubly difficult issues faced by women of color. Professor Kimberlé Crenshaw has provided valuable insights into the "racialization of sexual harassment" and the "pervasive stereotypes about black women . . . [that] shape the kind of harassment that black women experience . . . [and] influence whether black women's stories are likely to be believed."[17] Professor Emma Coleman Jordan has written about the combined impact of race, gender, and social class.[18] The present volume also represents an attempt to enhance our understanding of these difficult issues.[19] Eventually, new insights are bound to find their way into the law as courts learn to analyze the combined impact of race and sex on sexual harassment as experienced by women of color.

In the wake of the Hill-Thomas hearings some federal circuit courts began fine-tuning the law of sexual harassment and issued decisions that might have provided guidance to the Senate Judiciary Committee on how to conduct investigations. The Second Circuit issued a strong decision in July 1992 concerning the New York City Police Department.[20] After a woman officer reported that a male officer had sexually assaulted her brutally at gunpoint, the department refused to investigate *his* behavior but took after her with a vengeance. The court ruled that

> the relatively harsh disciplinary treatment [she] received from the NYPD when compared with the total absence of any investigation into [his] conduct, seems to us sufficiently egregious to . . . justify a jury's finding of an unconstitutional departmental practice of sex discrimination.[21]

Two months later, the Seventh Circuit decided a case brought by a harasser whose company had fired him for the harassment.[22] He sued for breach of contract and lost on a summary judgment motion after the employer presented detailed deposition testimony from the woman describing many "specific instances of sexual harassment."

> She told of [his] comments to her regarding her anatomy, of instances of unwelcome touching, and of his comments about his extramarital affairs with other women. She described these incidents in detail, relating the location, what was said, who was present, and how she felt. . . . She . . . described an incident where she had asked for a pay raise, and she remembered that he responded, "Well, you could be making more money if you perform favors, certain favors, on the side and you could receive bonuses. . . ." . . . She declined all of his invitations and frequently objected to his behavior, but to no avail. Instead, she testified that the frequency of his offensive behavior increased during the term of her employment.[23]

The man claimed that it was an error to decide the case on a summary judgment motion, and that he should have a trial because he had denied these allegations, thus creating a factual issue. The court responded that he was not entitled to a trial:

In . . . his deposition, he stated that he generally denied having sexually harassed any coworker. Given his unwillingness or inability to deny the specific allegations upon direct inquiry, his few denials of the broad accusations would not be sufficient evidence to support a jury verdict in his favor.[24]

Or consider a decision from the Third Circuit in June 1992.[25] The judges ruled that an arbitrator should not have reinstated an alleged harasser to the job from which he had been fired without a finding that he didn't do it. Even more important, the judges ruled that it was proper to require a different arbitrator to decide the case on remand, because the original arbitrator was "biased or partial towards [the alleged harasser]." The court gave some examples of the bias, including the arbitrator's characterization of the woman as "unattractive and frustrated," and his allowing questions such as "Would you think an average man would make a pass at a woman like that?"[26]

In short, some courts have begun to focus on what makes an effective investigation into sexual harassment. Calling the victim names, attacking her, failing to investigate the man's behavior, and accepting the man's general denials do not, in these courts' view, constitute a good-faith attempt to resolve the matter. I hope it's safe to say that the Senate has learned these lessons too.

The evolution of the Tailhook scandal indicates just how important honest investigations can be. After twenty-six navy women had to run the infamous gantlet of their male peers, the navy decided to investigate. Here's a news account of what one of these women endured:

> On each of the three nights of last September's convention, investigators found, groups of officers in civilian dress suddenly turned violent, organizing with military precision into drunken gangs that shoved terrified women down the gantlet, grabbing at their breasts and buttocks and stripping off their clothes. . . .
>
> Unsuspecting women were ambushed when they walked out of the elevator and turned right down the hallway into an ocean of unrelenting arms.
>
> Among them was a thirty-year-old navy lieutenant, a helicopter pilot who was an admiral's aide at the time. As she approached a group of officers in the hallway looking for some dinner companions, one officer shouted, "Admiral's aide! Admiral's aide," while another "grabbed me by the buttocks with such force that it lifted me off the ground and ahead a step," she later told naval investigators.
>
> Others grabbed her, too, and one man put his hands down her bra. . . .
>
> The lieutenant kicked and punched her assailants but was overpowered. After being pawed for about twenty feet of the hallway, she managed to escape through an open door into a hotel room.[27]

By April 1992, some fifteen hundred interviews later, the navy had found only two possible suspects, because the officers protected each other behind a "wall of silence." But then there was a new discovery. A witness interview indicating that Secretary of the Navy H. Lawrence Garrett III was at the scene had been deleted from the first report.[28] Shortly thereafter, Secretary Garrett resigned, and the Pentagon started a new investigation into how the first investigation had been conducted.[29] In the fall of 1992, the Pentagon's inspector general issued a scathing denunciation of that first attempt, finding that its major thrust was to protect the higher-ups.[30] Moreover, we learned that the man in charge of the first investigation, Rear Admiral Williams, had a rather limited opinion of women navy pilots. A lot of them are "go-go dancers, topless dancers or hookers," he said. Now Admiral Williams, along with two fellow admirals, is also out of a job.[31]

As we have seen, the legal legacy of the hearings was substantial. Since Anita Hill's ordeal before the Senate Judiciary Committee, there has been considerable progress on the issue of sexual harassment. The law now provides a vastly improved remedy. The law has also been strengthened and clarified. More and more women have gained the courage to speak up about their experiences. Lawyers are bringing new kinds of claims to court. We are starting to focus on the double-edged discrimination faced by women of color. Some judges have begun to demand real investigations, rather than the bogus inquiries that too often carried the day in the past. High government officials have lost their jobs for their failure to investigate, and we have learned that genuine investigation requires looking into the harasser's actions and refusing to call the woman names. The voters rejected one senator for his vote on the Thomas confirmation,[32] and another narrowly escaped defeat at the polls for his version of an investigation."[33] Indeed, the gender of the political landscape is changing as more women than ever before make their way into legislative bodies.

Anita Hill single-handedly changed American attitudes toward sexual harassment. Virtually overnight, by dint of her dignity, intelligence, and courage, she demolished the notion that sexual harassment is trivial. We can safely say that Professor Anita Hill has indeed been a catalyst for change, change that has just begun. And for that we are truly in her debt.

NOTES

1. 42 U.S.C. §§ 1981a(a) (right to damages) and 1981a(b)(3) (limiting damages, by size of employer, to: $50,000 (for employers of 14–100 employees); $100,000 (101–200 employees); $200,000 (201–500 employees); and $300,000 (over 500 employees)).

2. 20 U.S.C. §§ 1681–1688.

3. *Franklin* v. *Gwinnett County Public Schools*, __ U.S. __, 112 S. Ct. 1028, 1031, 117 L. Ed. 2d 208, 215 (1992).

4. Justice O'Connor spoke obliquely here, substituting the word "sex" for "bugger," the actual term Charles Hardy had used. Brief for the United States and the Equal Employment Opportunity Commission as Amicus Curiae, at 4, *Harris* v. *Forklift Systems, Inc.*, __ U.S. __ 114 S. Ct. 367, 126 L. Ed. 2d 295 (1993) (No. 92–1168). The Justice Department brief also mentioned other examples of Hardy's sexual innuendo. For example, "a former clerical employee . . . testified that Hardy would suggest turning down the air conditioning when a female employee wore a tight shirt because of the effect of the lower temperature on the women's breasts." Ibid. at n. 3.

5. *Harris* v. *Forklift Systems, Inc.*, __ U.S. __, 114 S. Ct. 367, 369, 126 L. Ed. 2d 295, 300 (1993).

6. 29 C. F. R. § 1604.11(a) (emphasis added).

7. 114 S. Ct. at 370–71, 126 L. Ed. 2d at 302.

8. Laura Blumenfeld, "One Year, A.H.," *Washington Post*, October 13, 1992, p. E5; Patricia Edmonds, "Year Later, Harassment's 'Real to More People,' " *USA Today*, October 2, 1992, p. 6A (reporting that 7,407 sexual harassment complaints had been filed with the EEOC from October 1, 1991, through June 30, 1992, compared to 6,883 for all of fiscal 1991). In August 1994, the EEOC reported that 10,532 complaints were filed in fiscal year 1992, another 11,908 in fiscal year 1993, and that there were 1,000 more complaints in the third quarter of fiscal year 1994 than there had been in the same quarter of fiscal year 1993. Telephone interview of Julie Pershan, EEOC public affairs specialist, by Jennifer Ellison, research assistant to Professor Ross (August 22, 1994).

9. Doug Crow, "Stroh's and Its Ads Square Off against an Angry Young Lawyer," *Star Tribune* (Minneapolis-St. Paul), November 10, 1991, p. 3B.

10. Ronald K. L. Collins, "Perspective on Advertising," *Los Angeles Times*, November 20, 1991, p. B7.

11. Diane Alters, "Ruling Clears Way for 3 Women Miners to File First-Ever Class-Action Suit on Sex Harassment," *Star Tribune* (Minneapolis-St. Paul), December 19, 1991, p. 1D; *Jenson* v. *Eveleth Taconite Co.*, 139 F.R.D. 657 (D. Minn. 1991).

12. *Jenson* v. *Eveleth Taconite Co.*, 824 F. Supp. 847, 879, 880, 888 (D. Minn. 1993).

13. Alaska Stat. § 23.10.440 (Supp. 1993); Cal. Gov't Code § 12950(a)-(c) (Deering Supp. 1994) (requiring information sheet to be distributed to each employee as well); Cal. Educ. Code § 212.6 (Deering Supp. 1994) (applies to educational institutions); Conn. Gen. Stat. § 46a–54(15)(A) (1993); Ill. Ann. Stat. ch. 775, para. 5/2-105(B)(5)(b) (Smith-Hurd Supp. 1994) (policy on posting applies only to state agencies); Minn. Stat. § 135A.15 (1992) (requiring posting of policy at appropriate campus locations for students and employees at postsecondary educational institutions); Tenn. Code Ann. § 4-3-124 (Supp. 1994) (applies to entities of state government); Tenn. Code Ann. § 4-3-905 (Supp. 1994) (employers in the state to make information about state sexual harassment law available to employees through posters, brochures, or pamphlets); Vt. Stat. Ann. tit. 21, § 495h(b) (Supp. 1993); 1994 Wash. Laws 214 (to be codified at Wash. Rev. Code 28A.640.020) (applies only to school districts).

14. Cal. Gov't Code § 12940(h)(3)(C) (Deering Supp. 1994) (clarifying that state prohibition on harassment includes sexual harassment, gender harassment, and harassment based on pregnancy, childbirth, or related medical conditions); Vt. Stat. Ann. tit. 21, § 495d(13) (Supp. 1993) (adding definition of sexual harassment); 1993 Wis. Laws 427 (to be codified at Wis. Stat. §§ 111. 32[13], 111.36[l][b], 111.36[l][br]) (amending the existing definition of sexual harassment law to add further details); Ill. Ann. Stat. ch. 775, para. 5/2-105(A)(4) (Smith-Hurd Supp. 1994) (applying to parties to public contracts and eligible bidders); Iowa Code Ann. § 19B. 12 (West Supp. 1994) (further requiring the adoption of rules, grievance procedures, and disciplinary procedures by the relevant state institutions, and guides for employees, students, and patients informing them of these rules and procedures); see also, Iowa Code Ann. § 2.11 (West Supp. 1994) (requiring each house of the state general assembly to develop prohibitions against sexual harassment and distribute such guides to its employees).

15. Cal. Penal Code § 13519.7 (Deering Supp. 1994) (requiring training sessions for law enforcement officers, and establishment of complaint guidelines for law enforcement officers who are victims of sexual harassment in the workforce); Conn. Gen. Stat. § 46a-54(15)(B) (1993) (requiring employers of fifty or more employees to have training sessions for supervisory employees); Ill. Ann. Stat. ch. 775, para. 5/2-105(B)(5)(c) (Smith-Hurd Supp. 1994) (applies only to state agencies); Tenn, Code Ann. § 4-3-1703(a)(4)

(Supp. 1994) (requiring state department of personnel to]help each entity of state government in planning and holding training workshops to prevent sexual harassment from occurring); Tenn. Code Ann. § 3-13-101(a)(10) (Supp. 1994) and § 16-3-502 (Supp. 1994) (requiring legislature and allowing supreme court, respectively, to establish policy to prevent sexual harassment, hold training workshops, and establish a hearing procedure); Tenn. Code Ann. § 49-7-122 (Supp. 1994) (requiring training on sexual harassment and a hearing process for all state higher education institutions); Vt. Stat. Ann. tit. 21, § 495h(f) (Supp. 1993) (encouraging training for employees, and additional training for supervisory and managerial employees covering their specific responsibilities to take corrective action).

16. Cal. Educ. Code 212.6 (Deering Supp. 1994) (requiring all educational institutions in California to have policy prohibiting sexual harassment of students or employees, and to make policy routinely available including by posting it at a prominent location); Cal. Educ. Code § 48900.2 (Deering Supp. 1994) (allowing suspension or expulsion from school of students above the third-grade level found by their principal to have committed sexual harassment); Conn. Gen. Stat. § 10a-55c (1993) (requiring each institution of higher education to have policy prohibiting sexual harassment, and procedures for students, employees, and others to report it and for informing victims of the outcome of resulting investigations or disciplinary proceedings); Iowa Code Ann. § 19B.12 (West Supp. 1994) (prohibiting state employees from sexually harassing either other state employees or students attending state educational institutions, and requiring rules, grievance procedures, disciplinary procedures, and guides for employees and students); Minn. Stat. §§ 126.70(2a)(8) and 126.77(1)(b)(1), (2), (7), (8) (1992) (encouraging public school districts to use curricula that address sexual harassment); Minn. Stat. § 127.46 (1992) (requiring each public school to develop a process for discussing its sexual harassment policy with students and employees); Minn. Stat. § 135A.15 (1992) (requiring posting of the sexual harassment policy, and numerous rights for employees and students who are sexual assault victims at postsecondary educational institutions); 1993 N. H. Laws 148 (creating a task force on sexual assault and sexual harassment at postsecondary institutions, with members to study the problems, coordinate resources addressed to them, and report back to the legislature and governor); Tenn. Code Ann. § 49-7-122 (Supp. 1994) (requiring training on sexual harassment and a hearing process for all state higher education institutions); 1994 Wash. Laws 213 (to be codified at Wash. Rev. Code § 28A.640.020) (defining sexual harassment and requiring each school district to adopt policy on it—including grievance procedures, remedies, and sanctions—covering employees, volunteers, parents, and students, with guidance from state superintendent of public instruction).

17. Kimberlé Crenshaw, "Race, Gender, and Sexual Harassment," *Southern California Law Review* 65 (1992): 1467, 1469–70; see also Kimberlé Crenshaw, "Whose Story Is It, Anyway? Feminist and Antiracist Appropriations of Anita Hill," in *Race-ing Justice, En-gendering Power*, ed. Toni Morrison (1992), p. 402.

18. Emma Coleman Jordan, "Race, Gender, and Social Class in the Thomas Sexual Harassment Hearings: The Hidden Fault Lines in Political Discourse," *Harvard Women's Law Journal* 15 (1992): 1.

19. For other authors who have addressed the subject, see generally the symposium issue *Gender, Race, and the Politics of Supreme Court Appointments: The Impact of the Anita Hill/Clarence Thomas Hearings, Southern California Law Review* 65 (1992): 1279; Morrison, *Race-ing Justice, En-gendering Power*; and Robert Chrisman and Robert L. Allen, eds., *Court of Appeal: The Black Community Speaks Out on the Racial and Sexual Politics of Clarence Thomas vs. Anita Hill* (1992).

20. *Sorlucco* v. *N.Y. Police Dep't.*, 971 F.2d 864 (2d Cir. 1992).

21. Ibid. at 873. The appellate court therefore reinstated the jury verdict in her favor, a verdict that had been set aside by the district court in response to the defendant's motion for judgment notwithstanding the verdict.

22. *Scherer* v. *Rockwell Int'l. Corp.*, 975 F.2d 356 (7th Cir. 1992).

23. Ibid. at 359.

24. Ibid. at 361.

25. *Stroehmann Bakeries, Inc.* v. *Local 776, Int'l. Bhd. of Teamsters*, 969 F.2d 1436 (3rd Cir.), *cert. denied*, __ U.S. 113 S. Ct. 660, 121 L. Ed. 2d 585 (1992).

26. Ibid. at 1446.

27. Eric Schmitt, "Wall of Silence Impedes Inquiry into a Rowdy Navy Convention," *New York Times*, June 14, 1992, p. Al.

28. Eric Schmitt, "Citing Scandal, Navy Group Cancels Annual Convention," *New York Times*, June 18, 1992, p. B11.

29. Eric Schmitt, "Navy Chief Quits amid Questions over Role in Sex-Assault Inquiry," *New York Times*, June 27, 1992, p. A1; Eric Schmitt, "Pentagon Takes Over Inquiry on Pilots," *New York Times*, June 19, 1992, p. A20.

30. John Lancaster, "Pentagon Blasts Tailhook Inquiry; Navy Leadership Faulted in Scandal," *Washington Post*, September 25, 1992, p. A1.

31. Ibid. Rear Admirals Williams and Cordon, who were respectively the commander of the Naval Investigative Service and the Navy's judge advocate general, were asked to resign, while Rear Admiral Davis, the Navy's inspector general, was reassigned.

32. Edward Walsh, "Sen. Dixon Loses in Stunning Upset," *Washington Post*, March 18, 1992, p. Al (recounting how now-Carol Moseley-Braun defeated then-Senator Alan Dixon in Illinois' three-way Democratic primary, with a strong percentage of Republican women voting for her).

33. Adam Clymer, "The 1992 Elections: Congress—The New Congress," *New York Times*, November 5, 1992, p. B6 (reporting that Sen. Arlen Specter narrowly won a third term with a 51 to 49 percent victory over Lynn Yeakel, a political newcomer who began her Senate race in reaction to Specter's conduct as a member of the Judiciary Committee during the Hill-Thomas hearings).

(U.S. SUPREME COURT DECISION, 1993)

O'CONNOR, J., delivered the opinion for a unanimous Court. SCALIA, J., and GINSBURG, J., filed concurring opinions.

I

Teresa Harris worked as a manager at Forklift Systems, Inc., an equipment rental company, from April 1985 until October 1987. Charles Hardy was Forklift's president.

The Magistrate found that, throughout Harris's time at Forklift, Hardy often insulted her because of her gender and often made her the target of unwanted sexual innuendos. Hardy told Harris on several occasions, in the presence of other employees, "You're a woman, what do you know" and "We need a man as the rental manager"; at least once, he told her she was "a dumb-ass woman." Again in front of others, he suggested that the two of them "go to the Holiday Inn to negotiate [Harris's] raise." Hardy occasionally asked Harris and other female employees to get coins from his front pants pocket. He threw objects on the ground in front of Harris and other women,

---

Teresa HARRIS, Petitioner, v. FORKLIFT SYSTEMS, INC., 114 S. Ct. 367 (1993).

and asked them to pick the objects up. He made sexual innuendos about Harris's and other women's clothing.

In mid-August 1987, Harris complained to Hardy about his conduct. Hardy said he was surprised that Harris was offended, claimed he was only joking, and apologized. He also promised he would stop, and based on this assurance Harris stayed on the job. But in early September, Hardy began anew: While Harris was arranging a deal with one of Forklift's customers, he asked her, again in front of other employees, "What did you do, promise the guy . . . some [sex] Saturday night?" On October 1, Harris collected her paycheck and quit.

Harris then sued Forklift, claiming that Hardy's conduct had created an abusive work environment for her because of her gender. The United States District Court for the Middle District of Tennessee, adopting the report and recommendation of the Magistrate, found this to be "a close case," but held that Hardy's conduct did not create an abusive environment. The court found that some of Hardy's comments "offended [Harris], and would offend the reasonable woman," but that they were not

> so severe as to be expected to seriously affect [Harris's] psychological well-being. A reasonable woman manager under like circumstances would have been offended by Hardy, but his conduct would not have risen to the level of interfering with that person's work performance.
>
> Neither do I believe that [Harris] was subjectively so offended that she suffered injury. . . . Although Hardy may at times have genuinely offended [Harris], I do not believe that he created a working environment so poisoned as to be intimidating or abusive to [Harris].

In focusing on the employee's psychological well-being, the District Court was following Circuit precedent. See *Rabidue* v. *Osceola Refining Co.*, 805 F.2d 611, 620 (CA6 1986), cert.* denied, 481 U.S. 1041, 107 S. Ct. 1983, 95 L.Ed.2d 823 (1987). The United States Court of Appeals for the Sixth Circuit affirmed in a brief unpublished decision, 976 F.2d 733 (1992).

We granted certiorari, 507 U.S. 959, 113 S. Ct. 1382, 122 L.Ed.2d 758 (1993), to resolve a conflict among the Circuits on whether conduct, to be actionable as "abusive work environment" harassment (no *quid pro quo* harassment issue is present here), must "seriously affect [an employee's] psychological well-being" or lead the plaintiff to "suffe[r] injury." Compare *Rabidue* (requiring serious effect on psychological well-being); *Vance* v. *Southern Bell Telephone & Telegraph Co.*, 863 F.2d 1503, 1510 (CA11 1989) (same); and *Downes* v. *FAA* 775 F.2d 288, 292 (CA Fed.1985) (same), with *Ellison* v. *Brady*, 924 F.2d 872, 877–878 (CA9 1991) (rejecting such a requirement).

---

*The U.S. Supreme Court receives many requests for *certiorari* (i.e., requests that they review cases brought before lower courts). The high court, at its discretion, may issue a writ requesting the record or a case for review. (*Ed.*)

II

[1, 2] Title VII of the Civil Rights Act of 1964 makes it "an unlawful employment practice for an employer . . . to discriminate against any individual with respect to his compensation, terms, conditions, or privileges of employment, because of such individual's race, color, religion, sex, or national origin." 42 U.S.C. § 2000e–2(a)(1). As we made clear in *Meritor Savings Bank, FSB* v. *Vinson*, 477 U.S. 57, 106 S. Ct. 2399, 91 L.Ed.2d 49 (1986), this language "is not limited to 'economic' or 'tangible' discrimination. The phrase 'terms, conditions, or privileges of employment' evinces a congressional intent 'to strike at the entire spectrum of disparate treatment of men and women' in employment," which includes requiring people to work in a discriminatorily hostile or abusive environment. Ibid., at 64, 106 S. Ct., at 2404, quoting *Los Angeles Dept. of Water and Power* v. *Manhart*, 435 U.S. 702, 707, n. 13, 98 S. Ct. 1370, 1374, 55 L.Ed.2d 657 (1978) (some internal quotation marks omitted). When the workplace is permeated with "discriminatory intimidation, ridicule, and insult," 477 U.S., at 65, 106 S. Ct., at 2405, that is "sufficiently severe or pervasive to alter the conditions of the victim's employment and create an abusive working environment," ibid., at 67, 106 S. Ct., at 2405 (internal brackets and quotation marks omitted), Title VII is violated.

[3] This standard, which we reaffirm today, takes a middle path between making actionable any conduct that is merely offensive and requiring the conduct to cause a tangible psychological injury. As we pointed out in *Meritor*, "mere utterance of an . . . epithet which engenders offensive feelings in an employee," ibid. (internal quotation marks omitted) does not sufficiently affect the conditions of employment to implicate Title VII. Conduct that is not severe or pervasive enough to create an objectively hostile or abusive work environment—an environment that a reasonable person would find hostile or abusive—is beyond Title VII's purview. Likewise, if the victim does not subjectively perceive the environment to be abusive, the conduct has not actually altered the conditions of the victim's employment, and there is no Title VII violation.

[4, 5] But Title VII comes into play before the harassing conduct leads to a nervous breakdown. A discriminatorily abusive work environment, even one that does not seriously affect employees' psychological well-being, can and often will detract from employees' job performance, discourage employees from remaining on the job, or keep them from advancing in their careers. Moreover, even without regard to these tangible effects, the very fact that the discriminatory conduct was so severe or pervasive that it created a work environment abusive to employees because of their race, gender, religion, or national origin offends Title VII's broad rule of workplace equality. The appalling conduct alleged in *Meritor*, and the reference in that case to environments "so heavily polluted with discrimination as to destroy completely the emotional and psychological stability of minority group workers," ibid., at 66, 106 S. Ct., at 2405, quoting *Rogers* v. *EEOC*, 454 F.2d 234, 238 (CA5 1971), cert. denied, 406 U.S. 957, 92 S. Ct. 2058, 32 L.Ed.2d 343 (1972), merely present some especially egregious examples of harassment. They do not mark the boundary of what is actionable.

[6] We therefore believe the District Court erred in relying on whether the conduct "seriously affect[ed] plaintiff's psychological well-being" or led her to "suffe[r] injury." Such an inquiry may needlessly focus the factfinder's attention on concrete psychological harm, an element Title VII does not require. Certainly Title VII bars conduct that would seriously affect a reasonable person's psychological well-being, but the statute is not limited to such conduct. So long as the environment would reasonably be perceived, and is perceived, as hostile or abusive, *Meritor, supra,* 477 U.S., at 67, 106 S. Ct., at 2405, there is no need for it also to be psychologically injurious.

[7] This is not, and by its nature cannot be, a mathematically precise test. We need not answer today all the potential questions it raises, nor specifically address the Equal Employment Opportunity Commission's new regulations on this subject, see 58 Fed.Reg. 51266 (1993) (proposed 29 CFR §§ 1609.1, 1609.2); see also 29 CFR § 1604.11 (1993). But we can say that whether an environment is "hostile" or "abusive" can be determined only by looking at all the circumstances. These may include the frequency of the discriminatory conduct; its severity; whether it is physically threatening or humiliating, or a mere offensive utterance; and whether it unreasonably interferes with an employee's work performance. The effect on the employee's psychological well-being is, of course, relevant to determining whether the plaintiff actually found the environment abusive. But while psychological harm, like any other relevant factor, may be taken into account, no single factor is required.

III

[8] Forklift, while conceding that a requirement that the conduct seriously affect psychological well-being is unfounded, argues that the District Court nonetheless correctly applied the *Meritor* standard. We disagree. Though the District Court did conclude that the work environment was not "intimidating or abusive to [Harris]," it did so only after finding that the conduct was not "so severe as to be expected to seriously affect plaintiff's psychological well-being," and that Harris was not "subjectively so offended that she suffered injury." The District Court's application of these incorrect standards may well have influenced its ultimate conclusion, especially given that the court found this to be a "close case."

We therefore reverse the judgment of the Court of Appeals.

Justice SCALIA, concurring.

Meritor Savings Bank, FSB v. *Vinson,* 477 U.S. 57, 106 S. Ct. 2399, 91 L.Ed.2d 49 (1986), held that Title VII prohibits sexual harassment that takes the form of a hostile work environment. The Court stated that sexual harassment is actionable if it is "sufficiently severe or pervasive 'to alter the conditions of [the victim's] employment and create an abusive working environment.' " Ibid., at 67, 106 S. Ct., at 2405 (quoting *Henson* v. *Dundee,* 682 F.2d 897, 904 [CA11

1982]). Today's opinion elaborates that the challenged conduct must be severe or pervasive enough "to create an objectively hostile or abusive work environment—an environment that a reasonable person would find hostile or abusive."

"Abusive" (or "hostile," which in this context I take to mean the same thing) does not seem to me a very clear standard—and I do not think clarity is at all increased by adding the adverb "objectively" or by appealing to a "reasonable person['s]" notion of what the vague word means. Today's opinion does list a number of factors that contribute to abusiveness, but since it neither says how much of each is necessary (an impossible task) nor identifies any single factor as determinative, it thereby adds little certitude. As a practical matter, today's holding lets virtually unguided juries decide whether sex-related conduct engaged in (or permitted by) an employer is egregious enough to warrant an award of damages. One might say that what constitutes "negligence" (a traditional jury question) is not much more clear and certain than what constitutes "abusiveness." Perhaps so. But the class of plaintiffs seeking to recover for negligence is limited to those who have suffered harm, whereas under this statute "abusiveness" is to be the test of whether legal harm has been suffered, opening more expansive vistas of litigation.

Be that as it may, I know of no alternative to the course the Court today has taken. One of the factors mentioned in the Court's nonexhaustive list—whether the conduct unreasonably interferes with an employee's work performance—would, if it were made an absolute test, provide greater guidance to juries and employers. But I see no basis for such a limitation in the language of the statute. Accepting *Meritor*'s interpretation of the term "conditions of employment" as the law, the test is not whether work has been impaired, but whether working conditions have been discriminatorily altered. I know of no test more faithful to the inherently vague statutory language than the one the Court today adopts. For these reasons, I join the opinion of the Court.

Justice GINSBURG, concurring.

Today the Court reaffirms the holding of *Meritor Savings Bank, FSB* v. *Vinson*, 477 U.S. 57, 66, 106 S. Ct. 2399, 2405, 91 L.Ed.2d 49 (1986): "[A] plaintiff may establish a violation of Title VII by proving that discrimination based on sex has created a hostile or abusive work environment." The critical issue, Title VII's text indicates, is whether members of one sex are exposed to disadvantageous terms or conditions of employment to which members of the other sex are not exposed. See 42 U.S.C. § 2000e–2(a)(l) (declaring that it is unlawful to discriminate with respect to, *inter alia*, "terms" or "conditions" of employment). As the Equal Employment Opportunity Commission emphasized, the adjudicator's inquiry should center, dominantly, on whether the discriminatory conduct has unreasonably interfered with the plaintiff's work performance. To show such interference, "the plaintiff need not prove that his or her tangible productivity has declined as a result of the harassment." *Davis* v. *Monsanto Chemical Co.*, 858 F.2d 345, 349 (CA6 1988). It suffices to prove that a reasonable person subjected to the discriminatory conduct would find, as the plaintiff did, that the harassment so altered working conditions as to "ma[k]e it more difficult to do the job." See ibid. *Davis* concerned race-based discrimination, but that difference does not alter the analysis; except in the rare case in which a bona fide occupational qualification is shown, see *Automobile Workers* v. *Johnson Controls, Inc.*, 499 U.S. 187, 200–207, 111 S. Ct. 1196, 1204–1208, 113 L.Ed.2d 158 (1991) (construing 42 U.S.C. § 2000e–2[e][1]), Title VII declares discriminatory practices based on race, gender, religion, or national origin equally unlawful.

The Court's opinion, which I join, seems to me in harmony with the view expressed in this concurring statement.

Hostile-Environment Sexual Harassment and the First Amendment

17 THE SEXUAL POLITICS OF THE FIRST AMENDMENT

CATHARINE A. MACKINNON

[The Dred Scott case] was a law to be cited, a lesson to be learned, judicial vigor to be emulated, political imprudence to be regretted, but most of all, as time passed, it was an embarrassment—the Court's highly visible skeleton in a transparent closet.
> —Don E. Ferrenbacher, *The Dred Scott Case: Its Significance in American Law and Politics*

Frankfurter is said to have remarked that Dred Scott was never mentioned by the Supreme Court any more than ropes and scaffolds were mentioned by a family that had lost one of its number to the hangman.
> —Bruce Catton, in John A. Garraty, ed., *Quarrels That Have Shaped the Constitution*

The Constitution of the United States, contrary to any impression you may have received, is a piece of paper with words written on it. Because it is old, it is considered a document. When it is interpreted by particular people under particular conditions, it becomes a text. Because it is backed up by the power of the state, it is a law.

Feminism, by contrast, springs from the impulse to self-

From Catharine A. MacKinnon, *Feminism Unmodified: Discourses on Life and Law* (Harvard University Press, 1987). Reprinted by permission of author and publisher.

respect in every woman. From this have come some fairly elegant things: a metaphysics of mind, a theory of knowledge, an approach to ethics, and a concept of social action. Aspiring to the point of view of all women on social life as a whole, feminism has expressed itself as a political movement for civil equality.

Looking at the Constitution through the lens of feminism, initially one sees exclusion of women from the Constitution. This is simply to say that we had no voice in the constituting document of this state. From that one can suppose that those who did constitute it may not have had the realities of our situation in mind.

Next one notices that the Constitution as interpreted is structured around what can generically be called the public, or state action. This constituting document pervasively assumes that those guarantees of freedoms that must be secured to citizens begin where law begins, with the public order. This posture is exalted as "negative liberty"[1] and is a cornerstone of the liberal state. You notice this from the feminist standpoint because women are oppressed socially, prior to law, without express state acts, often in intimate contexts. For women this structure means that those domains in which women are distinctively subordinated are assumed by the Constitution to be the domain of freedom.

Finally, combining these first two observations, one sees that women are not given affirmative access to those rights we need most. Equality, for example. Equality, in the words of Andrea Dworkin, was tacked on to the Constitution with spit and a prayer. And, let me also say, late.

If we apply these observations to the First Amendment, our exclusion means that the First Amendment was conceived by white men from the point of view of their social position. Some of them owned slaves; most of them owned women.[2] They wrote it to guarantee their freedom to keep something they felt at risk of losing.[3] Namely—and this gets to my next point—speech which they did not want lost through state action. They wrote the First Amendment so their speech would not be threatened by this powerful instrument they were *creating*, the federal government. You recall that it reads, "Congress shall make no law abridging ... the freedom of speech." They were creating that body. They were worried that it would abridge something they *did have*. You can tell that they had speech, because what they said was written down: it became a document, it has been interpreted, it is the law of the state.[4]

By contrast with those who wrote the First Amendment so they could keep what they had, those who didn't have it didn't get it. Those whose speech was silenced prior to law, prior to any operation of the state's prohibition of it, were not secured freedom of speech. Their speech was not regarded as something that had to be—and this gets to my next point—affirmatively guaranteed. Looking at the history of the First Amendment from this perspective, reprehensible examples of state attempts to suppress speech exist. But they constitute a history of comparative privilege in contrast with the history of silence of those whose speech has never been able to exist for the state even to contemplate abridging it.

A few affirmative guarantees of access to speech do exist. The *Red Lion* decision is one, although it may be slated for extinction.[5] Because certain avenues of speech are inherently restricted—for instance, there are only so many broadcast frequencies—according to the *Red Lion* doctrine of fairness in access to broadcast media, some people's access has to be restricted in the interest of providing access to all. In other words, the speech of those who could buy up all the speech there is, is restricted. Conceptually, this doctrine works exactly like affirmative action. The speech of those who might be the only ones there, is not there, so that others' can be.

With a few exceptions like that[6] we find no guarantees of access to speech. Take, for example, literacy. Even after it became clear that the Constitution applied to the states, nobody argued that the segregation of schools that created inferior conditions of access to literacy for blacks violated their First Amendment rights. Or the slave codes that made it a crime to teach a slave to read and write or to advocate their freedom.[7] Some of those folks who struggled for civil rights for black people must have thought of this, but I never heard their lawyers argue it. If access to the means of speech is effectively socially precluded on the basis of race or class or gender, freedom from state burdens on speech does not meaningfully guarantee the freedom to speak.

First Amendment absolutism, the view that speech must be absolutely protected, is not the law of the First Amendment. It is the conscience, the superego of the First Amendment, the implicit standard from which all deviations must be justified. It is also an advocacy position typically presented in debate as if it were legal fact. Consider for example that First Amendment bog, the distinction between speech and conduct. Most conduct is expressive as well as active; words are as often tantamount to acts as they are vehicles for removed cerebration. Case law knows this.[8] But the first question, the great divide, the beginning and the end, is still the absolutist question, "Is it speech or isn't it?"

First Amendment absolutism was forged in the crucible of obscenity litigation. Probably its most inspired expositions, its most passionate defenses, are to be found in Justice Douglas's dissents in obscenity cases.[9] This is no coincidence. Believe him when he says that pornography is at the core of the First Amendment. Absolutism has developed through obscenity litigation, I think, because pornography's protection fits perfectly with the power relations embedded in First Amendment structure and jurisprudence from the start. Pornography is exactly that speech of men that silences the speech of women. I take it seriously when Justice Douglas speaking on pornography and others preaching absolutism say that pornography has to be protected speech or else free expression will not mean what it has always meant in this country.

I must also say that the First Amendment has become a sexual fetish through years of absolutist writing in the melodrama mode in *Playboy* in particular. You know those superheated articles where freedom of speech is extolled and its imminent repression is invoked. Behaviorally, *Playboy*'s consumers are reading about the First Amendment, masturbating to the women, reading about the First Amendment, masturbating to the women, reading about the First Amendment, masturbating to the women. It makes subliminal seduction look subtle. What is conveyed is not only that using women is as legitimate as thinking about the Constitution, but also that if you don't support these views about the Constitution, you won't be able to use these women.

This general approach affects even religious groups. I love to go speaking against pornography when the sponsors dig up some religious types, thinking they will make me look bad because they will agree with me. Then the ministers come on and say, "This is the first time we've ever agreed with the ACLU about anything . . . why, what she's advocating would *violate the First Amendment*." This isn't their view universally, I guess, but it has been my experience repeatedly, and I have personally never had a minister support me on the air. One of them finally explained it. The First Amendment, he said, also guarantees the freedom of religion. So this is not only what we already know: regardless of one's politics and one's moral views, one is into using women largely. It is also that, consistent with this, First Amendment absolutism resonates historically in the context of the long-term collaboration in misogyny between church and state. Don't let them tell you they're "separate" in that.

In pursuit of absolute freedom of speech, the ACLU has been a major institution in defending, and now I describe their behavior, the Nazis, the Klan, and the pornographers. I am waiting for them to add the antiabortionists, including the expressive conduct of their violence. Think about one of their favorite metaphors, a capitalist metaphor, the marketplace of ideas. Think about whether the speech of the Nazis has historically enhanced the speech of the Jews. Has the speech of the Klan expanded the speech of blacks? Has the so-called speech of the pornographers enlarged the speech of women? In this context, apply to what they call the marketplace of ideas the question we were asked to consider in the keynote speech by Winona LaDuke: Is there a relationship between our poverty in speech and their wealth?

As many of you may know, Andrea Dworkin and I, with a lot of others, have been working to establish a law that recognizes pornography as a violation of the civil rights of women in particular. It recognizes that pornography is a form of sex discrimination. Recently, in a fairly unprecedented display of contempt, the U.S. Supreme Court found that the Indianapolis version of our law violates the First Amendment.[10] On a direct appeal, the Supreme Court invalidated a local ordinance by summary affirmance—no arguments, no briefs on the merits, no victims, no opinion, not so much as a single line of citation to controlling precedent. One is entitled to think that they would have put one there if they had had one.

The Court of Appeals opinion they affirmed[11] expressly concedes that pornography violates women in all the ways Indianapolis found it did. The opinion never questioned that pornography is sex discrimination. Interesting enough, the Seventh Circuit, in an opinion by Judge Frank Easterbrook, conceded the issue of objective causation. The only problem was, the harm didn't matter as much as the materials mattered. They are valuable. So the law that prohibited the harm the materials caused was held to be content-based and impermissible discrimination on the basis of viewpoint.

This is a law that gives victims a civil action when they are coerced into pornography, when pornography is forced on them, when they are assaulted because of specific pornography, and when they are subordinated through the trafficking in pornography. Some of us thought that sex discrimination and sexual abuse were against public policy. We defined pornography as the sexually explicit subordination of women through pictures or words that also includes presentations of women being sexually abused. There is a list of the specific acts of sexual abuse. The law covers men, too. We were so careful that practices whose abusiveness some people publicly question—for example, submission, servility, and display—are not covered by the trafficking provision. So we're talking rape, torture, pain, humiliation: we're talking violence against women turned into sex.

Now we are told that pornography, which, granted, does the harm we say it does, this pornography as we define it is protected speech. It has speech value. You can tell it has value as speech because it is so effective in doing the harm that it does.[12] (The passion of this rendition is mine, but the opinion really does say this.) The more harm, the more protection. This is now apparently the law of the First Amendment, at least where harm to women is the rationale. Judge LaDoris Cordell spoke earlier about the different legal standards for high-value and low-value speech, a doctrine that feminists who oppose pornography have always been averse to. But at least it is now clear that whatever the value of pornography is—and it is universally conceded to be low—the value of women is lower.

It is a matter of real interest to me exactly what the viewpoint element in our law is, according to Easterbrook's opinion. My best guess is that our law takes the point of view that women do not enjoy and deserve rape, and he saw that as just one point of view among many. Where do you suppose he got that idea? Another possible rendering is that our law takes the position that women should not be subordinated to men on the basis of sex, that women are or should be equal, and he regards relief to that end as the enforcement of a prohibited viewpoint.

Just what is and is not valuable, is and is not a viewpoint, is and is not against public policy was made even clearer the day after the summary affirmance. In the *Renton* case the Supreme Court revealed the conditions under which pornography can be restricted: it can be zoned beyond the city limits.[13] It can be regulated this way on the basis of its "secondary effects"—which are, guess what, property values. But it cannot be regulated on the basis of its primary effects on the bodies of the women who had to be ground up to make it.

Do you think it makes any difference to the woman who is coerced into pornography or who has just hit the end of this society's chances for women that the product of her exploitation is sold on the other side of the tracks? Does it matter to the molested child or the rape victim that the offender who used the pornography to get himself up or to plan what he would do or to decide what "type" to do it to had to drive across town to get it? It *does* matter to the women who live or work in the neighborhoods into which the pornography is zoned. They pay in increased street harassment, in an atmosphere of terror and contempt for what other neighborhoods gain in keeping their property values up.

Reading the two decisions together, you see the Court doing what it has always done with pornography: making it available in private while decrying it in public. Pretending to be tough on pornography's effects, the *Renton* case still *gives it a place to exist.* Although obscenity is supposed to have such little value that it is not considered speech at all, *Renton* exposes the real bottom line of the First Amendment: the pornography stays. Anyone who doesn't think absolutism has made any progress, check that.

Why is it that obscenity law can exist and our trafficking provision cannot? Why can the law against child pornography exist and not our law against coercion? Why aren't obscenity[14] and child pornography[15] laws viewpoint laws? Obscenity, as Justice Brennan pointed out in his dissent in *Renton*, expresses a viewpoint: sexual mores should be more relaxed, and if they were, sex would look like pornography.[16] Child pornography also presents a viewpoint: sex between adults and children is liberating, fulfilling, fun, and natural for the child. If one is concerned about the government taking a point of view through law, the laws against these things express the state's opposition to these viewpoints, to the extent of making them crimes to express. Why is a time-place-manner distinction all right in *Renton*, and not our forcing provision, which is kind of time-and-place-like and does not provide for actions against the pornographers at all? Why is it all right to make across-the-board, content-based distinctions like obscenity and child pornography, but not our trafficking provision, not our coercion provision?

When do you see a viewpoint as a viewpoint? When you don't agree with it. When is a viewpoint not a viewpoint? When it's yours.[17] What is and is not a viewpoint, much less a prohibited one, is a matter of individual values and social consensus. The reason Judge Easterbrook saw a viewpoint in our law was because he disagrees with it. (I don't mean to personify it, because it isn't at all personal; I mean, it is him, personally, but it isn't him only or only him, as a person.) There is real social disagreement as to whether women are or should be subordinated to men. Especially in sex.

His approach obscured the fact that our law is not content-based at all; it is harm-based. A harm is an act, an activity. It is not just a mental event. Coercion is not an image. Force is not a representation. Assault is not a symbol. Trafficking is not simply advocacy. Subordination is an activity, not just a point of view. The problem is, pornography is both theory and practice, both a metaphor for and a means of the subordination of women. The Seventh Circuit allowed the fact that pornography has a theory to obscure the fact that it is a practice, the fact that it is a metaphor to obscure the fact that it is also a means.

I don't want you to misunderstand what I am about to say. Our law comes nowhere near anybody's speech rights,[18] and the literatures of other inequalities do not relate to those inequalities in the same way pornography relates to sexism. But I risk your misunderstanding on both of these points in order to say that there have been serious movements for liberation in this world. This is by contrast with liberal movements. In serious movements for human freedom, speech is serious, both the attempt to get some for those who do not have any and the recognition that the so-called speech of the other side is a form of the practice of the other side. In union struggles, yellow-dog presses are attacked.[19] Abolitionists attacked slave presses.[20] The monarchist press was not tolerated by the revolutionaries who founded this country.[21] When the White Circle League published a racist pamphlet, it was found to violate a criminal law against libeling groups.[22] After World War II the Nazi press was restricted in Germany by law under the aegis of the Allies.[23] Nicaragua considers it "immoral" and contrary to the progress of education and the cultural development of the people to publish, distribute, circulate, exhibit, transmit, or sell materials that, among other things, "stimulate viciousness," "lower human dignity," or to "use women as sexual or commercial objects."[24]

The analogy Norma Ramos mentioned between the fight against pornography to sex equality and the fight against segregation to race equality makes the analogy between the Indianapolis case and *Brown* v. *Board of Education*[25] evocative to me also. But I think we may be at an even prior point. The Supreme Court just told us that it is a constitutional right to traffic in our flesh, so long as it is done through pictures and words, and a legislature may not give us access to court to contest it. The Indianapolis case is the *Dred Scott*[26] of the women's movement. The Supreme Court told Dred Scott, to the Constitution, you are property. It told women, to the Constitution, you are speech. The struggle against pornography is an abolitionist struggle to establish that just as buying and selling human beings never was anyone's property right, buying and selling women and children is no one's civil liberty.

NOTES

1. Isaiah Berlin distinguishes negative from positive freedom. Negative freedom asks the question, "what is the area within which the subject—a person or group of persons—is or should be left to do or be what [he] is able to do or be, without interference from other persons?" Positive freedom asks the question, "what, or who, is the source of control or interference that can determine someone to do, or be, this rather than that?" "Two Concepts of Liberty," in *Four Essays on Liberty* (1970), pp. 121–22. Is it not obvious that if one group is granted the positive freedom to do whatever they want to another group, to determine that the second group will be and do this rather than that, that no amount of negative freedom guaranteed to the second group will make it the equal of the first? The negative state is thus incapable of effective guarantees of rights in any but a just society, which is the society in which they are needed the least.

2. The analysis here is indebted to Andrea Dworkin, "For Men, Freedom of Speech, For Women, Silence Please," in *Take Back the Night: Women on Pornography*, ed. Laura Lederer (1982), pp. 255–58.

3. But cf. the words of framer William Livingston, who said, "Liberty of the press means promoting the common good of society, it does not mean unrestraint in writing." Livingston, "Of the Use, Abuse and Liberty of the Press," *Independent Reflector* (1754), quoted in Richard Buel, *The Press and the American Revolution* (1980), p. 69. Livingston's press was founded "to oppose superstition, bigotry, priestcraft, tyranny, servitude, public mismanagement and dishonesty in office." Quoted in Leonard W. Levy, *Emergence of a Free Press* (1985), p. 138. Levy, an absolutist, finds the theory that gave rise to the *Independent Reflector* "in fact reactionary if not vicious. . . . That a Framer could ever have held such views surprises" (p. 138).

4. There is a major controversy about the intent of the framers in relation to existing law and values of the colonial period. The controversy is discussed in T. Terrar, "The New Social History and Colonial America's Press Legacy: Tyranny or Freedom?" (unpublished manuscript, 1986).

5. *Red Lion Broadcasting Co.* v. *F.C.C.*, 395 U.S. 367 (1969). In *F.C.C.* v. *League of Women Voters*, 468 U.S. 364 (1984), the Supreme Court hints that it would be receptive to a challenge to the fairness doctrine on the basis that it impedes rather than furthers the values of the First Amendment, 376 n. 11, 378 n. 12.

6. *Schneider* v. *State*, 308 U.S. 147 (1939) (restricting street circulars because of litter is invalid if it is possible to clean them up).

7. Slave codes prohibited teaching slaves or free blacks to read, write, or spell and giving them reading materials and permitting meetings for schooling. Punishments for blacks included whipping; whites caught in the act could be fined and imprisoned but never whipped. Alabama: *Clay's Digest* 543, Act of 1832, § 10 (crime to teach black to spell, read, or write); North Carolina: *Revised Statutes* ch. 3, § 74 (1836–37) (crime to teach slave to read or write, except figures, to give or sell to slave a book or pamphlet); ch. 3, § 27 (slave who receives instruction receives thirty-nine lashes); Georgia: 2 *Cobb's Digest* 1001 (1829) (crime to teach black to read or write); Virginia: "Every assemblage of Negroes for the purpose of instruction in reading or writing shall be an unlawful assembly." *Virginia Code*, §§ 747–48 (1849); South Carolina: meetings including even one person of color "for the purpose of mental instruction in a confined or secret place are declared to be an unlawful meeting." Police can "break doors" and may lash participants sufficiently to deter them from future such acts. 7 *Statutes of South Carolina* 440 (1800). See generally George M. Stroud, *Sketch of the Laws Relating to Slavery* (1856, 1968 ed.), pp. 58–63. The slaves understood that literacy was as fundamental to effective expression as it was to every other benefit of equality: "It seemed to me that if I could learn to read and write, the learning might—nay I really thought it would, point out to me the way to freedom, influence, and real, secure, happiness." Slave narrative quoted in Thomas L. Webber, *Deep Like the Rivers: Education in the Slave Quarter Community* (1978), p. 144. The *Statutes of Louisiana* 208 (1852) state: "Whosoever shall make use of language in any public discourse from the bar, the bench, the stage, the pulpit, or in any place whatsoever, or whoever shall make use of language in private discourses or conversations, or shall make use of signs or actions, having a tendency to produce discontent among the free colored population of this state, or to excite insubordination among the slaves, or whosoever shall knowingly be instrumental in bringing into this state any paper, pamphlet or book having such tendency as aforesaid, shall, on conviction thereof before any court of competent jurisdiction, suffer imprisonment at hard labour not less than three years nor more than twenty-one years, or DEATH, at the discretion of the court" at 208.

8. The best examples are the laws against treason, bribery, conspiracy, threats, blackmail, and libel. Acts can also be expression, but are not necessarily protected as such. See, e.g., *Giboney* v. *Empire Storage & Ins. Co.*, 336 U.S. 490 (1946) (labor picketing can be enjoined on the ground the First Amendment does not cover "speech or writing used as an integral part of conduct in violation of a valid criminal statute"). Action "is often a method of expression and within the protection of the First Amendment . . ." but "picketing [is] 'free speech plus' [and] can be regulated when it comes to the 'plus' or 'action' side of the protest." *Brandenburg* v. *Ohio*, 395 U.S. 444, 455 (1969) (Douglas, J., concurring). See also *United States* v. *O'Brien*, 391 U.S. 367 (1968) (burning draft card not protected speech as symbolic protest); *Street* v. *New York*, 394 U.S. 576 (1969) (burning flag while speaking not punishable because speech is protected even though burning is crime); *Spence* v. *Washington*, 418 U.S. 407 (1974) (altering flag is protected speech despite flag desecration statute); *Clark* v. *Committee for Creative Non-Violence*, 468 U.S. 288 (1984) (sleeping in park to protest homelessness not protected as expressive conduct when it violates regulation against camping).

9. *Roth* v. *U.S.*, 354 U.S. 476, 508–14 ("The first amendment, in prohibitions in

terms absolute" at 514); *Memoirs* v. *Massachusetts*, 383 U.S. 413, 424–33 (concurring); *Miller* v. *California*, 413 U.S. 15, 37–47; *Paris Adult Theatres* v. *Slaton*, 413 U.S. 49, 70–73 (1973).

10. 106 S. Ct. 1172 (1986).

11. *American Booksellers* v. *Hudnut*, 771 F.2d 323 (7th Cir. 1985), *aff'd* 106 S. Ct. 1172 (1986).

12. 771 F.2d at 329.

13. *Renton* v. *Playtime Theatres*, 106 S. Ct. 925 (1986).

14. E.g., *Miller* v. *California*, 413 U.S. 15 (1973).

15. E.g., *New York* v. *Ferber*, 458 U.S. 747 (1982).

16. 106 S. Ct. at 933 n. 1 (Brennan, J., dissenting).

17. Laws against rape also express the view that sexual subordination is impermissible, and this is not considered repressive of thought, although presumably some thought is involved.

18. An erection is not a thought, either, unless one thinks with one's penis.

19. The most celebrated and equivocal example is the prosecution of unionist McNamara brothers for blowing up the virulently anti-union *Los Angeles Times*. The McNamaras pleaded guilty but doubt remains whether they did it. Although the bombing was criticized as inhumane (many people died), needlessly destructive, and instrategic, I found no argument within the movement that the *Times* should not have been attacked because it was "speech." See P. Foner, *History of the Labor Movement in the United States*, vol. 5, *The AFL in the Progressive Era* (1980), pp. 1910–15.

20. Abraham Lincoln ordered "copperhead" (northern pro-slavery) newspapers closed and editors jailed during the Civil War. The postmaster general barred some "copperhead" newspapers from the mail. Abolitionists "threatened, manhandled, or tarred editors, required changes in editorial policy, [and] burned print shops" of pro-slavery presses. Harold L. Nelson, *Freedom of the Press from Hamilton to the Warren Court* (1967), pp. xxvi–xxvii, 236–37.

21. For example, the Sons of Liberty in 1775 issued the following ultimatum to New York printers: "Sir, if you print, or suffer to be printed in your press anything against the rights and liberties of America, or in favor of our inveterate foes, the King, the Ministry and Parliament of Great Britain, death and destruction, ruin and perdition shall be your portion. Signed by Order of the Committee of Tarring and Feathering." Thomas Jones, *History of New York During the Revolutionary War*, ed. E. F. DeLancey (1879), quoted in Levy, *Emergence of a Free Press*, p. 175.

22. *Beauharnais* v. *Illinois*, 343 U.S. 250 (1952).

23. This was particularly true of the American-occupied zone. German publishers were licensed, and those who published materials inconsistent with the American objectives had their licenses revoked. They were kept under surveillance. Americans also imposed school reform and curriculum changes to reeducate German youth against the Nazi ideology. John Gimbel, *The American Occupation of Germany: Politics and the Military (1945–1949)* (1968), pp. 246–47. Positive steps were also taken. American propaganda efforts included radio and television campaigns against the harm of Nazism and attacks on neo-Nazis. Kurt P. Tauber, *Beyond Eagle and Swastika* (1967), p. 434. The British and American forces denied that they practiced censorship, but destructive criticism of the occupying powers was forbidden. Clara Menck, *A Struggle for Democracy in Germany*, ed. Gabriel L. Almon (1965), pp. 298–99.

24. *La Gaceta-Diario Oficial* (September 13, 1979), pp. 73–75, Ley General Provisional Sobre los Medios de Comunicacion Arto. 30 prohibits materials "que utilicen a la mujer como objeto sexual o comercial" ("that uses women as sexual or commercial

objects") Decree No. 48, August 17, 1979, p. 74. I make this reference not to hold up this language or this effort as an ideal to be strictly followed, but rather to remind leftists in particular that some efforts that they otherwise take as admirable do (even under conditions very different from those in the United States) consider that the use of women to sell things, as well as prostitution itself, is the opposite of the liberation of women as intended by their revolutions. It is also instructive to notice that an otherwise hard-headed revolutionary government with a lot to worry about does not regard the issue of sexual sale of women as either too unimportant to address or too moralistic for political concern.

25. *Brown* v. *Board of Education*, 347 U.S. 483 (1954).

26. *Dred Scott* v. *Sanford*, 60 U.S. (19 How.) 393 (1856).

18 TALKING DIRTY

THE EDITORS, *THE NEW REPUBLIC*

For all its luridness, absurdity, and brutality, the television trial of Clarence Thomas had at least one laudable side effect. It raised the public's awareness of sexual harassment in the workplace, and may even serve to discourage it in the future. As senators not previously known for their concern about women fell over each other to show their sensitivity to the nuances of sexual harassment, men around the country wondered whether they might be guilty of inappropriate conduct themselves. But by also revealing the elasticity of the legal definition of sexual harassment, the hearings could have another effect as well. They could ultimately cause harassment charges to be taken less seriously. Because the legal definition includes any unwanted "verbal conduct" that contributes to an "intimidating, hostile, or offensive working environment," it may lead to an outpouring of charges based less upon legitimate claims of harm than upon an increasingly powerful impulse to censor speech merely because it is offensive.

Invented in the 1970s by the feminist legal theorist Catharine MacKinnon, and endorsed in 1986 by the Supreme Court, the "hostile-environment" test threatens to trivialize legitimate claims of sexual harassment by equating sexual assaults with pinup calendars, and by diverting attention from genuine, harmful sex discrimination. It represents a radical new exception to the First Amendment axiom that speech cannot be punished just because it is offensive. Like restrictions on "hate speech," it punishes expression where it should punish harm. This would present a dilemma for civil libertarians if there weren't any other way to protect victims of real harassment. But there is.

The Civil Rights Act of 1964 says nothing about sexual harassment, and before the 1970s, courts dismissed the idea that offensive words—without physical, psychological, or economic harm—could add up to sex discrimination under Title VII. But in 1980, influenced by Professor MacKinnon's arguments, the Equal Employment Opportunity Commission adopted three tests for deciding whether "unwelcome verbal or physical conduct" violates the Civil Rights Act: first, is it "quid pro quo" behavior that makes submission to sex an implicit or explicit condition of advancement? Second, is it behavior that "unreasonably interferes with an individual's job performance"? And third, is it behavior that creates an "intimidating, hostile, or offensive working environment"?

We have no problems with the first two tests. But the third one is another matter. It relies heavily on the ambiguous term "verbal conduct," obscuring the most important distinction in First Amendment doctrine, which insists that the line between speech and conduct be drawn as precisely as possible. And in upholding the test, the Supreme Court never explained why unpleasant speech that *didn't* interfere with job performance could be regulated in any way. The ambiguous test then became unintelligible. Courts decided that legality of speech would depend, in retrospect, on whether a "reasonable woman" would have found that it created an "intimidating, hostile, or offensive" environment. This turns the First Amendment on its head. The Supreme Court has traditionally protected offensive speech because "one man's vulgarity is another man's lyric." Under the new rules, speech can be banned whenever one man's lyric becomes a reasonable woman's vulgarity. The fact that men and women often find different things funny (not to mention the fact that women themselves find different things funny) makes the "reasonable woman" standard even more perverse.

To prove the point, a federal appeals court found last January [1991] that even "well-intentioned compliments" from officemates can count as sexual harassment. An IRS agent in San Mateo, California, asked a fellow agent out to lunch twice, and after she declined, he declared his love in a poignant note praising her "style and elan," but promising to leave her alone if she asked. She sued and—because the court found that a "reasonable woman" would have found the note unwelcome—won. Days later a Florida district judge ordered the owner of a shipyard to stop his male welders from displaying pinup calendars and telling dirty jokes. His logic: "[B]anning sexist speech in the workplace does not censor such speech everywhere and for all time."

These cases are disturbing on two levels. First, they suggest that harassment claims tend to be trivial or imagined, when clearly most of them are not. It is impossible to wade through sexual harassment cases without being shocked by the sordidness—and the extent—of the abuse that many women experience at work. The scatology that runs throughout the opinions would make Long Dong

Silver blush. But if men are enjoined by courts from writing unwanted love letters, they will find it much harder to take real harassment seriously.

Second, it's scary to suggest that the rights of expression (including the right
to ask for dates) should be less protected at work than at home. Work is where
most Americans spend most of their waking hours; they must be free to express
themselves verbally without fear of prosecution. Professor MacKinnon is correct
when she argues that the logic of the "hostile-environment" exception cannot be
limited to the workplace, which is why it should apply neither in the office nor
outside of it.

The solution to this mess is a definition of sexual harassment that excludes
verbal harassment that has no other effect on its recipient than to create an
unpleasant working environment. Sexual harassment, as the ACLU [American
Civil Liberties Union] argues, should be limited to expression that is directed at
a specific employee and that "demonstrably hinders or completely prevents his
or her continuing to function as an employee." This would refine the existing test
for "unreasonable interference." Either version would cover legitimate claims.
As a 1989 note in the *Yale Law Journal* points out, *all* women who have successfully sued their supervisors (not their coworkers) for creating a "hostile environment" have also suffered some tangible economic harm, such as being fired.
Dropping the hostile environment standard wouldn't permit real harassment by
coworkers either. Even though it rarely presents an economic threat, such
assaults often interfere with job performance. The law against sexual harassment
would be strengthened, not weakened.

Assume, for example, that Anita Hill's charges are true. She would not need a
"hostile environment" test to make her case. She might have trouble proving "quid
pro quo" harassment, which occurs, according to the EEOC [Equal Employment
Opportunity Commission], when submission to (or rejection of) sexual advances is
used as the basis for employment decisions. She concedes that her refusal to date
Mr. Thomas and to watch bestiality videos didn't stop her from being promoted on
schedule. Ms. Hill could argue, however, that Mr. Thomas's advances "unreasonably interfered" with her job performance. She was sent to the hospital with nervous cramps, told her friends she had become depressed, and eventually left the
EEOC because she felt unable to continue. The judge in her case would still have
to make a difficult, subjective decision about how much the harassment had interfered with her job, and how much interference is "reasonable." But these are the
kinds of murky decisions that judges make every day, and they are far more appropriate than decisions about what a reasonable woman would find offensive.

What would be excluded from the legal definition of sexual harassment if
the "hostile-environment" test were abandoned? Only sexual expression that is
offensive but that has no detectable effect on job performance. That would
include most pinup calendars, most well-intentioned compliments, and even
some gross remarks. But trivial complaints like these are unusual. Sexual harassment lawyers say that cases of verbal harassment where the woman cannot prove
physical or psychological damage are rarely successful in court, even under the
"hostile-environment" test.

Abandoning the "hostile-environment" test is in the best interest of feminists as well as civil libertarians. The only realistic way to narrow the gap between what reasonable women and men perceive as harassment is to persuade men that unwanted advances can hurt women in tangible ways. A definition of harassment that diverts attention from that question makes relief for women all the more remote.

ROBINSON V. JACKSONVILLE SHIPYARDS, INC.

(UNITED STATES DISTRICT COURT, 1991)

FINDINGS OF FACT

Parties

1. Plaintiff Lois Robinson ("Robinson") is a female employee of Jacksonville Shipyards, Inc. ("JSI"). She has been a welder since September 1977. Robinson is one of a very small number of female skilled craftworkers employed by JSI. Between 1977 and the present, Robinson was promoted from third-class welder to second-class welder and from second-class welder to her present position as a first-class welder.

2. JSI is a Florida corporation that runs several shipyards engaged in the business of ship repair, including the Commercial Yard and the Mayport Yard. (The Court takes judicial notice of the closing and the reopening of the Commercial Yard operation subsequent to the trial of this case.) JSI does ship repair work for the federal government Department of the Navy. As a federal contractor, JSI has affirmative action and nondiscrimination obligations.

3. Defendant Arnold McIlwain ("McIlwain") held the office of president of JSI from the time Robinson was hired by the company through the time of the trial of this case. (The

---

Lois ROBINSON, Plaintiff, v. JACKSONVILLE SHIPYARDS, INC., et al, Defendants. 760 F. Supp. 1486 (M.D. Fla. 1991).

Court is aware from news reports that McIlwain no longer holds this office.) In that capacity he was the highest-ranking officer at JSI; as such he had supervisory authority over Robinson throughout her employment at JSI.

4. Defendant Lawrence Brown ("Brown") has been Vice-President for Operations at JSI since 1980. During the time relevant to this case, he oversaw the operations of the Commercial Yard and the Mayport Yard and formulated policies and regulations concerning the conduct and treatment of JSI employees at these two yards. He had and has supervisory authority over Robinson.

5. JSI is, in the words of its employees, "a boys club," and "more or less a man's world." Women craftworkers are an extreme rarity. The company's EEO–1 reports from 1980 to 1987 typically show that women form less than 5 percent of the skilled crafts. For example, JSI reported employing 2 women and 958 men as skilled craftworkers in 1980, 7 women and 1,010 men as skilled craftworkers in 1983, and 6 women and 846 men as skilled craftworkers in 1986. Henry Starling, a shift superintendent at the Commercial Yard, testified that on a busy shift he may see only 8 or 10 women, while seeing 150 men; on a quiet shift he may see no women at all. Leslie Albert, Lawanna Gail Banks, and Robinson each testified that she was the only woman in a crowd of men on occasions when each was sexually harassed at JSI. JSI has never employed a woman as a leaderman, quarterman, assistant foreman, foreman, superintendent, or coordinator. Nor has any woman ever held a position of vice-president or president of JSI.

6. Pictures of nude and partially nude women appear throughout the JSI workplace in the form of magazines, plaques on the wall, photographs torn from magazines and affixed to the wall or attached to calendars supplied by advertising tool supply companies ("vendors' advertising calendars"). Two plaques consisting of pictures of naked women, affixed to wood and varnished, were introduced into evidence and identified by several witnesses as having been on display for years at JSI in the fab shop area under the supervision of defendant [Ellis] Lovett.

7. Advertising calendars have been delivered for years to JSI by vendors with whom it does business. JSI officials then distribute the advertising calendars among JSI employees with the full knowledge and approval of JSI management. JSI employees are free to post these advertising calendars in the workplace. (It is not a condition of JSI's contracts with the vendors that the advertising calendars be posted.) A major supplier of advertising calendars to JSI is Whilden Valve and Gauge Repair, Inc.; Valve Repair, Inc. also does business with JSI and also delivers advertising calendars to the company. Generally speaking, these calendars feature women in various stages of undress and in sexually suggestive or submissive poses. Several male JSI employees corroborated the display of similar advertising calendars at JSI.

8. JSI has never distributed nor tolerated the distribution of a calendar or calendars with pictures of nude or partially nude men. Welding foreman Fred Turner noted it was accepted at the shipyards for vendors to supply calendars of nude women, but he had never known of a vendor distributing a calendar of nude men and, if one did so, he would think the "son of a bitch" was "queer."

9. JSI employees are encouraged to request permission to post most kinds

of materials; however, prior approval by the company is not required for the posting of advertising calendars with pictures of nude or partially nude women. JSI management has denied employees' requests to post political materials, advertisements, and commercial materials.

10. Bringing magazines and newspapers on the job is prohibited, but male JSI employees read pornographic magazines in the workplace without apparent sanctions. Although JSI employees are discouraged by management from reading on the job, they are not prohibited from tearing sexually suggestive or explicit pictures of women out of such magazines and displaying them on the workplace walls at JSI.

11. Management employees from the very top down condoned these displays; often they had their own pictures. McIlwain, for example, has been aware for years of *Playboy*- and *Penthouse*-style pictures showing nude women posted in the workplace; he refused to issue a policy prohibiting the display of such pictures. Both Brown and Stewart have encountered pictures of nude or partially nude women in the work environment at JSI. Nevertheless, both men have concluded, and agreed with each other, that there is nothing wrong with pictures of naked or partially naked women being posted in the JSI workplace.

CONCLUSIONS OF LAW

1. Five elements comprise a claim of sexual discrimination based on the existence of a hostile work environment: (1) plaintiff belongs to a protected category; (2) plaintiff was subject to unwelcome sexual harassment; (3) the harassment complained of was based upon sex; (4) the harassment complained of affected a term, condition, or privilege of employment; and (5) *respondeat superior*, that is, defendants knew or should have known of the harassment and failed to take prompt, effective remedial action. See *Meritor Savings Bank* v. *Vinson*, 477 U.S. 57, 66–69, 106 S. Ct. 2399, 2405–2407, 91 L.Ed.2d 49 (1986); *Henson* v. *City of Dundee*, 682 F.2d 897, 903–905 (11th Cir.1982); *Robinson* v. *Jacksonville Shipyards, Inc.*, 118 F.R.D. 525, 527-28 (M.D.Fla.1988).

2. Robinson indisputably belongs to a protected category.

3. The threshold for determining that sexually harassing conduct is unwelcome is "that the employee did not solicit or incite it, and . . . that the employee regarded the conduct as undesirable or offensive." *Henson*, 682 F.2d at 903 (citations omitted).

4. The relevant conduct in this case is the posting of pictures of nude and partially nude women in the workplace, the sexually demeaning remarks and jokes made by male workers, and harassment lacking a sexually explicit content such as the "Men Only" sign. The credible testimony of Robinson, corroborated by the observations of her supervisors and coworkers, attests to the offense she took at this behavior. Cf. *Vinson*, 477 U.S. at 68, 106 S. Ct. at 2406 ("the question whether particular conduct was indeed unwelcome presents difficult credibility determinations committed to the trier of fact"). Moreover, not a scintilla of

evidence suggests that she solicited or incited the conduct. Robinson did not welcome the conduct of which she complains.

5. The third element imposes a requirement that Robinson "must show that but for the fact of her sex, she would not have been the object of harassment." *Henson*, 682 F.2d at 904. This causation requirement encompasses several claims. For example, harassing behavior lacking a sexually explicit content but directed at women and motivated by animus against women satisfies this requirement. See *Andrews* v. *City of Philadelphia*, 895 F.2d 1469, 1485 (3d Cir.1990) ("The offensive conduct is not necessarily required to include sexual overtones in every instance"); *Lipsett* v. *University of Puerto Rico*, 864 F.2d 881, 905 (1st Cir.1988); *Hall* v. *Gus Constr. Co.*, 842 F.2d 1010, 1014 (8th Cir. 1988) ("Intimidation and hostility toward women because they are women can obviously result from conduct other than sexual advances"); *Hicks* v. *Gates Rubber Co.*, 833 F.2d 1406, 1415 (10th Cir.1987); *McKinney* v. *Dole*, 765 F.2d 1129, 1138 (D.C.Cir.1985). Second, sexual behavior directed at women will raise the inference that the harassment is based on their sex. E.g., *Huddleston* v. *Roger Dean Chevrolet, Inc.*, 845 F.2d 900, 904–905 (11th Cir.1988); *Sparks* v. *Pilot Freight Carriers, Inc.*, 830 F.2d 1554, 1561 (11th Cir.1987); see *Andrews*, 895 F.2d at 1485; *Lipsett*, 864 F.2d at 905; *Bennett* v. *Corroon & Black Corp.*, 845 F.2d 104, 106 (5th Cir.1988), *cert. denied*, 489 U.S. 1020, 109 S. Ct. 1140, 103 L.Ed.2d 201 (1989). A third category of actionable conduct is behavior that is not directed at a particular individual or group of individuals, but is disproportionately more offensive or demeaning to one sex. See *Henson*, 682 F.2d at 904; see also *Andrews*, 895 F.2d at 1485–86; *Waltman* v. *International Paper Co.*, 875 F.2d 468, 477 (5th Cir.1989), *rev'g* 47 Fair Empl.Prac.Cas. (BNA) 671 (W.D.La. 1987); *Lipsett*, 864 F.2d at 905; *Rabidue* v. *Osceola Ref. Corp.*, 805 F.2d 611, 627 (6th Cir.1986) (Keith, J., dissenting), *cert. denied*, 481 U.S. 1041, 107 S. Ct. 1983, 95 L.Ed.2d 823 (1987). This third category describes behavior that creates a barrier to the progress of women in the workplace because it conveys the message that they do not belong, that they are welcome in the workplace only if they will subvert their identities to the sexual stereotypes prevalent in that environment. That Title VII outlaws such conduct is beyond peradventure. Cf. *Price Waterhouse* v. *Hopkins*, 490 U.S. 228, 249–51, 109 S. Ct. 1775, 1790–91, 104 L.Ed.2d 268 (1989) (plurality opinion); ibid. at 262–67, 109 S. Ct. at 1797–99, 104 L.Ed.2d 268 (O'Connor, J., concurring in judgment) (use of gender stereotypes to evaluate female employees violates Title VII); *Griggs* v. *Duke Power Co.*, 401 U.S. 424, 431, 91 S. Ct. 849, 853, 28 L.Ed.2d 158 (1971) (Title VII was passed to remove "artificial, arbitrary, and unnecessary barriers to employment when the barriers operate invidiously to discriminate on the basis of . . . [an] impermissible classification").

6. The harassment of which Robinson complains was based upon her sex. The Findings of Fact reflect examples of the three aforementioned types of behavior. She suffered nonsexual harassing behavior from coworkers such as George Leach, who verbally abused or shunned her because she is a female. The "Men Only" sign also illustrates this type of harassment. She suffered incidents

of directed sexual behavior both before and after she lodged her complaints about the pictures of nude and partially nude women. The pictures themselves fall into the third category, behavior that did not originate with the intent of offending women in the workplace (because no women worked in the jobs when the behavior began) but clearly has a disproportionately demeaning impact on the women now working at JSI. The expert testimony of Dr. Fiske provides solid evidence that the presence of the pictures, even if not directed at offending a particular female employee, sexualizes the work environment to the detriment of all female employees.

7. The fourth element tests the impact of the harassing behavior on the employee and the work environment, separating the "mere utterance of . . . [a discriminatory] epithet which engenders offensive feelings in an employee," *Rogers* v. *EEOC*, 454 F.2d 234, 238 (5th Cir.1971), *cert. denied*, 406 U.S. 957, 92 S. Ct. 2058, 32 L.Ed.2d 343 (1972), and "the petty slights suffered by the hypersensitive," *Zabkowicz* v. *West Bend Co.*, 589 F.Supp. 780, 784 (E.D.Wis.1984), from actionable conduct under Title VII. To affect a "term, condition, or privilege" of employment within the meaning of Title VII, the harassment "must be sufficiently severe or pervasive 'to alter the conditions of [the victim's] employment and create an abusive working environment.' " *Vinson*, 477 U.S. at 67, 106 S. Ct. at 2405 (quoting *Henson*, 682 F.2d at 904). "This test may be satisfied by a showing that the sexual harassment was sufficiently severe or persistent 'to affect seriously [the victim's] psychological well-being.' " *Sparks*, 830 F.2d at 1561 (quoting *Henson*, 682 F.2d at 904). This "is a question to be determined with regard to the totality of the circumstances." *Henson*, 682 F.2d at 904. In the context of a racial harassment case, which is governed by the same standards under Title VII as a sexual harassment case, see *Patterson* v. *McLean Credit Union*, 491 U.S. 164, 109 S. Ct. 2363, 2374, 105 L.Ed.2d 132 (1989); *Risinger* v. *Ohio Bureau of Workers' Compensation*, 883 F.2d 475, 485 (6th Cir. 1989), the Eleventh Circuit elaborated on the evaluation of the totality of the circumstances:

> The prima facie showing in a hostile work environment case is likely to consist of evidence of many or very few acts or statements by the defendant which, taken together, constitute harassment. It is important to recognize that in assessing the credibility and weight of the evidence presented, the [trier of fact] does not necessarily examine each alleged incident of harassment in the vacuum. What may appear to be a legitimate justification for a single incident of alleged harassment may look pretextual when viewed in the context of several other related incidents.

> • • •

> . . . A hostile environment claim is a single cause of action rather than a sum total of a number of mutually distinct causes of action to be judged each on its own merits. . . . [T]he totality of the circumstances necessarily includes the severity, as well as the number, of incidents of harassment.

Vance, 863 F.2d at 1510–11 (footnote omitted).

8. Element four must be tested both subjectively and objectively. Regarding the former, the question is whether Robinson has shown she is an "affected individual," that is, she is at least as affected as the reasonable person under like circumstances. See *Robinson*, 118 F.R.D. at 530. The evidence reflects the great upset that Robinson felt when confronted with individual episodes of harassment and the workplace as a whole. Further, the impact on her work performance is plain. For essentially the same reasons that she successfully proved her case on the second element of this cause of action, Robinson likewise carries her burden as to the subjective part of the fourth element. (Defendants, having urged throughout these proceedings that Robinson is hypersensitive, appear to concede the point.) The contested issue in this case is the objective evaluation of the work environment at JSI.

9. The objective standard asks whether a reasonable person of Robinson's sex, that is, a reasonable woman, would perceive that an abusive working environment has been created. See *Vinson*, 477 U.S. at 67, 106 S. Ct. at 2405; *Andrews*, 895 F.2d at 1482; *Brooms* v. *Regal Tube Co.*, 881 F.2d 412, 419–20 (7th Cir.1989). The severity and pervasiveness aspects form a structure to test this hypothesis. As the prior quotations illustrate, the contours of what comprises "severe" and "pervasive" are not defined with precision. An interaction between the two is plain; greater severity in the impact of harassing behavior requires a lesser degree of pervasiveness in order to reach a level at which Title VII liability attaches. E.g., *Carrero* v. *New York Hous. Auth.*, 890 F.2d 569, 577 (2d Cir.1989). Moreover, the analysis cannot carve the work environment into a series of discrete incidents and measure the harm adhering in each episode. Rather, a holistic perspective is necessary, keeping in mind that each successive episode has its predecessors, that the impact of the separate incidents may accumulate, and that the work environment created thereby may exceed the sum of the individual episodes. "A play cannot be understood on the basis of some of its scenes but only on its entire performance, and similarly, a discrimination analysis must concentrate not on individual incidents but on the overall scenario." *Andrews*, 895 F.2d at 1484. It follows naturally from this proposition that the environment viewed as a whole may satisfy the legal definition of an abusive working environment although no single episode crosses the Title VII threshold.

10. The objective evaluation must account for the salient conditions of the work environment, such as the rarity of women in the relevant work areas. This important qualification explains why the Court places little value on the expert testimony of Drs. Mosher and Scott regarding the level of offensiveness to women of pornographic materials as measured in the abstract. Correspondingly, the need to identify the context in which harassing conduct arises weighs heavily in the Court's acceptance of the expert opinions of Dr. Fiske and Ms. Wagner.

11. A reasonable woman would find that the working environment at JSI was abusive. This conclusion reaches the totality of the circumstances, including the sexual remarks, the sexual jokes, the sexually oriented pictures of women, and the nonsexual rejection of women by coworkers. The testimony by Dr. Fiske and Ms. Wagner provides a reliable basis upon which to conclude that the cumu-

lative, corrosive effect of this work environment over time affects the psycho-logical well-being of a reasonable woman placed in these conditions. This corol-lary conclusion holds true whether the concept of psychological well-being is measured by the impact of the work environment on a reasonable woman's work performance or more broadly by the impact of the stress inflicted on her by the continuing presence of the harassing behavior. The fact that some female employees did not complain of the work environment or find some behaviors objectionable does not affect this conclusion concerning the objective offensive-ness of the work environment as a whole. See *Priest* v. *Rotary*, 634 F.Supp. 571, 582 (N.D.Cal. 1986); *Morgan* v. *Hertz Corp.*, 542 F.Supp. 123, 128 (W.D.Tenn. 1981), *aff'd*, 725 F.2d 1070 (6th Cir.1984).

12. The Court recognizes the existence of authority supporting defendants' contention that sexually oriented pictures and sexual remarks standing alone cannot form the basis for Title VII liability. The Court concludes that the rea-soning of these cases is not consistent with Eleventh Circuit precedent and is oth-erwise unsound.

(a) Defendants' authority, which hails from other jurisdictions, proceeds from premises that are inconsistent with authority that is binding on this Court. For example, the Sixth Circuit in *Rabidue* quoted with approval the conclusion of the district court that

> it cannot seriously be disputed that in some work environments, humor and lan-guage are rough hewn and vulgar. Sexual jokes, sexual conversations and girlie magazines may abound. Title VII was not meant to—or can—change this. It must never be forgotten that Title VII is the federal court mainstay in the struggle for equal employment opportunity for the female workers of America. But it is quite different to claim that Title VII was designed to bring about a magical transformation in the social mores of American workers.

805 F.2d at 620–21 (quoting in full 584 F.Supp. 419, 430). This conclusion but-tressed the appellate court's belief that "a proper assessment or evaluation of an employment environment" in a sexual harassment suit includes "the lexicon of obscenity that pervaded the environment of the workplace both before and after the plaintiff's introduction into its environs, coupled with the reasonable expec-tation of the plaintiff upon voluntarily entering that environment." Ibid. at 620. The *Rabidue* court further expounded on the social context argument:

> The sexually oriented poster displays had a de minimis effect on the plaintiff's work environment when considered in the context of a society that condones and publicly features and commercially exploits open displays of written and pictorial erotica at the newsstands, on prime-time television, at the cinema, and in other public places.

Ibid. at 622. These propositions, however, cannot be squared with the Eleventh Circuit's holding in *Walker* v. *Ford Motor Co.*, 684 F.2d 1355, 1359 and n. 2 (11th Cir.1982), that the social milieu of the area and the workplace does not diminish the harassing impact of racial slurs. (As previously noted, the analysis is not different for racial and sexual harassment claims.) The point is made more directly for sexual harassment claims in *Sparks*, wherein the appellate court explained that often "the whole point of the sexual harassment claim" is that behavior that "may be permissible in some settings . . . can be abusive in the workplace. . . ." 830 F.2d at 1561 n. 13; see also *Wyerick* v. *Bayou Steel Corp.*, 887 F.2d 1271, 1275 n. 11 (5th Cir.1989) ("heavy pollution defense" inconsistent with *Vinson* and *Henson*). A district court within the Eleventh Circuit recently concluded that a sexually hostile work environment was created in a police department when male officers subjected a female patrol officer to verbal abuse, "a plethora of sexually offensive posters, pictures, graffiti, and pinups placed on the walls throughout the Police Department," and "innumerable childish, yet offensive sexual and obscene innuendoes and incidents aimed at her on the basis of sex." *Sanchez* v. *City of Miami Beach*, 720 F.Supp. 974, 977 (S.D. Fla. 1989).

(b) The "social context" argument also lacks a sound analytical basis. Professor Kathryn Abrams has written an insightful critique of this argument:

> The *Rabidue* court's proposed standard is wholly inappropriate for several reasons. Not only did the court overestimate the public consensus on the question of pornography, but the fact that many forms of objectionable speech and conduct may be protected against interference by public authorities in the world at large does not mean that pornography should be accepted as appropriate in the workplace. Pornography in the workplace may be far more threatening to women workers than it is to the world at large. Outside the workplace, pornography can be protested or substantially avoided—options that may not be available to women disinclined to challenge their employers or obliged to enter certain offices. Moreover, while publicly disseminated pornography may influence all viewers, it remains the expression of the editors of *Penthouse* or *Hustler* or the directors of *Deep Throat*. On the wall of an office, it becomes the expression of a coworker or supervisor as well.
>
> In this context the effect of pornography on workplace equality is obvious. Pornography on an employer's wall or desk communicates a message about the way he views women, a view strikingly at odds with the way women wish to be viewed in the workplace. Depending upon the material in question, it may communicate that women should be the objects of sexual aggression, that they are submissive slaves to male desires, or that their most salient and desirable attributes are sexual. Any of these images may communicate to male coworkers that it is acceptable to view women in a predominately sexual way. All of the views to some extent detract from the image most women in the workplace would like to project: that of the professional, credible coworker.

Abrams, "Gender Discrimination and the Transformation of Workplace Norms," *Vanderbilt Law Review* 42 (1989): 1183, 1212 n. 118 (citation omitted); *accord Andrews*, 895 F.2d at 1485–86; *Lipsett*, 864 F.2d at 905 (adopting analysis of dissent in *Rabidue*); *Bennett*, 845 F.2d at 106; *Barbetta* v. *Chemlawn Servs. Corp.*, 669 F.Supp. 569, 573 and n. 2 (W.D.N.Y.1987); Ehrenreich, "Pluralist Myths and Powerless Men: The Ideology of Reasonableness in Sexual Harassment Law," *Yale Law Journal* 99 (1990): 1177, 1201–10; Strauss, "Sexist Speech in the

Workplace," *Harvard Civil Rights-Civil Liberties Law Review* 25 (1990): 1, 11–16. Professor Catherine MacKinnon makes the point in a pithy statement: "If the pervasiveness of an abuse makes it nonactionable, no inequality sufficiently institutionalized to merit a law against it would be actionable." C. MacKinnon, *Feminism Unmodified* (1987), p. 115.

(c) The "social context" argument cannot be squared with Title VII's promise to open the workplace to women. When the preexisting state of the work environment receives weight in evaluating its hostility to women, only those women who are willing to and can accept the level of abuse inherent in a given workplace—a place that may have historically been all-male or historically excluded women intentionally—will apply to and continue to work there. It is absurd to believe that Title VII opened the doors of such places in form and closed them in substance. A preexisting atmosphere that deters women from entering or continuing in a profession or job is no less destructive to and offensive to workplace equality than a sign declaring "Men Only." As the Fifth Circuit recently observed, "Work environments 'heavily charged' or 'heavily polluted' with racial or sexual abuse are at the core of the hostile environment theory." *Wyerick*, 887 F.2d at 1275. To implement fully the promise of Title VII, "the standards for assessing women's psychological harm due to harassment must begin to reflect women's sensitivity to behavior once condoned as acceptable." Note, "The Aftermath of *Meritor*: A Search for Standards in the Law of Sexual Harassment, *Yale Law Journal* 98 (1989): 1717, 1737–38.

(d) The *Rabidue* analysis violates the most basic tenet of the hostile work environment cause of action, the necessity of examining the totality of the circumstances. Excluding some forms of offensive conduct as a matter of law is not consistent with the factually oriented approach dictated by *Vinson, Henson,* and their progeny. The expert testimony in this case places the many instances of offensive behavior into a context that permits evaluation of the environment as a whole. The Court cannot ignore the expert testimony, or the Court's own perception of the work environment evaluated as a whole; it would have to do so in order to adopt the *Rabidue* conclusion that a sexually charged environment has only a "de minimis effect" on the psychological well-being of a reasonable woman who works in the skilled crafts at JSI.

13. The First Amendment guarantee of freedom of speech does not impede the remedy of injunctive relief. Accord *Davis* v. *Monsanto Chem. Co.*, 858 F.2d 345, 350 (6th Cir.1988), *cert. denied*, 490 U.S. 1110, 109 S. Ct. 3166, 104 L.Ed.2d 1028 (1989); *Jew* v. *University of Iowa*, 749 F.Supp. 946, 961 (S.D.Iowa 1990); cf. *EEOC* v. *Beverage Canners, Inc.*, 897 F.2d 1067, 1070 (11th Cir.1990) (upholding injunction directed to racially abusive language in workplace, without addressing free speech issues).

(a) First, JSI has disavowed that it seeks to express itself through the sexually oriented pictures or the verbal harassment by its employees. No First Amendment concern arises when the employer has no intention to express itself, see *Sage Realty*, 507 F.Supp. at 610 and n. 17, and JSI's action in limiting the speech options of its employees in the workplace, see FOF ¶¶ 20–21, establishes that the company may direct an end to the posting of materials without abridging its employees' free speech rights, cf. *May* v. *Evansville-Vanderburgh School Corp.*, 787 F.2d 1105, 1110 (7th Cir.1986) (because "workplace is for working," employer may lawfully withhold its consent for employees to engage in expressive activities).

(b) Second, the pictures and verbal harassment are not protected speech because they act as discriminatory conduct in the form of a hostile work environment. See *Roberts* v. *United States Jaycees*, 468 U.S. 609, 628, 104 S. Ct. 3244, 3255, 82 L.Ed.2d 462 (1984) ("[P]otentially expressive activities that produce special harms distinct from their communicative impact . . . are entitled to no constitutional protection"); *Hishon* v. *King & Spalding*, 467 U.S. 69, 78, 104 S. Ct. 2229, 2235, 81 L.Ed.2d 59 (1984); Strauss, "Sexist Speech in the Workplace," *Harvard Civil Rights-Civil Liberties Law Review* 25 (1990): 1, 38–41. In this respect, the speech at issue is indistinguishable from the speech that comprises a crime, such as threats of violence or blackmail, of which there can be no doubt of the authority of a state to punish. E.g., *Rankin* v. *McPherson*, 483 U.S. 378, 386–87, 107 S. Ct. 2891, 2897–99, 97 L.Ed.2d 315 (1987) (threat to kill the president is not protected by First Amendment); *United States* v. *Shoulberg*, 895 F.2d 882, 886 (2d Cir.1990) (threats to intimidate witnesses); see generally Greenawalt, "Criminal Coercion and Freedom of Speech," *Northwestern University Law Review* 78 (1983): 1081; Greenawalt, "Speech and Crime," *American Bar Foundation Res. Journal* (1980): 645. This treatment is consistent with the holding of *Pittsburgh Press Co.* v. *Human Relations Comm'n*, 413 U.S. 376, 93 S. Ct. 2553, 37 L.Ed.2d 669 (1973), that a ban on discriminatory help wanted advertisements did not offend the First Amendment. See also Smolla, "Rethinking First Amendment Assumptions About Racist and Sexist Speech," *Washington and Lee Law Review* 47 (1990): 171, 197 (transactional setting of sexual harassment opens sexist speech to regulation); cf. *Swank* v. *Smart*, 898 F.2d 1247, 1251 (7th Cir.) (casual chitchat while working is not protected speech), *cert. denied*, —— U.S. ——, 111 S. Ct. 147, 112 L.Ed.2d 113 (1990).

(c) Third, the regulation of discriminatory speech in the workplace constitutes nothing more than a time, place, and manner regulation of speech. The standard for this type of regulation requires a legitimate governmental interest unrelated to the suppression of speech, content neutrality, and a tailoring of the means to accomplish this interest. See, e.g., *United States* v. *O'Brien*, 391 U.S. 367, 377, 88 S. Ct. 1673, 1679, 20 L.Ed.2d 672 (1968). The eradication of workplace discrimination is more than simply a legitimate governmental interest, it is a compelling governmental interest. See *Rotary Int'l* v. *Rotary Club of Duarte*, 481 U.S. 537, 549, 107 S. Ct. 1940, 1947, 95 L.Ed.2d 474 (1987) (eliminating discrimination against women is compelling governmental interest); *Roberts*, 468 U.S. at 626, 104 S. Ct. at 3254 (compelling governmental interest lies in removing barriers to economic advancement and political and social integration that have historically plagued women). Given the circumstances of the JSI work environment, the method of regulation set forth in this order narrowly tailors the regulation to the minimum necessary to remedy the discrimination problem. To the extent that the regulation here does not seem entirely content neutral, the distinction based on the sexually explicit nature of the pictures and other speech does not offend constitutional principles. See *Renton* v. *Playtime Theatres, Inc.*, 475 U.S. 41, 48–49, 106 S. Ct. 925, 929–30, 89 L.Ed.2d 29 (1986); see also Sunstein, "Pornography and the First Amendment," *Duke Law Journal* 589 (1986): 616–17.

(d) Fourth, female workers at JSI are a captive audience in relation to the speech that comprises the hostile work environment. "Few audiences are more captive than the average worker. . . . Certainly, if employer-employee relations involve sufficient coercion that we justify regulation in other contexts, then this coercion does not suddenly vanish when the issue is submission to racist or sexist speech." Balkin, "Some Realism About Pluralism: Legal Realist Approaches to the First Amendment," *Duke Law Journal* 375 (1990): 423–24. The free speech guarantee admits great latitude in protecting captive audiences from offensive speech. See, e.g., *Frisby* v. *Schultz*, 487 U.S. 474, 487, 108 S. Ct. 2495, 2503, 101 L.Ed.2d 420 (1988); *FCC* v. *Pacifica Found.*, 438 U.S. 726, 744–51, 98 S. Ct. 3026, 3037–41, 57 L.Ed.2d 1073 (1978) (plurality opinion); *Lehman* v. *City of Shaker Heights*, 418 U.S. 298, 302–304, 94 S. Ct. 2714, 2716–18, 41 L.Ed.2d 770 (1974) (plurality opinion).

(e) Fifth, if the speech at issue is treated as fully protected, and the Court must balance the governmental interest in cleansing the workplace of impediments to the equality of women, the latter is a compelling interest that permits the regulation of the former and the regulation is narrowly drawn to serve this interest. Cf. *United States* v. *Paradise*, 480 U.S. 149, 171–85, 107 S. Ct. 1053, 1066–74, 94 L.Ed.2d 203 (1987) (performing similar analysis for race-conscious remedy to race discrimination). Other first amendment rights, such as the freedom of association and the free exercise of religion, have bowed to narrowly tailored remedies designed to advance the compelling governmental interest in eradicating employment discrimination. See, e.g., *Rotary Int'l*, 481 U.S. at 548–49, 107 S. Ct. at 1947–48; *EEOC* v. *Pacific Press*, 676 F.2d 1272, 1280–81 (9th Cir. 1982); *EEOC* v. *Mississippi College*, 626 F.2d 477, 488–89 (5th Cir.1980), *cert. denied*, 453 U.S. 912, 101 S. Ct. 3143, 69 L.Ed.2d 994 (1981); see also *Ellis* v. *Brotherhood of Ry. Airline & S.S. Clerks*, 466 U.S. 435, 455–56, 104 S. Ct. 1883, 1895–96, 80 L.Ed.2d 428 (1984) (governmental interest in industrial peace justifies interference with dissenting employees First Amendment rights resulting from allowing union shop).

(f) Sixth, the public employee speech cases lend a supportive analogy. If this Court's decree is conceptualized as a governmental directive concerning workplace rules that an employer must carry out, then the present inquiry is informed by the limits of a governmental employer's power to enforce workplace rules impinging on free speech rights. In the public employee speech cases, the interests of the employee in commenting on protected matters is balanced against the employer's interests in maintaining discipline and order in the workplace. See, e.g., *Finch* v. *City of Vernon*, 877 F.2d 1497, 1502 (11th Cir.1989). When an employee's exercise of free expression undermines the morale of the workforce, the employer may discipline or discharge the employee without violating the First Amendment. See, e.g., *Bryson* v. *City of Waycross*, 888 F.2d 1562, 1564–67 (11th Cir.1989). Analogously, the Court may, without violating the First Amendment, require that a private employer curtail the free expression in the workplace of some employees in order to remedy the demonstrated harm inflicted on other employees. Cf. *McMullen* v. *Carson*, 568 F.Supp. 937, 943–45 (M.D.Fla.1983) (finding no First Amendment violation in discharge of KKK member from police force because inter alia internal discipline and morale were threatened by potential for racial confrontations), *aff'd*, 754 F.2d 936 (11th Cir. 1985); *accord Rankin*, 483 U.S. at 391 n. 18, 107 S. Ct. at 2901 n. 18.

(g) Finally, defendants' reliance upon *American Booksellers Ass'n* v. *Hudnut*, 771 F.2d 323 (7th Cir.1985), *sum. aff'd*, 475 U.S. 1001, 106 S. Ct. 1172, 89 L.Ed.2d 291 (1986), is misplaced. Two concerns dominate that case. One is the broad definition of "pornography" in the Indianapolis ordinance. See 771 F.2d at 332. This issue is not present in this case because the affected speech, if it is speech protected by the First Amendment, is reached only after a determination that a harm has been and is continuing to be inflicted on identifiable individuals. The second concern raised in *Hudnut* is the underlying proposition of the Indianapolis ordinance that pornography conveys a message that is always inappropriate and always subject to punishment, regardless of the context in which it appears. See ibid. at 327–32. In this case, the context of the speech is the heart of the cause of action and the remedy goes no further than to regulate the time, place, and manner of the offensive speech. Cf. *Bryson*, 888 F.2d at 1567 (public employee may be discharged lawfully for uttering on-job speech which would be protected fully if uttered off-duty and in private).

In accordance with the foregoing, it is hereby

ADJUDGED:

That judgment shall be entered in favor of plaintiff Lois Robinson and against defendants Jacksonville Shipyards, Inc., Lawrence Brown, and John Stewart on the claim made pursuant to Title VII of the Civil Rights Act of 1964 . . .

PORNOGRAPHY, EQUALITY, AND A DISCRIMINATION-FREE WORKPLACE

A Comparative Perspective

THE EDITORS, HARVARD LAW REVIEW

Over the past two decades, various forms of antipornography legislation have been proposed on the local,[1] state,[2] and national[3] levels in the United States. Some of these measures have failed to be enacted[4] while others have been struck down as unconstitutional by federal courts.[5] However, the Canadian Supreme Court, in a 1992 decision that some commentators have hailed as groundbreaking,[6] upheld a statute criminalizing "obscenity" and redefined the term to encompass materials that degrade or subordinate women.[7] Recent U.S. Supreme Court free speech rulings may obstruct future attempts to follow Canada's lead and thus to eradicate pornography throughout the United States.[8] But the Court's landmark decision in *Meritor Savings Bank* v. *Vinson*,[9] which held that a hostile work environment could constitute actionable sex discrimination,[10] has opened the door for narrower—yet still significant—restrictions on pornography. Indeed, several lower federal courts have recently concluded that pornography in the workplace may serve as evidence supporting a claim for hostile environment sexual harassment under Title VII[11] of the Civil Rights Act of 1964. [12] In only one case decided so far, however, did a federal court find pornography in the workplace to be the primary offensive conduct in the creation of a discriminatory environment.[13] This Note argues that the eradication of porno-

From *Harvard Law Review* 106 (1993): 1075–92. Copyright © 1993 by The Harvard Law Review Association. Reprinted by permission.

graphic materials in the workplace is necessary to achieve the objectives of Title VII—that is, "an environment free from discriminatory ridicule and insult,"[14] where women can "achieve equality of employment opportunities."[15]

This Note adopts the feminist definition of pornography set forth in the Dworkin/MacKinnon civil rights antipornography ordinance. By that definition, pornography consists of "the graphic sexually explicit subordination of women through pictures or words" that also portray women in sexually degrading contexts, including submissive or servile poses, or sexualized in a manner involving violence.[16] Importantly, this definition properly restricts the scope of this Note's inquiry to the materials that most directly harm women.[17]

Part I explores the harms to women caused by pornography. Part II compares the societal responses to such harms in the United States and in Canada. Part III reviews precedents regarding sexual harassment and the use of pornography in the workplace, and describes a particularly compelling example of an instance where pornographic pictures were held to constitute a hostile working environment. Part IV explains how pornography in the workplace creates a hostile and discriminatory environment and therefore violates Title VII.

I. THE DIRECT EFFECTS OF PORNOGRAPHY ON WOMEN

Although much has been written and debated about the effects that pornography has upon men's attitudes and behavior,[18] precious little mention has been made in the legal literature about pornography's direct impact on women.[19] Nonetheless, evidence available from women's own accounts of their experiences with pornography indicate that pornography has a direct impact on women, apart from the attitudinal changes it may cause in men.[20]

Some women describe their experiences with pornography as positive. The Feminist Anti-Censorship Taskforce (FACT), for example, filed a brief against the Indianapolis City Council in *Hudnut*,[21] claiming that pornography may be a source of liberation and pleasure.[22] Most of the material that FACT wanted to protect, however, was not violent pornography that had been produced by and for men but rather feminist or lesbian erotica, which FACT feared would be targeted by the male-dominated legislature and judiciary.[23]

Although pornography may be pleasing to some women, it may terrorize others. For example, Andrea Dworkin describes a female response to a pornographic photograph of a woman, spread eagle, bound by ropes to the top of a jeep in *Hustler* magazine:

> The terror is implicit in the content of the photograph, but beyond that the photograph strikes the female viewer dumb with fear. One perceives that the bound woman must be in pain. The very power to make the photograph (to use the model, to tie her in that way) and the fact of the photograph (the fact that someone did use the model, did tie her in that way, that the photograph is published in a magazine and seen by millions of men who buy it specifically to see

such photographs) evoke fear in the female observer unless she entirely disso-
ciates herself from the photograph: refuses to believe or understand that real
persons posed for it, refuses to see the bound person as a woman like herself.
Terror is finally the content of the photograph, and it is also its effect on the
female observer.[24]

Pornography instills fear and humiliation in countless women.[25] Women who
have been raped or otherwise sexually abused[26] suffer even more profoundly
from forced exposure to pornography, largely because it validates and celebrates
the criminal behavior of which they have been victims,[27] and thus they are unable
to dissociate themselves completely from the women in the photographs.[28] It
seems clear that women, far more often then men, are likely to identify with the
subjects used in the production of the materials.[29]

This pain is particularly magnified for women who are coerced into the production of pornography and must suffer the enjoyment of a "permanent record"[30]
of their sexual abuse as someone else's sexual pleasure. Perhaps the most well-
known account of this pain is that of Linda Marchiano, who was kidnapped and
raped in the production of *Deep Throat*. "[E]very time someone watches the
film," she has testified, "they are watching me be raped."[31]

Pornography may also harm women by thrusting upon them insulting and
degrading views of their societal roles and their sexuality. Indeed, Robin West has
argued that pornography's greatest harm lies in its ability to define narrowly the
way in which women (and men) see themselves. Pornography enforces and legiti-
mates images of sexuality that exclude the perception of women as in sovereign
possession of their bodies and their own sexuality, and these images carry over to
a social structure of gender inequality as a whole.[32] Pornography degrades and
objectifies women; some reports suggest that women find nonviolent degrading
pornography more upsetting than the violent kind.[33] Pornography conveys a message to women of how the dominant (male) society views them;[34] it is not surprising that surveys reveal women to have far more negative views toward pornography than men.[35] To many women, pornography is hardly "harmless" and "fun."[36]

II. COMPARATIVE APPROACHES TO PORNOGRAPHY AND ITS DIRECT EFFECTS ON WOMEN

A. *Canada*

In Canada, as in the United States, feminists, libertarians, and others have
engaged in a contentious battle over the harm and constitutional implications of
pornography and its regulation.[37] Besides geographic proximity, Canada and the
United States share many sociological similarities.[38] Canada is governed under a
constitution similar to that of the United States.[39] Thus, the United States could
greatly benefit from a comparative examination of Canadian law.[40]

In its landmark ruling in *Butler* v. *Her Majesty the Queen*,[41] the Supreme
Court of Canada upheld the constitutionality of Canada's obscenity statute,

which criminalizes the publication and distribution of obscene materials, defined as those that have as a "dominant characteristic" the "undue exploitation of sex."[42] Donald Butler owned a store in Winnipeg that sold and rented "'hard core' videotapes and magazines as well as sexual paraphernalia."[43] Pursuant to an arrest warrant the police seized the entire inventory of Butler's store and charged him with 250 violations of Canada's criminal obscenity statute.[44] The trial court convicted him on eight counts relating to eight films and granted acquittals on the other 242 counts on the ground that most of the seized materials were constitutionally protected by the guarantee of freedom of expression in section 2(b) of the Canadian Charter of Rights and Freedoms.[45] The appellate court reversed the acquittals and entered convictions for all of the counts.[46]

The Canadian Supreme Court addressed two specific questions in *Butler*: whether a criminal ban on obscenity, interpreted to include pornography, infringed upon the guarantee of free expression, and, if so, whether such an infringement was "demonstrably justified" in a free and democratic society and therefore constitutionally valid under section I of the Charter as "a reasonable limit prescribed by law."[47] The court concluded that the obscenity law did infringe upon section 2(b) of the Charter because it sought to prohibit certain types of expressive activity on the basis of the content or meaning being conveyed.[48] Nonetheless, it held that the obscenity ban, interpreted to include pornography, was justifiable under Section I of the Charter because the overriding objective of the law was the avoidance of harm to society in general and to women in particular,[49] an interest sufficient to warrant a restriction on the freedom of expression.[50]

Notably, the Court expanded on the statute's scant definition of obscenity— "the undue exploitation of sex"—by focusing on the harms to society in general and to women in particular, stating that these "degrading or dehumanizing materials place women (and sometimes men) in positions of subordination, servile submission or humiliation. They run against the principles of equality and dignity of all human beings."[51] The Court also held that in pornography the appearance of participants' consent does not determine whether material is degrading or dehumanizing because "[s]ometimes the very appearance of consent makes the depicted acts even more degrading or dehumanizing."[52]

Moreover, the Canadian Supreme Court expressly recognized that pornography not only affects men and men's behavior, but also corrodes women's integrity and self-esteem. The Court wrote:

> [I]f true equality between male and female persons is to be achieved, we cannot ignore the threat to equality resulting from exposure to audiences of certain types of violent and degrading material. Materials portraying women as a class as objects for sexual exploitation and abuse have a negative impact on "the individual's sense of self-worth and acceptance."[53]

The Court also emphasized that "obscenity wields the power to wreak social damage in that a significant portion of the population is humiliated by its gross misrepresentations."[54] This acknowledgment of the difference between male and female perceptions of, depictions in, and attitudes toward pornography is arguably one of the greatest strengths of the Canadian decision. It treats pornography not as a mere idea, but as a concrete act of discrimination against women which degrades both their selfrespect and their social status.

B. The United States

By contrast with the course taken by its Canadian counterpart, the U.S. Supreme Court has never directly addressed pornography's harm to women. In a long line of cases the Court has analyzed the constitutionality of anti-obscenity laws almost exclusively by reference to pornography's impact on (and importance to) male consumers, and on the traditional moral fabric of heterosexual society.[55]

If the Court would view allegedly obscene material from the point of view of the participants and unwilling observers, however, it could better discern which materials were harmful and therefore justifiably regulable. Such was the case in *New York* v. *Ferber*,[56] in which the Court upheld a criminal ban on non-obscene child pornography—specifically, in that case, films depicting young boys masturbating[57]—on the ground that the state could rationally conclude that child pornography harms children.[58] Ferber thus carved out a new category of unprotected speech for child pornography. In so doing, it effectively equated child pornography with child abuse.[59]

Unfortunately, the Supreme Court has yet to apply similar insight to the pornography of women. The only federal court of appeals, however, to review the constitutionality of an antipornography law (as opposed to an anti-obscenity law) has acknowledged that pornography directly harms women. In *American Booksellers Association, Inc.* v. *Hudnut*,[60] judge Easterbrook, writing for a panel of the Seventh Circuit, explained:

> Depictions of subordination tend to perpetuate subordination. The subordinate status of women in turn leads to affront and lower pay at work, insult and injury at home, battery and rape on the streets. In the language of the legislature, "[p]ornography is central in creating and maintaining sex as a basis of discrimination. Pornography is a systematic practice of exploitation and subordination based on sex which differentially harms women. The bigotry and contempt it produces, with the acts of aggression it fosters, harm women's opportunities for equality and rights [of all kinds]."[61]

The court concluded, however, that the very fact that it harms women proves "the power of pornography as speech" and consequently justifies its protection under the First Amendment's Free Speech Clause.[62] The Supreme Court affirmed without comment.[63]

The *Hudnut* court's characterization of pornography as powerful yet harmful speech was, at the same time, both reminiscent of and contrary to the reasoning of the Canadian Supreme Court in *Butler*. On the one hand, both courts acknowledged the serious harms to women caused by pornography. But on the other hand, these two courts reached diametrically opposing results because of their differing approaches to gender equality. In the Canadian case, the Court looked to a constitutionally grounded guarantee of gender equality (encompassed by Section 28, the gender equality section, and Section I, allowing reasonable limits in a "free and democratic society") and held that the right to gender equality trumped the right to free expression.[64] By contrast, the Hudnut court, which of course could look to no express constitutional guarantee of gender equality and which chose to ignore the Fourteenth Amendment's Equal Protection Clause,[65] held that the right to free expression trumped women's right to equality.

One powerful analogy that the Hudnut court overlooked was that of the Equal Protection Clause[66] as interpreted by the Supreme Court in *Brown* v. *Board of Education.*[67] The *Brown* Court sought to eradicate racial segregation in the schools not on the grounds that it harmed traditional morality in society at large or that it inspired whites to commit acts of violence against Blacks, but rather because such discrimination "generate[d] a feeling of inferiority as to [Black children's] status in the community that may affect their hearts and minds in a way unlikely ever to be undone."[68] The system of racial discrimination that U.S. courts began to dismantle in the 1950s can be analogized to the system of sex inequality that pornography perpetuates today: both harm a group of human beings by reinforcing the view that its members are inferior and worthy of mistreatment.[69] Consequently, as Professor Catharine MacKinnon has argued, "making pornography actionable as sex discrimination would delegitimize the ideas the practice advances," just as "deinstitutionalizing segregation [did] a great deal to undermine the point of view it expressed."[70] Unfortunately, U.S. courts—unlike those in Canada[71]—have failed to recognize that the eradication of discriminatory messages is often both a necessary means and effect of eliminating discrimination, and that rights to free expression must sometimes be sacrificed in order to vindicate rights to equality.[72]

Another powerful analogy that the *Hudnut* court overlooked was that of the First Amendment as interpreted by the Supreme Court in Ferber. The Ferber Court's reasoning, which upheld the regulation of child pornography because it directly harmed children, could be extended to women. Contrary to fears expressed by civil libertarians, such a judgment need not rest on Victorian morals and condescending views toward women. Rather, it would rely upon an acknowledgment that women are systematically harassed, assaulted, raped, and killed,[73] and that women experience such treatment as part of an experience of social inequality based on gender.[74] Because men typically do not undergo these experiences,[75] they may not suffer from the same threat to equality and integrity that pornography poses to women.[76] To protect women from the terrorization of pornography is thus to grant them relief from discrimination, and social equality, rather than "special protection" in the paternalistic sense.

Despite the power of these analogies, the U.S. Supreme Court has given no indication that it is willing to treat the pornography of women as it has treated either racial segregation or child pornography. Yet, such a result should follow when the Court recognizes that pornography does harm women directly—most invidiously by expressing to women that they exist for the purpose of male gratification and that their proper place in society is that of sexual subservience to men.[77] Although the redress of these dignitary harms is currently close to impossible in U.S. society at large, a pocket of protection from these harms in the workplace has been created by Title VII of the Civil Rights Act of 1964.

III. PORNOGRAPHY IN THE WORKPLACE: THE CREATION OF A DISCRIMINATORY AND OFFENSIVE ENVIRONMENT

A. The Purpose and Meaning of Hostile Environment: Sexual Harassment under Title VII

Unlike Canada, the United States has not enacted an explicit constitutional guarantee of equal rights to women in all aspects of society.[78] Congress has, however, enacted the Civil Rights Act of 1964, which prohibits unlawful discrimination in the workplace. Title VII makes it unlawful "to discriminate against any individual with respect to his compensation, terms, conditions, or privileges of employment, because of such individual's race, color, religion, sex, or national origin."[79] In the 1986 case, *Meritor Savings Bank* v. *Vinson*,[80] a unanimous Supreme Court, in an opinion written by then-Justice Rehnquist, interpreted Title VII to prohibit sexual harassment.[81] The Court recognized two types of sexual harassment: "quid pro quo" sexual harassment—conditioning employment on "sexual favors"—and "hostile environment" sexual harassment—unwelcome sexual conduct which "unreasonably interfer[es] with an individual's work performance" or promotes an "intimidating, hostile, or offensive working environment." [82]

In recognizing a hostile environment as sexual harassment, the Court explicitly acknowledged that Title VII was aimed at "'the entire spectrum of disparate treatment of men and women' in employment," which includes psychological as well as economic and physical abuse.[83] Drawing from the context of racial harassment, the Court recognized that psychological and dignitary harms may not be trivial; rather, "[o]ne can readily envision working environments so heavily polluted with discrimination as to destroy completely the emotional and psychological stability of minority group workers"—which, according to the Court, includes women.[84]

The Meritor Court also noted that sexual conduct of a verbal, as well as physical nature may create a hostile environment in violation of Title VII.[85] Such verbal conduct, according to the Court, may be so demeaning that it interferes with an employee's ability to perform her job.[86] An employee should not be forced, simply because she is a woman, to "run a gauntlet of sexual abuse in return for the privilege of being allowed to work and make a living."[87] Consequently, "Title VII affords employees the right to work in an environment free from discriminatory intimidation, ridicule, and insult."[88]

B. Workplace Pornography and Hostile Environment Sexual Harassment

Although images of women as sexual objects may be pleasurable to some women when enjoyed in private, they can be particularly invidious when displayed at work, where a woman is striving to be treated as a "credible coworker."[89] Stories of women in nontraditional fields such as the trades demonstrate that pornography is often used by men in the workplace to send messages to the women that they do not belong there.[90] The existence of pornography in the workplace may undermine a woman's sense of self-worth and make the conditions of her employment either unbearable or devastating for her self-esteem.[91] It may drive women out of male-dominated workplaces that are badly in need of integration.[92]

Although many, if not most, women find pornography, particularly in workplace settings, to be insulting, intimidating, and degrading, courts generally have not held that pornography in the workplace, even when unwelcome and pervasive, constitutes hostile environment sexual harassment per se. Rather, most courts have cited pornography in the workplace as mere evidence of a hostile environment, if they found pornography to be worth mentioning at all,[93] and have focused primarily on other aspects of harassing behavior, such as offensive comments and sexist pranks.[94] That is, most courts found pornography to be evidence of discrimination in the workplace, rather than discrimination itself. The following case demonstrates that pornography in the workplace may in fact unreasonably interfere with a woman's ability to perform her job and consequently create a hostile working environment under Title VII.

C. Robinson v. Jacksonville Shipyards

In the spring of 1993, the U.S. Court of Appeals for the Eleventh Circuit will decide *Robinson* v. *Jacksonville Shipyards*,[95] in which a female welder sued her employer for sexual harassment. Lois Robinson worked as one of only a very few women who held a skilled crafts position at the shipyards.[96] Robinson worked in an environment immersed in pornography—photographs and plaques of nude women in submissive poses covered the walls—vendors who did business with the shipyards routinely distributed advertising calendars with "pinups" to employees, who were encouraged by their employer to post them at work.[97] Many pictures explicitly and violently demeaned women,[98] and none depicted men.[99] Several were placed either in Robinson's working area or on the box where she left her tools, or handed to her directly in front of male coworkers in order to humiliate her. For example, one of Robinson's coworkers taunted her with a photograph of a nude woman with long blond hair holding a whip. Because Robinson has long blond hair and worked with an instrument called a "whip," she understandably experienced the man's actions as a personal threat.[100] Robinson on numerous occasions complained to her employer that she found the pornographic pictures "degrading and humiliating" and that "they nauseated her," and requested that they be removed, but to no avail—her requests only prompted the male workers to bring in "hard pornography" instead.[101]

The men who worked at the shipyards acknowledged that the environment was a "boy's club," "more or less a man's world."[102] Federal District judge Melton took a different view of the work environment: a "visual assault on the sensibilities of female workers."[103] After hearing expert testimony concerning the effects of pornography on women in the workplace, the court held that a policy that allowed these materials to be displayed contradicted the spirit of Title VII—the creation of a workplace free of discrimination, where women are afforded equal opportunity to pursue a career.[104] Pornography, explained the court, "creates a barrier to the progress of women in the workplace because it conveys the message that they do not belong, that they are welcome in the workplace only if they subvert their identities to the sexual stereotypes prevalent in that environment."[105]

The Robinson court explicitly found that pornography in the workplace differentially harms women. It noted that pornography may threaten women in the workplace even more than it does in society at large.[106] It described pornography's impact on workplace equality:

> Pornography on an employer's wall or desk communicates a message about the way he views women, a view strikingly at odds with the way women wish to be viewed in the workplace. . . . It may communicate that women should be the objects of sexual aggression, that they are submissive slaves to male desires, or that their most salient and desirable attributes are sexual. . . . All of the views to some extent detract from the image most women in the workplace would like to project: that of the professional, credible coworker.[107]

The court concluded that such an atmosphere deters women from entering or remaining in a profession and is "no less destructive to and offensive to workplace equality than a sign declaring 'Men Only.' "[108] It is "absurd to believe that Title VII opened the doors of such places in form and closed them in substance."[109] The court ordered the shipyards to implement a sexual harassment prevention policy that mandated removing the pinups and other pornographic visuals.[110]

In confronting the shipyards' argument that a judicially imposed sexual harassment policy would violate its free speech right to pornography, Robinson resembles both *Butler* and *Hudnut*. The District Court in Robinson, however, explicitly rejected the applicability of *Hudnut*[111] and ultimately followed a *Butler*-like analysis in recognizing that speech rights sometimes must be sacrificed when the exercise of those rights harms others.[112]

IV. TOWARD CREATING A DISCRIMINATION-FREE WORKPLACE THROUGH THE ERADICATION OF WORKPLACE PORNOGRAPHY

Regardless of whether the Eleventh Circuit reverses or affirms Robinson, the case still presents a strong argument for the elimination of pornographic materials in the workplace, or in any place governed by a mandate of gender equality under Title VII. In determining the extent of the harm that pornographic materials inflict upon women in the workplace, the district court set out several well-reasoned and well-supported factors that other courts should consider. For example, the court recognized that women who work in virtually all-male workplaces will experience pornography as particularly threatening.[113] The negative consequences of extreme gender-imbalance in the workplace on women have been well documented;[114] such considerations are properly addressed in any hostile environment case. In addition, the court correctly noted that a gender-based power hierarchy in the workplace will magnify the harm of pornography there, because "the people affected by the sexualized working conditions are women, and the people deciding what to do about it are men."[115] Arguably, this factor resembles the Butler decision to the extent that the Supreme Court of Canada recognized a gender-based power imbalance in society as a whole.[116]

Further, *Robinson* correctly recognized that women constitute "captive audiences" in the workplace to the same extent as do men.[117] Most women, both single and married, work out of "pressing economic need"[118] and cannot afford to walk away from demeaning and hostile expression at work. Access to traditionally male, lucrative jobs, in fields such as the skilled trades, is crucial to the realization of gender equality.[119] When male employees fight adamantly for their "right" to use pornography at work, a crucial question to ask is "Why?" When pornography is recast from a woman's perspective[120] as the powerfully debilitating and terrorizing expression that it may be, arguments for its protection under *Hudnut* become arguments for its suppression under *Butler* and *Robinson*.

Finally, the Robinson court demonstrated the helpful nature of expert testimony in sexual harassment litigation. Since the law of sexual harassment is arguably one of the few legal remedies constructed both by and for women, courts and juries may benefit greatly from testimony that places women's reactions in the context of women's lived reality, rather than relying on harmful and outdated stereotypes.[121] Further, changing times call for changing burdens of proof; perhaps when certain characteristics of a workplace are shown to exist—such as a sex-skewed worker ratio and a gendered power hierarchy—courts should place the burden on the employer to prove that its conduct was not harmful or discriminatory.

To be sure, pornographic materials may not create an unreasonably offensive environment for all women in all work settings. The *Robinson* court, for example, recognized that a determination of whether pornography creates a hostile environment must be made by reference to the context in which the pornography appears.[122] In so doing, the court shifted the emphasis of the harms of pornography from a theoretical inquiry into the subordination of women in society, toward an empirical and experiential inquiry into the subordination of women in a particular working environment.[123] Validating women's accounts of their reactions to the conduct and expressive behavior that they encounter may mitigate the problem of essentialization of women's experience.[124] By crediting a woman's description of her experience, and focusing on a woman's account rather than on the abstract nature of harassing conduct, courts may begin to allow women to describe the nature of their pain in a forum where they might be believed and eventually be afforded relief.

V. Conclusion

Pornography may be speech—speech that many men and some women may claim to enjoy in private—but in the circumstances of a male-dominated workplace, pornography is an issue of power. Its elimination from the workplace would be a narrowly tailored and reasonable remedial measure that would infringe minimally on rights to free expression while having a great impact on women's rights to equality.[125] The right to work in a discrimination-free workplace is essential for women to obtain the equal employment status guaranteed by Title VII; moreover, it is a right that should be guaranteed to all individuals in any free and democratic society—including both Canada and the United States.

Notes

1. Ordinances have been proposed in the cities of Indianapolis, Indiana; Minneapolis, Minnesota; Cambridge, Massachusetts; Los Angeles, California; and Bellingham, Washington. See Andrea Dworkin, *Pornography: Men Possessing Women* (1989), pp. xxx–xxxi.

2. See, e.g., An Act to Protect the Civil Rights of Women and Children, Mass. H.B. 5194, 177th Gen. Ct., 1992 Reg. Sess., available in LEXIS, LEGIS Library, MACODE File.

3. See Pornography Victims' Compensation Act, S. 983, 102d Cong., 1st Sess. (1991).

4. For example, an antipornography ordinance was passed twice in Minneapolis, in 1983 and 1984, by two different city councils, and vetoed each time by the same mayor. See Dworkin, *Pornography*, p. xxx.

5. See, e.g., *American Booksellers Ass'n* v. *Hudnut*, 771 F.2d 323, 332 (7th Cir. 1985) (striking down the Indianapolis antipornography ordinance as an unconstitutional viewpoint- based restriction on speech), *aff'd without opinion*, 475 U.S. 1001 (1986).

6. See, e.g., Patrick Tivy and Southam News, "Porn Ruling is 'Historic,' " *Calgary Herald*, February 28, 1992, p. A1.

7. See *Butler* v. *Her Majesty The Queen*, [1992] 1 S.C.R. 452, 484–85, 509–10 (1992) (Can.).

8. See Cynthia G. Bowman, "Street Harassment and the Informal Ghettoization of Women," *Harvard Law Review* 106 (1993): 517, 546–48 (describing *R.A.V.* v. *City of St. Paul*, 112 S. Ct. 2538, 2550 [1992], as a potentially surmountable impediment to establishing viewpoint-based legislation such as regulation of street harassment or pornography).

9. 477 U.S. 57 (1986).

10. See ibid. at 66–67.

11. See 42 U.S.C. §§ 2000e to 2000e-17 (1988).

12. See *Andrews* v. *City of Philadelphia*, 895 F.2d 1469, 1485 (3d Cir. 1990);

Waltman v. *International Paper Co.*, 875 F.2d 468, 477 and n. 3 (5th Cir. 1989). But see *Rabidue* v. *Osceola Ref. Co.*, 805 F.2d 611, 622 (6th Cir. 1986) (dismissing the effect of pornography on the workplace as "de minimus"), *cert. denied*, 481 U.S. 1041 (1987).

13. See *Robinson* v. *Jacksonville Shipyards, Inc.*, 760 F. Supp. 1486, 1522, 1525–27 (M.D. Fla. 1991), *appeal docketed*, No. 91-3655 (11th Cir. July 12, 1991).

14. *Meritor Savings Bank* v. *Vinson*, 477 U.S. 57, 65 (1986).

15. *Griggs* v. *Duke Power Co.*, 401 U.S. 424, 429 (1971).

16. See, e.g., An Act to Protect the Civil Rights of Women and Children (see note 2), at §1. The act defines pornography as:

> [T]he presentation of women's [sexual] body parts . . . such that women are reduced to those parts, or the presentation of women: (a) as dehumanized sexual objects, things, or commodities; (b) as sexual objects who enjoy humiliation or pain; (c) as sexual objects experiencing sexual pleasure in rape, incest, or other sexual assault; (d) as sexual objects tied up or cut up or mutilated, bruised or physically hurt; (e) in postures or positions of sexual submission, servility, or display; (f) being penetrated by objects or animals; or (g) in scenarios of degradation, humiliation, injury, torture, shown as filthy or inferior, bleeding, bruised or hurt in a context that makes these conditions sexual.

Ibid., §i.

17. See Laurence H. Tribe, *American Constitutional Law*, 2d ed. (1988), §§ 12–17, pp. 920–21; Catharine A. MacKinnon, "Pornography as Defamation and Discrimination," *Boston University Law Review* 71 (1991): 793, 799–802; Martin Karo and Marcia McBrian, "The Lessons of *Miller* and *Hudnut*: On Proposing a Pornography Ordinance that Passes Constitutional Muster," *University of Michigan Journal of Law Reform* 23 (1989): 179, 179 n. 4; Cass R. Sunstein, "Pornography and the First Amendment," *Duke Law Journal* (1986): 589, 594–602.

18. See, e.g., Margaret Jean Intons-Peterson and Beverly Roskos-Ewoldsen, "Mitigating the Effects of Violent Pornography," in *For Adult Users Only*, ed. Susan Gubar and Joan Hoff (1989), pp. 218, 220–28 (overviewing the current research of the effects of pornography on men).

19. See Ann Russo, "Pornography's Active Subordination of Women: Radical Feminists Reclaim Speech Rights," in *Women Making Meaning*, ed. Lana F. Rakow (1992), pp. 144, 146 ("In the typical debates over pornography women's experiences and lives are usually invisible and socially meaningless").

20. See, e.g., Gloria Steinem, *Revolution from Within* (1990), p. 204.

21. *American Booksellers Ass'n* v. *Hudnut*, 771 F.2d 323, 332 (7th Cir. 1985), *aff'd without opinion*, 475 U.S. 1001 (1986).

22. See Nan D. Hunter and Sylvia A. Law, "Brief Amici Curiae of Feminist Anti-Censorship Taskforce, et al., in *American Booksellers Association* v. *Hudnut*," *University of Michigan Journal of Law Reform* 21 (1987–1988): 69, 74.

23. See ibid., p. 109.

24. Dworkin, *Pornography*, p. 27.

25. See, e.g., Susan Gubar, "Representing Pornography: Feminism, Criticism, and Depictions of Female Violation," in Gubar and Hoff, *For Adult Users Only*, pp. 47, 50–52 (describing René Magritte's *Le Viol* as pornographic "art" that may horrify women).

26. According to some studies, the majority of women may have been raped or otherwise sexually abused. See, e.g., Catharine A. MacKinnon, "Reflections on Sex Equality Under Law," *Yale Law Journal* 100 (1991): 1281, 1301–1302 and nn. 99–102 (reporting

statistics that reveal that 44 percent of women have been victims of rape or attempted rape, and 92.5 percent of women have been subject to sexual harassment).

27. See Catharine A. MacKinnon, "Francis Biddle's Sister," in *Feminism Unmodified* (1987), pp. 163, 171 ("Pornography sexualizes rape, battery, sexual harassment, prostitution, and child sexual abuse; it thereby celebrates, promotes, authorizes, and legitimizes them").

28. Ibid., p. 184; cf. Bowman, "Street Harassment and the Informal Ghettoization," p. 536 (describing the heightened injury suffered by rape victims who are subject to street harassment).

29. Sex-role identification is a well-established concept in the field of psychology. See, e.g., Henry Gleitman, *Basic Psychology* (1983), pp. 323–26 (describing a variety of theories which account for this process).

30. *New York* v. *Ferber*, 458 U.S. 747, 759 (1982).

31. Public Hearings on Ordinances to Add Pornography as Discrimination Against Women, Minneapolis City Council, Government Operations Comm., December 12–13, 1983, quoted in Dworkin, *Pornography*, p. xvi.

32. See Robin West, "Pornography as a Legal Text," in Gubar and Hoff, *For Adult Users Only*, pp. 108, 116.

33. See, e.g., "A New Way of Looking at Porn," *Glamour* (April 1992): 54 (describing studies revealing women's negative views toward pornography).

34. See Kathleen Mahoney, "The Canadian Constitutional Approach to Freedom of Expression in Hate Propaganda and Pornography," *Law and Contemporary Problems* 55 (1992): 77, 101 (describing the "true essence of discrimination" as how members of a disadvantaged group are "viewed by members of the dominant majority").

35. See, e.g., Doris-Jean Burton, "Public Opinion and Pornography Policy," Gubar and Hoff, *For Adult Users Only*, pp. 133, 135 (describing surveys which demonstrate that nearly half of all women surveyed would like pornography to be entirely illegal, while less than a third of the men surveyed agreed).

36. Harry Hurt III, "Zipless Sex: Or Why Men Love Pornography," *Self* (November 1992): 169, 184 (suggesting that pornography is merely harmless "fantasy").

37. See, e.g., Kathleen A. Lahey, "The Canadian Charter of Rights and Pornography: Toward a Theory of Actual Gender Equality," *New England Law Review* 20 (1984–1985): 649–51, 664–72; Kelly Toughill, "Women Take Aim at Civil Liberties Group," *Toronto Star*, August 30, 1992, p. A1.

38. See Mahoney, "The Canadian Constitutional Approach to Freedom of Expression," p. 86.

39. However, the Canadian constitution, unlike that of the United States, has an equal rights amendment for women. See note 47.

40. See Mahoney, "The Canadian Constitutional Approach to Freedom of Expression," p. 105 ("The *Butler* decision is a welcome development in the law that other countries and the international human rights community should contemplate if they are genuinely serious about women's human rights, violence against women, and women's equality"); see also Mary Ann Glendon, "A Beau Mentir Qui Vient de Loin: The 1988 Canadian Abortion Decision in Comparative Perspective," *Northwestern University Law Review* 83 (1989): 569, 591 (noting the "great opportunity afforded [to the United States] by the developing jurisprudence under the Canadian Charter").

41. [1992] 1 S.C.R. 452 (1992) (Can.).

42. Criminal Code, R.S.C. ch. C-46, § 163(8) (1985) (Can.) ("For the purposes of this Act, any publication a dominant characteristic of which is the undue exploitation of sex, or of sex and any one or more of the following subjects, namely, crime, horror, cru-

elty and violence, shall be deemed to be obscene"); see also ibid. § 163(1) (making it an offense to produce or distribute such materials).

43. *Butler*, [1992] 1 S.C.R. at 461. Donald Butler's store contained mainly visual materials in which women were presented as "used, hurt, or abused for sex for men." Factum of the Intervener Women's Legal Education and Action Fund at 1, *Butler*, [1992] 1 S.C.R. 452 (1992) (Can.).

44. See *Butler*, [1992] 1 S.C.R. at 461–62.

45. See ibid. at 463 (citing *Irwin Toy Ltd.* v. *Quebec [Attorney General]*, [1980] 1 S.C.R. 927 (1989) (Can.); see also Can. Const. (Constitution Act, 1982) pt. 1 (Canadian Charter of Rights and Freedoms), § 2(b) ("Everyone has the following fundamental freedoms: . . . freedom of thought, belief, opinion and expression, including freedom of the press and other media of communication . . .").

46. *Butler*, [1992] 1 S.C.R. at 465–66 (citing 50 C.C.C.3d 97, 124–25 [Man. Q.B. 1989], *appeal dismissed and cross-appeal allowed*, 6o C.C.C.3d 219 [Man. C.A. 1990]).

47. Ibid. at 471. Section 1 of the Charter of Rights and Freedoms, the Canadian analog to the U.S. Constitution's Bill of Rights, provides that limitations upon constitutional rights may be allowed if they can be "demonstrably justified in a free and democratic society." Can. Const. (Constitution Act, 1982) pt. 1 (Canadian Charter of Rights and Freedoms), § 1.

The Canadian Charter of Rights and Freedoms also contains an equality section, which, unlike other national and international instruments that exist to prohibit discrimination, contains express equality guarantees, an open-ended list of prohibited bases for discrimination, and an affirmative action provision that allows beneficial programs for disadvantaged groups or individuals. See ibid. § 15. Section 28, the gender equality section, states that, "[n]otwithstanding anything in this Charter, the rights and freedoms referred to in it are guaranteed equally to male and female persons." Ibid. § 28. Although the United States Constitution does not have an Equal Protection Amendment for women, Section 28 might be viewed as Canada's analogue to the Equal Protection Clause of the Fourteenth Amendment and to Title VII.

48. See *Butler*, [1992] 1 S.C.R. at 489.

49. See ibid.

50. See ibid. at 498–99.

51. Ibid. at 479.

52. *Butler*, [1992] 1 S.C.R. at 479.

53. Ibid. at 497 (quoting *Regina* v. *Red Hot Video Ltd.*, 45 C.R.3d 36, 43–44 [B.C.C.A. 1985]).

54. Ibid. at 501. The court rejected the argument offered by the British Columbia Civil Liberties Association that pornography "celebrates both female pleasure and male rationality." Ibid. at 500 (quoting Robin West, "The Feminist-Conservative Anti-Pornography Alliance and the 1986 Attorney General's Commission on Pornography Report," *American Bar Foundation Res. Journal* 4 [1987]: 681, 696. Instead, the Court concluded that this description "ignore[s] . . . the realities of the pornography industry." *Butler*, [1992] 1 S.C.R. at 500.

55. See *Barnes* v. *Glen Theatre, Inc.*, 111 S. Ct. 2456, 2462 (1991) (plurality opinion); *Miller* v. *California*, 413 U.S. 15 (1973); *Jacobellis* v. *Ohio*, 378 U.S. 184, 197 (1964) (Stewart, J., concurring); Catharine A. MacKinnon, "Not a Moral Issue," in *Feminism Unmodified* (1987), pp. 146, 157 and n. 57 (listing sources).

56. 458 U.S. 747 (1982).

57. See ibid. at 752.

58. See ibid. at 757–58. The *Ferber* Court stated that prevention of sexual exploita-

tion and child abuse constituted a government objective of "surpassing importance" and accepted the legislative judgment that child pornography harms minors. First, the Court reasoned, "the use of children as subjects of pornographic materials is harmful to the physiological, emotional, and mental health of the child." Second, the distribution of child pornography harms children by creating a "permanent record" of the child's participation, and such harm is exacerbated by the circulation of the materials. Third, this harm is not mitigated by any serious literary, artistic, or political value. And fourth, the best means of reducing pornographic exploitation of children is to attack the economic incentive in the distribution and production of such materials. Further, the *Ferber* Court expressly recognized that the *Miller* obscenity standard was not useful in determining whether children were hurt by pornography. See ibid. at 757–65.

59. See Lahey, "The Canadian Charter of Rights and Pornography," p. 674; Mahoney, "The Canadian Constitutional Approach to Freedom of Expression," p. 92.

60. 771 F.2d 323 (7th Cir. 1985), *aff'd without opinion*, 475 U.S. 1001 (1986).

61. Ibid. at 329 (footnote omitted) (quoting *Indianapolis, Ind., Code* § 16-1[a][2]). Notably, the Seventh Circuit cited national studies conducted in Great Britain and Canada, as well as in the United States for the proposition that pornography harms women. See ibid. at 329 n. 2.

62. Ibid. at 329.

63. See 475 U.S. 1001 (1986). Chief Justice Burger, and Justices Rehnquist and O'Connor would have granted certiorari. See ibid.

64. See Mahoney, "The Canadian Constitutional Approach to Freedom of Expression," p. 102.

65. U.S. Constitution, Amendment 14, § I ("No State shall . . . deny to any person . . . the equal protection of the laws").

66. See MacKinnon, "Pornography as Defamation and Discrimination," pp. 810–15 (arguing that an equality approach should have been applied in *Hudnut*).

67. 347 U.S. 483 (1954).

68. Ibid. at 494; see Tribe, *American Constitutional Law*, § 12-5, at 821 (stating that the Court invalidated segregation because it "unavoidably communicated a social message of black inferiority").

69. See MacKinnon, "Pornography as Defamation and Discrimination," pp. 812–13.

70. Ibid.

71. see supra pp. 1079–82.

72. But cf. *Roberts* v. *United States Jaycees*, 468 U.S. 609, 622–29 (1984) (recognizing sex equality as a compelling state interest sufficient to integrate a private all-male organization); *Pittsburgh Press Co.* v. *Pittsburgh Comm'n on Human Relations*, 413 U.S. 376, 391 (1973) (upholding an ordinance prohibiting newspapers from printing sex-designated "help wanted" ads).

73. According to FBI statistics, on average a woman is battered every fifteen seconds, and a woman is raped every five minutes. See S. Rep. No. 545, 101st Cong., 2d Sess., pt. 3(A), at 28 (1990); Federal Bureau of Investigation, U.S. Dept. of Justice, *Uniform Crime Reports for the United States* 4 (1991). The Supreme Court has acknowledged the extent of such harms to women. See *Planned Parenthood* v. *Casey*, 112 S. Ct. 2791, 2826–28 (1992) (providing statistics on domestic violence).

74. Often it is not clear whether violence is inflicted on women because they are women or because they were simply in the "wrong place at the wrong time." Judith G. Greenberg, Introduction to Mary Joe Frug, *Postmodern Legal Feminism* (1992), p. ix (problematizing this very question). It is clear, however, that these injuries are often

inflicted as a part of the production of pornography, for which women have been "beaten, forced to commit sex acts, imprisoned, bound and gagged, and tortured." Sunstein, "Pornography and the First Amendment," p. 595 (citing U.S. Department of Justice, Attorney General's Commission on Pornography, Final Report pt. IV, ch. 2, § B[3][b], at 866–69 [1986]).

75. But see Gary David Comstock, *Violence against Lesbians and Gay Men* (1991), pp. 106–109. Gay men are more likely to undergo these experiences because they, like women, are subject to abuse due to gender-role stigmatization.

76. Cf. Bowman, "Street Harassment and the Informal Ghettoization of Women," p. 521 (arguing that when the law fails to protect women from a harm that men do not share, it leaves women in a "Hobbesian wilderness" from which men are protected by the laws and by the male-dominated society).

77. See supra pp. 1078–79.

78. See generally Barbara A. Brown, Thomas I. Emerson, Gail Falk, and Ann E. Freedman, "The Equal Rights Amendment: A Constitutional Basis for Equal Rights for Women," *Yale Law Journal* 80 (1970): 871 (discussing the need for, and potential benefits of, an ERA).

79. 42 U.S.C. § 2000(e)-2(a)(1) (1988).

80. 477 U.S. 57 (1986).

81. See ibid. at 66.

82. Ibid. at 65–66 (citing Equal Employment Opportunity Commission Guidelines on Discrimination Because of Sex: Sexual Harassment, 29 C.F.R. § 1604.11[a] [1985]).

83. Ibid. (quoting *Los Angeles Dep't of Water and Power* v. *Manhart*, 435 U.S. 702, 707 n. 13 [1978]).

84. Ibid. at 66 (citing *Rogers* v. *EEOC*, 454 F.2d 234, 238 [5th Cir. 1971]).

85. See ibid. at 65.

86. See ibid. at 67.

87. Ibid. (quoting *Henson* v. *Dundee*, 682 F.2d 897, 902 [11th Cir. 1982]).

88. Ibid. at 65.

89. Kathryn Abrams, "Gender Discrimination and the Transformation of Workplace Norms," 42.

90. See, e.g., Brief of Amicus Curiae Equal Rights Advocates at 4, *Robinson* v. *Jacksonville Shipyards*, 760 F. Supp. 1486 (M.D. Fla. 1991), *appeal docketed*, No. 91-3655 (11th Cir. July 12, 1991). See generally Wendy Pollack, "Sexual Harassment: Women's Experience vs. Legal Definitions," *Harvard Women's Law Journal* 13 (1990): 36–44 (describing harassment faced by women in the construction industry).

91. Even the American Civil Liberties Union, which vehemently opposed the Dworkin/MacKinnon antipornography ordinance in *Hudnut*, has argued that pornography may create a harassing environment for women in some workplaces. See Brief for Amicus Curiae American Civil Liberties Union at 15–16, 18, *Robinson* v. *Jacksonville Shipyards*, 760 F. Supp 1486 (M.D. Fla. 1991), *appeal docketed*, No. 91-3655 (11th Cir. July 12, 1991).

92. See Naomi Wolf, *The Beauty Myth* (1991), pp. 51–52 (describing pornography in the workplace as one of the systematic means by which men send women messages of their worthlessness); William Petrocfelli and Barbara Kate Repa, *Sexual Harassment on the Job* (1992), 3/13–3/14 .

93. See *Rabidue* v. *Osceola Refining Co.*, 805 F.2d 611, 622 (6th Cir. 1986) (finding that pornography in the workplace had a "de minimis effect").

94. See, e.g., *Andrews* v. *City of Philadelphia*, 895 F.2d 1469, 1485 (3d Cir. 1990) (finding the posting of pornographic pictures in common areas and in the plaintiff's work

spaces to be evidence of a hostile environment); *Waltman* v. *International Paper Co.*, 875 F.2d 468, 476–77 (5th Cir. 1989) (considering sexual graffiti evidence of a hostile work environment).

95. 760 F. Supp. 1486 (M.D. Fla. 1991), *appeal docketed*, No. 91-3655 (11th Cir. July 12, 1991).

96. See ibid. at 1493. The shipyard employed 2 women and 958 men as skilled craftsworkers in 1980, 7 women and 1,010 men as skilled craftsworkers in 1983, and 6 women and 846 men as skilled craftsworkers in 1986. See ibid.

97. See ibid. at 1493–94.

98. See ibid. at 1493, 1495–99. For example, one picture displayed a woman's torso with a meat spatula pressed onto her pubic area and another showed a nude woman with the words "USDA Choice" printed on her stomach. See ibid. at 1495. In addition, the employees hung a dart board with a drawing of a woman's breast on which the woman's nipple served as the bull's-eye. See ibid. at 1497. A life-size picture of a nude woman was drawn on a wall; another drawing depicted a nude woman with fluid coming from her genital area. See ibid.

99. See ibid. at 1494 (quoting one foreman as saying that if he ever saw a calendar with pictures of nude men, he would throw it in the trash, and another as saying that if he saw a vendor distributing a calendar with pictures of nude men, he would think the "son of a bitch" was "queer").

100. See ibid. at 1496.

101. Ibid. at 1514–15.

102. Ibid. at 1498. After Robinson complained about a graphic calendar in the ship-fitter's trailer, male workers retaliated by posting a sign on the trailer's door that read "MEN ONLY." See ibid.

103. Ibid. at 1495.

104. See ibid. at 1535–36.

105. Ibid. at 1523.

106. See ibid. at 1527 (citing Abrams, "Gender Discrimination and the Transformation of Workplace Norms," p. 1212 n. 118).

107. Ibid.

108. Ibid.

109. Ibid.

110. See ibid. app., at 1542. The sexual harassment policy mandated by the court defined harassing depictions as materials that are "sexually suggestive, sexually *demeaning*, or pornographic." Ibid. (emphasis added). It defined "sexually suggestive" in part as "posed for the obvious purpose of displaying or drawing attention to private portions of his or her body." Ibid. This definition incorporates both the Canadian and Dworkin/MacKinnon definitions of materials that harm women. See supra pp. 1075, 1080–81.

111. See ibid. at 1536 (distinguishing *Hudnut* because "the affected speech, if it is speech protected by the first amendment, is reached only after a determination that a harm has been and is continuing to be inflicted on identifiable individuals"). Had the *Hudnut* court interpreted the antipornography ordinance as it was written, it would have reached an identical conclusion. That is, the ordinance creates only a civil cause of action for damages for coercion or assault that stems from a particular piece of pornography. Cf. An Act to Protect the Civil Rights of Women and Children, see note 2 (providing for the same causes of action as the statute at issue in *Hudnut*).

112. See ibid. ("[T]he Court may, without violating the First Amendment, require that a private employer curtail the free expression in the workplace of some employees in order to remedy the demonstrated harm inflicted on other employees.")

113. See ibid. at 1503 (citing the testimony of Dr. Susan Fiske).

114. See generally Rosabeth M. Kanter, *Men and Women of the Corporation* (1977), pp. 208–42 (describing the psychological harms caused by numerical male dominance in the workplace); Barbara Gutek, *Sex and the Workplace* (1985), pp. 15–16 (discussing the harm of sex-role spillover).

115. *Robinson*, 760 F. Supp. at 1504.

116. Cf. Gerd Brantenberg, *Egalia's Daughters*, trans. Louis Mackay (1995), pp. 249–50 (demonstrating the use of pornography as a tool by the dominant gender in a sex-hierarchical society by describing the pornography of men in a fictional female-dominated society).

117. See *Robinson*, 760 F. Supp. at 1535–36.

118. See, e.g., Committee on Labor and Human Resources, 96th Cong., 2d Sess., Legislative History of the Pregnancy Discrimination Act of 1978 (Comm. Print 1979), p. 61.

119. See, e.g., Kimberlé Crenshaw, "Race, Gender, and Sexual Harassment," *Southern California Law Review* 65 (1992): 1467, 1475 (arguing that "the social opportunities of millions of women are bounded and policed through subordinating gender practices such as sexual harassment" that exclude women from the trades even more than they do from the ranks of professional education).

120. The *Robinson* court explicitly adopted the perspective of the "reasonable woman." See 760 F. Supp. at 1524. This is a welcome trend. See, e.g., *Ellison* v. *Brady*, 924 F.2d 872, 879 (9th Cir. 1991) (adopting the perspective of the reasonable woman because "a sex-blind reasonable person standard tends to be male-biased and tends to systematically ignore the experiences of women").

121. See, e.g., Susan D. Ross, "Proving Sexual Harassment: The Hurdles," *Southern California Law Review* 65 (1992): 1451, 1453–58.

122. See *Robinson*, 760 F. Supp. at 1504–1505.

123. See Amy Horton, "Of Supervision, Centerfolds, and Censorship: Sexual Harassment, the First Amendment, and the Contours of Title VII," *University of Miami Law Review* 46 (1991): 403, 434.

124. Cf. Abrams, "Gender Discrimination and the Transformation of Workplace Norms," p. 1209 (arguing that courts should accord primary weight to a woman's reactions to sexual behavior and focus their attention on the victim's response, rather than on the harassing conduct in the abstract).

125. For an excellent overview of the First Amendment issues at stake in sexual harassment litigation, see generally Horton, "Of Supervision, Centerfolds, and Censorship," at 410–52.

CONTRIBUTORS

MARTHA R. BURT, Human Resources Policy Center, Urban Institute, Washington, D.C.

ALBA CONTE, attorney, Santa Barbara, California.

BILLIE WRIGHT DZIECH, Language Arts, University of Cincinnati, Ohio.

VAUGHANA MACY FEARY, Department of Philosophy, Fairleigh Dickinson University, Madison, New Jersey.

LOUISE F. FITZGERALD, Department of Psychology, University of Illinois at Urbana-Champaign.

MICHAEL W. HAWKINS, attorney, Dinsmore and Shohl, Cincinnati, Ohio.

LEANOR B. JOHNSON, Department of Family Resources and Human Development, Arizona State University, Tempe.

ELISABETH A. KELLER, School of Law, Boston College, Newton, Massachusetts.

CATHARINE A. MACKINNON, School of Law, University of Michigan, Ann Arbor.

CAMILLE PAGLIA, Liberal Arts, University of the Arts, Philadelphia, Pennsylvania.

ELLEN FRANKEL PAUL, Social Philosophy and Policy Center, Bowling Green State University, Ohio.

SUSAN DELLER ROSS, School of Law, Georgetown University, Washington, D.C.

SANDRA S. TANGRI, Department of Psychology, Howard University, Washington, D.C.

EDMUND WALL, Department of Philosophy, East Carolina University, Greenville, North Carolina.